Helots and their masters in Laconia and Messenia: histories, ideologies, structures

Edited by N. Luraghi and S. E. Alcock

D1381603

Center for Hellenic Studies
Trustees for Harvard University
Washington, D.C.
Distributed by Harvard University Press
Cambridge, Massachusetts, and London, England
2003

Helots and their masters in Laconia and Messenia: histories, ideologies, structures,
edited by N. Luraghi and S.E. Alcock

Copyright © 2003 Center for Hellenic Studies, Trustees for Harvard University
All Rights Reserved.
Published by Center for Hellenic Studies, Trustees for Harvard University, Washington, D.C.
Distributed by Harvard University Press, Cambridge, Massachusetts and London, England
Production editor: Jennifer Reilly
Production: Kristin Murphy Romano
Cover design and illustration: Michael J. Horsley
Printed in Baltimore, MD by Victor Graphics

Editorial Team
Senior Advisers: W. Robert Connor, Gloria Ferrari Pinney, Albert Henrichs, James O'Donnell, Bernd Seidensticker
Editorial Board: Gregory Nagy (Chair), Christopher Blackwell, Casey Dué, Mary Ebbott, Anne Mahoney, Leonard Muellner, Ross Scaife
Managing Editor: Gregory Nagy
Executive Editors: Casey Dué, Mary Ebbott
Production Editors: M. Zoie Lafis, Ivy Livingston, Jennifer Reilly
Web Producer: Mark Tomasko

Library of Congress Cataloging-in-Publication Data:
  Helots and their masters in Laconia and Messenia : histories,
  ideologies, structures / edited by N. Luraghi and S.E. Alcock.
     p. cm.
  Includes bibliographical references and index.
  ISBN 0-674-01223-2
  1. Helots—Greece—Lakōnia. 2. Helots—Greece—Messēnia.
  3. Lakōnia (Greece)—Social conditions. 4. Messēnia (Greece)—Social conditions.
  I. Luraghi, Nino. II. Alcock, Susan E. III. Title.
  DF261.L2H45 2003
  938'.9—dc22   2003019543
  23456789

Acknowledgments

This volume originates from a workshop held at Harvard University on March 16-17, 2001. The majority of the essays in this book were there presented for the first time, in some cases in a significantly different form from that assumed in the end. In an attempt at countering the isolationist tendencies that so often plague ancient history, the organizers invited scholars from different fields to offer a commentary on the workshop's papers. Orlando Patterson's observations have been transformed into the volume's concluding essay, but the organizers would also like to express their gratitude to Michael McCormick (Harvard University) for his lively and thoughtful contribution to the event's proceedings. The workshop was made possible by the generous financial support of the Arthur F. Thurnau Professorship (University of Michigan) and of the Loeb Fund of the Department of the Classics (Harvard University). The editors are grateful to both their home institutions for this assistance. Ana Galjanic (Harvard University) has also been helpful in the preparation of the manuscript.

One of the workshop's principal goals was to bring together scholars who manifestly possessed different views of many aspects of the history and sociology of Helotage. In the course of the workshop and thereafter, while every contributor has revised her or his positions in the light of our discussions, not surprisingly no consensus has emerged. This volume testifies to a diversity of approaches that open up new avenues of interpretation. The editors are convinced that such provocative variety constitutes an ideal starting point toward future researches. The contributors to this volume have delved deep into the intricacies of the arguments they were dealing—or sometimes struggling—with, and the result is, we think, a series of extremely engaging pieces, that will repay the patient reader.

The last word on the Helots will never be spoken, and it is in the nature of the evidence that whatever is said about them has to be tentative, temporary, indeed controversial. Since scholarly views of the history of their masters have been undergoing radical transformations over the last decades, to an important extent thanks to the work of the scholars assembled in this volume, it is indeed high time to start assembling the materials and ideas for a reassessment of the history of the Helots. Such is the ambition of the present volume.

S. E. Alcock & N. Luraghi
Ann Arbor-Cambridge
April 2003

Table of contents

Introduction

One

Researching the helots:
details, methodologies, agencies

Susan E. Alcock

This introductory essay, tidily enough for a volume divided in three parts, likewise possesses a tripartite structure—of details, methodologies, and agencies. These rubrics combine to outline and to argue why a collection of essays on "helots and their masters" is a valid and timely exercise.

Details . . .

. . . details. Or better, lack of details. Reading or re-reading past and current scholarship about helots and about any or all aspects of their lives, one is apt to come across a plethora of qualifying parenthetical phrases—"if we had the details", "whatever the details", "despite a lack of detail". This simple observation underlines something those interested in the problem often loudly deplore, but perhaps have not sufficiently internalized: the fact that—in detail—we don't know a great deal about helots.

That may seem a maximally bathetic statement to make about a well-known, much bewailed gap in our sources. Yet the situation does govern the essential framework of our debate about this ancient group, and it requires a care in analysis that perhaps has not always been met. Sins of commission and omission in past (and present) scholarship could easily, if undiplomatically, be cited, as some individuals push and stretch our fragile and entirely non-indigenous sources for all that they are worth (and perhaps a bit more), while others accept silence as justification for neglect.

Nor is it simply the holes in our evidence that leave the helots so invitingly open to interpretation and re-interpretation. What we know, or what we think we know, is also caught up in wider webs of attitudes and contradictions. Helots appear betwixt and between: between free men and slave, akin and yet not akin to those who rule them, of uncertain and debated origin, arguable remnants of a more energetic, admirable diaspora population. Willing (on occasion) to fight for those who despise them. A passive-aggressive people; long-term losers who ultimately triumph. No wonder different scholars, working within different intellectual and political paradigms, react to different aspects of these formulations. And thus schools develop, of continualists versus discontinualists, maximalists versus minimalists, those pro-the worker versus those pro-the establishment . . . More than most topics in ancient history, the helots can become a kind of Rorschach test. We report what we see in sometimes uncomfortably revealing, and often quite personal, ways.

That propensity, obviously, will never disappear, and—equally obviously—the helots merely lie at the far end of a spectrum we travel all the time. Yet what a lack of detail demands, it can be argued, is a more careful and appropriate selection of targets for investigation. Some long-engaged controversies will remain forever opaque: the historicity and chronology of the "Messenian Wars", for example, is one apt candidate. In general, one could question the productive return on what seems too often an endless recycling and reshuffling of our scant textual sources in various forms of intellectual gymnastics, trying to solve mysteries unsolvable with our problematic evidence.

A perceived need to recast approaches to the "helot problem" is one theme that connects all the contributions to this volume. Each author, however, does this in his own way. Paul Cartledge, for one, explicitly embraces that "personal" quality of response to the helots, while also reviewing how a mirage-like image has allowed their use in a variety of seemingly inappropriate, but emotionally powerful, situations—from Spartacus to South African apartheid. His own visceral reaction to the helot predicament leads him to query other, revisionist views that either reconsider the uniqueness of that predicament or that minimize the scope of its horrors.[1] Issues of status, treatment, and revolt, he no doubt rightly forecasts, are "three major pressure-points of current and likely future scholarly discussions of the Helots and the Helot experience in the Classical fifth and fourth centuries" (p. 17).

Nigel Kennell advances things in a quite different direction by not focussing, as is the scholarly wont, on those same fifth and fourth centuries BC. Kennell instead explores the later years of helotage in Laconia, offering (as far as is possible) a reconstruction of affairs following the Messenian liberation by scrupulously tracing the vicissitudes of Hellenistic history in Sparta.[2] Evidence is hardly richer

....

[1] See, for the first, aspects of Ducat 1990; Hodkinson 1992; Luraghi 2001, 2002; for the second, Roobaert 1977; Talbert 1989; Whitby 1994; contra Cartledge 1991, 1993 (with Hodkinson's response, 2000: 116-117), 2001.

[2] See also Kennell 1999.

for this period than for earlier times: the Laconian helots remain "on the shadowy margins of a society famous for its obsession with secrecy" (p. 103). Still, attention paid to these frequently neglected stages in the history of helotage is welcome. The distinctions, or similarities, between helot life in Laconia and Messenia are increasingly emerging as a point for fruitful analysis; Kennell's piece is salutary for any who thought the dynamics of the Spartan-helot relationship ended with Epaminondas.

Methodologies

Other contributions to the volume pioneer alternative ways to research (re-search?) the helot problem. One strategy is not merely to recycle the sources, but to read them far more stringently, to assess them as socially and temporally contextualized, as ideological and imaginative products. Indeed, almost all of the authors do just that, most visibly perhaps Luraghi and Hall. Here Luraghi directly takes on past tendencies to "flatten" our sources to fit what has become the generally approved *vulgata* on the origins of helotry. He reviews (with a fine-tooth comb) the extant relevant texts in their particular contexts and as

> reacting to the cultural and political environment in which they were composed. In this perspective, the ancient sources themselves preserve all their importance as evidence . . . not for the origins of Helotry and the early history of Laconia and Messenia, but rather, for the way in which the changing political map of the southern Peloponnese challenged subsequent Greeks to rethink the crucial "time of the origins" . . . (p. 135)

This rigorous exposure of our data, Luraghi believes, allows critical (in every sense) revision of the *communis opinio,* not least in regard to notions such as the existence of early Messenian ethnic identity and solidarity, and the standard "mass enslavement" model of helot origins.

This last position manifestly sets a collision course between Luraghi and the contribution of Hans van Wees, "Conquerors and serfs: wars of conquest and forced labour in archaic Greece". Setting these two, side by side, is an ample and intriguing demonstration of how radically divergent conclusions can still be reached with (approximately) the same limited data set. Van Wees, picking up on a point also raised by Cartledge about the general invisibility of ancient dependent populations, sees nothing peculiar about the Messenian helots. Indeed, he argues for a similar, if even more badly documented, phenomenon of "conquest serfs" in several parts of the Greek world (e.g. Sicyon, Argos, Thessaly, Crete, the colonial world). Van Wees sums up his argument coolly—"Sparta's conquest of Messenia was no anomaly, but merely the most spectacular and best attested instance of a form of imperialism characteristic of archaic Greece" (p. 72)—and blames both poor sources and disciplinary disinclinations for our failure to recognize this fact before. Readers can sample both Luraghi and van Wees, observe the methodological rules followed and fundamental assumptions revealed, and draw their own conclusions—which may be to remain agnostic on the "truth" of helot origins.

Central to van Wees' argument is his refusal to view helots in isolation, but to keep them aligned with other dependent peoples. Part of his paper employs parallels from outside the ancient world, from the Spanish domination of the land, labor and lives of Central American populations, to inform his thinking. This explicitly comparative methodology is being taken to another level by Stephen Hodkinson's project, "Sparta in comparative historical perspective, ancient to modern", of which his paper here is a first salvo.[3] Hodkinson begins by acknowledging our evidentiary problems, and proposes turning to the history and sociology of certain other systems of unfree labour (particularly serfdom in Russia, slavery in the American South, and slavery in pre-colonial Africa) "to map out some plausible broad contours for the operation of helotage, even if much of the detailed topography must necessarily remain obscure" (p. 249). The focus of this particular discussion revolves around Spartiate-helot relations within the agrarian economy, in particular trying to investigate how helotry worked "on the ground" along dimensions such as relationships to the land, supervision and absenteeism, residence and communities, and leadership and politics. The emphasis here is on using comparative evidence to suggest and support likely possibilities, not to shoehorn the ancient case into identikit solutions. Data from a variety of sources, however individually scanty, are then employed to see what fits, and what fails to fit, those "plausible broad contours". This methodological stratagem promises one significant way to escape the trap of our evidence and to season our understanding of helots and their masters. In a divergent fashion, Raaflaub's dialogue with Orlando Patterson's *Freedom in the Making of Western Culture*—about the possible impact of slavery and helotage on the rise of the "freedom ethos" in Greece (Raaflaub remains unconvinced)—also engages the helots in wider intellectual and social arguments.[4]

Another very positive visible development is the growing body of relevant archaeological data. No individual paper deals first and foremost with the material world of the helots, but a gratifying number (indeed virtually all of the papers in the volume) not only cite, but actively employ, recent archaeological discoveries in their analysis. "Helot archaeology", in any rounded sense, still lies some distance in

....

[3] Hodkinson, rightly, acknowledges the early example of comparative work provided by Cartledge's 'Rebels and *Sambos*' (2001, originally published in 1985).

[4] Patterson 1991; see also Raaflaub 1985.

the future with the excavation of their homes and their graves, the study of their bones, the analysis of their diets. Material studies of other dependent populations make clear what could some day be ours.[5]

What is beginning to emerge, however, is a kind of regional perspective on the world of the helots. Archaeological survey projects have been conducted in both Laconia and Messenia, and the resulting settlement and land use patterns are highly provocative about, among other things, the potential differences between helot life in those two regions (or at least the parts intensively explored by the Laconia Survey and the Pylos Regional Archaeological Project).[6] Hodkinson pushes the evidence hardest; the difference between the nucleated settlement of Messenia and the more dispersed patterns visible in Laconia, for example, allows significant inferences about the structure, relative "autonomy", and operation of these different communities "on the ground". In addition to this regional perspective, archaeological evidence for tomb cult at various ancient Messenian sites is also successfully drawn into the picture.[7] These interpretive forays into the archaeology of historical Messenia may do much to encourage additional work, balancing out the trend either to emphasize the prehistoric occupation of the region or to focus on post-liberation Messene.[8]

Agencies

In another context, I commented on how our paucity of sources, combined with (as several other authors here note) their usual peripheral appearance on the edges of Spartan history, tends to leave helots "a largely undifferentiated mass whose inner workings seem hidden and unknowable".[9] Without getting into the debate, actively stirred up here, about the inception and nature of helot (especially Messenian helot) identity and corporate unity, it is essential to avoid the (unstated) assumption that helots were not active social agents, who—possessing their own attitudes and memories, invisible as these are to us—at least attempted to direct their own fates. Silence on the part of our ancient sources about such attempts (Pausanias is a remarkable culprit) cannot be allowed to render helots as faceless and passive—or perhaps even as "understudies", in Figueira's interesting term for the *Neodamôdeis*.[10]

....

[5] See, for example, Ferguson 1991, 1992; McDavid 1999; Orser 1988; Singleton 1985; Singleton and Bograd 1995.

[6] Laconia: Cavanagh et al. 1996. Pylos: Davis et al. 1997; Davis 1998; *The Pylos Regional Archaeological Project: Internet Edition* (http://river.blg.uc.edu/prap/PRAP.html).

[7] See also Alcock 2002a: 132-75, 2002b.

[8] Spencer 1998.

[9] Alcock 2002a: 137, referring specifically to the Messenian helots.

[10] Figueira 1999: 226. On Pausanias, see Alcock 2001.

All the papers in this volume, in their various ways, contribute to repelling this danger. Figueira and Scheidel, in their discussions of helot demography, serve to improve understanding of the parameters of the Spartiate-helot relationship in one very fundamental way—their relative numbers and the inferences for interaction that can be based upon that foundation. Both concur in moving toward a lower estimate for the helot population than was once the norm (neatly laid out by Figueira). Despite that shared substantive conclusion, the papers operate in very different fashions. In a dense web of argument, Figueira weaves together as much of the textual evidence as possible with other relevant factors, while also reviewing, very helpfully, other recent assaults (including his own) on this problem. Scheidel, by contrast, prefers a "simplified" model, stripping the elements in his calculations down to the barest of bones and cautiously allowing for wide "bands of probability" in his answers. The pair make for a wonderful methodological comparison. The fact that their conclusions are (hearteningly) rather similar, while reducing somewhat the looming "menace" of the helot threat, still leaves us to understand a system of exploitation—operative over a significant territory and within particular social and ideological constraints—where masters were outnumbered.

A more intimate view into the agency of the helots of Messenia, and of the diaspora population of the Messenians, is given by Hall. Allowing for shifting constructions of group identity, he seeks "to account for the possible historical circumstances in which the Messenians gained, maintained and chartered cognizance both of their own identity and of their affiliation to a broader Dorian ethnocommunity" (p. 142). Open acceptance of such strategic dynamism, over time and between groups, empowers both the diaspora—who (Hall suggests) claimed Dorian ancestry as a counter to Spartan superiority—and the helots, who may have allied themselves with a proud Akhaian heritage. The completed "Dorianization" of the reunited group came about in the changed circumstances of post-liberation Messenia.[11] Whether one accepts all of Hall's contentions, introducing such flexibility and mobility into the self-imaging of the Messenians is surely correct.

༈

It is unlikely that the helots will ever shed that quality of Rorschach test, and indeed it might be a shame, given their evocative history, that they ever should. Still, this volume directs us towards new ways of analyzing and of envisioning these people.

....

[11] For another view of the 'evolution of Messenian identity', see Figueira 1999.

In part, this involves the nature of our questions: accepting our lack of detail about helots and helot life should discourage grand and totalizing narratives. Instead, the way forward seems to be through encouragement of alternative methodologies, such as the use of comparative data sets or of archaeology, to unpick more nuanced questions, in more localized fashions. Perhaps most fundamental of all is the need to reconsider our own starting assumptions, to grant the helots both capacities and hopes that the usual suspects of our sources have steadfastly denied to them.

Such reconsideration—recasting the terms of debate about helots and helotage— was the point of the original workshop organized by the editors, and remains the point of this volume. It is certainly a methodological puzzle. It is inescapably a political challenge. It is arguably a moral obligation.[12]

---

[12] As Cartledge notes, 'a faint and distant echo of that battle cry of freedom lies behind the present scholarly project' (p. 15).

Susan E. Alcock

Bibliography

Alcock, S. E. 2001. "The Peculiar Book IV and the Problem of the Messenian Past." In S. E. Alcock, J. F. Cherry and J. Elsner (eds.), *Pausanias: Travel and Memory in Roman Greece*. Oxford and New York: 142-153.

———. 2002a. *Archaeologies of the Greek Past: Landscape, Monuments and Memories*. Cambridge.

———. 2002b. "A Simple Case of Exploitation: The Helots of Messenia." In P. Cartledge, E. E. Cohen and L. Foxhall (eds.), *Money, Labour and Land: Approaches to the Economies of Ancient Greece*. London and New York: 185-199.

Cartledge, P. 1991. "Richard Talbert's Revision of the Sparta-Helot Struggle: A Reply." *Historia* 40: 379-381.

———. 1993. "Classical Greek Agriculture: Recent Work and Alternative Views." *Journal of Peasant Studies* 21: 127-136.

———. 2001. "Rebels and *Sambos* in Classical Greece: A Comparative View." Revised reprint in *Spartan Reflections*. London: 127-152. (Originally published in P. Cartledge and F. D. Harvey [eds.], *CRUX: Essays in Greek History presented to G. E. M. de Ste. Croix,* London, 1985: 16-46).

Cavanagh, W., J. Crouwel, R. W. V. Catling and G. Shipley. 1996. *The Laconia Survey: Continuity and Change in a Greek Rural Landscape. Vol. 2. Archaeological Data*. (Annual of the British School at Athens, Supplementary Volume 27). London.

Davis, J. L., S. E. Alcock, J. Bennet, Y. G. Lolos, and C. W. Shelmerdine. 1997. "The Pylos Regional Archaeology Project. Part I: Overview and the Archaeological Survey." *Hesperia* 66: 391-494.

Davis, J. L. (ed.). 1998. *Sandy Pylos: An Archaeological History from Nestor to Navarino*. Austin.

Ducat, J. 1990. *Les Hilotes*. (Bulletin de correspondance hellénique, Supplément 20). Athens and Paris.

Ferguson, L. G. 1991. "Struggling with Pots in Colonial America." In R. H. McGuire and R. Paynter (eds.), *The Archaeology of Inequality*. New York: 28-39.

———. 1992. *Uncommon Ground: Archaeology and Early African America, 1650-1800*. Washington, D.C.

Figueira, T. J. 1999. "The Evolution of the Messenian Identity." In Hodkinson and Powell 1999: 211-244.

Hodkinson, S. 1992. "Sharecropping and Sparta's Economic Exploitation of the Helots." In J. M. Sanders (ed.), ΦΙΛΟΛΑΚΩΝ: *Lakonian Studies in Honour of Hector Catling*. London: 123-134.

_____. 2000. *Property and Wealth in Classical Sparta*. London.

Hodkinson, S., and A. Powell (eds.) 1999. *Sparta: New Perspectives*. London.

Kennell, N. 1999. "From Perioikoi to Poleis: The Laconian Cities in the Late Hellenistic Period." In Hodkinson and Powell 1999: 189-210.

Luraghi, N. 2001. "Der Erdbebenaufstand und die Entstehung der messenischen Identität." In D. Papenfuß and V. M. Strocka (eds.), *Gab es das griechische Wunder? Griechenland zwischen dem Ende des 6. Und der Mitte des 5. Jahrhunderts v. Chr.* Mainz: 279-301.

_____. 2002. "Becoming Messenian." *Journal of Hellenic Studies* 122: 45-69.

McDavid, C. 1999. "From Real Space to Cyberspace: Contemporary Conversations about the Archaeology of Slavery and Tenancy." *Internet Archaeology* 6 (http://intarch.ac.uk/journal/issue6/mcdavid_toc.html)

Orser, C. E., Jr. 1988. "Toward a Theory of Power for Historical Archaeology: Plantations and Space." In M. P. Leone and P. B. Potter, Jr. (eds.), *The Recovery of Meaning: Historical Archaeology in the Eastern United States*. Washington and London: 313-343.

Patterson, O. 1991. *Freedom*. Vol. 1. *Freedom in the Making of Western Culture*. New York.

Raaflaub, K. 1985. *Die Entdeckung der Freiheit*. (Vestigia 37). Munich.

Roobaert, A. 1977. "Le danger hilote?" *Ktema* 2: 141-155.

Singleton, T. A. (ed.). 1985. *The Archaeology of Slavery and Plantation Life*. Orlando.

Singleton, T. A., and M. D. Bograd. 1995. *The Archaeology of the African Diaspora in the Americas*. (Guides to the Archaeological Literature of the Immigrant Experience in America 2). Ann Arbor.

Spencer, N. 1998. "The History of Archaeological Investigations in Messenia." In Davis 1998: 23-41.

Talbert, R. 1989. "The Role of the Helots in the Class Struggle at Sparta." *Historia* 38: 22-40.

Whitby, M. 1994. "Two Shadows: Images of Spartans and Helots." In A. Powell and S. Hodkinson (eds.), *The Shadow of Sparta*. London and New York: 87-126.

Two

Raising hell? The Helot Mirage—a personal re-view[1]

Paul Cartledge

The first instalment of Larry Gonick's idiosyncratic and insufficiently known *Cartoon History of the Universe*, entitled "From the Big Bang to Alexander the Great", was published in the dynamic year of 1989. In one particularly teasing cartoon a sexy and uninhibited Spartan wife makes a prospective male Helot lover an offer: "Wanna raise hell, Helot?"—an offer it appears he would very much want to refuse.[2] That is one side of the Helot "mirage", no doubt, playing to the both ancient and modern image of Spartan women as initiators of dangerous sexual liaisons outside marriage, allegedly from as early as the supposed Partheniai "affair" of the later eighth century BCE.[3] But there is another side to the mirage, and, dare I say, an upside. For the Helots, being rightly perceived as of fundamental historical importance, have also been far from neglected by interested outsiders, from the time of the Athenians Kritias (deadly serious) and Eupolis (presumably somehow

....

[1] The original version of this paper was delivered as a curtainraising address on 16 March 2001 before the workshop held the following day. I have tried to retain something of the original's oral flavour in this printed version. To the directors of the workshop, Sue Alcock and Nino Luraghi, I am deeply indebted for their invitation, hospitality and constant intellectual provocation (in the best possible sense). To my fellow-participants, especially perhaps Orlando Patterson, I am most grateful for comradeship and lively interchange. Of other living fellow-labourers in the vineyard of Lakonian studies, apart from those present at the Workshop and in this volume, I owe most to Anton Powell, who is the dedicatee of Cartledge 2002c. See now Powell 2002: ch. 6 ('Life in Sparta').

[2] In August 2001 I delivered a paper on the Helots at the California State University at Fresno, thanks to the kind invitation of Victor Hanson; I used as my visual prompts a selection of Gonick's cartoons, a source apparently unfamiliar even to a Californian audience. Of course, Gonick, a non-specialist, sometimes gets his 'facts' wrong, but more often than not he is faithful at least to the spirit of the original sources, and he has clearly done a great deal of effective background homework. For further recognition, see now Alcock 2002: 139 n. 13 and Fig. 4.3.

[3] The issue of Spartan women's sexuality and alleged sexual liberality, as presented in the ancient sources (visual as well as verbal) and interpreted by modern historians, is addressed in Cartledge 2001d; cf. now Pomeroy 2002 (though unfortunately, at pp. 159-161, she misrepresents my position rather grossly). On the Partheniai see, e.g., Kunstler 1983.

comic) in the late fifth century BCE to the latest contemporary scholarship (entirely lacking in humour).[4]

Let us begin by naming names, because—whatever Shakespeare's Romeo might have claimed to the contrary—there is, sometimes, quite a lot in a name. It is for a start a remarkable fact, though too rarely remarked as such, that the Greek word *heilôs* (alternatively *heilôtês*) has spawned some distinctive and revealing linguistic progeny, both among the ancient Greeks themselves, and in our own English language. In antiquity, it generated not only an adjective, *heilôtikos*, but also, more extraordinarily, a generic verb *heilôteuein* that meant to be, or behave like, Helots—as if the meaning of "Helot" was itself pretty transparently clear.[5] (Alas, if it was so to the ancient Greeks, it certainly is not now to us—as we shall see in section I below.) In more modern times Lord Byron, typically, gave the word a humorous twist when he wrote of the ferociously learned but notoriously crapulent Trinity College Cambridge classicist, Richard Porson, that he "could hiccup Greek like a helot". That was a coded reference to the Spartans' regular practice, recorded in Plutarch's *Life of Lykourgos* 28, of compelling Helots, who were native Greek speakers, to get disgustingly drunk on unmixed wine and then displaying them before the young in their *suskania* (communal dining groups or messes) as examples of behaviour utterly inappropriate for a properly brought up Spartan.[6]

....

[4] In the ancient 'mirage' (the term is originally that of Ollier 1933-43) the Helots may be conveniently traced and tracked through the index to Rawson 1991: s.v.; cf. for the fifth and fourth centuries, Klees 1991-1992. The first scholarly modern study of ancient Sparta as a whole was by J. C. F. Manso; his 3-volume opus (Leipzig, 1800-1805) contains a typically sober appendix on the Helots (vol. I, Beylage 10, pp. 135-155). For pre-1800 'Forschung', see Schulz-Falkenthal 1986, 1987. For an excellent general overview of scholarly Sparta research, see Christ 1986. Recent highlights include Oliva 1971, together with his 1986 review of the literature on the Helot question, Ducat's outstanding synthetic study (1990), and Hodkinson 2000: ch. 4 ('Helotage and the exploitation of Spartan territory').

To give some indication of the pace of current research and level of current interest, I note that in the time that elapsed between my delivering the original oral version of this paper and my writing up this version for publication the sixth chapter of Ducat 1990 appeared in English translation with some editorial comment (Ducat 2002); my 'Rebels and *Sambos*' article (originally 1985) was reprinted with a new introduction and supplementary bibliography (Cartledge 2001a—see further section II below); and major new discussions of Messenian Helot settlement patterns, arising out of the collaborative Pylos Regional Archaeology Project (PRAP) that she co-directs (see below, text and n. 40), were published by Susan Alcock (2002a, 2002b: esp. ch. 4). See also her study of Pausanias's 'Messeniaka' (book IV of the *Periegesis*): Alcock 2001. Disappointingly, though, Koliopoulos 2001 in his study of Spartan 'high strategy' manages to overlook the Helots almost completely.

[5] Ste. Croix 1981: 149 does properly emphasise this.

[6] The Byron passage is cited and documented in Cartledge 1998: 106. The Plutarch passage is translated as text D8a in Appendix 4 of Cartledge 2001b: 305. That Appendix contains translations of only 'some' ancient sources; some others not included there will be translated and/or discussed below. On Spartan education, see now Griffith 2001 *passim*.

Byron's philhellenism took the shape of a fairly uncomplicated admiration of a heroic and exemplary ancient Greek past. References to Marathon and Thermopylae tripped easily from his silver tongue. On the eve of another, less glorious war, the professional classicist Louis Macneice produced one of the most striking and jarring poems of the last century, the long and meditative *Autumn Journal* of 1939. It was, he wrote there of the ancient world, "all so unimaginably different/ and all so long ago". The larger immediate context (the end of section IX) from which those two familiar lines are taken bears full citation:

And when I should remember the paragons of Hellas

    I think instead

Of the crooks, the adventurers, the opportunists,

    The careless athletes and the fancy boys,

The hair-splitters, the pedants, the hard-boiled sceptics

    And the Agora and the noise

Of the demagogues and the quacks; and the women pouring

    Libations over graves

And the trimmers of Delphi and the dummies at Sparta and lastly

    I think of the slaves.

And how one can imagine oneself among them

    I do not know;

It was all so unimaginably different

    And all so long ago.

"[A]nd lastly . . . the slaves": it is probably never otiose, in an intellectual sense, to be reminded of them and their key role in making Greek culture, especially in connection with "the dummies of Sparta".[7] But against Macneice's hard-boiled and essentially pessimistic invocation it is at any rate intriguing to set another much less well known poem of the 1930s, "Spartacus" by James Leslie Mitchell, who is better known, as a novelist, under his pen name Lewis Grassic Gibbon. Here is part of the poem's apostrophe to the eponymous rebel slave leader:

....

[7] Cartledge 1993.

From out the darkling heavens of misty Time

Clear is thy light, and like Ocean's chime

Thy voice. Yea, clear as when unflinchingly

Thou ledst the hordes of helotry to die

And fell in glorious fight, nor knew the day

The creaking crosses fringed the Appian Way—

Sport of the winds, O ashes of the strong!

But down the aeons roars the helots' song . . .

Perhaps it was the assonance of "Sparta" and "Spartacus" that prompted Mitchell's poetically forceful but historically deeply misleading assimilation of two very different sorts of unfreedom, the chattel slavery of Spartacus and his gladiators and the Helotage imposed by the Spartans.

However that may be, Grassic Gibbon's novel *Spartacus* was published in 1933, most baneful among twentieth-century years, and he himself was part of the widespread movement of intellectually-minded communist revolutionaries who found in the rising led by Spartacus in 73 BCE both inspiration and legitimation for their calls for the liberation of the "enslaved" proletariat two millennia later. Of course, the Spartacist League and its distant followers like Mitchell/Grassic Gibbon were a little too misty-eyed about the true nature of Spartacus's revolt.[8] But at least a faint and distant echo of that battle cry of freedom lies behind the present scholarly project, led by Susan Alcock and Nino Luraghi, and that is yet another side of the Helot mirage worth commemorating and indeed celebrating. For I am one of those who firmly believe that historians should not be ashamed to nail their colours to moral masts, to decry unfreedom and cry up liberation whenever and wherever they can—with all due respect, of course, for the evidence and for the generally accepted historiographical norms and principles for interpreting it.

But even if that belief of mine is not widely shared, it is hard to dispute that the moment in 370/69 BCE when many thousands of Greeks, Messenian Helots, were at last set free, into not just personal but—for the adult males— political emancipation, was a turning-point in historiographical perception. For, as Pierre Vidal-Naquet conclusively established, the liberation of the Messenian Helots by Epameinondas provoked a historiographical *coupure*. In an area of Greek life that was generally rather murky conceptually and linguistically (as

....

[8] Shaw 2001: esp. 14-24.

well as morally) speaking, Theopompus of Chios's apparently original distinction between slaves bought individually for cash on the market and peoples or ethnic groups collectively enslaved in and on their native land represented a major intellectual breakthrough.[9]

To that observation of Vidal-Naquet's I would add that the liberation of the Messenian Helots may well also have marked a change of sensibility, at least among the more sensitive intellectual Greeks. "God", opined the contemporary rhetor and philosopher Alkidamas, a pupil of Gorgias, had "made no man a slave". According to our source for that opinion, a scholiast on Aristotle's *Rhetoric* 1373b18, Alkidamas's general statement had been prompted specifically by the Messenians' liberation. It was progressive and enlightened Sophistic views like that, presumably, which helped to provoke from Aristotle his philosophically as well as morally retrogressive defence of "natural" slavery.[10]

What is more, the Messenian revolt and liberation of 370/69 changed the course of Spartan and so all Greek history. We have to look only a little further down the line, chronologically, to see just how great was their impact. Sparta, formerly the greatest power on the Greek mainland, was already by 360 condemned to isolationist impotence. Two illustrations, both deft strokes of Macedonian foreign policy, will have to suffice. One of the smartest of Philip II's many smart diplomatic moves was to leave Sparta in 338/7 deliberately in the cold outside the framework of what moderns refer to as the League of Corinth.[11] One of the most telling of his son Alexander the Great's authentic *bons mots* was the inscription that he caused to be appended to the dedication to Athena of the 300 panoplies that he sent back to Athens after the Battle of the Granikos in 334: "Alexander son of Philip and the Greeks—except the Spartans—[*sc.* dedicate these spoils taken] from the barbarians who inhabit Asia".[12]

....

9 Vidal-Naquet 1986. Victor Hanson (2000: 17-120) has recently, and I think rightly, celebrated Epameinondas as one of history's great liberators. Further on the historiography of Greek slavery, ancient and modern: Hunt 1998; Cartledge 2002a.

10 Alkidamas = Text E1 in Garnsey 1996: 75-76. Garnsey 1996: 107-127 is a useful discussion of the notoriously difficult Aristotelian defence of a doctrine of 'natural' slavery, on which see also Cartledge 2002b: 135-141.

11 The story is best told in one of the greatest achievements in the field of ancient Greek history of the last generation, Guy Griffith's study of the reign of Philip II of Macedon, his contribution to Hammond and Griffith 1979: see esp. pp. 616-619.

12 Arrian *Anabasis* I.16.7. C. P. Cavafy, no less brilliantly, picked up on and indeed developed that trope for his own age in one of his very best poems, 'In the Year 200 B.C.' (1931). In case it should be wondered why Alexander dedicated precisely 300 suits of armour, surely this was because he was intending a calculatedly cruel reminder of Sparta's long past glory days of resistance to Persia at Thermopylae in 480 BCE led by King Leonidas and his 300 (on which, incidentally, Cavafy also wrote hauntingly).

In the remainder of this necessarily very brief Helotological *tour d'horizon*, I shall focus on what I see as the three major pressure-points of current and likely future scholarly discussions of the Helots and the Helot experience in the Classical fifth and fourth centuries. In order to do so, I shall be privileging very deliberately the contemporary evidence of Thucydides and Aristotle, who have—or in my view ought to enjoy—a better than average reputation for empirical reliability and analytical acuteness (though not necessarily, in all respects, for moral sensitivity).

1. Status

As I understand them, several leading students of the Helots today—Ducat, Hodkinson and Luraghi among them—wish to deny, or at any rate to minimise, the gulf in status between Helots and all (or most) other slaves (or peoples and individuals labelled as *douloi* or an equivalent term) in Classical Greece.[13] That is, they wish to emphasise, rather, individual ownership (in so far as that term is strictly applicable in any ancient Greek context) and control of Helot *douloi,* with all that that might be taken to imply for, for instance, an internal "market" in Helots, as opposed to any supposed ownership and control by the Spartans collectively. The well-known and much discussed statements of Strabo (first century BCE/CE) and Pausanias (late second century CE), which seem to be saying that Helots were somehow enslaved to the community as such, or at any rate more so than to an individual Spartan master or mistress, seem to stand against them.[14] But these are dismissed or finessed on the grounds that they apply, if at all in a strict sense, only to the post-revolutionary times of the later third century BCE onwards, that is, to the period after the revolutions of Agis IV and Kleomenes III, and, therefore, only to the Lakonian Helots.[15] Against which revision I wish to lodge a protest, on two grounds mainly, using Thucydides and Aristotle respectively as my witnesses to what I take to be the truth of the matter in the Classical era.

Thucydides at 5.34 makes it unambiguously clear that at least some Helots were then (421 BCE) manumitted, not through private sale or gift by individual

....

[13] Ducat 1990: esp. ch. III ('La relation de propriété'); Hodkinson 2000: esp. ch. 4, and this volume; Luraghi, this volume, and 2002. I do not discuss here the question of the origins of Helotage, whether in Lakonia or Messenia, but I note Luraghi's confident assertion, this volume, that 'mass enslavement of an indigenous population is an inherently unlikely explanation' (p. 109).

[14] The texts are respectively Cartledge 2001b: 303 (C.11) and 301 (B.7b).

[15] See ch. 4 of Cartledge and Spawforth 2001 (a bibliographically updated reissue of the corrected 1991 paperback reprint of the 1989 original).

masters (or mistresses), but publicly by formal act of the collective entity that we usually call the Spartan State:[16]

> The Spartans decreed that the Helots who had fought with Brasidas should be free and allowed to live where they liked, and not long afterwards settled them with the *Neodamôdeis* at Lepreion, which is situated on the border between *Lakonikê* and *Eleia*; Sparta being at this time at enmity with Elis.

This is far from being the only evidence for the fact of the manumission of Helots, which, indeed, was practised by the Spartans with considerable managerial art and skill. I would argue, furthermore, that it was precisely because (at least some) Helots were collectively, centrally and publicly manumitted that a group of freedmen like the Neodamodeis could come into existence uniquely here. For although the Helots, while they were Helots, might intelligibly be lumped together with some other Greek and non-Greek servile collectivities such as the Penestai of Thessaly, as they are by Aristotle in a fragment from his lost *Lakedaimoniôn Politeia*,[17] the Neodamodeis would appear to have no analogues elsewhere whatsoever, and no ancient source compares them in any respect to any other collectivity of manumittees. They were, to adapt the label "between free people and *douloi*" applied by the second-century CE Greek lexicographer Pollux (3.83) to the Helots and other supposedly comparable servile peoples Greek and non-Greek, between full citizens and Helots. Practically speaking, in other words, whatever the technical legal position may have been, the Neodamodeis were liable for collective public duty on their ex-masters' terms and at their ex-masters' pleasure, and so suffered collectively, for military purposes of various sorts, something like the condition of *paramonê* imposed on certain individual ex-chattel slaves in the Hellenistic period.[18]

It remains to consider Aristotle *Politics* 1263a31-7:

> Such a system [sc. of private acquisition/possession (*ktêsis*), but use in common among friends] exists even now in outline in some cities . . . : for example, in Lakedaimon they use each other's *douloi* almost as if they were their own, and horses and dogs likewise, and similarly with produce in the countryside if they require provisions on a journey.

....

[16] For once, 'state' is probably an accurate enough term. Sparta, odd in this as in so many ways, was not entirely or straightforwardly a 'stateless political community', as all other Greek *poleis* probably were (on this I agree with my former pupil, Dr. Moshe Berent: see Berent 1994).

[17] Arist. fr. 586 Rose: '[the Kallikyrioi at Syracuse] are like the Spartans' Helots, the Thessalians' Penestai, and the Cretans' Klarotai'. See generally Lotze 1959 and 1985. See also van Wees, this volume.

[18] Cartledge, *Der Neue Pauly* 8 (2000) 823, s.v. 'Neodamodeis'; cf. Christien 2000: 147-149.

Isn't Aristotle making it clear that *ktêsis*—acquisition, and so possession or owner-ship—of Helots was private, but use of them, ideally among friends, common? He is indeed, though unfortunately he does not state explicitly how in his view the *ktêsis* was effected or maintained. But I note, first, that this is stated in the present tense; he may therefore be talking about Lakonian Helots only, since he is writing well after the liberation of Messenia, and about conditions when the *ancien régime* was on the slide or at least being relaxed. And I note, second, another passage of the *Politics* a little later on (1264a8-11):

> In the upshot no other regulation will have been introduced [in the ideal Kallipolis of Plato's *Republic*] except the exemption of the Guardians from farming—a measure that even now [or now too] the Spartans are undertaking/attempting to introduce (*poiein*).

This formally implies that at least some Spartans were in practice farming, despite the (legally enforceable?) attempt to exempt them from that (otherwise peculiarly Helot) function, in the same way that the ruling philosopher Guardians of Plato's ideal Kallipolis were supposed to be likewise exempted. Again, that situation would not comport with the continued enforcement of a strict "Lykourgan" regime at Sparta. In other words, how far can we legitimately press Aristotle on the individual ownership as opposed to communal control of Helots? Beyond him, there is no other usable and directly relevant ancient testimony.

Which brings me back, finally in this section, to Thucydides. No doubt, as Figueira has ably argued, the Athenians had their reasons for inventing their own Helot mirage, typically stressing the Helots' collective ethnic solidarity rather than their class solidarity in opposition to the Spartans.[19] The Spartans, likewise, had their own reasons for insisting on the servility, the slave status, of the Helots. Nevertheless, the public use of *douleia* as a collective abstract for concrete in their treaty with the Athenians of 421—as reported, surely accurately, in Thucydides 5.23.3—is I think quite remarkable. Again, there is a great deal in a name. That the word *douleia* was available for use at all, and that it had a unique and unambiguous reference to the Helots, for me these are the key points. Nor do I need to dwell here on the precise nature of the treaty reference, to which I shall be returning. I merely remark that the Athenians were swearing, unilaterally, to aid the Spartans in case the *douleia* should revolt.[20] No other slaves in Greece taken in the mass, apart

....

[19] Figueira 1999.

[20] That is, to be more precise, revolt *again*; but the legal basis of the Athenians' assistance to the Spartans during the Helot revolt of the 460s is obscure, and, besides, that aid had been unhappily repudiated (see esp. Thuc. 1.102.3), which may perhaps partly explain the attempt at unilateral quasi-legal codi-fication in an otherwise bilateral treaty of defensive alliance.

perhaps from the Penestai of Thessaly, could plausibly have been so labelled in an official document.[21]

In short, H.W. Singor seems to me to get the Helots' status just about exactly right when he writes: "The helots never were degraded to the position of slaves of their respective masters though they remained enslaved as a nation to the collectivity of the Spartan state".[22]

2. Treatment

An important part of what is at stake for modern scholars who wish to explain as well as understand this near-unique historical phenomenon is the general question of how important the Helots were to the entire Spartan political and social and cultural regime, and especially how much of a threat they posed to that regime on a regular, everyday basis—as opposed to the searingly manifest episodes of concerted and open revolt such as those in the 460s and in 370/69. In short, how, and how well or ill, were the Helots as a rule treated?[23]

Much hangs, in this debate, on one's reading of Thucydides 4.80.3, which irritatingly is not unambiguous:

> Fear of their numbers and obstinacy prompted the Spartans to take the action which I shall now relate. For [either] Spartan policy had always been determined by the necessity of taking precautions against the Helots [or] in the Spartans' relations with the Helots the central issue had always been to keep them under surveillance.

Either, then, Thucydides is saying that, as a general principle of governance, Spartan policy had always been determined by the necessity of taking precautions against the Helots. *Or* he is making a more restricted claim, about the centrally and fundamentally precautionary nature of the Spartans' dealings with the Helots. Whichever of those readings is correct, the ambiguity must not be allowed to obscure the fact that his usage of "always" is deliberately emphatic: the Greek word *aiei* appears first in the sentence. This gives a special significance to the circumstance that it is in this same passage that Thucydides goes on to relate as an illustration of that general state of affairs an instance of extreme Spartan surveillance involving, allegedly, the calculatedly

....

21 On the Penestai, see comprehensively Ducat 1994.

22 Singor 1993: 41.

23 What follows is an adapted and, I hope, strengthened version of my new introduction to Cartledge 2001b. Manso (1800: 146) claimed the credit for being the first to appreciate the true significance of Thuc. 4.80.

duplicitous slaughter of a round 2000 Helots. Those modern scholars who wish to play down the importance of the Helot "danger" to Sparta or the determining influence of that perceived danger on the whole Spartan regime tend mostly to favour the second, more minimal translation of Thucydides 4.80.3 given above, though even that is a concession too far in the eyes of those who are prepared even to deny the historicity of that reported massacre.[24] In the sharpest possible contrast Thucydides, the contemporary historian himself, not only believed the massacre to have happened but deemed it to be and presented it as an illustration of a general rule of Spartan behaviour towards the Helots: "always", as—e.g.—in this particular instance. So, not only is the fundamental and essential nature of the Spartan regime at scholarly stake here, but so too are Thucydides's judgment and reputation.

What, then, might Thucydides's source(s) for this story have been (as usual, he doesn't tell us explicitly), and might there have been any ideological or other kind of motive that could have led him to abandon in this case what seem to have been his usual high standards of verification and authentication and so to fall for a contrived and malicious anti-Spartan fiction? As for the first issue, it is vital to take the full measure of his very rare confession, in connection with the numbers of the Spartan dead at the battle of Mantineia in 418, that he could not estimate the Spartans' casualties with any accuracy "on account of the secrecy of their *politeia*" (5.68.2). *Politeia* is also, alas, ambiguous: it could mean either the Spartan state authorities specifically in 418 or the Spartans' political arrangements more generally (roughly our "constitution") or, most generally of all, their whole way of life. But for the purpose of interpreting 4.80.2-4 the key inference to be made from 5.68.2 is that in the case of the Helot massacre the awkwardly probing and sceptical Thucydides did *not* feel such qualms of doubt or ignorance, even though that deceitful outrage had been accomplished, as he rather sensationally reported it, in total secrecy.[25] From what, to him, reliable witness or witnesses could he have received and believed such a report?

Speculation should be kept on the tightest of reins. If we exclude Spartan or Perioikic deserters or defectors on the grounds that they were probably either thin on the ground or non-existent, the likeliest potential sources, direct or indirect, are

....

[24] For instance, Roobaert 1977; Talbert 1989 (to which I replied in Cartledge 1991); and Whitby 1994. Whitby's new collection (2002, index s.v. 'helots') does not seriously reopen this particular issue.

[25] As he put it, 'No one ever knew how each of them perished'. For the chilling significance of the phrase 'each of them', see Vidal-Naquet 1992: 102-109. On the deceitfulness involved, see Hesk 2000: 31 n. 39.

[26] Such fugitive Helots had two main routes of escape from Sparta's own home territory potentially open to them: either via the fortified position occupied by the Athenians at Pylos in Messenia since 425 (it was the capture of this that in 424, according to Thuc. 4.80.3, provoked the Spartans to extreme fear of Helot 'obstinacy' [*skaiotês*] and numbers), or *via* the 'sort of isthmus' in the Malea peninsula in Lakonia opposite the island of Kythera that the Athenians occupied and fortified in 413, precisely as a place 'to which the Helots might desert' (Thuc. 7.26.2).

fugitive Helots.[26] Or, if one requires Athenian or Athenian-connected intermediaries, one's thoughts might well go to the ex-Helot Messenians settled by the Athenians at Naupaktos in *c.* 460 and used profitably by the Athenian general Demosthenes (who was surely known to Thucydides personally) both during and after the Pylos success of 425. Why, finally, did Thucydides choose to find the witness or witnesses reliable and believable?

Pro-Athenian patriotic prejudice on big issues such as overall war-guilt has been alleged against Thucydides, though not in my view sustainably.[27] It is, on the other hand, utterly implausible that he should have shared any such fellow-feeling for slaves or Helots as may—perhaps—have been entertained by Athenian ideological democrats.[28] The most economical and satisfying explanation of Thucydides 4.80.2-4 would therefore seem to me to be that the reported massacre of some 2000 Helots at some (unspecified) time before 424 fitted into a pattern already in the eyes of Thucydides firmly established and rigorously tested: a pattern of Spartan precaution to the point of paranoia towards the Helots that might entail exemplary punishments of outstanding brutality. Thucydides' overall method of historical presentation may in my view appropriately be characterised as paradigmatic. Accordingly, his chilling description at 4.80.2-4 of the massacre of (in round figures) 2000 Helots, whenever exactly that happened, should therefore be read as his paradigm case of the Spartans' regular treatment of the Helots.

Why should he have so considered it? Thucydides does not mention the Spartan Krypteia (first explicitly attested by Plato and Aristotle), though a version of it undoubtedly existed in his day, nor does he cite the annual declaration of war on the Helots by the Ephors (also first attested by Aristotle), though this too has a good chance of having been in force already in the late fifth century.[29] But he had no necessary cause or obligation to cite them and if, as is likely enough, he nevertheless knew of them, they will have been part and parcel of a reassuringly coherent and consistent picture. Thucydides does, on the other hand, cite and cite emphatically the Spartans' seemingly paranoid dismissal of the Athenians "alone of their allies"

....

[27] On this big issue see now Powell 2002: 436-448 (Appendix, in successful rebuttal of E. Badian, entitled 'Did Thucydides write 'pure fiction'? Ancient history and modern passion').

[28] Thucydides on the Helots is perhaps something of an exception to the rule, convincingly identified by Peter Hunt (1998), that all the major Greek historians underemphasised the role of slaves and the unfree in Greek warfare.

[29] On the sources for the Krypteia, see Lévy 1988; cf. Jeanmaire 1913; Ducat 1997a, 1997b; Cartledge, *Der Neue Pauly* 6 (1999) 872, s.v.; Handy 2001. Griffith (2001: 51 n. 92) rightly distinguishes between the Krypteia's Helot-policing function, restricted perhaps to a specially selected elite squad, and the test in survival skills applied to all immediate pre-adults. On the Ephors in general, and specifically their annual declaration of war on the Helots (Aristotle fr. 543 Gigon), see Ste. Croix 1981: 48, 149; and now Richer 1998: 249-251.

(1.102.3) during the Pentekontaëtia, at the time of the great (mainly Messenian) Helot revolt sparked by the earthquake of *c*. 465. Moreover, in the course of his Peloponnesian War narrative, he relates a number of telling instances of the Spartans murdering free Greeks.[30] He thereby and in other ways testifies crucially to the physical violence that was a striking feature, both literally and metaphorically, of Spartan behaviour at home and abroad.[31] An *a fortiori* inference by the reader, so far as the Spartans' treatment of unfree Helots was concerned, would therefore seem entirely justifiable, and I am confident that Thucydides intended just such an implication.

In short, I—still—see no good reason not to believe the authenticity of the report of the massacre at Thucydides 4.80.2-4, and every reason to regard this extreme and typically deceitful precautionary measure as powerful evidence of an all too vivid perception, on the part at least of the Spartans, of the genuine existence of a Helot "danger".

3. Revolt

The original version of my essay on Helot revolt was published in a *Festschrift* that I co-edited for G. E. M. de Ste. Croix, one of the most distinguished students of ancient Greek and Roman servitude in the past half-century.[32] For him, slavery and other forms of unfree labour constituted the basis, in a marxist sense, of Graeco-Roman civilisation and culture, and he devoted his unusually powerful mind to studying them in all their manifestations, ideological as well as material, since his time as a mature undergraduate student in the late 1940s at University College London, where he was influenced above all by the teaching of A. H. M. Jones.[33]

Slave revolt, or rather its apparent absence from the world of chattel slavery in Classical Greece, is that essay's theme. But this is just one aspect of a vast subject, the importance of which remains in my view still somewhat underappreciated, or at any rate understudied, by historians of ancient Greece generally. Peter Hunt's 1998 monograph on the use of slaves in Greek warfare, and the (non)mentions of that use by the great fifth- and fourth-century Greek historians, is of course a

....

[30] At 2.67.3, the Spartans reportedly murdered neutrals as well as Athenian and allied traders at the outset of the war; at 3.68.2, they massacred at least 200 Plataians in 427; and at 5.83.2, they killed all available freemen of Peloponnesian Hysiai in 419 (on this last, see Dover 1973: 39).

[31] Hornblower 2000.

[32] Cartledge and Harvey 1985. What follows here is partially based on my new introduction to Cartledge 2001b; see also Cartledge 2002a.

[33] Ste. Croix on slavery: see items 9 and 40 of the 'Select Bibliography' in Cartledge and Harvey 1985: viii-xii, in addition to Ste. Croix 1981 (*op. cit.*, item 45) *passim*. For the influence of Jones on Ste. Croix, see 'Editors' Preface', *ibid. xv*.

shining recent exception to that general neglect—but it is the sort of exception that goes to prove the rule.[34]

My essay of 1985 was also an evangelistical exercise in comparativist method, owing most in its original form to the work of Eugene Genovese on slave revolt in the Americas and something to the systematising historical sociology of slavery of Orlando Patterson.[35] The essay is divided into two parts. In the first and longer one I attempt to apply systematically to Classical Greece those of the criteria for successful servile revolt elaborated by Genovese that I deem relevantly applicable. Here, in other words, I am attempting to account for a null case, the *non*-occurrence in Greece of servile revolt—as opposed to servile *resistance*, which is to be assumed and can indeed be sufficiently documented. In the second part of the essay, I apply those same criteria of Genovese's to the Helots of Sparta, both those of Lakonia and those of Messenia. As was notorious in antiquity and is still a matter for rightful preoccupation today, this servile group—or rather perhaps groups—did actually manage to revolt, more than once, and indeed not merely to revolt but, with a great deal of help from their friends (or at any rate their Spartan masters' enemies), to achieve full collective civic freedom (for the adult males of the new *polis* of Messene) as well as individual personal liberty.[36]

No doubt there were many in classical Greece who had special reasons for wanting to end Sparta's Helotage, and for being prepared to take the appropriate action when the opportunity offered. But I hope it is not controversial to claim that there must also have been something special about the condition or situation of the Helots that both provided the opportunity and prompted the capacity and willingness of outsiders to exploit it. What exactly that special factor or special factors was or were is the issue before us: was it relative numbers? the nature of the terrain? the mode of social and economic existence? ethnicity, i.e. ethnic self-consciousness? or a combination of some or all of those? In my original article of 1985 I concluded that the single most important variable in this complex multivariate process was what Genovese called in shorthand "the master-slave relationship", that is, the factor comprising slave ideology and psychology (both the masters' and the slaves'). I should like now to nuance that conclusion a little further by drawing especially on the work of Walter Scheidel (this volume) and Susan Alcock.[37] I shall argue, in effect, that it is a combination of status and treatment (as I understand them) that will give us the key to unlock the conundrum.

....

[34] See Cartledge 2002a.
[35] Genovese 1979; Patterson 1982.
[36] The story is told briefly in Cartledge 1987/2000: 384-385.
[37] Esp. Alcock 2002a.

The Helots, at any rate the Helots of Messenia, were an unfree people, not just a random collection of individually owned slaves.[38] They were moreover an unfree *Greek* people—and the fact that the very utterance of that phrase in a context of Greek domestic politics, as opposed to one of external imperial domination, sticks in the gullet is a fair index of just how rare (though not unique) this situation was, and how crucial their condition was in preparing them ultimately for freedom, or rather liberation. Even after the liberation of the Messenian Helots, indeed, Plato could speak of the situation of the remaining, Lakonian Helots as deeply controversial, and his pupil Aristotle, writing up to twenty years later, could liken them to an enemy constantly sitting in wait, as if in ambush, for the disasters of their masters.[39] That constituted a unique situation in ancient Greece, a giant exception within the overall framework of the classical Greek servile regime. But for it to become actively operational, material conditions had also to be favourable.

The shrinking size of the master class through a process laconically defined by Aristotle as *oliganthrôpia*—shortage of military manpower—had become conspicuous at least as early as the first phase of the Peloponnesian War.[40] The disproportion between the number of Helots and the number of adult male Spartan citizens, though never precisely quantifiable, can only have increased from the early fifth-century peak of the latter to the demise of Sparta as a great power a century later. Scheidel's composite mean estimate (really a "guesstimate") of 30,000 able-bodied adult male Helots in the early fifth century suggests that they then outnumbered their Spartiate counterparts by some four to one. To that we should now add the findings, admittedly preliminary and of course provisional and tentative, of the PRAP survey, to the effect that Messenian Helots lived in agglomerated settlements rather than on dispersed farmsteads: "Community dwelling not only helps to explain pragmatic things (such as how helots could plan rebellion), but provides the day-to-day context for other forms of communication as well . . . [S]uch dwelling together also affirmed emotional ties of kinship and of common concern which could, potentially, ignite into violent resistance."[41] This returns us to our starting point, the key factor of "the master-slave relationship".

. . . .

38 Though, as Alcock (1999: 337) rightly observes, 'It is possible . . . that the 'Messenians'—as a unified entity, with a self-awareness of group identity—were only created *with* conquest' (italics in the original); cf. Figueira 1999; Hall, this volume.

39 Plato *Laws* 776c = Cartledge 2001b: Appendix 4, Text A2a. Aristotle *Pol.* 1269a36-b5 = Cartledge 2001b: Appendix 4, Text E2a.

40 Cartledge 2001b: ch. 14, at 266.

41 Alcock 2002: 143, from a section, 'Spartan Messenia' (pp. 134-152), of chapter 4 ('Being Messenian').

ह

To conclude these brief reflections on the Helot mirage, I revisit the issue of terminology. The word "helot" is still quite often used figuratively in contemporary English to describe, classify or sympathise with any unusually oppressed, disenfranchised, even enslaved persons, such as, for example, the black indigenous population of South Africa under the former apartheid regime.[42] Actually, it is probably too glib to refer to any oppressed or even enslaved peoples today as "Helots". Nevertheless, this is an aspect of the Helot mirage that I for one would not wish entirely to discourage. For the Helots' (in part self-produced) liberation raises up, to borrow Ernst Bloch's ringing phrase, *das Prinzip Hoffnung*,[43] a principled hope of better times to come not only in the next world, if there is a next world, but in this world too.

....

[42] This was a fact remarked on by the late and much lamented Elizabeth Rawson in her splendid work on 'The Spartan Tradition in European Thought' (1991: 366).
[43] On Bloch's two-volume work (1959), see briefly Hobsbawm 1973: ch. 14.

Bibliography

Alcock, S. E. 1999. "The Pseudo-History of Messenia Unplugged." *Transactions of the American Philological Association* 129: 333-341.

_____. 2001. "The Peculiar Book IV and the Problem of the Messenian Past." In S. E. Alcock, J. F. Cherry and J. Elsner (eds.), *Pausanias: Travel and Memory in Roman Greece.* Oxford and New York: 142-153.

_____. 2002a. "A Simple Case of Exploitation? The Helots of Messenia." In P. Cartledge, E. Cohen and L. Foxhall (eds.), *Money, Labour and Land: Approaches to the Economies of Ancient Greece.* London and New York: 185-199.

_____. 2002b. *Archaeologies of the Greek Past. Landscape, Monuments, and Memories.* Cambridge.

Berent, M. 1994. "The Stateless Polis". Unpublished Ph.D. thesis, University of Cambridge.

Bloch, E. 1959. *Das Prinzip Hoffnung.* Two volumes. Frankfurt am Main.

Cartledge, P. 1987/2000. *Agesilaos and the Crisis of Sparta.* London and Baltimore.

_____. 1991. "Richard Talbert's Revision of the Sparta-Helot Struggle: A Reply." *Historia* 40: 379-381.

_____. 1993. "'Like a Worm i' the Bud?' A Heterology of Classical Greek Slavery." *Greece & Rome* 40: 163-180.

_____. 1998. "Classics for the Third Millennium." In S. Ormrod (ed.), *Cambridge Contributions.* Cambridge: 103-121.

_____. 2001a. "Rebels and *Sambos* in Classical Greece: A Comparative View." Revised reprint in Cartledge 2001c. London: 127-152. (Originally published in P. Cartledge and F. D Harvey [eds.], *CRUX: Essays in Greek History presented to G. E. M. de Ste. Croix,* London, 1985: 16-46).

_____.2001b. *Sparta and Lakonia: A Regional History 1300-362 BC.* Second edition. London and New York.

_____. 2001c. *Spartan Reflections.* Berkeley, Los Angeles and London.

_____. 2001d. "Spartan Wives: Liberation or Licence?" In Cartledge 2001c: 106-126. (Originally published in *Classical Quarterly* n.s. 31 [1981] 84-105).

_____. 2002a. "Greek Civilisation and Slavery." In T. P. Wiseman (ed.), *Classics in Progress.* London: 247-62.

_____. 2002b. *The Greeks: A Portrait of Self and Others.* Second edition. Oxford.

_____. 2002c. *The Spartans: An Epic History.* London.

Cartledge, P., and F. D. Harvey (eds.). 1985. *CRUX: Essays in Greek History Presented to G. E. M. de Ste. Croix.* London.

Cartledge, P., and A. J. S. Spawforth. 2001. *Hellenistic and Roman Sparta: A Tale of Two Cities.* Revised edition. London and New York.

Christ, K. 1986. "Spartaforschung und Spartabild" in K. Christ (ed.), *Sparta* (Wege der Forschung 622). Darmstadt: 1-72.

Christien, J. 2000. "Sparte: les années de gloire." In M.-C. Amouretti, J. Christien, F. Ruzé, and P. Sineux. *Le regard des Grecs sur la guerre. Mythes et réalités.* Paris: ch. 7.

Dover, K. J. 1973. *Thucydides.* (Greece & Rome New Surveys in the Classics 7). Oxford.

Ducat, J. 1990. *Les Hilotes.* (Bulletin de correspondance hellénique, Supplément 20). Athens and Paris.

_____. 1994. *Les Pénestes de Thessalie.* (Annales Littéraires de l'Université de Besançon 512). Paris.

_____. 1997a. "La cryptie en question." In P. Brulé and J. Oulhen (eds.), *Esclavage, guerre, économie en Grèce ancienne. Hommages à Yvon Garlan.* Rennes: 43-74.

_____. 1997b. "Crypties." *Cahiers du Centre Gustave Glotz* 8: 9-38.

_____. 2002. "The Obligations of Helots." In Whitby 2002:196-211. English translation of Ducat 1990: ch. 6.

Figueira, T. 1999. "The Evolution of the Messenian Identity." In S. Hodkinson and A. Powell (eds.), *Sparta: New Perspectives.* London: 211-44.

Garnsey, P. 1996. *Ideas of Slavery from Aristotle to Augustine.* Cambridge.

Genovese, E. D. 1979. *From Rebellion to Revolution: Afro-American Slave Revolts in the Making of the Modern World.* Baton Rouge and London.

Griffith, M. 2001. "Public and Private in Early Greek Education." In Y. L. Too (ed.), *Education in Greek and Roman Antiquity.* Leiden: 23-84.

Hammond, N. G. L., and G. T. Griffith 1979. *A History of Macedonia.* Vol. 2. *550-336 BC.* Oxford.

Handy, M. 2001. "Studien zur spartanischen *Krypteia.*" Unpublished M.A. thesis, Universität Graz.

Hanson, V. D. 2000. *The Soul of Battle: From Ancient Times to the Present Day, How Three Great Liberators Vanquished Tyranny.* New York

Hesk, J. P. 2000. *Deception and Democracy in Classical Athens.* Cambridge.

Hobsbawm, E.J. 1973. *Revolutionaries.* London.

Hodkinson, S. 2000. *Property and Wealth in Classical Sparta.* London.

Hornblower, S. 2000. "Sticks, Stones and Spartans: The Sociology of Spartan Violence." In H. van Wees (ed.), *War and Violence in Ancient Greece.* London: 57-82.

Hunt, P. 1998. *Slaves, Warfare and Ideology in the Greek Historians.* Cambridge.

Jeanmaire, H. 1913. "La cryptie lacédémonienne." *Revue des études grecques* 26: 121-150.

Klees, H. 1991-1992. "Zur Beurteilung der Helotie im historischen und politischen Denken der Griechen im 5. und 4. Jh. v. Chr." *Laverna* 2: 27-52; 3: 1-31.

Koliopoulos, K. 2001. ʿΗ ὑψηλὴ στρατηγικὴ τῆς ἀρχαίας Σπάρτης *(750-192 π. Χ.).* Athens.

Kunstler, B. L. 1983. "Women and the Development of the Spartan Polis: A Study of Sex Roles in Classical Antiquity". Unpublished Ph.D. thesis, Boston University.

Lévy, E. 1988. "La kryptie et ses contradictions." *Ktéma* 13: 245-252.

Lotze, D. 1959. Μεταξὺ ἐλευθέρων καὶ δούλων. *Studien zur Rechtsstellung unfreier Landbevölkerungen in Griechenland bis zum 4. Jahrhundert v. Chr.* Berlin.

_____. "Zu neuen Vermutungen über abhängige Landleute im alten Sikyon." In H. Kreissig and F. Kühnert (eds.), *Antike Abhängigkeitsformen.* Berlin: 20-28. (Reprinted in Lotze 2000: 57-68).

_____. 2000. *Bürger und Unfreie im vorhellenistischen Griechenland. Ausgewählte Aufsätze.* Ed. by W. Ameling and K. Zimmermann. Stuttgart.

Luraghi, N. 2002. "Helotic Slavery Reconsidered." In A. Powell and S. Hodkinson (eds.), *Sparta: Beyond the Mirage.* London: 229-50.

Manso, J. C. F. 1800-1805. *Sparta. Ein Versuch zur Aufklärung der Geschichte und Verfassung dieses Staates.* Three volumes. Leipzig.

Oliva, P. 1971. *Sparta and her Social Problems.* Amsterdam and Prague.

_____. 1986. "Die Helotenfrage in der Geschichte Spartas." Reprinted in K. Christ (ed.), *Sparta.* (Wege der Forschung 622). Darmstadt: 317-26. (Originally published in J. Herrmann and I. Sellnow [eds.], *Die Rolle der Volksmassen in der Geschichte der vorkapitalistischen Gesellschaftsformen,* Berlin 1975).

Ollier, F. 1933-1943. *Le mirage spartiate*. Two volumes. Paris.

Patterson, O. 1982. *Slavery and Social Death*. Cambridge, MA.

Pomeroy, S. 2002. *Spartan Women*. New York.

Powell, A. 2002. *Athens and Sparta: Constructing Greek Political and Social History from 478 BC*. Second edition. London and New York.

Rawson, E. 1991. *The Spartan Tradition in European Thought*. Originally published 1969. Oxford.

Richer, N. 1998. *Les Éphores. Études sur l'histoire et sur l'image de Sparte (VIIIe-IIIe siècles avant Jésus-Christ)*. Paris.

Roobaert, A. 1977. "Le danger hilote?" *Ktéma* 2: 141-55.

Ste. Croix, G. E. M. de. 1981. *The Class Struggle in the Ancient Greek World: From the Archaic Age to the Arab Conquests*. London and Ithaca.

Schulz-Falkenthal, H. 1986. "Die spartanische Helotie als Gegenstand der Forschung vom Anfang des 16. bis zum Ende des 17. Jahrhundert." *Wissenschaftliche Zeitschrift der Martin-Luther-Universität Halle-Wittenberg. Gesellschafts- und Sprachwissenschaftliche Reihe* 35.3: 96-107.

———. 1987. "Die spartanische Helotie als Gegenstand der Forschung im 18. Jahrhundert." *Wissenschaftliche Zeitschrift der Martin-Luther-Universität Halle-Wittenberg. Gesellschafts- und Sprachwissenschaftliche Reihe* 36.5: 82-101.

Shaw, B. D. (ed.). 2001. *Spartacus and the Slave Wars: A Brief History with Documents*. New York.

Singor, H. W. 1993. "Spartan Land Lots and Helot Rents." In H. Sancisi-Weerdenburg et al. (eds.), *De agricultura: In memoriam Pieter Willem de Neeve*. Amsterdam: 31-60.

Talbert, R. 1989. "The Role of the Helots in the Class Struggle at Sparta." *Historia* 38: 22-40.

Vidal-Naquet, P. 1986. "Reflections on Greek Historical Writing about Slavery." In *The Black Hunter*. Baltimore and London: 168-188.

———. 1992. "Assassins of Memory." In P. Vidal-Naquet, *Assassins of Memory: Essays on the Denial of the Holocaust*. New York: 99-142, 177-191.

Whitby, M. 1994. "Two Shadows: Images of Spartans and Helots." In A. Powell and S. Hodkinson (eds.), *The Shadow of Sparta*. London and New York: 87-126.

Whitby, M. (ed.). 2002. *Sparta*. Edinburgh.

Part I

Helotic histories

Three

Conquerors and serfs:
wars of conquest and forced labour in archaic Greece

Hans van Wees

In many parts of the Greek world, the typical agricultural labourer was neither a free man nor a slave, but something in between. The Greeks, for once, did not have a word for it, but we may call this status "serfdom".[1] Such serfs are generally regarded as creatures of the Dark Age, a primitive form of unfree labour destined to be replaced by the more modern institution of chattel slavery in the archaic period. Serfs were created for the last time in mainland Greece, it is thought, when the Messenians were forced into servitude by Spartan conquest around 700 BC. Some believe that most serf populations originated when Dorian invaders subjugated the native inhabitants of Greece, from 1100 BC onwards, in which case the Messenians were exceptional in being conquered so late. Others imagine that serfs were poor, vulnerable families who had fallen into a state of bondage to rich landowners over the centuries, in which case the Messenians were exceptional in being conquered at all.[2]

....

[1] "Serf" and "serfdom" are used here, not in any of their technical senses, but merely as a convenient shorthand to denote a slave-like status which does not entail outright chattel slavery.

[2] Dorian conquest: e.g. Lotze 1959: 69-77; Murray 1993: 153; cf. section 3, below. A process of internal subjection was assumed as the norm by Moses Finley, who placed helots and other groups "between free men and slaves" in the same bracket as debt-bondsmen, clients, and *coloni*, labelling all of these as "the half-free *within*" (1964: 128-130), an "*internal* [labour] force" (1973: 66-70). Finley left room for "force of arms" as a means of creating a "half-way type" of unfree labour (1973: 66), no doubt with Messenian helots and colonial serf populations in mind, but his argument requires that conquest was the exception. He stressed the contrast between exploitation of an internal labour force, which created a "spectrum of statuses", and exploitation of an externally acquired labour force (chattel slaves), which created a sharp polarization of free and unfree (e.g. 1959: 98; 1964: 132): this contrast would have been fatally undermined if "internal" labour forces had in fact often been subjected outsiders as well. Ian Morris adopted Finley's model (while applying it to earlier historical developments: 1987: esp. 187, 196); other scholars nod towards Finley's approach—and are sceptical about the historicity of the Dorian conquest—but end up merely suspending judgment: e.g. Austin and Vidal-Naquet 1977: 65, 86; Snodgrass 1980: 87-91 (esp. p. 89: "rightly or wrongly"); Garlan 1988: 95-96 ("whichever of the two solutions is favoured").

A reconsideration of the evidence will show that statuses "between free men and slaves" were not a relic of the Dark Age, and that the Messenian case was far from unique. The serf populations in the Greek world known to us were indeed created by conquest, not by a process of internal differentiation—but these conquests took place in the archaic age, specifically in the period c. 750-550 BC, not in the legendary age of the Dorian migrations.[3]

The process was, as we shall see, similar in many ways to the imposition of servitude on the natives of Central and South America by their sixteenth-century Spanish conquerors, whose attitudes call to mind the Spartan ethos: "Let the dogs work and die, said these men."[4]

1. Serfdom in three archaic empires

Even our best evidence for serfdom in early Greece is severely limited and has only reached us through the filter of classical and hellenistic historiography. Yet it is enough to show that at least three groups of serfs in the Peloponnese were created by conquest in the archaic age: Sparta's Messenian helots, Sicyon's "*katônakê-wearers*", and the "naked people" of Argos.

The Messenian helots

The earliest surviving account of the subjection of the Messenians appears in the near-contemporary poems of Tyrtaeus, which said that Theopompus, king of Sparta, occupied "Messene" after a twenty-year war of conquest in the time of "the fathers of our fathers" (F 5.1-6 West), probably the early seventh century.[5] As Tyrtaeus pictured it, some Messenians abandoned their homes (F.5.7-8), but those who stayed were forced to present half of their annual harvests to the Spartans, "labouring under the heavy burdens which they carry for their masters under

---

[3] This chapter adopts several of the important new ideas about the history of Messenian helotage recently developed by Nino Luraghi (and summarised by him in this volume), but also takes issue with some of his ideas, above all his contention that "in Greek history, there is not a single case of a city being conquered and its citizens being kept there as slaves of the conquerors" (2002: 237) and indeed that "mass enslavement of an indigenous population is an inherently unlikely explanation" for the origins of serfdom (this volume, p. 109; cf. 2002: 236).

[4] So Alonso de Zorita in his *Brief and Summary Relation of the Lords of New Spain, c. 1570* (1963: 217-218). Orlando Patterson singled out the Spanish conquest of the Americas as a rare modern example of enslavement "*en masse* and *in situ*" (1982: 110, 113).

[5] The most convincing chronology of the Messenian Wars is established by Parker 1993.

miserable compulsion, like donkeys" (F 6), and to mourn at Spartan funerals, "both the men and their wives uttering lamentations for their masters" (F 7).[6]

The poet does not seem to have called the Messenians "helots" (*heilôtai*), and perhaps this label was not applied to them until later, but their status was clearly already "between free men and slaves" and as such a form of serfdom. Families ("men and their wives") and presumably communities were left intact, but assigned to individual Spartan "masters" to whom they owed burdensome material and symbolic tributes. Forced lamentation at the death of people with whom one had "no connection or relation" (Aelian *VH* 6.1) was deemed particularly humiliating— it is a role played elsewhere by slave women, ostensibly mourning their master but crying "each for her own sorrows" (*Iliad* 19.301-2).[7]

Spartans and Messenians fought again in Tyrtaeus' own day, and the poet's allusion to the earlier conquest by Theopompus shows that the Spartans regarded their campaign as a war against rebellious subjects. It is possible, of course, that Theopompus' conquests had not extended to all of Messenia, and that the Spartans were in fact engaged in further expansion. At least one ancient school of thought held that the Messenians were not finally subjected until the end of this war, c. 600 BC.[8] After their defeat, according to Pausanias, some Messenians emigrated to Sicily,

....

6 Luraghi (this volume, pp. 114-5; cf. 2002: 235-6) notes that FF 6 and 7 do not name the Messenians and might refer to some other "dependent labour force"; he also points out that the only explicit statement in Tyrtaeus about the inhabitants of "Messene" (which, Luraghi points out, may not have meant the entire region later known as Messenia) is that they *left* their land. While this is true, we should give some weight to the fact that Pausanias (4.14.1-5) and his probable source Myron of Priene, who knew the whole poem, thought that FF 6 and 7 *did* refer to Messenians. It is, moreover, highly likely that FF 5, 6 and 7 were closely linked in the original text: in F 5.7, the people who leave their farmlands are introduced with the words *hoi men*, which suggests that they are the first half of a contrasting pair, indicated by the common *men* . . . *de* construction (used by Tyrtaeus in FF 4.3-5, 10.29, 11.5-6 and 11-14, 23.8-10 West). If so, the poem will have continued by introducing (with the words *hoi de*) a second group of inhabitants of "Messene", who did not flee, but stayed behind and accepted servitude, a status then colourfully described in FF 6 and 7 (cf. Hodkinson, this volume, p. 256).

7 For the label "helots", see below. Individual masters: Hodkinson 2000: 113-116; Luraghi, this volume, p. 114: "people held in a relation of personal dependence, rather than a submitted community". Forced lamentation for individual masters is to be distinguished from the duty to mourn at royal funerals mentioned by Herodotus (6.58), although Pausanias conflates the two by explaining "masters" as "kings and other officials" (4.14.4; cf. Hodkinson 2000: 237-238; Ducat 1990: 60). The perception of forced mourning as particularly "slavish" led Herodotus to stress that in Sparta even representatives of (free) citizen families and (free) perioikic communities mourned at royal funerals "under compulsion", a custom paralleled only among (slavish) barbarians; that (unfree) helots were also compelled to do so was unremarkable to him and he mentions this only in passing. For the same reason, Aelian stressed that the Spartans imposed the duty to lament on "free" Messenian women, i.e. women who had been free until the moment of conquest: one should not infer that Aelian thought that the Messenians remained free even after their defeat (contra Luraghi 2002: 236).

8 Plutarch *Moralia* 194b and Aelian *VH* 13.42, with the discussion of this date in Parker 1993.

while the rest were captured and "assigned to the helot class" (4.23.1), "paying tribute under compulsion as helots" (4.24.5). Many details of this story, however, are incompatible with a late seventh-century date, and if there is any truth in them at all they must derive from events in the aftermath of a Messenian revolt c. 490 BC.[9] The flight abroad of substantial numbers of Messenians whenever a revolt was crushed would have left the Spartans with a reduced labour force, and not surprisingly the signs are that smaller-scale desertion was a constant problem. Spartan masters would surely have needed to make up for such losses by importing chattel slaves or other forms of dependent labour. A gradual intermingling of natives and others would explain why, according to Thucydides, "most", but apparently not all, of the helots who rebelled in 464 BC were "descendants of the old Messenians who had been enslaved once" (1.101.2). It would also explain how Isocrates could claim in a piece of pro-Spartan rhetoric that the inhabitants of Messenia were not "truly Messenians" at all, but mere slaves (*Archidamus* 28).[10]

Along with its composition, the status of the population of Messenia is likely to have changed, even if our lacunose evidence makes it impossible to tell precisely how and when. Pausanias apparently thought that the status of "helot" was not actually imposed on the Messenians until after their final subjection, and that the serfdom imposed upon them after the initial conquest by Theopompus had not been quite the same thing. His comment that initially they had paid "no fixed tributes" (4.14.4), but a proportion of their crops, suggests that this was for him the key difference: helots *did* pay fixed sums of tribute.[11] This claim may be based on some knowledge of the status of Messenian helots in the archaic period, but may unfortunately equally well be based on projecting back into the past the position of late third-century Laconian helots.[12] Either way, it seems probable that agricultural

....

[9] Attested only by Plato *Laws* 692d, 698e, but see esp. Shaw 1999: 275-276, and Hunt 1998: 28-31.

[10] Another wave of emigration occurred a generation later, c. 460 BC, when defeated Messenian rebels left to settle in Naupactus (Thucydides 1.103.1-3); a Spartan treaty with Tegea forbidding the allies to harbour Messenians may reveal early worries about a draining away of manpower (Aristotle F 592 Rose; for its interpretation and possible dates, see Braun 1994, and Hall, this volume, pp. 151-2). The importation of chattel slaves and other dependents is plausibly suggested by Luraghi. The prominence and persistence of tomb cult in Messenia, noted in this volume by Hall, p. 160, and Hodkinson, p. 274, does suggest a general continuity of habitation, and indeed, as Hall attractively suggests, an attempt by the native population to identify themselves as "Achaeans".

[11] As pointed out by Luraghi 2002: 236 with n. 25 ("it must be the sharecropping arrangement that made this condition . . . different from Helotry"), and this volume, p. 131, noting the contrast between Pausanias 4.14.4-5 and 4.23.2, 24.5. Cf. Kiechle 1959: 57-62.

[12] Pausanias' source here was the third-century author Myron of Priene (4.6.2), whose understanding of the position of helots may well have been based primarily on the Laconian helots of his own day (*FGrHist* 106 FF 1-2). The fixed tribute obligations of the latter are described by Plutarch *Lycurgus* 8.4, 24.3 and *Moralia* 239e (with the discussion in Hodkinson 2000: 89, 125-126).

tributes were not fixed once and for all in the early seventh century, but were adjusted or even completely restructured from time to time, especially in the wake of revolts.

Other changes included the abolition of compulsory mourning for Spartan masters, which was confined to royal funerals. Compulsory military service in the Spartan army as light-armed attendants may not have been obligatory from the outset, but introduced later.[13] The limited rights which Sparta's serfs enjoyed— their masters were not allowed to sell them "across the border", set them free, or exact more than the established tribute—may also have been formulated over time rather than granted from the start.[14] Indeed, it has been attractively suggested that a formally defined status of "helot" may not have existed until the sixth century when a series of reforms of Spartan society and politics perhaps included the impo- sition of the standardised position and name of "helot" on an agricultural workforce which had previously comprised a wide variety of forms of dependent labour.[15]

Whatever the changes, there can be little doubt that the Messenians experi- enced fundamentally the same regime from the first conquest to their liberation some three centuries later in 370 BC: a state of serfdom imposed as a result of conquest.

Not long after Messenia regained its independence, we find the first expres- sions of the remarkable idea that its original subjection had taken place, not under king Theopompus, but several centuries earlier, only a generation or two after the Dorian migration[16] Since we have unambiguous evidence to the contrary in the fragments of Tyrtaeus, scholars rightly reject this notion out of hand. The fact that such a legendary story of conquest could be conjured up in defiance of a clear state- ment by a famous contemporary poet, however, shows how powerful were the forces of mythmaking and imaginative historiography—an issue to which we shall return when investigating the allegedly even earlier origins of Sparta's Laconian helots, the *penestai* of Thessaly and the serfs of Crete.

....

[13] Funerals: Hodkinson 2000: 264 n.5 (see also n. 7 above). Military service: the 35,000 helots mobilised by Sparta in 479 BC must have included Messenians (Herodotus 9.28-9).

[14] No sale or manumission: Ephorus *FGrHist* 70 F 117. No excess tribute: Plutarch *Moralia* 239e. See Ducat 1990: 57-59, and Hodkinson 2000: 117-118, 126. The "curse" laid on the overexploitative might well have applied when rents were proportional rather than a fixed share: see below, p. 70.

[15] So Luraghi 2002: 233-234, 240-241; for another reconstruction of changes in Messenian helot status, see Figueira, this volume, pp. 220-7.

[16] Isocrates *Archidamus* 22-3, claimed that the Spartans "acquired the territory after besieging the Messenians" in the first generation after the Dorian migration; Ephorus dated the "enslavement" of the Messenians another generation or more later, but still well before the war won by Theopompus (*FGrHist* 70 F 116, with Diodorus 15.66.2-3 and Nicolaus of Damascus *FGrHist* 90 F 31, 34).

The "katônakê-wearers" of Sicyon

"There were some slaves called the *katônakê*-wearers among the Sicyonians, whose position was similar to the *epeunaktai*", Theopompus noted in his *Histories* (*FGrHist* 115 F 176). The author of a local history of Sicyon, Menaechmus, agreed (*FGrHist* 131 F1). The *katônakê* was widely regarded as typical slave dress, "a thick woollen garment with sheepskin stitched onto it at the bottom".[17] The *epeunaktai*, "by-sleepers", as Theopompus fortunately explained later, were Laconian helots who had been allowed to marry Spartan citizen women when the Spartans had suffered heavy manpower losses in the Messenian War, and who had later been granted citizen status (F 171). The *katônakê*-wearers were therefore helot-like serfs, who at some point in time had been allowed to marry into citizen families and become free men.[18]

Yet another fragment of Theopompus says that "they were forced to wear the *katônakê* by the tyrants, so that they would not come to town" (F 311). We need not take too seriously the suggested rationale for making people wear sheepskin-trimmed cloaks. The idea that they would be too ashamed of their clothes to show themselves in public and would therefore stay on the farm was clearly inspired by the fourth-century notion that tyrants liked to keep their subjects dispersed and hard at work to stop them from plotting. What is left is the claim that Sicyon's rural serf population was created or regulated by "the tyrants", i.e. the Orthagorid dynasty of c. 650-550 BC. Much later sources making similar claims are unfortunately muddled and confuse the tyrants of Sicyon with the tyrants of Athens, but it seems unlikely that Theopompus shared in that confusion, and there is no reason to doubt that he reported a genuine local tradition about the origins of Sicyon's serfs.[19]

Other stories about the tyrants of Sicyon tell of their protracted war against neighbouring Pellene. Orthagoras' rise to power was said to have been due to his successes in this war (*P.Oxy.* 1365.28-45). More importantly, Cleisthenes, who ruled c. 570 BC, was according to Aristotle "a warlike man" who ultimately

....

[17] Aristophanes *Lysistrata* 1150-6; *Ecclesiazusae* 724. Description: Pollux 7.68.

[18] The point of the comparison between them and *epeunaktai* cannot be simply that they were slaves who had become citizens: if that is what Theopompus was trying to say, he could have said so, or at least picked a less arcane comparison, such as the Spartan *neodamôdeis*.

[19] Pollux 7.68 says that the *katônakê* became compulsory dress "in Sicyon under the tyrants and in Athens under the Peisistratids". The idea that this happened in Athens as well surely derived from an over-literal reading of Aristophanes' *Lysistrata* 1150-6, which speaks *metaphorically* of Athenians wearing the slave's *katônakê* under the tyrants but the free man's cloak after their liberation. Once this parallel had been drawn, others were invented: instead of *katônakophoroi* Sicyon's serfs are called *korynêphoroi* in various lists (Pollux 3.83; Stephanus of Byzantium s.v. *Chios*; *Etymologicum Gudianum* s.v. *Heilôtai*), on the analogy with Peisistratus' body-guard of that name (cf. Whitehead 1981; Lotze 1985 = Lotze 2000: 57-68). Theopompus' fragments as they stand are free from this muddle, and the mix-up is likely to be the result of several centuries of further speculation, compilation, and epitomizing.

"destroyed" the city of Pellene, "and some say that Pellene was not only enslaved by Cleisthenes . . . but that their captured wives and daughters were reduced to prostitution".[20] The story seemed shocking even in antiquity ("this is most savage . . . not even among barbarians is this acceptable", exclaimed Aelian, *VH* 6.1.4) and whatever the precise historical events behind the tradition, there was clearly more to this war than skirmishing over strips of borderland. Sicyonian expansion did not stop there: its next victims were Pellene's neighbour Donoussa, which was destroyed, and Donoussa's neighbour Aigeira, which according to legend used a herd of goats with torches tied to their horns to beat back the assault (Pausanias 7.26.2, 6). The conquerors held on to their new territories for only about two generations. Pellene was refounded on a new site and is known to have been organising its own games soon after the Persian Wars.[21]

It seems obvious that we should put two and two together and identify Sicyon's serf population as the "enslaved" Pelleneans and Donoussans, subjected to Sicyon's short-lived empire and forced to submit to humiliations of which wearing slave dress was only the least.

Supporting evidence for this identification comes from Herodotus' initially baffling story about the reforms instigated by Cleisthenes of Sicyon (5.68):

> He changed the names of the Dorian tribes, so that the Sicyonians and the Argives would not have the same ones. In doing so, he also made a great mockery of the Sicyonians, for he gave them names which derived from the words "pig" and "ass" with changed endings, with the exception of his own tribe, which he gave a name derived from his own position of power. The latter, then, were called Rulers of the People (*archelaoi*), but the others Swine People (*hyatai*), Donkey People (*oneatai*) and Pig People (*choireatai*). The Sicyonians used these names for the tribes not only while Cleisthenes ruled but for another sixty years after his death. Then, after discussion, they changed them to the usual Hylleis, Pamphyloi and Dymanates, but added a fourth which they gave a name derived from Aigialeus, son of Adrastus, and called Aigialeis.

As Herodotus tells it, the story is very odd. How could Cleisthenes give four new names to three old tribes? Why would a ruler with a reputation as a popular leader want to insult the majority of his potential supporters? Why would the Sicyonians have put up with their insulting labels for half a century after the fall of the tyranny?

---

[20] Aristotle *Politics* 1315b17 ("warlike man") and as cited in *P.Oxy.* 1241, col.iii.2-12 (on Pellene).

[21] Zenobius 1.57. Games: Pindar *Olympian* 7.86, 9.98, 13.109; *Nemean* 10.44 (468-464 BC).

Who were the Aigialeis assigned to a new tribe when the rest eventually reverted to their old tribal system?

The answer to the last question provides a clue about the true nature of these reforms. We know that in Cleisthenes' day *Aigialeis*, "shore-dwellers", was what the Sicyonians called the inhabitants of Pellene, Donoussa, Aigeira and the other cities along the north coast of the Peloponnese, inhabited by people better known to us as Achaeans, who were said to be descendants of Aigialeus, just as Herodotus claimed (Alcman F 149 Page). The fourth tribe, then, evidently contained Achaeans incorporated into the Sicyonian political community. These Achaeans were surely the remnant of Pelleneans and others enslaved two generations earlier. When Pellene regained its independence, around 500 BC, the Sicyonians must have decided to admit the rest of their Achaean subjects to citizenship, probably by the gradual extension of citizen-rights to Achaeans marrying into Sicyonian families. Not until the reign of the tyrant Euphron in the 360s BC were the last remaining serfs enfranchised.[22]

With this as a starting point, we can begin to understand what had happened under Cleisthenes. When he subjected neighbouring communities, he added insult to injury by giving their defeated inhabitants shameful names—the "donkeys" reminiscent of Messenians laden with tribute like beasts of burden, the "swine" and "pigs" emblematic of extreme rusticity—just as he prescribed for them a shameful style of dress. The conquering citizens of Sicyon, on the other hand, united against their new subjects, adopted the appropriate title "leaders of the people". This explains how there could be more names than there had been tribes, why these names were offensive, and why they continued in use long after Cleisthenes' death yet were ultimately abolished: the system lasted for as long as the Sicyonians retained power, but was abandoned as soon as their micro-empire fell apart.

If this is right, Herodotus badly misunderstood the nature of Cleisthenes' actions. One can see how the misunderstanding might have come about. Herodotus never mentioned Cleisthenes' conquests, and may not have been aware of them. His information here derived largely from Athenian stories in which Cleisthenes made an occasional appearance. He thus saw events in Sicyon from an Athenian perspective and imagined that the tyrant carried out reforms similar to those of his grandson, Cleisthenes of Athens, who had introduced new names for the Athenian tribes. Both men had wanted to set their city apart from others in this way—so Herodotus guessed—but Cleisthenes of Sicyon, being a tyrant, had given

....

[22] Xenophon *Hellenica* 7.3.8, as convincingly explained by Cartledge 1980: 209-211. Theopompus' use of *epeunaktai* as an analogy also suggests that not all serfs were emancipated at once, and that rights of intermarriage played a key role. Compare also the serfs of Argos and Heraclea, below.

his reform a characteristically tyrannical twist by imposing humiliating names on most of his fellow-citizens.[23] Stripped of this Athenocentric and anti-tyrannical interpretation, the true meaning of the story emerges: it was a record of how Sicyon won and lost its serfs.[24]

The "naked people" of Argos

Ancient lists of statuses "between free men and slaves" regularly include the *gumnêtes* or *gumnêsioi*, "the naked people", of Argos.[25] They are almost certainly to be identified with a group variously called "slaves" or *perioikoi*, "dwellers-around", who were temporarily granted citizen-rights in the early fifth century when thousands of Argive soldiers had been massacred by the Spartans after the battle of Sepeia.[26] According to Herodotus,

> Argos was so bereft of men that their slaves [*douloi*] controlled all their affairs, governing and managing things, until the sons of those who had fallen [in the battle of Sepeia] reached adulthood. Then these men won back Argos for themselves and threw them out. And the slaves, having been forced out, took Tiryns in a battle. For a while they lived in harmony with one another, but then the *mantis* Kleandros . . . joined the slaves; he persuaded the slaves to attack their masters. After that there was war between them for a long time, until the Argives with difficulty won the victory.[27]

A different account was given by Aristotle, who said that the Argives "were forced to admit some of the *perioikoi* to citizenship" (*Politics* 1303a6-8), and by the local historian Socrates of Argos, who insisted that after the battle "in order to remedy the shortage of men, they made the women marry, not slaves, as Herodotus claims, but the best of the *perioikoi*, who were made citizens" (*FGrHist* 310 F 6). Aristotle

....

[23] See Ducat's excellent analysis (1976) of the biases which shaped Herodotus' version of this story and his suggestion that it originally referred to the naming of Sicyon's serfs; but cf. n. 24 below.

[24] Contra Ducat 1976, who assumes that this serf population was created, not by conquest, but by a process of internal differentiation which was formalised by Cleisthenes. This interpretation leaves unanswered the questions of why a "popular" tyrant (Aristotle *Politics* 1315b18) would want to antagonise his own (potential) supporters, and who the Aigialeis might have been. I would reject the theory that Cleisthenes championed the non-Doric element of the Sicyonian population, and that his power rested on exploiting "ethnic" tensions (Andrewes 1956: 58-61).

[25] Lists, as cited in n.19 above, plus Eustathius, on Dionysius *Periegesis* 533.

[26] So e.g. Tomlinson 1972: 68, 73-75, 99; Vidal-Naquet 1986: 210. I see no basis for Lotze's argument (1959: 54; cf. 1971; adopted by Snodgrass 1980: 89; Morris 1987: 187) that the "naked people" might have been serfs once but were free citizens by the beginning of the archaic period.

[27] Herodotus 6.83. Diodorus 10.26 and Pausanias 2.20.8 uses the term *oiketai*, which could simply mean "slaves", but could also refer more specifically to serfs: see below, at n.78.

41

used the term *perioikoi* to mean a subject rural population which cultivated land for its masters—in his ideal city, all farming would be done "by slaves or barbarian *perioikoi*" (*Politics* 1330a25-31)—and elsewhere we find *perioikoi* used as a synonym for "helots".[28] Clearly, Herodotus' story was simply a hostile version of the same tale: with conservative outrage and exaggeration, his sources condemned the admission of rural serfs to citizenship as a surrender of all power to mere "slaves".

At about the same time that Sicyon lost most of its serfs and enfranchised the rest, Argos thus also enfranchised its serf population, as a result of a severe military crisis. In both cases the right to marry into citizen families was a key element of the process. In Argos, an attempt was made soon afterwards to undo the reform, leading to a civil war during which the ex-serfs based themselves in Tiryns and which ended with the destruction of Tiryns by Argos, shortly after 468 BC. Although some Tirynthians took refuge in other cities, we are told that the rest were made citizens of Argos.[29] The serfs, despite being defeated, thus ended up being re-enfranchised after all. This is why, within a few years of these events, the three Dorian tribes of Argos were joined by a fourth, the Hyrnathioi. As at Sicyon, the newly enfranchised serfs were accommodated by the creation of a new tribe just for them.[30] The name was surely chosen to suggest that the members of this tribe were a junior branch of the Argive family: whereas the Dorian tribes were named after sons of Heracles, the Hyrnathioi were named after Hyrnetho, a daughter of Argos' founding king Temenos.[31]

What obligations the "naked people" had to their masters while they remained in subjection we do not know, except that they were somehow similar to those of helots. It does seem, however, that the serfs were allotted to individual Argive masters, judging by a dedication made by Callippus, "an Argive leader and his

....

[28] Isocrates 4.131 proposes to make the barbarians *perioikoi* of Greece, whereas in *Ep.* 3.5 he proposes to make the barbarians helots of the Greeks (as noted by Ste. Croix 1981: 160). Cretan serf populations are also called *perioikoi* by Aristotle, see below at n.78.

[29] Tiryns was still independent in 479 BC (Herodotus 6.83; 9.28, 31) and in 468 BC when there was an Olympic victor from Tiryns (*P.Oxy* 222). Tirynthians made citizens after destruction of city: Pausanias 2.25.7 (their major cult statue was also taken by Argos and placed in the Heraion, Pausanias 2.17.5). Tirynthians fleeing: Herodotus 7.137; cf. Ephorus *FGrHist* 70 F 56 (to Halieis); Strabo 8.6.11 (to Epidaurus, confirmed by inscription discussed below).

[30] Stephanus of Byzantium *Ethnikon* s.v. *Dymanes,* lists the three Dorian tribes and says "the Hyrnethia was added to these, according to Ephoros" (*FGrHist* 70 F 15). Hyrnathioi are first attested in two inscriptions of c. 460-450: *IG* 4.517 (*LSAG* 164-165, 170 no. 32 = *Nomima* I.86) and Piérart 1992: 235 (*Nomima* I.65). Also in *IG* 4.487-488 (and 600-602, of Roman imperial date). Hyrnathioi did not yet exist (or have citizen rights) c. 575-550 BC, when Argive magistrates were numbered in multiples of three, implying three tribes only: *IG* IV.614; *SEG* XI.314 (*LSAG* 156-158, 168 nos. 7-8; *Nomima* I.87, 88). The parallel with Sicyon is noted by Lotze 1971: 104 = 2000: 79.

[31] For Hyrnetho, see below, with n. 94.

woikiatai", i.e. his serfs, in the temple of Apollo Maleatas at Epidaurus between 475 and 450 BC. Callippus described himself as a "suppliant of the Epidaurians", and the dedication may be a monument to a dramatic story of a master taking the side of his serfs and fleeing with them to Epidaurus when the Argives put down the revolt.[32]

How and when had Argos acquired its "naked people"? In the archaic period, Argos enjoyed a great reputation as a conquering state. A much-quoted Delphic oracle praised the "linen-corsleted Argives, goads of war" as the best soldiers in Greece, with the Chalcidians of Euboea second-best (*Anthologia Palatina* 14.73). This boast would have been acceptable only in the period between 700 and 550 BC, when the cities of Euboea had lost their former prominence, and the Spartans had not yet established their reputation for invincibility. Herodotus says that, until the Spartans ousted them, the entire east coast of the Peloponnese south of Argos "as far as Cape Malea belonged to the Argives, both the territory on the mainland and the island of Cythera and the rest of the islands" (1.82.2). This territory, or a large part of it, was known as Cynouria, and Herodotus adds that "the Cynourians are autochthonous and seem to be the only Ionians [in the Peloponnese], but they have become Dorianized as a result of being ruled by the Argives and the passage of time" (8.73.3). One of the towns in this area, Hysiae, was according to Pausanias (2.24.8) already under Argive control in 669 BC, and was still regarded as "an Argive place" in the late fifth century.[33]

To the east, all the towns in the Argolid except Mycenae are said to have been "subject" to Argos by the early fifth century (Diodorus 11.65.2). Herodotus' account of the battle of Sepeia confirms that Tiryns and Nauplia were at the time controlled by Argos: the Spartans would not have invaded "in the area of Tiryns and Nauplia", and the Argives would certainly not have marched out to fight a battle "near Tiryns", if these towns had not been regarded as part of Argive territory (6.77). The fact that no city in the Argolid other than Mycenae sent troops to fight the Persians in 480 and 479 BC, although a small contingent from Tiryns, presumably rebellious serfs, joined in on the latter occasion, supports the claim that Mycenae alone remained independent.[34] There were stories about Argive military intervention in the eastern Argolid as early as the seventh century, but Tiryns at any rate was not subjected until the sixth. The oracle praising Argive valour refers to Argos as situated "between Tiryns and Arcadia", implying that Tiryns was not yet

....

[32] *LSAG* 444F, 445 = *Nomima* II.28: "Callippus, suppliant/ son of Eucles/ of the Epidaurians/ from Apollo/Pythius, an Argive/ leader [*archos*] and serfs". See Lambrinoudakis 1980: 57-59.

[33] Thucydides 5.83.2. The date of Argos' battle against the Spartans at Hysiae is probably not reliable: for a radical re-dating, see Shaw 1999.

[34] Herodotus 7.202; 9.28.4. A Mycenaean decree from c. 525 BC also implies that the city was still independent (*IG* IV.493 = *Nomima* I.101); cf. Hall 1995: 610-611.

part of Argos, and a decree issued by the *dêmos* of Tiryns c. 600 BC shows that the city was indeed still independent at that time.[35]

Finally, Pheidon, king and tyrant of Argos, was said to have "reconquered" the parts of the Peloponnese which had supposedly been allotted to his ancestor Temenos after the Dorian migration but had subsequently been lost—an unsubtle attempt to justify conquest (Ephorus *FGrHist* 70 F 115). Herodotus' date for Pheidon in the early sixth century, as a slightly older contemporary of Cleisthenes of Sicyon (6.127), places him just around the time when Tiryns was presumably subjected, while the range of earlier dates attributed to Pheidon by ancient and modern scholars can in various ways be linked to earlier stages of Argive expansion.[36] However one chooses to reconstruct the chronology and extent of Argos' conquests, there can be no doubt that the Argives subjected a number of neighbouring cities, beginning at the earliest around 700 BC, like Sparta, and at the latest in the early sixth century, like Sicyon.[37]

Once again, it seems obvious to connect Argos' possession of a serf population with its history of conquest: the "naked people" were defeated enemies who were not massacred, sold into slavery, or expelled, but were allowed to live in their native communities, subject to the sort of demands that Sparta made on its helots. Tiryns became the base from which the serfs waged war on Argos because Tiryns was the largest and best fortified of the towns reduced to servitude. The connection is made explicitly by Herodotus when, after noting that the Cynourians "have become Dorianized as a result of being ruled by the Argives", he adds "being Orneatai and *perioikoi*" (8.73.3). Despite modern attempts to explain this phrase otherwise or declare it corrupt, its natural sense, adopted by all earlier commentaries, is that the

....

[35] Decree: *SEG* 30.380 = *Nomima* I.78. Its significance, and the implications of the oracle, are noted by Hall 1995: 587; contra e.g. Tomlinson 1972: 77-78. Van Effenterre's suggestion (*Nomima* I, p. 296) that the decree should be down-dated and interpreted as the product of a carnivalesque, topsy-turvy regime instituted during the revolt of the "slaves" is imaginative, but hardly very plausible. Argos is said to have destroyed Asine at the end of the First Messenian War (Pausanias 2.36.5; 3.7.4; 4.14.3) and Nauplia after the Messenian Revolt (Pausanias 4.24.4, 27.8, 35.2) after which Argos took Nauplia's place in the Calaurian amphictyony (Strabo 8.6.14): in each case, according to tradition, the settlement was destroyed and its population driven out, rather than reduced to serfdom..

[36] Ephorus placed Pheidon tenth in line from Temenos, which put the subjection of the Argolid in the early eighth century, but his inclination to date conquests early is evident from his treatment of the helots in Messenia (above) and Laconia (below). On the ancient trend to date Pheidon (and others) ever further back in time, and the corollary that Herodotus' date is more reliable than the others, see Drews 1983; cf. Koiv 2001. Pheidon was linked with seventh-century Argive expansion by Andrewes 1956: 39-42.

[37] Jonathan Hall's demonstration (1995) from archaeological evidence that the Argive Heraion was not fully under Argive control until c. 450 BC fits very well with the fact that Mycenae was not conquered (and destroyed) by Argos until c. 460 BC. His claim that Tiryns and the eastern Argolid were not subjected until then either seems harder to maintain, in view of the literary evidence.

Cynourians were ruled by the Argives "*because* they were *perioikoi*": the very term used by Aristotle and Socrates to describe the people whom Herodotus elsewhere calls "slaves". The only problem lies in the reference to "Orneatai" as apparently yet another name for the subject population—unattested elsewhere and inexplicable, since the city of Orneai, although not far from Argos, was neither in Cynouria nor subject to Argos until 416 BC.[38] Perhaps Herodotus or a scribe mistakenly substituted "Orneatai" for "Hyrnathioi", the obscure tribal name by which the former serfs had come to be known by Herodotus' day.

In short, Argos acquired a serf population by means of conquest in the archaic period, but had to give it up when a shortage of manpower forced them to enfranchise at least some of the serfs. A subsequent attempt to disenfranchise them again led to protracted warfare, ending in the 460s with the "dissolution" of Tiryns, Hysiae, "and any other little settlement in the Argolid not worth mentioning" (Pausanias 8.27.1) and the complete absorption of the former serfs into the citizen community of Argos, where they were registered as members of the Hyrnathioi tribe. The Argives soon put their new manpower to the test in war, defeating their sole remaining rival in the Argolid, Mycenae, which was razed to the ground while its people were sold into chattel slavery rather than reduced to serfdom.[39]

2. Greek colonists and "barbarian" serfs

When the likes of Isocrates and Aristotle imagined Greeks living off the labour of "barbarian *perioikoi*",[40] they were not merely fantasising but drawing on the experience of several Greek settlements overseas. According to Herodotus, the elite of "so-called land-sharers" (*gamoroi*) in Syracuse employed "slaves called Kyllyrians"

....

[38] Orneai was an independent ally of Argos in 418 (Thucydides 5.66.2, 72.4) and once fought independently against Sicyon (Pausanias 10.18.4; Plutarch *Moralia* 401d), but was destroyed by Argos in 416 (Thucydides 6.7) which rules out the idea that Orneai was one of Argos' earliest conquests and gave a collective name to all *perioikoi* acquired later (so Rawlinson 1880; Stein 1881; Macan 1908; and How and Wells 1928, ad loc., all following the interpretation of K.O. Müller in *Die Dorier*—non vidi). Orneai lay some distance to the northwest of Argos, while Cynouria lay to the south, which rules out the idea that Herodotus, as an afterthought to his sentence, was simply explaining where the Cynourians lived: "they are the people of Orneai and their neighbours" (Larsen 1936: col. 822; Gschnitzer 1958: 79 n.23). Masaracchia 1990, ad loc., declares the passage corrupt (and the Penguin translation of the *Histories* simply omits it).

[39] The war against Mycenae is described in some detail by Diodorus 11.65.1-5; cf. Strabo 8.6.19. Diodorus lists the war under Olympiad 78 (468 BC), but also says that it happened shortly after the Messenian revolt which began in 464 (11.65.3), which would make better sense: the Argives first end the war with their former serfs before they attack their old, independent rival. That Pausanias lumps the destruction of Mycenae together with the dissolution of the subject towns proves nothing about the chronology or nature of these wars; he also includes the destruction of Orneai, which happened much later (8.27.1); cf. the chronologically mixed list in Strabo (8.6.11).

[40] See above, p. 42, with n. 29.

who joined forces with the common people to rise up in a briefly successful revolt against the upper classes in the 480s (7.155). These must be the same people referred to as "Kallikyrians" and compared to Spartan helots in the Aristotelian *Constitution of the Syracusans* (F 586 Rose). We have no further details, but it seems obvious that during or after the foundation of Syracuse—traditional date 733 BC— Greek settlers reduced the native Sicilian population to servitude by force, and kept them in submission at least until the early fifth-century revolt.

Something similar happened when the Megarians founded Byzantium, c. 660 BC, since we are told by the third-century historian Phylarchus that the relationship between Byzantines and native Bithynians was the same as that between Spartans and helots (*FGrHist* 81 F 8).

Another century later the founding of Heraclea on the Black Sea in 559 BC created the most famous group of barbarian serfs, the Mariandynians, whose tribute payments earned them the nickname "gift-bearers" (*dôrophoroi*). The hellenistic poet Euphorion described them as "trembling before their masters" (F 83) and they "could even be sold, but not beyond the borders" (Strabo 12.3.4; cf. Poseidonius *FGrHist* 87 F 8). They were compared to helots from Plato onwards and Aristotle alluded to them as an example of *perioikoi* cultivating the land and liable to military service—in the navy—but excluded from citizenship.[41] Just as in Sicyon, they were ultimately enfranchised in the 360s by a tyrant leading a popular uprising against the rich. Justin described in lurid detail how the tyrant, Clearchus, forced noble women to "marry their own slaves", and how these women killed themselves—sometimes after killing their new husbands on the wedding night—rather than suffer such humiliation (16.5.1-4). His story is marked by hostile exaggeration in the manner of Herodotus' account of "slaves taking power" in Argos, and need imply no more than that Clearchus abolished serf status and legalised marriage between ex-serfs and citizens. Intermarriage was clearly still as sensitive an issue for the elite as it had once been in Sicyon and Argos.

These three Greek settlements overseas may be the only ones where barbarian serfs are explicitly attested, but the fact that we have only a single chance reference to their existence in a city as prominent as Byzantium suggests that our evidence reveals, as Nick Fisher put it, "only a few tips of a large number of nasty icebergs" (1993: 33).

One further instance of "colonial" serfdom perhaps just breaks the surface in Herodotus' account of Cyrene, a city which in around 570 BC, two generations after its foundation, attracted large numbers of additional settlers by promising a distribution of land at the expense of its neighbours, the native Libyans, who "were deprived

....

[41] Plato *Laws* 777c; Aristotle *Politics* 1327b12-15; cf. Athenaeus 263ce (for Euphorion, Poseidonius, and Callistratus *FGrHist* 348 F 4); Pollux 3.83; Pausanias Atticus K9, 33, with Ducat 1990: 33.

of their territory and treated with great *hubris* by the Cyrenaeans" (4.159). This choice of words may suggest subjection rather than expulsion. In any case, when the Libyans' resistance had been crushed, they were evidently reduced to some subordinate status, because we are told that about two decades later, c. 550 BC, they "revolted from the Cyrenaeans" (4.160). In the fighting which ensued, 7,000 Cyrenaean hoplites are said to have fallen, and the immediate response was a reform in which all settlers, old and new, were grouped into three tribes: one for "all the islanders", one for "the Peloponnesians and Cretans", and one for "the Theraians and the *perioikoi*" (4.161). It is hard to see who these *perioikoi* might have been if not Libyans, or why they would have been given citizenship if they had not previously already been a subject part of the community, rather than merely neighbours.[42] The most plausible scenario for these events again runs parallel to events at Sicyon and Argos: conquest creates a serf population, but eventually a major military setback leads to the loss of much conquered territory, the enfranchisement of the remaining serfs, and a tribal reform.[43]

3. Serfs, *perioikoi* and the "Dorian migration"

The forms of serfdom investigated so far were all created between the late eighth and the late sixth century BC. Of much earlier origin, some ancient authors said, were Sparta's Laconian helots and the Thessalians' *penestai*. Theopompus of Chios, proudly claiming for his home town the invention of chattel slavery, believed that the Spartans and Thessalians

> formed their slave population from the Greeks who were already living in the territory which they now control—the Spartans from the Achaeans, the Thessalians from the Perrhaebians and Magnetes—and they call the enslaved "helots" and "*penestai*", respectively (*FGrHist* 115 F122).

These conquests were part of the "Dorian migration", which supposedly reached Thessaly 60 years after the Trojan War and Laconia 20 years later (Thucydides 1.12.3). Some modern scholars not only accept this story of origin but extend it to the serf populations of Crete.[44] A second feature which Sparta and the cities of Thessaly and Crete had in common was their control of subject communities

....

[42] Contra Shipley 1997: 218.

[43] For other possible cases, where the evidence seems to me insufficient, see n. 100, below.

[44] So e.g. Willetts (1955: 47) who envisages a Dorian League invading Crete c. 1200 BC, but not establishing its overall dominance until about 800 BC (pp. viii, 231). There is uncertainty about the details of Theopompus' story: he elsewhere (F 13) seems to imply that not all Laconians but only the people of Helos were native Achaeans (below, p. 49), and it is conceivable that he imagined that the enslavement of the Perrhaebians had taken place even *before* the Trojan war (below, pp. 53-4).

which were clearly distinct from the serfs, but confusingly referred to by the same name we have seen used elsewhere for serf populations: *perioikoi*. The evidence for an early origin of serfdom in these three regions can easily be shown not to stand up to scrutiny, and a good case can be made that it was in fact primarily through conquests at a much later date that serfs and *perioikoi* were created.

Helots and perioikoi *in Laconia*

Theopompus' story about the origins of Laconian helots in the Dorian migration is contradicted not only by archaeology—which finds no evidence of large-scale population movements, let alone violent incursions[45]—but also by at least three rival literary traditions.

The earliest surviving account is that of the late fifth-century historian Antiochus of Syracuse. He made the creation of Laconian helots contemporary with the subjection of Messenia: "during the Messenian War, those of the Lacedaemonians who did not join the expedition were judged slaves and named helots" (*FGrHist* 555 F 13). As well as a much later date, this version offers a wholly different reason for the servitude of the Laconians: far from being conquered by outsiders, they were punished for disobeying their own government.[46]

A second story comes from the late fourth-century historian Ephorus, who offered a variant of the Dorian migration story: the native population of Laconia had not been subjected by the invaders but emigrated to Ionia, allowing the Dorians to resettle the region. In the next generation, king Agis of Sparta deprived the other Laconian towns of their political rights, reducing them to the status of *perioikoi*. All complied, except the people of Helos. When the latter were defeated in war, they agreed to serve as slaves "on certain conditions" and thus became the first helots (*FGrHist* 70 F 117). Something very much like this story was in antiquity the most widely accepted account of the origins of the helots.[47]

....

[45] E.g. Snodgrass 2001: 296-323; Osborne 1996: 33-37; Hall 1997: 114-128.

[46] For detailed discussion, see Luraghi, this volume, pp. 115-7; despite his reservations, it does appear from the phrase "they were named helots" that Antiochus was referring to the first creation of this status (as argued by Vidal-Naquet 1986: 177, and Ducat 1990: 7-8, 67).

[47] It is worth stressing the implication of Ephorus' account, as summarised by Strabo (8.5.4), that the Laconian helots were mostly Dorians (contra Luraghi, this volume, p. 125): after the native Achaeans had left the country, the whole of Laconia, including Helos, was divided up amongst those who had taken part in the conquest, i.e. Dorians; their relatively small numbers, however, were filled out by accepting "volunteers from abroad as fellow-settlers". The popularity of Ephorus' account, or something similar, is attested by Plutarch, who said that "*most*" authors attributed the subjection of Helos to Soos, Agis' co-ruler (*Lycurgus* 2.1); Plutarch elsewhere recounted an episode from a war against helots set at the same early date (just before the foundation of Melos: *Moralia* 247ad; cf. Polyaenus 7.49). On Ephorus' notion of a "contract of servitude", see Ducat 1990: 70-76.

The third rival account appears in the work of Pausanias, who unfortunately does not reveal his source. We are told that, for centuries after the Dorian migration, the invaders controlled no more than Sparta itself. Only in the course of the eighth century did they conquer the rest of Laconia,[48] and made most of its people *perioikoi*. Finally, in the reign of the kings who also started the first Messenian War, the Spartans reached the southern plain of Helos and conquered its native inhabitants: these were the first people to be made helots.[49]

In short, two stories treated Laconian helots as pre-Dorian Greeks subjected by conquest, either 700 BC (Pausanias) or 1100 BC (Theopompus), and the other two treated them as fellow-Dorians made subject to Sparta in punishment for disobeying legitimate orders from their king, either 700 BC (Antiochus) or 1100 BC (Ephorus). The utter incompatibility of the four stories is proof enough that our sources had no reliable information on the origins of Laconian helots or *perioikoi*. Specifically, the old legend of the Dorian migration, current since at least the late seventh century (Tyrtaeus F 2 West), probably did not say anything about the invaders creating helots or *perioikoi*, or else it would surely not have been necessary or possible to invent so many different accounts. So far as we know, Ephorus and Theopompus in the late fourth century were the first to connect the origin of helotage and the Dorian migration, and this is probably no accident of survival: the link may never have been made until the liberation of Messenia encouraged historians to establish a clear chronological distance between Messenian helots, now free, and Laconian helots, still enslaved.[50]

More significant than these stories of origin, it has been argued, is the fact that Laconian helots had no distinct ethnic identity. They were simply "helots", whereas the Messenian serfs were regarded as both "helots" and "Messenians"— their revolt of 464 BC was for Sparta a "war against the Messenians".[51] Some have inferred that the Laconian helots had lost their original ethnic identity and must therefore have been conquered many centuries before the Messenians were. Others would conclude that the Laconian helots had no distinct identity because they had never been a distinct community: they were the lower classes who had become dependent farmers.[52]

....

[48] Pausanias 3.2.5 and 3.7.3; 3.2.6 (with 19.6, 22.6) and 3.7.4.
[49] Pausanias 3.2.7, 3.20.6 and 3.7.5.
[50] In parallel with the development of a story about a very early conquest of Messenia (above, p. 37).
[51] "War against Messenians", rather than "helots": Herodotus 9.35, 64; Thucydides 1.101.2. This is not to say, of course, that Messenians' sense of identity simply remained intact throughout the period of their subjection: it was clearly contested and developed in a variety of ways: see esp. Figueira 1999.
[52] Early conquest: e.g. Cartledge 2002: 83-84. Lower class origins are implied by Luraghi 2002: 240-241, and those who argue for a general process of internal differentiation (cf. n. 2, above).

The lack of a distinct ethnic identity among Laconian serfs, however, does not tell us anything about the date or means of their subjection. The inhabitants of the entire Eurotas valley from Sparta in the north to Helos in the south shared an ethnic identity as Lacedaemonians from a very early date, since the region was known as Lacedaemon probably already in the Mycenaean age, and certainly by the time of Homer.[53] Laconian helots thus counted as Lacedaemonians, not because their original identity had gradually faded into that of their conquerors, but because this *was* their original identity. Early Iron Age Lacedaemon was presumably, as so many parts of Greece continued to be, an "ethnic" region consisting of essentially independent settlements, competing and cooperating in a variety of ways, until the Spartans succeeded in politically unifying the region under their rule. It is quite conceivable that the process of establishing Spartan control entailed the reduction of some Lacedaemonian communities to serfdom and that this occurred only a short time before the conquest of Messenia. It is even possible that the Spartans expanded southwards into Laconia and eastwards into Messenia at the same time.

Notable differences between Laconian and Messenian helots are perhaps beginning to emerge from archaeological evidence, but these still tell us nothing about their respective origins. Survey in the area of ancient Pylos has shown that Messenians here lived in villages or towns, whereas a survey of the plain near Sparta revealed few concentrated settlements, so that Laconian helots here probably lived in small groups on Spartan estates, rather than in their own communities.[54] The greater integration of the Laconian serfs might be attributed to conquest at a much earlier date, or taken to show that they were not conquered populations at all but the Spartan lower classes. Yet it is equally possible that the explanation lies in different histories rather than different origins. As the Spanish American experience shows (below, pp. 66-71), patterns of exploitation may quickly diverge after conquest, as the new rulers leave distant subjects largely to their own devices while closer to home they intervene more harshly, to the point of breaking up native communities.

More complete integration of the Laconian helots explains why they proved comparatively loyal to Sparta when a Theban army liberated Messenia in 370 BC. Thousands took up a Spartan offer of freedom in exchange for military service against the invaders, rather than rebelling and taking the Thebans' side (Xenophon, *Hellenica* 6.5.28-9). The extent of their loyalty should in any case not be overestimated: they had probably rebelled on previous occasions; the Spartans would not have made their offer if they had not seriously feared another uprising; and the

....

[53] Mycenaean Lacedaemon: Hall 2000: 85. Homer: *Iliad* 2.581-90; *Odyssey* 3.326, 4.1, 21.13.

[54] For estate management in Laconia and Messenia, see Hodkinson, this volume, esp. pp. 225-6, 263-9 for his interpretation of survey findings; cf. Luraghi 2002: 231-232.

choice between immediate individual freedom and the hope of future collective freedom could never have been easy, even for the most rebellious helot. In short, nothing of what we know about Laconian helots helps us determine how they became serfs. What we know about Sparta, on the other hand, strongly favours the idea that they were subjected by conquest. The eighty or more communities in Lacedaemonia and Messenia which ranked as *perioikoi* paid great honour to the kings of Sparta—granting them royal estates, offering royal tributes, and sending representatives to mourn at their funerals—and in military matters at least were wholly controlled by the Spartan government, which might also intervene in their internal judicial affairs. They were thus subject to all, or almost all, of the duties of citizens, but without enjoying in return the citizens' political and social privileges.[55] A few perioikic communities were established by the Spartans themselves when they granted land to refugees from sacked allied cities, and these clearly accepted their inferior status voluntarily, in exchange for a place to live. But for the dozens of communities who already had their homes in Lacedaemonia it is difficult to see what would have induced them to accept perioikic status except force, or the threat of force.[56]

A few scraps of poetry hint that Sparta's relation with its *perioikoi* in the early archaic period was indeed openly based on force. In the *Odyssey*, Menelaus says that he had planned to reward his loyal ally Odysseus by inviting him to leave Ithaca "with his entire people" and come to live in a new city to be built for him near Sparta, "when I have destroyed one of the surrounding cities which I myself rule" (4.169-77). The notion that a king would find space for new settlers by destroying a town already in his power makes little sense unless these towns were imagined as controlled by virtue of conquest. Similarly, when the historical Spartans granted land to refugee allies, they gave them parcels of conquered territory.[57] In this light, it may be significant that the earliest surviving reference to the Dorian migration claims only that the kings were ordained by the gods to govern the city of Sparta, not all of Lacedaemonia (Tyrtaeus F 2.12-13; cf. 4.3-4). Perhaps power over the wider region was still regarded as based on might, rather than on right, as was claimed later.

Outside Lacedaemonia, the Spartans expanded in the course of the seventh century to occupy Messenia in the west, and by the middle of the sixth century had

---

....

[55] Royal estates: Xenophon *Spartan Constitution* 15.3. Tribute: [Plato] *Alcibiades* I 123a; Strabo 8.5.4 (and perhaps Hesychius s.v. *kalamê*), despite the scepticism of Cartledge 2002: 155. Mourning: see n. 7 above. On perioikic status, see further Shipley 1997: 201-216.

[56] See e.g. Hall 2000: 83-85; Cartledge 2002: 84-86. Land grants to allies, see below, n. 57.

[57] Pausanias 4.14.3 (Asine), 24.4 (Nauplia); Thucydides 2.27 (Aegina). The parallel explains the *Odyssey* passage, which has puzzled some commentators, who have unnecessarily suggested that the verb *exalapazein*, "destroy", here uniquely means "to empty" or "to evacuate" (e.g. West 1988, ad loc.).

seized Cynouria in the east, a substantial territory whose inhabitants had previously been reduced to serfdom by Argos, as we have seen. Herodotus reported that in the sixth century the Spartans had also tried to occupy all of Arcadia in the north, but had suffered a series of defeats. It would seem that this brought about a change of direction in Spartan warfare. Instead of aiming at outright conquest, the Spartans now sought to forge a network of subordinate allies, but by then "most of the Peloponnese had already been subjected by them" (Herodotus 1.68).[58]

Sparta's history of military activity within and outside Lacedaemonia, and the fact that after conquest serfdom was imposed upon the Messenians, presumably retained for the Cynourians, and probably intended for the Arcadians, makes it difficult to escape the conclusion that Laconian serfdom was also the product of conquest. The simplest scenario would be that the Spartans in the course of expansion reduced their victims to the status of either *perioikoi* or helots, depending on circumstances at which we can now only guess. Alternatively, we might imagine an early stage of expansion during which Sparta's nearest neighbours were made *perioikoi*, and a later stage during which more distant victims in the southern plains of the Eurotas valley, and outside Laconia, were mostly forced into serfdom.

The latter scenario would help explain why almost all the literary accounts of the origins of the Laconian helots, despite their otherwise extreme divergence, agree that the first helots were the inhabitants of Helos.[59] This is usually dismissed as a mere punning etymology deriving *heilôs* from *Helos*, although even ancient grammarians felt that there was a problem with the intrusive iota. Yet it is striking, given the fondness of ancient Greek scholars for inventive etymologies, that no one ever offered a different explanation of their name, such as the obvious possibility favoured by some modern scholars of deriving helot from *helein*, the aorist of the verb for "to take", "to capture".[60] The exceptional unanimity may suggest that there was a strong

[58] Herodotus 1.82 (Cynouria) and 1.66 (Arcadia), with e.g. Cartledge 2002: 118-123.

[59] For Pausanias, Helos was still inhabited by pre-Dorian natives (3.2.7) when it was destroyed by the Spartans, and its inhabitants were "the first to be called Helots, after what they really were", i.e. inhabitants of Helos (3.20.6); similarly Ephorus *FGrHist* 70 F 117 ("the Heleioi, who held Helos") and Theopompus *FGrHist* 115 F 13 ("the Heleatai who used to live in a place called Helos in Laconia"). Hellanicus *FGrHist* 4 F 188 and "many" others (Harpocration s.v. *heilôteuein*) said that the helots were "the first to be defeated of those who lived in the city Helos". Only Antiochus' version, in the brief paraphrase that survives, does not refer to Helos, though it is conceivable that in the full version the people of Helos were named as the Lacedaemonians who refused to serve against Messenia. (If so, we would have to conclude that Antiochus did not regard them as the fathers of the Partheniai, whose story follows immediately, or that Antiochus, like Polybius [12.6b] but unlike others, regarded the Partheniai as sons of helots: see Ogden 1997: 73-74, contra Nafissi 1999: 254-255; Luraghi, this volume, pp. 115-6).

[60] Modern etymology: e.g. Cartledge 2002: 83. For ancient discussions, see Ducat 1990: 9-10, noting that "curiously this etymology remains implicit".

tradition about the conquest of Helos.[61] The plain of Helos was "the largest and finest territory in Laconia" (Polybius 5.19.7) and indeed comprised the bulk of Laconia's agricultural land. It seems quite possible that the Spartans first found it desirable and feasible to introduce serfdom when they conquered this prosperous farming region, just as they did in the even more prosperous plains of Messenia.[62]

Since the first archaeological evidence of settlements on the sites of Sparta and the later perioikic towns does not appear until 950 BC, Sparta's first conquests could hardly have taken place before that time. The first serfs may have been made at any time between about 900 and 700 BC. If conquest unfolded in the two stages sketched above, the first helots will have been created nearer the end of this period. Coincidentally or otherwise, the late date offered by two traditions—perhaps widely accepted before historians began to date these events back to the Dorian migration—may not have been far wrong.[63]

Penestai and perioikoi *in Thessaly*

Ancient lists and lexica often cite "the *penestai* of the Thessalians" as a parallel to the helots. These serfs were privately owned in large numbers: Menon of Pharsalus joined a siege army in 477 BC with 200 or 300 horsemen, "his own *penestai*". Like the helots and Mariandynians, they were employed as an agricultural workforce, liable to service in the army and navy, and protected from excessive exploitation by a rule which said that they could not be legally killed or "taken out of the country" by their masters.[64]

According to Theocritus' *Idylls*, *penestai* received "monthly rations" (16.34-5). Other authors compared them with early Athenian wage labourers and, unfavourably, with Roman clients; some very late sources oddly described the *penestai* as "slaves working for a wage".[65] These descriptions all suggest bonded

....

[61] Even if the conquest was historical, the explanation of the name "helot" built on it was surely false.

[62] Contra Vidal-Naquet 1986: 178 (an "absurd story"). The Helos plain: Hodkinson 2000: 138-140.

[63] Neither Antiochus nor Pausanias had any reason to invent a late date. The creation of helots is of no relevance to the story about the Partheniai which Antiochus tells. The date adopted by Pausanias forced him to assume that the Dorian migration originally reached Sparta but not the rest of Laconia, and in effect resumed four centuries later, which is curious in itself and clashes with the legend that in the Dorian migration the whole of Laconia had fallen to the kings of Sparta. If these authors nevertheless stuck with their date, perhaps they did so because it was supported by a strong tradition.

[64] Ducat 1994: 75-86; Menon's *penestai*: Demosthenes 13.23; 23.199; cf. Ducat 1994: 24-29, 71-72. Private ownership: also Theocritus *Idylls* 16. 34-35; Euripides *Phrixos* F 830 Nauck[2]. Military service also: Xenophon *Hellenica* 6.1.11 (Ducat 1994: 62-63); *IG* IX 2, 234, lines 1-3 (late third century BC; Ducat 1994: 107-113). Restriction of masters' power: Strabo 12.3.4; Archemachus *FGrHist* 424 F 1; Photius and Suda s.v. *penestai* (= Pausanias Atticus). On the possibility of manumission, see Ducat 1994: 72-73.

[65] Rations: see Ducat 1994: 46-48, citing Hesiod *Works & Days* 766-767. Labourers, clients: Dionysius of Halicarnassus 2.9; cf. Euripides F 830 N[2] (*latris*). "Waged slaves": scholia on Aristophanes *Wasps* 1274; *Etymologicum Gudianum* s.v. *heilôtes*. See also Ducat 1994: 17-18, 30-36, 71-72.

labourers dependent on their masters for distributions of food, and perhaps later money. The hellenistic historian Archemachus, by contrast, claimed that *penestai* "pay their contributions" (*suntaxeis*) and that "many are wealthier than their own masters". Strabo similarly speaks of *penestai* at Larisa paying "tributes" (*phoroi*).[66] Here *penestai* are not mere labourers but bonded tenants or sharecroppers, like Tyrtaeus' Messenians or the "gift-giving" Mariandynians. The most likely explanation is that the category *penestai* covered a range of unfree statuses. Rural serfs may have paid tributes, while domestic serfs drew rations; quite possibly, the position of *penestai* varied from city to city. Alternatively, the discrepancy may reflect major changes over time: perhaps the serfs turned from unfree labourers into dependent farmers in the course of the classical period.[67]

It would not be surprising if over the centuries the *penestai* did indeed attain greater independence from their masters. They had a reputation for being particularly "difficult and full of big ideas" and are said to have "frequently attacked the Thessalians". Although we happen to know of only one plotted revolt, repeated uprisings may eventually have won the serfs some concessions.[68] Strabo seems to imply that the *penestai* of Larissa were set free by Philip II of Macedon, presumably when he intervened in Thessalian civil strife in the late 340s. Philip is said to have supported the common people in these conflicts, so this might be yet another instance of a popular uprising against the elite resulting in the liberation of serfs, as in fifth-century Syracuse and fourth-century Sicyon and Heraclea. Elsewhere, *penestai* remained serfs until well into the hellenistic period.[69]

Theopompus' story of origins—that the *penestai* were created when the Thessalians first entered the region and subjected the Perrhaebians and Magnetes native to eastern Thessaly—is usually, and plausibly, taken to refer to the time of the Dorian migration. It should be noted, however, that Strabo, who also claimed that the *penestai* were descended from native Perrhaebians reduced to serfdom, said that they had been conquered by their neighbours, the Lapiths, a generation or two

....

[66] Archemachus *FGrHist* 424 F 1; Strabo 9.5.19-20 (where the word *penestai* is not used, but they are clearly meant; see also n. 69 below). Archemachus' account is apologetic in tone and could perhaps be dismissed as an idealising misrepresentation of the position of the *penestai* (see Ducat 1994: 14-16), but Strabo's comment cannot be explained away on those grounds.

[67] Theocritus is probably drawing on the poetry of Simonides (Ducat 1994: 46-48), and may reflect an archaic situation; Strabo and Archemachus may have projected back a later situation.

[68] Quotations: Aristotle *Politics* 1264a35, 1269a37; cf. Plato *Laws* 776cd, 777c. Plotted revolt in 406: Xenophon *Hellenica* 2.3.36 (Ducat [1994: 103-104] is surely too sceptical when he suggests that this episode may have been the only basis for claims that the *penestai* were particularly rebellious).

[69] Strabo 9.5.19, claiming that tributes were levied "until Philip took power", presumably referring to his interventions in the late 340s (see e.g. Hammond 1994: 118-119). Polyaenus 4.2.19 claims that Philip tended to intervene on the side of "the people". See Ducat 1994: 107-113, on enfranchisement of *penestai* in the second century BC in Pharsalus.

before the Trojan War, rather than by Dorian invaders two generations after the fall of Troy. Some Perrhaebians took refuge in the mountains, but those who stayed behind became serfs (9.5.12, 19-20). Perhaps this is what Theopompus had in mind as well, or else we have two rival versions of this tradition.

Another tradition drew on the story, first found in Thucydides (1.12.3), that the Boeotians had once lived in Arne in western Thessaly, from where they were driven out by the Thessalians sixty years after the Trojan War. Others dated these events two or four generations after the fall of Troy.[70] Some added that not all Boeotians had left: some stayed behind "because they liked the country" and accepted a position of serfdom, as we are told in a fragment of Archemachus' *History of Euboea* (*FGrHist* 424 F 1) which gives no date. This tradition flagrantly contradicted the *Iliad* which placed the Boeotians in Boeotia already during the Trojan War (2.494-510). Thucydides hypothesized that "a section" of the Boeotians had moved into the region long before the rest followed. Later sources had an even more ingenious explanation: the Boeotians did live in Boeotia, but were driven out to Thessaly by Pelasgian and Thracian invaders during the Trojan War, only to return again two or more generations later.[71] The most radical solution to the chronological problem appeared in the work of Pausanias Atticus, which referred to "the Boeotians who, having been defeated in Arne by Haemon, did not flee the slavery imposed upon them, but stayed until the third generation". Haemon, father of Thessalus, ancestor of all Thessalians, dates long before the Trojan War, and this story thus claims that the Boeotians had once been serfs, but had escaped subjection, left Thessaly, and occupied Boeotia well before the Trojan War.[72]

A third strand of tradition, attested in a couple of commentaries on Aristophanes' *Wasps* (1274), claims that the *penestai* were neither Perrhaebians nor Boeotians but close relatives of the Thessalians: descendants of a certain Penestes, himself descended from Thessalus.

Thessalian serfs were thus credited with an even greater variety of ethnic and historical origins than Laconian helots. The notion that the *penestai* were a junior branch of the Thessalian family tree was probably invented only after serfdom had been abolished in Thessaly: it is very reminiscent of the revision of myth in Sicyon and Argos, where new tribal names implied that ex-serfs were descended from

....

[70] Two generations: Strabo 9.2.3; cf. 9.2.5, 29. Four generations: Diodorus 19.53.7-8.

[71] Strabo 9.2.3, 25, 29; Diodorus 19.53.7-8.

[72] Pausanias Atticus Π 16 (p. 204 Erbse) (= Photius and Suda s.v. *penestai*). For Haemon, see Strabo 9.5.23. Discussion in Ducat 1994: 38-40; cf. 93-98. I would reject his suggestion that the details of this version are garbled and can be dismissed as mere mistakes. For *penestai* as Boeotians, see also Polyaenus 1.12; cf. Philocrates *FGrHist* 601 F 2.

Aigialeus and Hyrnetho, respectively.[73] The idea that *penestai* were Boeotians must have developed after c. 700 BC: the poet of the *Iliad* made an effort to take account of migration legends in constructing the geography of Greece at the time of the Trojan War,[74] and he would not have had his Boeotia already populated by Boeotians if he had known of a story which placed the Boeotians in Thessaly at the time. This tradition may have evolved as a result of sixth-century attempts by the Thessalians to occupy Boeotia (see below), creating an awkward historiographical problem, imaginatively solved by scholars from Thucydides onwards. Finally, the claim that eastern Thessalian serfs were Perrhaebians and Magnesians is unobjectionable in itself, but the suggestion that they were subjected before the Trojan War, at the hands of the legendary Lapiths (best known for fighting Centaurs) leaves no doubt about its mythical nature. In short, we can put no more faith in these traditions than in the tales about Laconian helots.

It may nevertheless be significant that all these accounts assumed that the Thessalians acquired their slaves by conquest. So did ancient dictionary definitions of *penestai*, such as the one offered by Ammonius in *On Similar and Different Words*: "among the Thessalians, a *penestes* is someone enslaved through war, just like the helots among the Laconians".[75] Since the cities of Thessaly engaged in campaigns of conquest in the archaic period, just like Sparta, Sicyon and Argos, serfs and *perioikoi* may well have been created in war at this time.

In the classical period, the inhabitants of the mountain ranges encircling the Thessalian plains were all deemed "subjects" of Thessaly. They included Perrhaebians, Magnetes, Achaeans of Phthia, Dolopes, and others, adding up to a very large number of communities. They were liable to provide contingents of light infantry and pay tribute "as it had been set under Scopas" when ordered to do so by the rulers of Thessaly (Xenophon *Hellenica* 6.1.9, 12, 19). Their obligation was thus not to individual Thessalian cities, but to the rulers of Thessaly as a whole, just as the obligations of Spartan *perioikoi* seem to have been primarily to the kings. Rivalry between the cities meant that at times no single ruler held power, so the Thessalian *perioikoi* retained greater freedom of action than their counterparts in Sparta, and counted as semi-independent states (Herodotus 7.132, 185). Still, they were subjects, and had been reduced to this status through protracted warfare,

....

[73] It may be significant that the commentaries note that "this system of *penestai* had been *dissolved* and afterwards they called poor men and labourers *penestai*"; Ducat (1994: 17-20), however, argues that this idea was an invention by the scholiasts, based on a misunderstanding of Aristophanes' joke.

[74] As noted by Andrewes 1971: 34; see further van Wees 1999a: 14-15 = 2002: 108-110.

[75] Ammonius 386, p. 100 Nickau. Cf. Athenaeus 264a: "those who are not slaves by birth, but were taken in war"; *Suda* s.v. *penestai*: "those who had been defeated in the war and served and became the slaves of the victors"; also Theopompus *FGrHist* 115 F 122b: "free men who serve as slaves".

judging by Aristotle's comment that the *penestai* had found it easy to revolt while their masters "were still fighting their neighbours, the Achaeans, Perrhaebians and Magnetes" (*Politics* 1269b6). If, as seems reasonable to assume, the regulation of tribute payments by Scopas marked the end of these wars, the *perioikoi* would probably not have been finally subjected until c. 600 BC.[76] Thessalian expansion did not stop there. According to Plutarch, the Thessalians had once "ruled Greece up to Thespiae" in southern Boeotia, until defeated in battle at the fortress Keressos, c. 575 BC. They had also controlled Phocis, until thrown out by a ferocious *intifada* known as the "Phocian despair" in which the rebels killed their Thessalian rulers and vowed to commit mass suicide rather than surrender. The Thessalians attempted to regain control over Phocis right up to the Persian wars, suffering at least two massacres at the hands of Phocian guerillas, and ultimately bringing in the Persian army to exact an extremely violent revenge.[77]

So much for the history of *collective* Thessalian conquest, which perhaps began when the Thessalian cities were unified under a leader known as Aleuas the Red who institutionalised the mobilisation of Thessalian forces (Aristotle F 498 Rose). *Individual* Thessalian cities are likely to have engaged in campaigns of conquest against neighbours long before the region was more or less unified, and indeed to have continued waging such wars afterwards. Local wars may over the centuries have resulted in larger settlements seizing the territories of their weaker neighbours, and reducing the inhabitants to serfdom. The precise conditions would presumably have varied from place to place, but developments were sufficiently similar across the region to create in Thessaly a relatively small number of dominant cities, each surrounded by a large territory cultivated by their subject *penestai*.

....

[76] The best-known Scopas was the exceptionally rich patron of Simonides, in the late sixth century (Simonides FF 4, 32 Diehl; Athenaeus 438c; Plutarch *Moralia* 527c; *Cato Maior* 18; Cicero, *De Oratore* 2.86.352). His grandfather is referred to as "the old Scopas" (Athenaeus ibid.; Quintilian, *Institutio Oratoria* 11.2.14), which means that he, too, was well-known for something: this must have been the victories in war implied, and the consequent regulation of tribute referred to, by Xenophon.

[77] Boeotia: Plutarch *On the Malice of Herodotus* 33; *Life of Camillus* 19.2; cf. Pausanias 9.14.2. The battle of Keressos was linked to the battle of Leuctra in various ways, and clearly had a similar historical significance in Boeotian eyes, so it is not unlikely that the fairly precise date given in the second passage—"more than 200 years before" Leuctra, i.e. c. 575 BC—was remembered in local tradition. That Plutarch in the first passage dates the same event to "a short while" before the Persian Wars is no obstacle to accepting this date: it suited Plutarch's rhetorical and polemical point to play down the chronological distance, and in the long view of an author writing six centuries after the war, another century earlier may well have seemed "a short while". Wars with Phocis: Plutarch *Moralia* 244ae; Herodotus 8.27-28; Pausanias 10.1.3, 10-11; Polyaenus 6.18.2, 8.65; Polybius 16.32. For the nature and chronology of archaic Thessalian expansion, see Helly 1995; Ellinger 1993; Ducat 1973.

Dependent statuses in Crete

"The *perioikoi* cultivate the land for the Cretans", said Aristotle. "From all the crops and livestock which come in from the public estates and from the tributes paid by the *perioikoi*, one part is allocated to the gods and to common expenditures, and the rest goes to the public messes, so that everyone—women, children and men—may be fed from communal resources".[78] Later authors tacitly corrected Aristotle's terminology, pointing out that in Crete, as in Sparta and Thessaly, the word *perioikoi* referred to subject communities, not serfs. The serfs proper were generically known as "serfs" (*woikeis*) and "slaves" (*douloi*), but subdivided into the categories of publicly owned *mnoia* and privately owned *a(m)phamiotai* or *klarôtai*, "the allotted".[79]

Cretan serfs were often compared to helots and *penestai*, with whom they are said to have shared the condition that they could not legally be sold "beyond the borders" (Strabo 12.3.4). In other respects, they appear to have enjoyed greater rights than serfs elsewhere. Surviving laws show that, while the land which they worked and the houses in which they lived were owned by their masters, the serfs could own movable property, including livestock, and might gain ownership of the estate itself in the event that their masters left no heirs. Male serfs were even allowed to marry citizen women, a practice which elsewhere met with much resistance, as we have seen.[80] This relative freedom was presumably what Aristotle had in mind when he claimed that Cretans "grant their slaves all other rights of this kind and forbid them only to exercise in the *gumnasia* and to own weapons" (*Politics* 1264a21-2). Whether the *klarôtai* were thereby also exempted from following their masters to war, in contrast to helots and *penestai*, is not clear, but they do seem to have been exempt from domestic service. Athenaeus tells us that house-servants in Crete were called *chrusônetai*, "bought with gold", which must mean that they were chattel slaves, rather than serfs (263e).

We know very little more about the economic burdens imposed on the serfs, except that in hellenistic Lyttus "each slave [*doulos*] contributed an Aeginetan stater" to the common messes (Dosiadas *FGrHist* 458 F 2). The demand for money is noteworthy, and was probably a recent development; it is hard to tell whether this

....

[78] *Politics* 1272a1, 18-22; cf. 1271a29; the term *perioikoi* is used also at 1271b31, 1272b19; that many cities all over Crete have their own *perioikoi* is made clear at 1269b3.

[79] See Sosicrates *FGrHist* 461 F 4 and Dosiadas *FGrHist* 458 F 3, cited with other passages at Athenaeus 263f-264a. The term *klarôtai* is attested in Ephorus *FGrHist* 70 F 29 and Aristotle F 586 Rose; *mnoia* occurs in an archaic poem (see below); *woikeus* and *doulos* are used in inscribed Cretan laws, esp. the Gortyn Code. For a recent discussion of the terminology, see Link 2001, who shows that *woikeus* and *doulos* are used as synonyms, and questions the validity of the distinction between private and public slaves made by our (late) sources.

[80] See Willetts 1955: 49-51, for the evidence from the Gortyn Code and other laws.

payment was required instead of, or on top of, agricultural tribute. *Perioikoi*, at any rate, continued to pay tribute in kind: hellenistic Praisos took 10% of Stalai's revenues from harbour dues, fisheries and purple production, later reduced to 5%, while Gortyn demanded 10% of all Kaudos' annual harvests (excluding vegetables), plus fixed quantities of salt and juniper berries.[81] Clearly the conditions of exploitation in Crete, as elsewhere, developed over time and varied from place to place.

Crete had its own legend of a Dorian invasion, and some scholars have sought the origins of the serfs here. As Herodotus tells the story, after the Trojan War the population of the island was nearly wiped out by famine and plague, and the people currently known as Cretans were the few survivors joined by many later immigrants (7.170-1). Late fourth-century sources specify that these immigrants came from Sparta and Argos two generations after the Dorian migration. The Spartan settlers were a group of people who had once lived in Lemnos and Imbros and were either non-Greek Pelasgians or half-Greeks of mixed Pelasgian and Athenian descent. They had moved to Sparta and settled in Amyclae for a while, but after a failed rebellion were forced to leave for Crete, settling at Lyttus (or Lyctus) and Gortyn under the leadership of the Spartan Pollis. At the same time, and also as a result of civil strife, Althaemenes led a group of "Dorians and some Pelasgians" from Argos to settle in Rhodes and at ten sites in Crete, including Knossos and Tylissos.[82]

In complete contrast to these widely-attested stories stood the lone account of the fourth-century historian Andron of Halicarnassus, according to whom "Dorians, Achaeans and Pelasgians" had migrated to Crete straight from their homeland of Doris in Thessaly, under the leadership of Tectaphos, son of Doros, son of Hellen, long before the Trojan War and even before the reign of Minos, "when Cres ruled the island" (*FGrHist* 10 F 16). This unusual story was clearly pure invention, designed to explain Homer's famous description of Crete:

> It has infinitely many people and ninety cities. Their languages are all different but mingled together. There are Achaeans, there are great-hearted Eteocretans, there are Cydonians, and Dorians in three groups, and noble Pelasgians (*Odyssey* 19.172-7).

The Eteocretans and Cydonians were regarded as aboriginal peoples,[83] but the presence in Crete of Achaeans, Pelasgians, and above all Dorians at a time before the

......

[81] Chaniotis 1996: 160-168 and texts 64 (early 3rd century) and 69 (late third/early second century).

[82] See Aristotle *Politics* 1271b25-33; Ephorus *FGrHist* 70 F 117-18, 146, 149; Konon *FGrHist* 26 F 1.36, 1.47; Nicolaus of Damascus *FGrHist* 90 F 28; Plutarch *Moralia* 247bf, 296bd. Spartan traditions: Malkin 1994: 76-80; Argive colonies: Graham 1964: 154-165.

[83] Strabo 10.4.6; implicit already in Herodotus 7.170 where the only remaining groups of Cretan natives are from Praisos (Eteocretans) and Polichna (Cydonians).

Dorian migration posed a problem. Andron radically posited that all three groups mentioned by Homer must have moved to Crete from mainland Greece near the beginning of the island's history.

The mainstream tradition also shows signs of having been elaborated to accommodate the evidence of Homer. The claim that Argives settled at ten sites is explicitly derived from a reference in the *Iliad* to "Crete of a hundred cities" (2.649): since the *Odyssey* spoke of only ninety, some deduced that ten cities had been destroyed in the island while the Cretan army was fighting at Troy, but Ephorus argued that the reference in the *Iliad* was to a later time, and that ten new cities had been founded by Althaemenes (*FGrHist* 70 F 146). Moreover, the link made in the *Odyssey* between Dorians and "noble Pelasgians" is probably responsible for the curious idea that the Argives brought along "some Pelasgians" and the even odder notion that most of the settlers from Amyclae were not actually Spartans but (half-)Pelasgians.[84]

At least part of these stories were thus later invention, and it is quite possible that they were wholly invented—created for the very purposes which they served in the classical period, when they were cited by politicians to justify intervention in Crete and used by scholars to explain the similarities between Spartan and Cretan customs.[85]

Moreover, the Cretan stories differed from the tradition about Thessaly and Sparta insofar as they did not suggest that the invaders subjected the natives by force. The hellenistic author Konon insisted that the Spartans had occupied the site of Gortyn "without meeting any resistance" and had "settled it together with the neighbouring Cretans" (*FGrHist* 26 F 1.36), implying the sort of peaceful coexistence also suggested by Herodotus' story that the previous inhabitants of Crete were all but extinct when the new settlers arrived. Lyttus was an exception: it was said that the colonists here fought fierce battles against the natives and after the foundation of Lyttus "also took control of other cities"—the latter presumably the towns of *perioikoi* which, according to Aristotle, still retained their ancestral customs.[86]

Even if these traditions had some historical basis, then, they only explain the origins of serfs and *perioikoi* in Lyttus, not of the subject populations in the other cities supposedly settled by Sparta and Argos, let alone of those which existed elsewhere

....

[84] This last conceit was evidently developed by adapting a story told by Herodotus about a different group of half-Pelasgians, who came from Lemnos, settled in Sparta—on Mount Taygetus this time—and left after a failed rebellion to settle abroad, some colonising Thera under Spartan leadership, others migrating to Triphylia (4.145-8); cf. Malkin 1994: 73-85, who argues for its historicity.

[85] Malkin (1994: 79-80) argues that they do refer to historical colonisations; but his eighth century date rests on the assumption that the helots who feature in these stories are Messenians (pp. 77-78): in fact they are Laconian helots and the date is shortly after the Dorian migration (see above, n. 47).

[86] Plutarch *Moralia* 247ef (a story about the class of funerary experts called "cremators", *katakautai*, allegedly formed to deal with the many casualties) and 296bd; Aristotle *Politics* 1271b25-33.

in Crete.[87] If *klarôtai* were nevertheless categorically defined as "native rural serfs *enslaved through war*" (Athenaeus 263e), this can hardly mean a one-off Dark Age mass enslavement, but must refer to many separate, local and piecemeal reductions to serfdom which resulted from the many wars which Cretan cities fought against one another over the centuries.

Little is known about the details of Cretan military and political history before the mid-fourth century BC, but the Cretans certainly had a reputation for bellicosity to rival Sparta's: "in Sparta and Crete the system of education and the majority of laws are largely designed with a view to war", both observing a rigid separation between the warrior class and those who cultivated the land for them (Aristotle, *Politics* 1324b7-9; 1329b1-5). Archaic Cretan attitudes to war are revealed by the so-called *Song of Hybrias*, which boasts:

> I have great wealth: a spear, a sword, and the fine leather shield which protects one's skin. For with this I plough, with this I harvest, with this I trample the sweet wine from the vines, with this I am called master of the serfs (*mnoia*).

> Those who dare not hold a spear, a sword, and the fine leather shield which protects one's skin all cower at my knee and prostrate themselves, addressing me as "Master" and "Great King" (*Skolion* 909 Page).

This drinking song does not merely claim that warriors live off the agricultural labour of serfs and are treated with the greatest respect, but strongly implies that good fighters will *make* serfs of the weak. The *Song of Hybrias* thus affords a unique glimpse of an archaic ideology which regards the imposition of serfdom as a legitimate and admirable goal of war. It must remain uncertain when serfs first appeared in Crete, but it seems clear that serf populations continued to be created through conquest in the archaic age.

4. Serfdom and conquest: some other candidates

In the cities and regions we have considered so far, the presence of a dependent labour force "between free men and slaves" is explicitly attested by ancient evidence, and in each case we can plausibly trace its origins back to archaic—in some cases perhaps earlier—conquests. In several other areas we have either clear evidence for a serf population, but without any indication of its possible origins, or evidence for

---

[87] Ephorus *FGrHist* 70 F 149 already pointed out that Cretan cities which were *not* "colonies" of Sparta nevertheless had the same institutions; he also explicitly spoke of serfs at Cydonia (F 29); see above, nn. 78-79, for the presence of serfs in all parts of Crete.

archaic wars of conquest resulting in some form of subjection without clear evidence that this entailed the imposition of serfdom. None of these cases can stand by itself, but their cumulative effect is to suggest that the archaic period saw many communities at least temporarily reduced to serf or perioikic status.

Locris and Phocis

An early fifth-century bronze plaque recording the conditions upon which colonists from the cities of Eastern Locris and from Chaleion in Western Locris are to settle in Naupactus stipulates that any magistrate who fails to uphold the regulations is to be punished with confiscation of "his *klêros* and his *woikiatai*". This is evidently not just another way of saying "his property", but specifically a landed estate with cultivators who are tied to it: the *woikiatai* are serfs.[88] Although this is our only explicit evidence, the existence of serfs in Eastern and Western Locris, and probably Phocis as well, is indirectly confirmed by Timaeus' claim that Locrians and Phocians did not employ chattel slaves until the mid-fourth century, when the wife of Philomelos bought herself two maidservants. Previously, he said, house-servants had been *hired*, among the younger and poorer citizens (*FGrHist* 566 F 11). It would be quite remarkable if these two peoples, unlike all their neighbours, had done without any sort of unfree labour for so long. Much more probably, they did not use chattel slaves because they used serfs instead. As in Crete, serfs engaged only in agricultural labour, leaving domestic service to hired staff, and later also to chattel slaves.

A warlike tradition was certainly maintained well into the classical period by the Western Locrians at least, who lived what Thucydides described as "the ancient life" of constant raiding by land and sea, and retained the old custom of bearing arms at all times,[89] but we do not know whether their wars ever extended to the subjection of neighbouring communities.

Megarian tears

A classical story explained the proverbs "Godlike Corinth" and "Megarian tears" as follows:

> The Megarians were colonists of the Corinthians and in many ways had to yield to the Corinthians on account of the might of this city. The Corinthians ordered them to do many other things, and when one of the Bacchiads died (since these were governing the city), it was compulsory

---

[88] Tod no. 24; for translation see Graham 1964: 226-228; Fornara 1983: 47-49. For *woikiatai* as serfs, see e.g. Vidal-Naquet 1986: 212; compare also the Argive inscription cited above, n. 32.

[89] Thucydides 1.5.1-6.2; on bearing arms see van Wees 1998. A mid-fifth century treaty between two West Locrian cities attempts to control mutual raiding: Tod I, no. 34; see Fornara 1983: 87-88.

for Megarian men and women to come to Corinth and join the lamentations for the dead man. Thus the Corinthians omitted no form of *hubris*...⁹⁰

There were other versions of the tale, recorded centuries later in proverb collections, which said that the Megarians went to Corinth to lament on only one occasion, at the death of the daughter of their king Clytius, who had married a certain Bacchius of Corinth (Zenobius 5.8), or that it was a Megarian queen who once forced her people to make lamentation at their own king's funeral (Diogenianus 6.34; Apostolius 11.10). These later versions are easily understood as attempts to clean up the earlier story, from a Megarian point of view, by removing the stigma of once having been so humiliated by their neighbours. The original tale, however, is not so easily explained away. It was of no significance to the explanation of the expression "godlike Corinth", which actually hinged on a confrontation between a Corinthian envoy and irate Megarians and did not need an invented period of Bacchiad domination to make sense. It also seems too elaborate to have been invented just to account for the expression "Megarian tears", especially since a simpler explanation—that the Megarians were famous garlic growers (Zenobius 5.8; Apostolius 11.10)—lay to hand.⁹¹

The parallel with the obligations imposed on Sparta's subjects suggests that during the period of Bacchiad rule, c. 750-650 BC, the Corinthians reduced their neighbours to either serf or perioikic status. Other traditions confirm that "in ancient times", when Megara was merely a collection of villages rather than a city-state, the Corinthians were always trying to "subject the Megarians to themselves" and that unnamed "enemies", who were surely the Corinthians, once "cut off much land", later restored to Megarian control by Orsippus in the late eighth century. It appears, then, that Corinth did not merely exercise political pressure on a supposed "colony" but resorted to outright war in occupying all or part of the Megarid.⁹²

....

⁹⁰ The story is attributed to Demon (*FGrHist* 327 F 19), but may go back to Ephorus (*FGrHist* 70 F 19). For further details of the sources and their variants, see Salmon 1972: 197-198.

⁹¹ John Salmon took the opposite view, arguing that "Zenobius . . . has circumstantial detail [i.e. the name Clytius, 'famous' ?] which is not likely to have been invented" and that "Demon has written a garbled version of the tradition preserved by Zenobius" (1972: 198), but this seems less plausible.

⁹² As suggested by Hammond 1954: 97. Early Corinthian imperialism: Plutarch *Moralia* 295bc; land "cut off" and restored by Orsippus: *IG* VII.52 (Orsippus was credited with an Olympic victory in 720 BC). Plutarch's list of Megarian villages suggests that the Perachora region, later part of Corinthian territory (e.g. Xenophon *Hellenica* 4.5.1-5), was once part of Megara, and Strabo (8.6.22) said the same about Crommyon. Archaeology has uncovered many Corinthian-made artefacts in Perachora and Corinthian-style burials in Crommyon in the eighth century, but that does not tell us who was in control: Megara at the time used "only orthodox Corinthian ware" and its burial customs are unknown (Coldstream 1977: 86, 172), so that we cannot tell whether the graves and artefacts came from Corinth or Megara (contra Salmon 1972, 1984: 48).

It is hard to say whether the Megarians were temporarily reduced to *perioikoi*, obliged to send mourners to the funerals of Bacchiad kings, or even to the position of serfs, each family forced to weep crocodile tears at their master's funeral—but both scenarios are possible.

The "dusty feet" of Epidaurus

The citizen body was comprised of 180 men, from among whom they elected councillors called *artunoi*. The majority of the people lived in the countryside. They were called "dusty-feet" (*konipodes*) because, as one can guess, they were recognized by their dusty feet when they came up to the city (Plutarch *Moralia* 291de).

Although Plutarch does not say so, it is tempting to see in this mockingly-named rural population another group of serfs.[93] There may be some indirect support for this in legends which claimed that Epidaurus, not Argos, was really entitled to the inheritance of Temenos and had always championed the region's other Dorian and Dryopian cities against Argive aggression. Most significantly, Epidaurus claimed to be the true home and final resting place of Hyrnetho, Temenos' daughter, the notional ancestor of Argos' serfs.[94] Couched in mythical terms, this was surely the Epidaurians' way of expressing their ambition to take over Argos' leading status and its subject population. Such expansionist behaviour by Epidaurus went a long way back into the archaic period. Neighbouring Aegina was at an early stage claimed as a "colony" of Epidaurus, and the Aeginetans were forced "amongst other things" to submit all their disputes to Epidaurian judges (Herodotus 5.83; 8.46), suggesting a dependent status similar to Sparta's *perioikoi*.

Against this background, it would not be at all surprising if the "dusty-feet" were indeed serfs, acquired through conquest in the archaic period. Epidaurus at some point dropped one of the standard Dorian tribal names, Pamphyloi, while introducing two others, Azantiaioi and Hysminates, and it is conceivable that these tribes were created to incorporate the serfs when they were finally enfranchised, just as had happened in Sicyon and Argos.[95]

Hollow Elis and the "yokels" of Pisa

The defining feature of the history of archaic Elis was the protracted warfare between the people of "Hollow" Elis in the northwest of the region and their neighbours, the

....

[93] So Garlan 1988: 95, 99; Fisher 1993: 33.

[94] Pausanias 2.19.1, 2.23.3, 2.28.3, 2.29.5; Nicolaus of Damascus *FGrHist* 90 F 30.

[95] New tribal names: *IG* 4².1.28 (146 BC), 96, 102-103, 106, 108. See Jones 1987: 107-111.

inhabitants of Pisa or Pisatis. This traditional history concentrated on the issue of who controlled the sanctuary at Olympia. The Eleans claimed that they had been in charge of Olympia and its Games from the days of the Dorian migration onwards, but that the Pisatans had repeatedly, and on occasion successfully, tried to oust them. At some point in the early sixth century, probably c. 580 BC, Elis finally regained firm control. Given that Olympia actually lay within the territory of the Pisatans, we are clearly dealing with a history written by the victors: a distorted, legitimising account of the Eleans' conquest of Pisatis and seizure of its main sanctuary. Strabo and Pausanias both believed that the Eleans at the same time also occupied part or all of Triphylia, the region south of Pisatis, and that they everywhere "uprooted" inhabitants, "pulled down many settlements" and "exacted tributes".[96]

Pausanias also reported a war between Elis and a coalition of Pisatans, "other *perioikoi*" and Arcadians, which was fought after the Persian Wars (5.4.7) and brought Elis enough spoils to fund the construction of the classical temple of Zeus at Olympia (5.10.2). This war must have taken place in the 470s or 460s, which fits Herodotus' remark that "the Eleans sacked the majority" of Triphylian cities "in my time" (4.148). Elis eventually lost control of Triphylia after being defeated by the Spartans around 400 BC, while the Pisatans eventually regained their independence in an Arcadian-backed uprising in 364 BC.[97]

The towns of Triphylia, all but one of them acquired by the Eleans as "spoils of war", were clearly tribute-paying *perioikoi* of the type we have found in Sparta, Thessaly and Crete. The status of the Pisatans, however, was different: the Spartans set free the *perioikoi*, but refused to liberate the Pisatans on the grounds that they were "yokels" (*chôritai*), "not fit to be in charge" of the sanctuary at Olympia.[98] If the Pisatis was a particularly rustic region at the time, this was probably not because it had remained undeveloped—Strabo stresses that it had once had eight cities, most of which he names (8.3.31-2)—but because the Eleans had made it so. In other words, Elis had done much more here than impose tributes on defeated communities: direct and drastic intervention had reduced Pisatis to a thinly settled agricultural area and, quite possibly, its population to serf-like dependents.

If so, developments in early classical Elis may have run parallel to those in Argos. The synoecism of Elis in 471 BC and the synoecism of Argos at much the

......

[96] Strabo 8.3.30 = Ephorus *FGrHist* 70 F 115 (cf. Strabo 8.3.2 and 33), mentioning tribute and dating the final conquest to after the Second Messenian War. Pausanias 6.22.2-4 (cf. 5.6.4, 5.8.5, 5.16.5-6), giving a date not long after 588; the first appointment of two Elean presidents to run the Games in 580 (5.9.4) suggests a similar date; Eusebius (*Chronica* I 194ff Schöne) has Pisatan control end in 572. The payment of tribute (of one talent) by one of the towns is confirmed by Thucydides 5.31.2-4.

[97] Xenophon *Hellenica* 3.2.23-31 (Triphylia), 7.4.28-9; Pausanias 5.9.6, 6.4.2, 6.8.3, 6.22.3 (Pisatis).

[98] *Hellenica* 3.2.31 and 3.2.23 for *perioikoi* as "spoils of war". Cf. Roy 1997: 291-292.

same time may both have been attempts to deal with rebellious subjects by integrating them into the community, in part by concentrating a greater proportion of the population in the dominant city, and in part by incorporating them into the city's political organisation: the Pisatans formed four out of Elis' twelve tribes.[99] As in Argos, the enfranchisement of former subjects may well have been followed immediately by renewed expansionist campaigns, leading to the further conquests in Triphylia recalled by Herodotus. Unlike Argos' *gumnêtes*, however, Elis' subjects did not fully merge into the citizen-body, and finally reasserted their independence in the same decade which saw the liberation of serfs in Messenia, Sicyon and Heraclea.

ᛞ

Among the many obscure groups of people in ancient Greece of whom we catch an occasional glimpse, there may have been yet other serf populations—the Gergithes, perhaps, or the Ellopians or Kylikranes—but the evidence in these cases is too tenuous to inspire any confidence.[100] Even without adding to our tally, however, we have found up to a dozen cities and regions other than Sparta which employed serfs and other subject populations acquired by conquest. The Messenian helots were clearly not alone in the Greek world—nor, as we shall see, were the conquest serfs of Greece without parallel in history.

5. Helots and Indians: forced labour in a conquest society

A few hundred Spanish soldiers took only a couple of years to conquer the vast territories of Central America, with a native population of at least two million. Fifty years after the conquest, a mere 2,300 Spanish citizens and their households still ruled over about half a million Indians, scattered over a thousand settlements. Despite their overwhelming superiority in numbers, the natives—not only in Central America but also in the Caribbean, Mexico and South America— submitted to the heavy burden in tribute payments and forced labour imposed upon them by the invaders. With variations in the nature and level of exactions, the system remained in place for a century, always aggravated by gratuitous abuse from

....

[99] Synoecism: Diodorus Siculus 11.54.1; Strabo 8.3.2; cf. Moggi 1976: 157-66. The loss of Pisatis in 364 led directly to a reduction of the number of Elean tribes from 12 to 8 (Pausanias 5.9.6), so by this date, at any rate, the Pisatans belonged to the tribes, and probably simply formed four distinct tribes. For a discussion of the synoecism and its effect on Elis' subjects, see Roy 1997: esp. 286-289.

[100] Gergithes of Miletus: Garlan 1988: 105 (but Gorman 2001: 102-107, is rightly sceptical). Ellopians of Euboea: Asheri 1975: n.28 (tentatively). Kylikranes of Trachis: Asheri 1975; Ducat 1994: 108-109.

the sort of people who believed that "if water were lacking to irrigate the Spaniards' farms, they would have to be watered with the blood of the Indians".[101]

Conquered settlements were simply allocated to Spanish officers and soldiers by a system of grants known as *encomienda*, which gave the *encomenderos* the right to impose tribute and labour obligations on "their" Indians. The natives were legally free men, subjects of the crown, but differed from slaves only in "the manner in which they had been acquired, and not the manner in which they were used", being "made to work for the Spaniards without pay, and . . . whipped and aggrieved in other ways, as if they were slaves".[102]

Tributes took the form of levies of agricultural produce and home-made commodities. For example, the following tribute was owed to Pedro de Alvarado, the conqueror of Guatemala, personally. Each year, his Indians between them were expected to provide 500 measures of cacao beans, 100 pairs of sandals, 60 reed mats, and 60 gourds. Every fifteen days, they gave him 40 striped Indian mantles, 20 jackets, 20 loincloths, 10 chickens, 5 turkeys, 90 bushels of maize, a bushel of beans, a bushel of chili peppers, a bushel of salt, and a jug of honey. Every Friday, they presented him with 40 eggs and a basket of crabs.[103]

A source of as much deprivation as the levy itself was the obligation to carry the tribute to the *encomendero's* place of residence, which required Indians to walk distances of up to a hundred miles with heavy loads. Contemporaries commented on the suffering caused:

> They have been exhausted by their journeys to carry tribute every year to the Spaniards' towns. They came a great distance . . . and brought with them but a little poor food. When they arrived, worn out and famished, they were made to fetch water and wood, sweep the house and stables, and take out rubbish and manure. They were kept at such labour two, three, or more days without being given food, so that they were forced to eat the food they had brought from home, if anything was left, and so had nothing for the journey home. This is still being done (Zorita [1963] 209).

A century after the conquest, another observer echoed Tyrtaeus in speaking of Indians carrying burdens "like donkeys" and noted that "in most cases they are

....

[101] So a Spanish colonial judge, quoted in Zorita 1963: 217. For the population figures, see the statistics in Sherman 1979: 3-8, 347-370.

[102] Quotations from Kramer 1994: 3, and Sherman 1979: 321 (cf. p. 85; and at p. 136 a contemporary is cited for the judgment that "the *encomienda* Indians . . . were no better off than slaves").

[103] Kramer 1994: 247; cf. p. 221.

treated harshly and are belabored and kicked and beaten, without turning against those who maltreat them".[104]

The labour obligations imposed in addition to the tribute were no less burdensome. Pedro de Alvarado demanded "fifteen Indians to serve in the city", and compulsory domestic service in Spanish households remained normal practice, *servicio ordinario*. Forced labour was also used in public works, both for major construction projects and on a routine basis: one Spanish town required 30 Indians to attend three times a week to clean the "palace", and also demanded the services, once a week, of 46 grass-cutters, 3 wetnurses, and 6 men to clean the latrines in the city jail.[105] Finally, the natives were compelled to join military expeditions:

> Yet another multitude has been killed off and continues to be killed off by being taken as carriers on conquests and expeditions, and still others to serve the soldiers . . . In the New Kingdom of Granada I heard many Spaniards say that one could not lose one's way between that country and the province of Popayán because it was marked with the bones of dead men (Zorita [1963] 209-10).

On de Alvarado's expedition to Peru, "depending on his status, a soldier could take from 2 to 8 Indians to serve him", a figure which lends some support to Herodotus' notorious claim that during Pausanias' campaign at Plataea every Spartan was escorted by seven helots.[106]

The roles and treatment of Indians were thus almost identical to those of conquest serfs in ancient Greece, and whatever the legal niceties of their position, the status of both was in practice clearly "between free men and slaves", and they long remained so despite often living at great distances from their masters and greatly outnumbering the conquerors.

In Central America a small number of conquerors were able to exploit a vast population in part because tribute and labour were being demanded by native chieftains even before the Spanish arrived. At first, the conquerors operated entirely through this traditional hierarchy, with local "lords" passing on to them the bulk of the levies.[107] The situation was not quite the same in Greece, but here too conquerors must have built on pre-conquest regimes. Where land ownership was concentrated in the hands of few and estates were largely worked by share-croppers, for example,

....

[104] Sherman 1979: 337-338; cf. 92-93. Further abuses: Zorita 1963: 213-215.
[105] Lutz 1994: 22-23; cf. Kramer 1994: 220-221 and 247 (Alvarado); Sherman 1979: 85-128, 191-259, and 305-313 on the services demanded from Indian women in particular.
[106] Sherman 1979: 59, 106; cf. Herodotus 9.28-29.
[107] Kramer 1994: 210-218; Sherman 1979: 85-86, 263-275.

it would have been relatively simple for conquerors to demand agricultural tribute: little would change for the cultivators, except that they handed over their produce to more distant landlords. Precisely such a regime existed in seventh-century Athens, and probably also in other parts of Greece, especially in regions with large and fertile agricultural plains, such as southern Laconia, Messenia, Thessaly or Elis.[108] A region dominated by independent family farms, by contrast, could not be exploited without drastic, structural, interventions. The nature of the pre-conquest regime was surely a key factor in deciding whether a defeated enemy was to be reduced to serfdom or suffer some other fate.

Over time, the Spanish rulers of Central America began to intervene more in the structure of Indian communities. The *encomenderos* not only undermined the power of native chiefs by usurping their tribute and humiliating them in front of their subjects, but increasingly by-passed the chiefs altogether, levying tribute in person or through their own agents. At the same time, the Spanish crown extended the administration of justice through its magistrates rather than the native elite. Most chiefs ended up impoverished and lapsed into the status of commoner.[109] Within decades of the conquest, moreover, the *encomenderos* most directly involved in managing their domains were arranging for the wholesale resettlement of Indian communities in order to concentrate the workforce nearer their agricultural estates.[110]

We have seen hints that in Greece, too, regimes of exploitation were subject to change. The limited evidence makes it impossible to trace these developments, but what happened after the Spanish conquest may provide a useful model. When a Greek city was conquered, a large section of the native elite would take refuge abroad, rather than submit to the new rulers, but some will usually have remained behind. A gradual undermining by the conquerors of local political and social structures would help explain how communities which were once stratified and politically organised could be reduced to villages with a barely differentiated population of serfs. As suggested earlier, historical changes and divergences in degrees of exploitation and intervention could also account for real social and economic differences between serf populations, as between Messenian and Laconian helots.

The single biggest problem encountered by the Spanish colonial administration was to prevent *encomenderos* from negating the gains of conquest through overexploitation. "The conquest of Central America and the two decades after it bear more resemblance to a large raid than to an occupation" because most *conquistadores* had come

....
[108] On archaic Greek regimes of landownership, see van Wees 1999b, 1999c: 2-6; Link 1991.
[109] Sherman 1969: 263-303, esp. 276-277; cf. Kramer 1994: 210.
[110] MacLeod 1973: 121-122; Lutz 1994: 20-22; Kramer 1994: 213-216.

"to accumulate booty or wealth as rapidly as possible so that they could return to wealth and prestige in Spain" (MacLeod 1973, 47). They did not want to settle down as the master of an *encomienda* which demanded some care and attention in exchange for unspectacular tributes. Not only did colonising expeditions literally turn into slave raids, but many *encomenderos* resorted to illegally seizing their peers' and their own tribute-paying Indians and selling them into slavery, leaving some regions virtually depopulated. The Spanish government responded with law after law prohibiting the sale of Indians. Since masters would find excuses to travel abroad with large Indian retinues, only to sell their attendants as soon as they reached a remote enough area, the law ultimately forbade them to take Indians outside their native regions at all.[111] The parallel with Greek rules against selling serfs abroad (or manumitting them—at a price) is irresistible. Rather than a "contract" made with the defeated enemy, as the sources present it, or a humanitarian measure, these restrictions were imposed by conquering communities to ensure that the greed of individual citizens did not deplete the native labour force to the point where the occupied land became impossible to exploit.[112]

The first generation of conquerors in Central America were more or less free to set their own tribute and labour requirements, and constantly quarreled amongst themselves over mutual infringements between neighbouring *encomiendas*. The Spanish government later acted to prevent disunity amongst the rulers and overexploitation of the ruled by imposing a "redistribution of Indians" (*repartimiento*), checks on labour demands and maximum tributes. It also became compulsory to pay Indians a small wage for what was nevertheless forced forced labour, a point which may throw some light on what ancient sources meant when they described *penestai* as "slaves working for a wage". More generally, these developments support the claim that in Sparta excessive exploitation of serfs was punishable by a curse.[113]

One sixteenth-century observer asked the King to fix a maximum annual tribute, because

> the *encomenderos* should receive as much tribute as suffices for a decent living, and not what is needed to gratify luxurious and extravagant taste in clothing, food, household service, and the like (Zorita [1963] 254-5).

....

[111] Sherman 1979: 39-63, esp. 47-48; MacLeod 1973: 47, 50-56; Zorita 1963: 202.

[112] On the "contract of servitude" in the sources, see Ducat 1990: 70-76, 1994: 72, who points out that in fact such measures are vital to any system which does not have an external supply of labour.

[113] Conflict among conquerors: Kramer 1994: 201, 213-216; Sherman 1979: 43. Government controls: Sherman 1979: 9-12, 88-89, 129-188. *Repartimiento*: Sherman 1979: 191-259. Curse: see above, n.14.

The idea that the greed of the colonial elite which threatened the stability of Spanish rule was driven by private conspicuous consumption of wealth no doubt holds true for Greece as well. The Spartans tried to get to the root of the problem by not only limiting the amount of tribute but also restricting the display of wealth itself, imposing sumptuary restrictions precisely on "clothing, food, household service, and the like". If Sparta managed to cling on to its helots when several neighbouring states lost their serfs, it may be in part because, by the beginning of the classical period if not earlier, the Spartans had created a notably "austere" form of the leisured lifestyle enjoyed by all Greek elites, especially in conquest states.[114]

"Attempts by a conquering group to enslave a conquered people *en masse* and *in situ*", Orlando Patterson has observed, "were almost always disastrous failures". He concedes that "such attempts . . . lasted much longer than is generally acknowledged" and that Spanish rule in the Americas was among "the most sustained and, not surprisingly, the most frightening" (1982: 110, 112). Since the system outlined here lasted only for about a century, before gradually turning into a different regime of exploitation which instead relied heavily on debt-bondage,[115] the long centuries of serfdom in Laconia, Thessaly and Crete remain remarkable.

But their persistence is certainly not inexplicable. The Spanish system ultimately "failed" not because it was impossible to control the natives, but partly because virulent diseases wiped out much of the labour force, and, even more importantly in the long run, because the surplus of cacao beans and cloth produced by the native economy did not satisfy the conquerors. The search for greater profits led to the creation of a mining industry, large agricultural estates, and vast cattle ranches—all of which operated more effectively with hired labourers and debt-bondsmen.[116] In Greece, conquerors did not spread fatal diseases and were apparently content to do little more than siphon off native produce. Without the pressures that ultimately transformed Spanish rule, there is no reason why a Greek conquest state which judiciously applied punishments and rewards, and tempered exploitation with self-restraint, could not retain control over large numbers of serfs for many centuries.

....

[114] For reassessments of the evidence usually taken to show that the Spartan culture of "austerity" was established by the mid-sixth century, see Hodkinson 1998 (dedications) and Powell 1998 (iconography), who show that the transformation may well have taken place significantly later.

[115] The change was gradual, so there is room for debate as to how long the forced labour system lasted, but Sherman (1979: 12, 337-338) sees its essentials still in place in 1630s, i.e. more than a century after the first conquests in mainland Central America in 1523.

[116] MacLeod 1973: 124-128 (Central America); Keith 1976: 130-136 (Peru); Frank 1979: 4-7 (Mexico).

6. Conclusion: helots in context

Sparta's conquest of Messenia was no anomaly, but merely the most spectacular and best attested instance of a form of imperialism characteristic of archaic Greece. In large parts of northern Greece (Thessaly, Locris and Phocis), most of the Peloponnese (Sicyon, Argos, Corinth, Epidaurus and Elis, as well as Sparta and Messenia), all of Crete, and parts of the colonial world (Syracuse, Byzantium, Heraclea, and Cyrene) communities succeeded in reducing their Greek or barbarian neighbours to the status of serfs or *perioikoi*. The earliest datable conquests of this type were made by Corinth and Syracuse in the eighth century BC, which is perhaps also when Sparta conquered Laconia and Argos began subjecting its neighbours. In none of the other areas need expansion have begun earlier. The latest datable wars which resulted in the creation of serfs fell in the decades 580-560 BC, when Sicyon, Elis and Heraclea first established their power. At the very same time Argos probably entered a new phase of conquest, the Thessalians reached the limits of their expansion, and the Spartans tried but failed to do to Arcadia what they had done to Messenia.

The subjects of Corinth, Cyrene and Sicyon reasserted their independence after no more than two generations, and the early decades of the fifth century marked a turning point as serf populations revolted all over the Greek world. Sicyon lost most of its *katônakê*-wearers around 500 BC; Argos struggled with its *gumnêtes* from the 490s to the 460s; the *kullurioi* of Syracuse rebelled in the 480s; the "yokels" of Pisatis tried to escape Elean control in the 470s or 460s. It was also "not long" before 480 BC that the Phocians fought their life-or-death struggle for independence against the Thessalians. The helot revolts which Sparta faced in 490 and 464 BC thus formed part of a broader historical pattern.[117] But Sparta differed from others in its response. The other Peloponnesian states ended up enfranchising their serfs, and Argos and Elis turned their newly enhanced manpower to further wars of conquest—which now no longer led to the creation of serfs. Sparta, by contrast, forced its helots and *perioikoi* back into subjection and drew back from aggressive warfare, let alone territorial expansion.

Another wave of liberations occurred a century later, in the years 370-364 BC, when outside intervention set free the Messenians and Pisatans, while popular uprisings led by tyrants led to the emancipation of the Mariandynians and probably the remnant of Sicyon's serfs, all in quick succession. The spread of chattel slavery in Locris and Phocis, and the apparent liberation of *penestai* at Larissa by

[117] For these revolts, see above, at nn. 9-10.

Philip II, in the course of the next two decades suggest a wider historical trend against the exploitation of serf labour. Again Sparta was part of these developments, and again it went against the flow by tenaciously hanging on to its remaining serfs, albeit at the cost of manumitting several thousand Laconian helots.

One may wonder why, if conquest serfdom was widespread in archaic Greece, it is so poorly attested that scholars have been virtually unaware of it. The reasons are simple. First, ancient authors took slaves and serfs very much for granted and often barely mentioned them.[118] Secondly, for most of the states which employed serfs we have very little evidence of any kind, let alone evidence for their use of unfree labour; conversely, we only know as much as we do about the conquest of Messenia because we are relatively well informed about Sparta in general. Thirdly, many forms of serfdom were already a thing of the past by the mid-fifth century when we first have contemporary historical sources; by the late fourth century, when the likes of Aristotle, Theopompus and Ephorus were writing, there were hardly any serf populations left in Greece except in Laconia, Thessaly and Crete. Classical authors thus had very little evidence to go on even if they did deign to write about serfs. Fourthly, these authors obscured what little historical evidence there might have been about the origins of the few remaining serf populations by appealing to, or indeed inventing, legends about migrations which had taken place just before or after the Trojan War.

These problems with the sources are compounded by a disinclination among scholars to see wars of conquest and widespread serfdom in archaic Greece, because these phenomena do not fit current models of archaic warfare and the exploitation of labour, respectively.

The common modern perception of archaic Greek warfare is that it was "agonal", that is to say, highly ritualised and restricted, aiming for minor territorial gains at best, not at the wholesale subjection of neighbouring states.[119] I would argue that this is too narrow a notion of warfare in archaic Greece. The evidence presented here shows clearly that wars of conquest did occur, and we must accordingly broaden our picture of war in the archaic Greek world to encompass a variety of forms ranging from restricted combat with limited objectives to all-out campaigns aimed at the subjection or destruction of the enemy.[120]

------

[118] See Hunt 1998.

[119] See esp. Hanson 1995, 1998: 202-205, 2000; Ober 1985, 1996; Pritchett 1974: 147-189; Detienne 1968: 123.

[120] See several important studies by Peter Krentz (1997, 2000, 2002); also van Wees, forthcoming.

Current orthodoxy on the history of unfree labour in archaic Greece, derived from the model developed by Moses Finley, holds that forms of dependent labour "between free men and slaves" were a relic of the Dark Age, and, so far from still being created in the archaic age, were abolished in all the more progressive parts of Greece from c. 600 BC onwards, when their place was taken by chattel slavery.[121] This model rests almost entirely on *a priori* assumptions rather than evidence, and although the assumptions are plausible enough in themselves, I would suggest that they are disproved by the cumulative weight of evidence assembled here, tenuous as most individual pieces may be. What we find instead is not a development from primitive serfdom to developed chattel slavery, but the simultaneous spread of conquest serfdom and chattel slavery throughout the archaic period.

This process was no doubt driven by the greed of the Greek upper classes.[122] The archaic elite reduced their share-croppers, hired labourers, debtors and clients to abject poverty, which meant that when they turned to war as a means of further self-enrichment, their impoverished fellow-citizens would be only too happy to join them, in the hope of alleviating their own lot. Depending on the circumstances, such campaigns might result in the acquisition of either land, or chattel slaves, or land with a serf labour force attached. In archaic Greece all these options were open, and serfdom was by no means an uncommon fate for a defeated enemy. It was only in the classical period—in the early fifth century in some areas, the mid-fourth century in others, and not until later still in Laconia, Thessaly and Crete—that serfdom began to disappear by stages and chattel slavery prevailed.[123]

....

[121] See Finley 1959: 114-115, 1960: 149, 1964: 132, 1965: 166, 1973: 70, 1980: 146, 1982: 271-273; he is followed by, for instance, Snodgrass 1980: 87-95; Vidal-Naquet 1986: 163-164; Garlan 1988: 39-40; Manville 1991: 132-133; Garnsey 1996: 4; more cautiously also by Ducat 1990: 78; Fisher 1993: 15-21. Even scholars who fundamentally disagree with Finley's approach and concepts have tended to accept the essentials of his model (Ste. Croix 1981: 141-142; Cartledge 1988: 36). I am aware of only one recent challenge to Finley's ideas: Rihll 1996.

[122] So also Luraghi 2002: 240-241, and cf. Link 1991.

[123] Earlier incarnations of this paper were delivered at the Harvard conference, the Triennial meeting in Oxford and at research seminars in London and Oxford. The response from organisers and participants on each occasion has had a profound influence on the argument and shape of this final version, and I am grateful to all concerned, notably to Simon Corcoran, Jonathan Hall, Rebecca Flemming and, above all, Nino Luraghi for their particularly detailed and insightful comments.

Bibliography

Andrewes, A. 1956. *The Greek Tyrants*. London.

———. 1971. *Greek Society*. Harmondsworth.

Asheri, D. 1975. "Eracle, Eraclea e i Cylicranes: mitologia e decolonizzazione nella Grecia del IV a.c." *Ancient Society* 6: 33-50.

Austin, M., and P. Vidal-Naquet. 1977. *Economic and Social History of Ancient Greece*. Berkeley and Los Angeles.

Braun, T. 1994. "ΧΡΗΣΤΟΥΣ ΠΟΙΕΙΝ." *Classical Quarterly* 44: 40-45.

Cartledge, P. 1980. "Euphron and the *douloi* Again." *Liverpool Classical Monthly* 5: 209-211.

———. 1988. "Serfdom in Classical Greece." In L. Archer (ed.), *Slavery and Other Forms of Unfree Labour*. London: 33-41.

———. 2002. *Sparta and Lakonia: A Regional History 1300 to 362 BC*. Second edition. London and New York.

Chaniotis, A. 1996. *Die Verträge zwischen kretischen Poleis in der hellenistischen Zeit*. Stuttgart.

Coldstream, N. 1977. *Geometric Greece*. London.

Detienne, M. 1968. "La phalange: problèmes et controverses." In J.-P. Vernant (ed.), *Problèmes de la guerre en grèce ancienne*. Paris: 119-142.

Drews, R. 1983. *Basileus: The Evidence for Kingship in Geometric Greece*. New Haven.

Ducat, J. 1973. "La confédération Béotienne et l'expansion Thébaine à l'époque archaïque." *Bulletin de correspondance hellénique* 97: 59-73.

———. 1976. "Clisthène, le porc et l'âne." *Dialogues d'histoire ancienne* 2: 359-368.

———. 1990. *Les Hilotes*. (Bulletin de correspondance hellénique, Supplément 20). Athens and Paris.

———. 1994. *Les Pénestes de Thessalie*. (Annales Littéraires de l'Université de Besançon 512). Paris.

Ellinger, P. 1993. *La légende nationale phocidienne: Artémis, les situations extrêmes et les récits de guerre d'anéantissement*. (Bulletin de correspondance hellénique. Supplément 27). Athens and Paris.

Hans van Wees

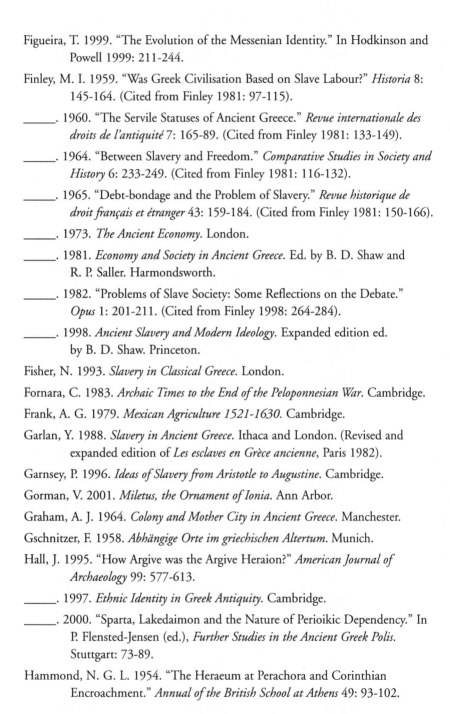

Figueira, T. 1999. "The Evolution of the Messenian Identity." In Hodkinson and Powell 1999: 211-244.

Finley, M. I. 1959. "Was Greek Civilisation Based on Slave Labour?" *Historia* 8: 145-164. (Cited from Finley 1981: 97-115).

———. 1960. "The Servile Statuses of Ancient Greece." *Revue internationale des droits de l'antiquité* 7: 165-89. (Cited from Finley 1981: 133-149).

———. 1964. "Between Slavery and Freedom." *Comparative Studies in Society and History* 6: 233-249. (Cited from Finley 1981: 116-132).

———. 1965. "Debt-bondage and the Problem of Slavery." *Revue historique de droit français et étranger* 43: 159-184. (Cited from Finley 1981: 150-166).

———. 1973. *The Ancient Economy*. London.

———. 1981. *Economy and Society in Ancient Greece*. Ed. by B. D. Shaw and R. P. Saller. Harmondsworth.

———. 1982. "Problems of Slave Society: Some Reflections on the Debate." *Opus* 1: 201-211. (Cited from Finley 1998: 264-284).

———. 1998. *Ancient Slavery and Modern Ideology*. Expanded edition ed. by B. D. Shaw. Princeton.

Fisher, N. 1993. *Slavery in Classical Greece*. London.

Fornara, C. 1983. *Archaic Times to the End of the Peloponnesian War*. Cambridge.

Frank, A. G. 1979. *Mexican Agriculture 1521-1630*. Cambridge.

Garlan, Y. 1988. *Slavery in Ancient Greece*. Ithaca and London. (Revised and expanded edition of *Les esclaves en Grèce ancienne*, Paris 1982).

Garnsey, P. 1996. *Ideas of Slavery from Aristotle to Augustine*. Cambridge.

Gorman, V. 2001. *Miletus, the Ornament of Ionia*. Ann Arbor.

Graham, A. J. 1964. *Colony and Mother City in Ancient Greece*. Manchester.

Gschnitzer, F. 1958. *Abhängige Orte im griechischen Altertum*. Munich.

Hall, J. 1995. "How Argive was the Argive Heraion?" *American Journal of Archaeology* 99: 577-613.

———. 1997. *Ethnic Identity in Greek Antiquity*. Cambridge.

———. 2000. "Sparta, Lakedaimon and the Nature of Perioikic Dependency." In P. Flensted-Jensen (ed.), *Further Studies in the Ancient Greek Polis*. Stuttgart: 73-89.

Hammond, N. G. L. 1954. "The Heraeum at Perachora and Corinthian Encroachment." *Annual of the British School at Athens* 49: 93-102.

_____. 1994. *Philip of Macedon*. London.

Hanson, V. D. 1995. *The Other Greeks*. New York.

_____. 1998. *Warfare and Agriculture in Classical Greece*. Revised edition. Berkeley.

_____. 2000. "Hoplite Battle as Ancient Greek Warfare: When, Where and Why?" in H. van Wees (ed.), *War and Violence in Ancient Greece*. London: 201-232.

Helly, B. 1995. *L'état thessalien: Aleuas le Roux, les tétrades et les tagoi*. Paris.

Hodkinson, S. 1998. "Laconian Artistic Production and the Problem of Spartan Austerity." In N. Fisher and H. van Wees (eds.), *Archaic Greece: New Approaches and New Evidence*. London: 93-117.

_____. 2000. *Property and Wealth in Classical Sparta*. London.

Hodkinson, S., and A. Powell (eds.). 1999. *Sparta: New Perspectives*. London.

How, W. W., and J. Wells. 1928. *A Commentary on Herodotus*, Vol. 2. *(Books V-IX)*. Corrected reprint. Oxford.

Hunt, P. 1998. *Slaves, Warfare and Ideology in the Greek Historians*. Cambridge.

Jones, N. F. 1987. *Public Organization in Ancient Greece: A Documentary Study*. (Memoirs of the American Philosophical Society 176). Philadelphia.

Keith, R. 1976. *Conquest and Agrarian Change*. Cambridge, MA.

Kiechle, F. 1959. *Messenische Studien. Untersuchungen zur Geschichte der Messenischen Kriege und der Auswanderung der Messenier*. Kallmünz.

Koiv, M. 2001. "The Dating of Pheidon in Antiquity." *Klio* 83: 327-347.

Kramer, W. 1994. *Encomienda Politics in Early Colonial Guatemala, 1524-1544*. Boulder.

Krentz, P. 1997. "The Strategic Culture of Periclean Athens." In C. Hamilton and P. Krentz (eds.), *Polis and Polemos: Essays on Politics, War, and History in Ancient Greece in Honor of Donald Kagan*. Claremont: 55-72.

_____. 2000. "Deception in Archaic and Classical Greek Warfare." In H. van Wees (ed.), *War and Violence in Ancient Greece*. London: 167-200.

_____. 2002. "Fighting by the Rules: The Invention of the Hoplite *agôn*." *Hesperia* 71: 23-39.

Lambrinoudakis, W. 1980. "Staatskult und Geschichte der Stadt Epidaurus." *Archaiognosia* 1: 39-63.

Larsen, J. A. O. 1937. "Perioikoi." *Realenzyklopädie der classischen Altertumswissencahft*. 19.1: 816-833.

Link, S. 1991. *Landverteilung und sozialer Frieden im archaischen Griechenland.* Stuttgart.

_____. 2001. "*Dolos* und *woikeus* im Recht von Gortyn." *Dike* 4: 87-112.

Lotze, D. 1959. Μεταξὺ ἐλευθέρων καὶ δούλων. *Studien zur Rechtsstellung unfreier Landbevölkerungen in Griechenland bis zum 4. Jahrhundert v. Chr.* Berlin.

_____. 1971. "Zur Verfassung von Argos nach der Schlacht bei Sepeia." *Chiron* 1: 95-109.

_____. 1985. "Zu neuen Vermutungen über abhängige Landleute im alten Sikyon." In H. Kreissig and F. Kühnert (eds.), *Antike Abhängigkeitsformen.* Berlin: 20-28.

_____. 2000. *Bürger und Unfreie im vorhellenistischen Griechenland. Ausgewählte Aufsätze.* Ed. by W. Ameling and K. Zimmermann. Stuttgart.

Luraghi, N. 2002. "Helotic Slavery Reconsidered." In A. Powell and S. Hodkinson (eds.), *Sparta: Beyond the Mirage.* London: 227-248.

Lutz, C. 1994. *Santiago de Guatemala 1541-1773. City, Caste, and the Colonial Experience.* Norman and London.

LSAG = Jeffery, L. H. 1990. *The Local Scripts of Archaic Greece. A Study of the Origin of the Greek Alphabet and its Development from the Eighth to the Fifth Centuries BC.* Revised edition by A. Johnston. Oxford.

Macan, R. W. 1908. *Herodotus: The Seventh, Eighth and Ninth Books.* Vol. 1.2. London.

MacLeod, M. 1973. *Spanish Central America: A Socioeconomic History, 1520-1720.* Berkeley.

Malkin, I. 1994. *Myth and Territory in the Spartan Mediterranean.* Cambridge.

Manville, P. B. 1991. *The Origins of Citizenship in Ancient Athens.* Princeton.

Masaracchia, A. 1990. *Erodoto: La battaglia di Salamina. Libro VIII delle storie.* Second edition. Milan.

Moggi, M. 1976. *I sinecismi interstatali greci.* Vol. 1. Pisa.

Morris, I. 1987. *Burial and Ancient Society: The Rise of the Greek City-State.* Cambridge.

Murray, O. 1993. *Early Greece.* Second edition. London.

Nafissi, M. 1999. "From Sparta to Taras: *nomima, ktiseis* and Relationships between Colony and Mother City." In Hodkinson and Powell 1999: 245-272.

Nomima I = H. van Effenterre and F. Ruzé (eds.). 1994. *Nomima: recueil d'inscriptions politiques et juridiques de l'archaïsme grec.* Vol. 1. *Cités et institutions.* Rome.

Ober, J. 1985. *Fortress Attica: Defense of the Athenian Land Frontier.* Leiden.

_____. 1996. "The Rules of War in Classical Greece." In J. Ober, *The Athenian Revolution: Essays on Ancient Greek Democracy and Political Theory.* Princeton: 53-71.

Ogden, D. 1997. *The Crooked Kings of Ancient Greece.* London.

Osborne, R. 1996. *Greece in the Making c. 1200-479 BC.* London.

Parker, V. 1993. "Some Dates in Early Spartan History." *Klio* 75: 45-60.

Patterson, O. 1982. *Slavery and Social Death: A Comparative Study.* Cambridge, MA.

Piérart, M. (ed.). 1992. *Polydipsion Argos.* (Bulletin de correspondance hellénique, Supplément 23). Athens and Paris.

Powell, A. 1998. "Sixth-century Laconian Vase-painting: Continuities and Discontinuities with the 'Lykourgan' Ethos." In N. Fisher and H. van Wees (eds.), *Archaic Greece: New Approaches and New Evidence.* London: 119-146.

Pritchett, W. K. 1974. *The Greek State at War.* Vol. 2. Berkeley.

Rawlinson, G. 1880. *History of Herodotus.* Fourth edition. London.

Rihll, T. 1996. "The Origin and Establishment of Ancient Greek Slavery." In M. L. Bush (ed.), *Serfdom and Slavery: Studies in Legal Bondage.* London: 89-111.

Roy, J. 1997. "The *perioikoi* of Elis." In M. H. Hansen (ed.), *The Polis as an Urban Centre and as a Political Community.* (Acts of the Copenhagen Polis Centre 4). Copenhagen: 282-320.

Ste. Croix, G. E. M. de. 1981. *The Class Struggle in the Ancient Greek World.* London.

Salmon, J. 1972. "The Heraeum at Perachora and the Early History of Corinth and Megara." *Annual of the British School at Athens* 67: 159-204.

Shaw, P.-J. 1999. "Olympiad Chronography and 'Early' Spartan History." In Hodkinson and Powell 1999: 273-309.

Sherman, W. 1979. *Forced Native Labor in Sixteenth-Century Central America.* Lincoln.

Shipley, G. 1997. "'The Other Lakedaimonians': The Dependent Perioikic Poleis of Laconia and Messenia." In M. H. Hansen (ed.), *The Polis as an Urban Centre and as a Political Community*. (Acts of the Copenhagen Polis Centre 4). Copenhagen: 189-281.

Snodgrass, A. M. 1980. *Archaic Greece: The Age of Experiment*. London.

_____. 2001. *The Dark Age of Greece*. Edinburgh. (Originally published 1971).

Stein, H. 1881. *Herodotos. Band IV, Buch VII*. Berlin.

Tomlinson, R. 1972. *Argos and the Argolid*. London.

van Wees, H. 1998. "Greeks Bearing Arms." In N. Fisher and H. van Wees (eds.), *Archaic Greece: New Approaches and New Evidence*. London: 333-378.

_____. 1999a/2002. "Homer and Early Greece." In I. de Jong, *Homer: Critical Assessments*. London: 1-32. (Corrected reprint in *Colby Quarterly*: 94-117).

_____. 1999b. "The Mafia of Early Greece." In K. Hopwood (ed.), *Organised Crime in Antiquity*. London: 1-51.

_____. 1999c. "Tyrtaeus' *Eunomia*: Nothing to Do with the Great Rhetra." In Hodkinson and Powell 1999: 1-41.

_____. Forthcoming. *Greek Warfare. Myths and Realities*. London.

Vidal-Naquet, P. 1986. *The Black Hunter*. Baltimore and London.

West, S. 1988. *A Commentary on Homer's Odyssey*. Vol. I. Cambridge.

Whitehead, D. 1981. "The Serfs of Sicyon." *Liverpool Classical Monthly* 6: 37-41.

Willetts, R. 1955. *Aristocratic Society in Ancient Crete*. London.

Zorita, A. de. 1963. *The Brief and Summary Relation of the Lords of New Spain* (c. 1570). Translated by B. Keen as *Life and Labor in Ancient Mexico*. New Brunswick.

Four

Agreste genus: Helots in Hellenistic Laconia

Nigel M. Kennell

In the aftermath of the battle of Leuctra, Sparta lost a third of its territory, comprising over half its arable land, and the majority of its helots. While their fellows west of Taygetus soon established a free state, Laconian helots, with no similar collective identity invented or genuine to differentiate themselves from their masters, remained under Spartan domination for centuries more. This was not for lack of spirit. Laconian helots joined in a general revolt in the wake of Leuctra, and the majority of the helots who crossed over to the Theban army as it advanced on Sparta must have been Laconian.[1] On the other hand, helots responded to a Spartan call to arms in return for a pledge of freedom in such numbers that they aroused suspicion and fear among the Spartiates.[2] The revolt petered out or was repressed, and the fate of the helot volunteers is unknown.

Despite the massive disruption in the lives of most Spartans the loss of Messenia must have caused, especially among those whose principal holdings had been located there, the lot of the helot in the middle of the fourth century remained the same as it had been for hundreds of years. According to Aristotle, helots still farmed for the Spartans as the *penestai* did for the Thessalians and due to their harsh treatment were still prone to revolt.[3] The continued existence of helots well into the next century is solidly attested: in the spring of 272 BC when the army of king Pyrrhus was bearing down on Sparta accompanied by the pretender Cleonymus, that man's friends and helots, we are told, decorated his house as if to welcome the invader to dinner.[4] Helots also appear in the accounts of king Cleomenes' preparations for the battle of Sellasia in 222 and in Nabis' attempts to suppress dissent

....

[1] Xen. *Hell.* 7.2.2.
[2] Xen. *Hell.* 6.5.28-29.
[3] Aristot. *Pol.* 2.9.2 1269a, 10.5 1271b, 10.16 1272b.
[4] Plut. *Pyrrh.* 27.3.

prior to his showdown with the Romans in 195. These sources number less than ten. But even this meager harvest provokes questions on two matters of interest: the end of helotage in Laconia and the status of helots in later Spartan society.

The history of Sparta in the third and second centuries is marked by a series of attempts, all ultimately unsuccessful for a variety of reasons, to restore Sparta to the predominant military position the city once held. Areus I, king from 309/8 to (probably) 265, and Nabis, last ruler of an independent Sparta (c. 207-192), both aimed for that goal by endeavoring to transform Sparta into a Hellenistic state *comme les autres*, while the two more famous kings Agis IV (c. 244-241) and Cleomenes III (c. 235-222) drew upon and elaborated the Lycurgan legend. Helots, however, simply did not enter into their calculations: no Spartan reformer or revolutionary ever seems to have decided to tap the immense manpower resources they represented to renew the Spartiate class. Not even Nabis, whose changes to the citizen body were radical, attempted it. Although some have mistakenly thought that he "liberated the helots", the evidence that he freed any helots at all is at best slight, as we shall see.

Areus need not detain us because we have no means of determining what impact his modernization policy had upon Laconia's helot population. One might speculate that it facilitated even greater concentration of landed wealth and consequently brought more helots under the control of fewer masters. By the middle of the third century, if the images of an extremely polarized society that have come down to us from Phylarchus are more or less accurate in general outline, the role of the helots had changed significantly. With the land owned by a small minority of *plousioi*, perhaps as few as one hundred, helots no longer provided a significant portion of their agricultural produce to support contributions from a broad range of Spartiates to the *sussitia* who thus maintained their status among the *homoioi*.[5] Instead, as the helots were now working for far fewer Spartiates than before, they would have produced for their masters a surplus increased far beyond what was needed for their survival and for their masters' contributions to the *sussitia*. Although, as Stephen Hodkinson pointed out, this pattern of ownership had existed in Laconia well before Leuctra, the loss of Messenia must have exacerbated it.[6] As the trend continued, it produced a vicious circle which caused more and more Spartiates to fail to make their contributions to the *sussitia*, because they did not own sufficient land from which to obtain the produce. *Sussitia* thus would have failed, and land passed into the ownership of fewer and fewer people, whose messes

....

[5] Plut. *Agis* 6.
[6] Hodkinson 2000: 65-112.

now became theaters for unreserved display of disposable income. In addition, the Spartan aristocracy's obsession with breeding and racing horses suffered no setback after 370: Isocrates in the *Archidamus* has Agesilaus' son say that Spartans were still rearing teams of voracious horses, in spite of being a people under dire compulsion and lacking even daily necessities.[7] The economic implications of such land use are important; for, although large areas of land for pasturage were needed, fewer helots could manage the herds than were necessary in the more labor-intensive activity of farming. For their masters, horse-breeding and animal husbandry in general significantly mitigated the impact of Leuctra. The helots' role thus changed from providing the broad economic foundation for a warrior class to being producers of wealth for a small elite.

Upon ascending the throne, the young king Agis IV set out to redress the gross imbalances that had arisen in Sparta by instituting quite radical reforms, in the distribution of land for example, which he justified as a return to the ideals of the legendary lawgiver Lycurgus.[8] He aimed at replenishing the Spartiate class by enfranchising perioeci and mercenaries who had sufficient means to live as gentlemen, were healthy, and of military age, but did not consider extending the offer of citizenship to the helots.[9] On the other hand, his policy of land redistribution that was eventually brought to fruition by Cleomenes certainly touched the lives of helots who had worked for generations on the vast estates of the elite. Although no ancient source alludes to this aspect of the reforms and no modern study has addressed it, the pooling of all land owned by Spartans and its allotment as equal *klêroi* to the renewed Spartiate citizen body must have entailed a considerable increase in manpower needs as the old economies of scale were lost.

The Spartans could have addressed this problem in one of three ways: either the mass of helots might simply have been divided up and assigned along with the *klêroi* to new masters; the helots might have continued to work the same land as before, even though it was now subdivided, with the produce from each of the *klêroi* within the larger unit going to its respective Spartiate owner; or the helots might have stayed with their original masters, leaving the new *klêros*-owners without helots of their own to fend for themselves. This last solution is impossible, in light of the 'Lycurgan' ideology of the revolutionary kings. The first solution would have produced an outcome more or less matching the situation before Leuctra, as it has been recently

....
[7] Isoc. 6.55.
[8] Plut. *Agis* 6.2, 10.2, 19.5; Hodkinson 2000: 43-45.
[9] Plut. *Agis* 8.3: ἀναπληρωθῆναι δὲ τούτους ἔκ τε περιοίκων καὶ ξένων, ὅσοι τροφῆς μετεσχηκότες ἐλευθερίου καὶ χαρίεντες ἄλλως τοῖς σώμασι καὶ καθ' ἡλικίαν ἀκμάζοντες εἶεν.

reconstructed, when Spartiates actually owned helots on their land, albeit with certain restrictions on their rights as property owners.[10] But it would have been horrendously complicated to put into effect, as it required breaking up at least some pre-existing helot communities and dispersing their members into smaller units over wide areas to work the scattered *klêroi*. It also remains unclear whether, after centuries of land passing into the hands of fewer and fewer owners, the helot population had the numbers to make the exploitation of *klêroi* in this way economically viable.

I think the second solution is the most logical and is the one which fits the almost non-existent evidence for the status of helots following the reigns of Agis and Cleomenes. One vital testimonium for this period has only recently been recognized as such. It appears in a passage of Strabo we will have occasion to revisit later, in which he provides a capsule history of helotage:

> Ephorus says that . . . the other (sc. Laconians) submitted, but the Heleians, who held Helos (called Helots) rose up and were swiftly defeated in war and enslaved under certain conditions, namely that it was not permitted for an owner to free them or sell them beyond the borders, and that this was called The War Against the Helots. Agis' regime instituted helotage, which lasted almost until the Roman domination; for the Lacedaemonians held them as sort of public slaves, establishing residences for them and particular tasks (κατοικίας τινὰς αὐτοῖς ἀποδείξαντες καὶ λειτουργίας ἰδίας).[11]

Hodkinson recognized that the sentence referring to Agis I's institution of the *heilôteia* cannot have come from Ephorus, as it begins with the statement that there were helots until the time of the Romans.[12] The syntax of the passage confirms this insight. The material taken from Ephorus is presented in indirect discourse, whereas the sentence in question was written in *oratio recta* and is undoubtedly from Strabo himself. Although this information is therefore irrelevant to the study of helots in the archaic and classical periods, it is of great value for our understanding of helotage after Cleomenes III. In contrast to the earlier period, helots were now state-owned, lived in communities dictated by the state, and provided some of the services normally associated with public slaves in other cities. Such explicit codification of the status of the helot would conform well with Cleomenes' program of reform, in which traditional practices were reconstituted and reshaped to produce new versions of the citizen training system and the *sussitia*.[13]

....

[10] Hodkinson 2000: 113-117.
[11] Strab. 8.5.4 (365).
[12] Hodkinson 2000: 117-118.
[13] Kennell 1995: 98-114.

The smooth operation of the renewed *sussitia* depended on all members being able to provide contributions in kind from their own land. Since the Lycurgan ethos prevented Spartans from sowing and reaping themselves, *sussitia* depended ultimately on helots. Thus, any distribution of land intended to revivify the common messes must inevitably have entailed a corresponding reform of the *heilôteia*. Along with losing (or giving up) their land, the Spartan elite also lost control of many helots. The state took their place, regulating where helots might live to ensure a stable pool of labor for the new *klêros*-holders and utilizing them for certain public duties beneath the dignity of the revived Spartiate class. After Cleomenes, individual Spartans could not own helots, but they were able to make use of the products of their labor on the land assigned to them. One final advantage of this "minimalist" version of Cleomenes' land reforms is that it would have taken only a short time to implement and could have been in place soon after he launched his coup against the ephors in 227.

Spartan military successes over the next few years, combined with the threat Cleomenes' ideas posed to property owners elsewhere in Greece, soon provoked the Achaean League to seek help from its old enemy Macedon. This alliance turned the tide against Cleomenes despite some astonishing Spartan victories, such as the sack of Megalopolis in 223. All ended with the massive defeat at Sellasia and Cleomenes' subsequent flight into Egyptian exile.[14] In 223/2, just before the battle of Sellasia, helots again had the promise of freedom dangled before them. Through this offer, made for the first time since Leuctra and under similar duress, Cleomenes raised 500 talents from the 6000 helots who could afford the price of 5 Attic minae each.[15] The sum has been thought high but, as has been pointed out, it is within the range of manumission fees paid by slaves elsewhere.[16] He also notes that helots who had worked on the large estates before redistribution might have had ample opportunity to amass capital from the sale of produce that was surplus to their own or their masters' needs. Cleomenes armed 2000 of the newly-liberated hoplites in the Macedonian style to confront Antigonus' elite troops.[17]

The fate of these ex-helots after Antigonus Doson's swift settlement of Spartan affairs remains unclear. Much remains unclear about the settlement as a whole. Polybius describes it twice. In his narrative of the reign of Cleomenes he polishes it

....

[14] Plut. *Cleom.* 23.3-25.1.

[15] Plut. *Cleom.* 23.1: ὁ Κλεομένης τῶν μὲν εἰλώτων τοὺς πέντε μνᾶς Ἀττικὰς καταβαλόντας ἐλευθέρους ἐποίει καὶ τάλαντα πεντακόσια συνέλεξε, δισχιλίους δὲ προσκαθοπλίσας Μακεδονικῶς ἀντίταγμα τοῖς παρ' Ἀντιγόνου λευκάσπισιν, ἔργον ἐπὶ νοῦν βάλλεται μέγα καὶ πᾶσιν ἀπροσδόκητον.

[16] Cartledge and Spawforth 1989: 56; Daubies 1971: 675.

[17] The doubts of Ducat (1990: 160) and Daubies (1971: 668) as to the correct translation of Plut. *Cleom.* 23.1 (see above n. 15) are unfounded. The asymmetrical positions of μέν and δέ are a result of the suppression of the second τῶν εἰλώτων (see Kühner-Gerth II.2 268).

off in a single sentence: "Securing Sparta after his assault Antigonus for the rest treated the Lacedaemonians with magnanimity and humanity, and having restored the ancestral *politeuma* within a few days withdrew with his forces from the city".[18] Later, in assessing the character of Philip V after his vicious destruction of Thermon in 218, Polybius compares Antigonus' behavior towards the defeated Spartans.

After defeating Cleomenes king of the Lacedaemonians in a pitched battle, Antigonus secured Sparta as well. But although as master he could treat the city and its citizens as he wished, he so refrained from ill-treating those who had come into his power that, on the contrary, he returned their ancestral *politeuma* and freedom, and after being responsible for very great benefactions both publicly and privately for the Lacedaemonians, he left for his own country.[19]

The meaning of *politeuma*, the key word in both passages, has been the subject of some debate, especially since Cleomenes himself claimed to be reviving Sparta's traditional or ancestral constitution (*politeia*).[20] Against Shimron's contention that Polybius used *politeuma* strictly to denote governmental institutions in contrast to *politeia*, which he used for social institutions in general, Walbank argued that the words were essentially synonymous.[21] According to him, Polybius blamed Cleomenes for destroying the Lycurgan constitution which had survived, albeit in disarray, even Leuctra. Antigonus re-instituted the ephorate, which Cleomenes had abolished tyrannically in 227, and which Polybius evidently believed was genuinely Lycurgan. However, Walbank did agree with Shimron's distinction between the purely governmental and the social aspects of Cleomenes' program. But on the crucial question of which, if any, reforms Antigonus left in place, he remained agnostic: "Whether in fact on this occasion some of Cleomenes' measures remained in force is a matter that can only be determined independently".[22]

....

18 Polyb. 2.70.1: Ἀντίγονος δ' ἐγκρατὴς γενόμενος ἐξ ἐφόδου τῆς Σπάρτης τά τε λοιπὰ μεγαλοψύχως καὶ φιλανθρώπως ἐχρήσατο τοῖς Λακεδαιμονίοις τό τε πολίτευμα τὸ πάτριον αὐτοῖς καταστήσας ἐν ὀλίγαις ἡμέραις ἀνέζευξε μετὰ δυνάμεων ἐκ τῆς πόλεως.

19 Polyb. 5.9.9: Ἀντίγονος ἐκ παρατάξεως νικήσας μάχῃ Κλεομένην τὸν βασιλέα τῶν Λακεδαιμονίων ἐγκρατὴς ἐγένετο καὶ τῆς Σπάρτης, αὐτός τε ὢν κύριος ὃ βούλοιτο χρῆσθαι καὶ τῇ πόλει καὶ τοῖς ἐμπολιτευομένοις τοσοῦτον ἀπεῖχε τοῦ κακῶς ποιεῖν τοὺς γεγονότας ὑποχειρίους ὡς ἐκ τῶν ἐναντίων ἀποδοὺς τὸ πάτριον πολίτευμα καὶ τὴν ἐλευθερίαν, καὶ τῶν μεγίστων ἀγαθῶν αἴτιος γενόμενος καὶ κοινῇ καὶ κατ' ἰδίαν Λακεδαιμονίοις, οὕτως εἰς τὴν οἰκείαν ἀπηλλάγη.

20 Shimron 1972: 553-555; Polyb. 2.47.3; 4.81.14.

21 Walbank 1966: 303-312.

22 Walbank 1966: 312 n. 41.

Nonetheless, Shimron's idea that there was a distinction between *politeia* and *politeuma* has more support than Walbank allowed, although the words do not have the meanings he thought they did. We can invoke the authority of Aristotle in the *Politics*: "Since *politeia* and *politeuma* mean the same thing, *politeuma* is the sovereign authority in cities; and it is necessary for that sovereign authority to be either an individual, a few people, or the many".[23] *Politeuma* here is "government," "state," or, more precisely, "the body of citizens with full rights of participation in government".[24] Walbank quoted this passage only partially in his rebuttal to Shimron, omitting everything after the first clause and thus passing over the subtle but important difference between the two words. Aristotle moves from the more general term *politeia*, "constitution," or "rights of citizenship," to a discussion of the more specific *politeuma*. Their meanings did overlap in general usage, like the modern "state" and "constitution," and Aristotle uses that blurring to his advantage, but there was a real distinction between the two. This distinction can be seen quite easily in epigraphical texts. For example, in the decree of the Smyrnaeans ratifying their *sumpoliteia* with Magnesia ad Sipylum from the middle of the third century, the *dêmos* is described as having "given citizenship (*politeia*) to the inhabitants of Magnesia," while later in the document the new citizens are characterized as "those who are being registered in the citizen body" (τοὺς καταχωριζομένους εἰς τὸ πολίτευμα).[25] In a letter to the people of Larissa, Philip V describes their need for new citizens:

> Petraios, Anankippos, and Aristonous, when they were on the embassy, revealed to me that your city too was in need of more inhabitants due to the wars. Therefore, until I think of others who are worthy of being citizens with you (ἀξίους τοῦ παρ' ὑμῖν πολιτεύματος), for the present I order that you vote that citizenship be given (δοθῆι πολιτεία) to those Thessalians or other Greeks who are living with you.[26]

Through a *sumpoliteia* agreement at the end of the third century, the Milesians enfranchised all citizens of Seleucia/Tralles who lived there up to the date of the

....

23 Aristot. *Pol.* 3.7.1 1279a: ἐπεὶ δὲ πολιτεία μὲν καὶ πολίτευμα σημαίνει ταὐτόν, πολίτευμα δ' ἐστὶ τὸ κύριον τῶν πόλεων, ἀνάγκη δ' εἶναι κύριον ἢ ἕνα ἢ ὀλίγους ἢ τοὺς πολλούς.
24 Miller 1995: 150. See also the discussion of Chrimes 1949: 16-18.
25 *I. Smyrna* II.1 573 I, lines 35, 36; II, line 72.
26 *IG* IX.2 517, lines 4-7: Πετραῖος καὶ Ἀνάγκιππος καὶ Ἀριστόνους ὡς ἀπὸ τῆς πρεσβείας ἐγένοντο, ἐνεφάνιζόν μοι ὅτι καὶ ἡ ὑμέτερα πόλις διὰ τοὺς πολέμους προσδεῖται πλεόνων οἰκητῶν· ἕως ἂν οὖν καὶ ἑτέρους ἐπινοήσωμεν ἀξίους τοῦ παρ- ὑμῖν πολιτεύματος, ἐπὶ τοῦ πάροντος κρίνω ψηφίσασθαι ὑμᾶς ὅπως τοῖς κατοικοῦσιν παρ' ὑμῖν Θεσσαλῶν ἢ τῶν ἄλλων Ἑλλήνων δοθῆι πολιτεία.

grant and allowed anyone who became a citizen of Seleucia by decree but who did not live there or was given citizenship (δοθῆι . . . πολιτεία) later also to become Milesian during a grace period of ten years following the original enrollment of the Seleucians into the citizen body (ἀπὸ τῆς πρὸς τὸ πολίτευμα προσγραφῆς).[27] In the *sumpoliteia* with Herakleia neither Milesians nor Herakleians who had not been resident in either city for more than five years were allowed to be enrolled in the citizen community (προσγραφῆναι πρὸς τὸ πολίτευμα) of the other city. As a rule, the inscriptions distinguish between the rights of citizenship (*politeia*), which can be granted to outsiders, and the community of citizens (*politeuma*), into which the new citizens were then enrolled. The difference resulted in the words acquiring in the Roman period two quite different meanings—magistracy (*politeia*) and community (*politeuma*).[28] Plutarch uses the latter word with almost exactly this meaning when noting the general decline of the state due to pervasive corruption just before the accession of Agis IV (ἐγκεκλικότων ἤδη τῇ διαφορᾷ τοῦ πολιτεύματος ὁμαλῶς ἁπάντων). Polybius also observes this distinction. His summary of the declaration of war against the Aetolians that opened the Social War in 220 contains a pledge to liberate states which were unwilling members of the Aetolian League and to "reestablish them in their ancestral states (ἀποκαταστήσουσιν εἰς τὰ πάτρια πολιτεύματα), with their own territory and cities, ungarrisoned, untaxed, and free, enjoying their traditional constitutions and laws (πολιτείαις καὶ νόμοις χρωμένους τοῖς πατρίοις)".[29] On occasion Polybius' usage comes close to that found in inscriptions. In Book 3 he specifies how in his narrative he will touch on the "development of the Rhodian state" (τῆς αὐξήσεως τοῦ Ῥωδίων πολιτεύματος). In a letter Laodice III recounts the benefactions of Antiochos III to the city of Iasos in Caria: "he granted you liberty and laws and for the rest has shown that he will develop the state (συναύξειν τὸ πολίτευμα) and will lead it to a better condition".[30] Polybius' use of *politeuma* thus coincides with Aristotle's definition and with the epigraphical record. Both it and *politeia* can denote systems of government, but whereas *politeia* emphasizes the legal and administrative structure of government, *politeuma* is concerned with the body of citizens who have effective control of that system.

To return, at last, to Antigonus' settlement in Sparta. In both passages Polybius says that Antigonus restored the ancestral *politeuma*, which must mean at the very least that he restored the citizen body to its original, pre-Cleomenean configuration,

....

[27] *Milet* I.3 143a, lines 17-23.
[28] *Politeia: IG* IV 716, πᾶσαν πολιτείαν ἐπιφανῶς ἐκτελέσαντα; *politeuma: IG* XIV 701, ἱερατεύσασας τοῦ πολιτεύματος τῶν Φρύγων.
[29] Polyb. 4.25.7.
[30] Polyb. 3.3.7; *I. Iasos* 93, line 10.

stripping the perioeci and mercenaries of their citizenship and possibly reinstating those wealthy Spartans who were in exile. Any hopes the helots freed by Cleomenes had to become full citizens would have been dashed. In the strictly constitutional sphere, his changes seem to have been minimal: the restoration of the ephorate is the single action that can be plausibly attributed to Antigonus.[31] The dyarchy was no more, Cleomenes' new magistracy, the patronomate, and his reformed *agogê* were both allowed to remain in place, thus winning Antigonus Polybius' admiration for his light-handed treatment of the defeated enemy[32] For what it is worth, Pausanias later claimed that Cleomenes' constitution, except for the monarchy, lasted until his own time.[33]

As for the unfortunate ex-helots, we should not just assume that they simply reverted to their former status. When Philopoemen stripped many people of their Spartan citizenship in 188 he conspicuously did not re-enslave those who obeyed his order to forsake Laconia. As Philopoemen's attitude to Sparta was much harsher and more unforgiving than Antigonus' appears to have been, it is not unreasonable to suppose that the Macedonian victor took similar or even milder sanctions against the new citizens than did the Achaean three decades later.

Antigonus' gentleness with Sparta was not entirely altruistic. As events during the next few years would show, there was still a base of support for Cleomenes among the population, and Doson may have thought it wise not to provide that faction with too many ready-made grievances around which to rally. But grievances there were, enough to provide the pretender Cheilon with ammunition for his attempted coup four years later against the ephors' choice of Lycurgus as king.[34] Although the uprising soon collapsed when he failed to win significant public support for a program of debt cancellation and land redistribution, Cheilon must have gambled that these issues would again strike a chord among Spartans at large. That the populace turned against Cheilon upon hearing his announcements in the agora may have been due more to his connections with Achaea and Macedon, with whom Sparta was then at war, than to its own satisfaction with the status quo.[35] Assuming that Cheilon had not completely misread the situation, it would appear that by 218 Sparta was again suffering from grossly unequal ownership of land. This inequality, I believe, was caused by the disenfranchisement of Cleomenes' new

....

[31] Shimron 1972: 60-63.
[32] On the survival of some of Cleomenes' reforms, see Cartledge and Spawforth 1989: 58, 201; Kennell 1985: 6-7.
[33] Paus. 2.9.3.
[34] Polyb. 4.81.1-11.
[35] Shimron 1972: 74-75.

citizens and the subsequent freeing-up of substantial lots of land that had consti-tuted their *klêroi*. Whether or not those exiled under Cleomenes returned after Sellasia, the action taken by wealthier Spartans to acquire the newly available lots to re-establish their estates would have had serious consequences for the Cleomenean ideal of complete equality among Spartan citizens. It is doubtful that the renewed imbalance in land ownership altered the status of the helots. Our only sure source for their post-Cleomenean status, Strabo, gives no indication that they remained "sort of public slaves" only for the five years of the revolutionary regime. During the unrest and turmoil of the next decade, nothing appears in our sketchy evidence to suggest that helots took part in any agitation to improve their position in Spartan society. The stasis between the remnants of Cleomenes' party and their enemies was confined exclusively to Spartan citizens. Despite a succession of exil-ings, massacres, and the like, we hear of no helot revolt.

Stable government returned to Sparta when Nabis came to power c. 207. His regime lasted until his murder in 192, making it the longest since that of Areus I. Polybius apparently treated Nabis' rule at Sparta in some detail, but unfortunately only fragments of his account have survived, along with sizeable portions of Livy's *History* which are derived from him. Polybius is far from an unbiased source; he saw in Nabis the embodiment of everything he despised in a ruler: exiling the rich, freeing slaves, engaging in aggressive military adventurism abroad and physical intimidation of his opponents at home, all the while depending on mercenaries to enforce his will.[36] Polybius' loathing has influenced all the ancient sources pertaining to Nabis' career and has made difficult an unbiased assessment of his program (or even if he had one).

Like Areus I, Nabis evidently pursued a Hellenistic, rather than purely Spartan, model of kingship. He styled himself thus, minted coins with his portrait, had roof tiles stamped with his title, and was addressed as king in documents from other states.[37] To Polybius he was simply a tyrant, responsible for a lengthy and burden-some tyranny at Sparta. To the Romans, who had quickly become adept in the murky world of Greek politics, he was a Saddam Hussein figure, a useful tool at first, with his occupation of neighboring Argos fully tolerated, but when his actions no longer coincided with the Romans' new policy of Greek self-determination in 196, he was subjected to the full onslaught of an allied coalition the Romans gathered against him in 195.

....

36 Polyb. 13.6.1-3; 16.13.1.
37 Tile stamp: *IG* V.1 885; coins: Grunauer-von Hoerschelmann 1978, Group IX, with Furtwängler 1985; international relations: *SIG*³ 584.

Nabis himself recognized that his policies of both land reform and liberation of slaves were inimical to Roman sensibilities.[38] He was not mistaken: Titus Flamininus called them "certainly not in themselves trivial" (*non quidem nec ipsa mediocria*).[39] Most modern scholars have concentrated on Nabis' enlargement of the citizen body. Almost without exception they have credited Nabis with the liberation of helots, some even with the abolition of helotage itself, to achieve this end.[40] Nabis' liberation of helots has become as established a "fact" as any can be in the shadowy history of Hellenistic Sparta. But it rests upon a single assumption, that the word "slave" (δοῦλος, οἰκέτης, or *seruus*) whenever it is used in connection with Spartan affairs normally is equivalent to "helot".[41]

Nabis did liberate slaves, of that there can be no doubt. Polybius and Livy, again our most important sources, are explicit and consistent. Polybius asserts "He liberated the slaves;" and Livy has Flamininus say to Nabis, "You say that charges of having called slaves to freedom and dividing land up for poor people have been made against you".[42] Like other kings and tyrants Nabis expanded the citizen body by liberating slaves and enrolling foreigners as citizens. The process, known in Greek as ἀναπλήρωσις, comes to us through Livy's Latin version as *multitudinem . . . auctam*.[43] The enrollment of foreigners, particularly mercenaries who had done their host city service, was quite common. The "Thessalians and other Greeks" that Philip V referred to in his letter to the city of Larissa were almost certainly mercenaries. During the later third century the Milesians gave citizenship to a large number of Cretan mercenaries and their families.[44] At Sparta, as I have mentioned, Cleomenes provided a precedent by enfranchising mercenaries who had served him. Polybius does not say explicitly that Nabis gave his mercenaries citizenship, but it is the logical conclusion to be drawn from his statement that the tyrant gave the property and wives of those he exiled to the most conspicuous of the others in Sparta and to mercenaries. In the language of international relations, he granted the mercenaries the rights of γῆς καὶ οἰκίας ἔγκτησις and ἐπιγαμία. Nabis thus ensured that their ownership of the property was recognized at Sparta under his regime and that any offspring of their unions with Spartan women would be Spartan citizens too.[45]

....

38 Liv. 34.31.11, 14.
39 Liv. 34.32.9.
40 E.g. Shimron 1972: 89; Ducat 1990: 171-172; Mendels 1979: 319; Cartledge and Spawforth 1989: 69-70. Abolition of helotage: Texier 1975: 34-35.
41 E.g. Oliva 1971: 271; Texier 1974: 194; Mendels 1979: 319; Cartledge and Spawforth 1989: 69-70.
42 Polyb. 16.13.1: ἠλευθέρωσε τοὺς δούλους; Liv. 34.32.9: seruorum ad libertatem uocatorum et egentibus hominibus agri diuisi crimina tibi obici dicebas.
43 Liv. 34.31.14.
44 *Milet* III 33-38. See also Launey 1950: 652-675.
45 Shimron (1972: 141-142) came to a similar conclusion.

Finally, there is welcome epigraphical support for intermarriage with citizen women in the form of a few grave inscriptions erected by women with impeccable Spartan names for their foreign, mercenary husbands.[46] Polybius accused Nabis of liberating "slaves" and marrying off the wives and daughters of his opponents to them as well in a passage whose problematic nature was only recognized by Ducat.[47] He pointed to the contradictions between it and the lengthier account of Nabis' policy in book thirteen, where Polybius says Nabis married off only the wives not to slaves, but to the most renowned of the rest of the Spartans and to the mercenaries.[48] Ducat therefore sensibly discounts the charge as *une généralization passionnée et excessive*. This leaves Livy's descriptions of the events during the last years of Nabis' reign from 195-192 and of the measures taken against Sparta by the Achaean general Philopoemen in 188 as the only accurate means of determining the extent of Nabis' liberation of slaves at Sparta.

As already remarked, Livy has both Nabis and Flamininus mention the liberation of slaves as a major irritant in the talks they conducted in 195 before the new walls of Sparta. From the context, we can deduce that the liberation of Spartan slaves and the redistribution of Laconian land are meant, but the terms of the peace treaty Nabis finally accepted after several days of Roman attacks make it equally clear that the only slaves to be returned to their masters were those from Argos or Messene.[49] The Romans demanded no substantive change in Sparta's internal affairs. Although they did deal a severe blow to Spartan prestige and power by drastically reducing the navy and removing the maritime cities of Laconia from Spartan control, Flamininus manifestly was only interested in removing Sparta as a major player and potential threat in international power politics. Livy tells us that Nabis was not displeased that the Romans did not require the return of any exiles; in fact they only insisted that the wives of exiles be given the option of leaving to join their husbands—an indication perhaps that not all were dissatisfied with their present marriages.[50]

....

[46] Steinhauer 1992: 239-245.

[47] Polyb. 16.13.1: "Ότι κατὰ τὴν Πελοπόννησον τίνα μὲν ἐξ ἀρχῆς προαίρεσιν ἐνεστήσατο Νάβις ὁ τῶν Λακεδαιμονίων τύραννος, καὶ πῶς ἐκβαλὼν τοὺς πολίτας ἠλευθέρωσε τοὺς δούλους καὶ συνῴκισε ταῖς τῶν δεσποτῶν γυναιξὶ καὶ θυγατράσιν; Ducat 1990: 171.

[48] Polyb. 13.6.1-3: ὁ δὲ τῶν Λακεδαιμονίων τύραννος Νάβις, ἔτος ἤδη τρίτον ἔχων τὴν ἀρχήν, ὁλοσχερὲς μὲν οὐδὲ πράττειν οὐδὲ τολμᾶν διὰ τὸ πρόσφατον εἶναι τὴν ὑπὸ τῶν Ἀχαιῶν ἧτταν τοῦ Μαχανίδου, καταβολὴν δ' ἐποιεῖτο καὶ θεμέλιον ὑπεβάλλετο πολυχρονίου καὶ βαρείας τυραννίδος. διέφθειρε γὰρ τοὺς λοιποὺς ἄρδην ἐκ τῆς Σπάρτης, ἐφυγάδευσε δὲ τοὺς κατὰ πλέον πλούτῳ διαφέροντας ἢ δόξῃ προγονικῇ, τὰς δὲ τούτων οὐσίας καὶ γυναῖκας διεδίδου τῶν ἄλλων τοῖς ἐπιφανεστάτοις καὶ τοῖς μισθοφόροις.

[49] Liv. 34.35.4, 6.

[50] Liv. 34.35.7, 36.2.

If Flamininus did not interfere in Sparta's internal affairs in 195, the same cannot be said of Philopoemen in 188. The treaty imposed by the Romans in 195 did not settle anything, as public resentment against the loss of the maritime cities, especially the port of Gythium, was bitter. Several years of war and unrest followed as the Spartans first lost their war of recovery to the Achaeans in 193, their leader with the assassination of Nabis by his faithless Aetolian allies in 192, their independence with the city's forcible incorporation into the Achaean League that same year, and their way of life after a failed attempt to occupy a perioecic town and leave the League in 188. Unlike Flamininus in 195, Philopoemen had a score to settle seven years later. Flamininus' aims had been to reduce the damage Nabis could do on the international stage; Philopoemen's were to "humble the city of the Spartans".[51] His settlement was consequently much harsher and more interventionist: Sparta's walls were to be torn down, the Belminatis given up, the Cleomenean *agogê* (now considered equivalent to the Lycurgan system) was to be abolished, the constitution was to be altered to conform to Achaean norms, mercenaries were to be dismissed, and all those made citizens by the tyrants were to be expelled.[52]

Livy mentions these people twice, the first time as *quae seruitia tyranni liberassent (ea magna multitudo erat)*, the second as *Lacedaemoniis adscriptos (ita enim uocabant qui ab tyrannis liberati erant)*.[53] In the same context, Plutarch calls them ὅσοι δ᾽ ἦσαν ὑπὸ τῶν τυράννων ἀποδεδειγμένοι πολῖται τῆς Σπάρτης.[54] The consistent references to tyrants in the plural, rather than to a single tyrant, surely echo the language of Polybius in reporting the Achaean actions. Historians have attempted either to identify these tyrants with some of the leaders of Sparta between Cleomenes and Nabis or to discount the plural completely and associate the term solely with Nabis. But "tyrants" as used here is a propaganda term, without precise constitutional significance: one person's tyrant could be another's king. Lycurgus, the first king after the period of direct Macedonian rule, was accused of gaining the throne through bribery and Livy refers to him explicitly *primus tyrannus Lacedaemone*, yet only a few chapters later he has Flamininus style Lycurgus' son Pelops as *rege iusto ac legitimo*.[55] Again relying on Polybius, he also calls Machanidas, Lycurgus' successor, *tyrannus Lacedaemoniorum*.[56] To his supporters and to the Romans, when it suited them, Nabis was king of Sparta, to his enemies he was the worst tyrant of them all. Therefore, the

....

51 Polyb. 21.32C.3.
52 Cartledge and Spawforth 1989: 78-79; Kennell 1992: 198-202.
53 Liv. 38.34.2, 6.
54 Plut. *Philop.* 16.4.
55 Liv. 34.26.14, 32.1.
56 Liv. 27.29.9.

reference to all those liberated and/or made citizens by the tyrants reveal nothing about the policies of any particular Spartan leader. We are left with Nabis' reference to his own liberation of slaves. Were they then the only ones expelled by the Achaeans? Livy certainly implies as much when he defines the expression *Lacedaemoniis adscripti* as the Spartan name for those who had been liberated by the tyrants.[57] In the earlier passage, these same people are simply "whatever persons the tyrants had freed from slavery".[58] In his version, Plutarch refers to ἀποδεδειγμένοι πολῖται τῆς Σπάρτης without mentioning their servile status.[59] Those who take Livy at his word have interpreted *Lacedaemoniis adscripti* as a special term reserved for the ex-slaves, whom they identify as ex-helots, which showed that they were not completely integrated into the citizen body and continued to constitute a separate group, analogous to the *neodamôdeis* of old.[60] But there is nothing special about the word *adscripti*. Livy used *adscribere* elsewhere for the enrolling of Roman colonists; here it is the Latin equivalent of a Greek term.[61] A literal back-translation of *adscribere* is προσγράφειν, which is one of a number of verbs that designates the enrolling of new citizens. In 182 the Milesians passed a treaty of *sumpoliteia* with the city of Pidasa, which gave the Pidaseans who were to be enrolled as new citizens (Πιδασέων τοὺς προσγραφησομένους) exemption from liturgies for ten years.[62] In a *sumpoliteia* at Xanthus, the *prutaneis* have the duty of enrolling the new citizens (προσγραφέτωσαν) into tribes and demes as soon as possible.[63] On Delos and Tenos, when foreign benefactors were made citizens, they also received the right to be enrolled (προσγράψασθαι) in the tribe and phratry of their choice.[64] Lists of ephebes from Chaeronea marking their coming of age are headed, "These were enrolled from the ephebes into the brigades" (οἵδε προσεγράφησαν ἐξ ἐφήβων εἰς τὰ τάγματα).[65] In Polybius' original text the expression he used was most likely οἱ προσγραφέντες πρὸς τοὺς Λακεδαιμονίους. From the epigraphical

....

[57] Liv. 38.34.5.
[58] Liv. 38.24.2.
[59] Plut. *Philop.* 16. 4-9.
[60] Ducat 1990: 171-172; Texier 1974: 195; Papazoglou 1993: 18.
[61] E.g. Liv. 6.30.9: *noui coloni adscripti;* 31.49.6: *hi colonos Venusiam adscripserunt;* 35.9.8: *nouos colonos adscribere possent.*
[62] *Milet* I 3 149, lines 35-36. See also 150, line 59.
[63] Bousquet and Gauthier 1994: 321, lines 21-22.
[64] Delos: *IG* XI.4 547. Tenos: *IG* XII.5 798; cf. 799, 804-806.
[65] *IG* VII 3294, 3296, 3297. See also Diodorus Siculus 12.11.2; 20.36.3. Other terms for the enrollment of citizens include καταχωρίζεσθαι (*I. Smyrna* II.1 573 II, line 60) and πολιτογράφειν (*SIG*³ 742, line 40 (Ephesus); *OGIS* 229 (Smyrna); Polyb. 32.7.3.

parallels, it is clear that the phrase carried no connotation of inferior or separate status with it beyond that of belonging to a group of newly-enrolled citizens. Sometimes, to be sure, certain restrictions were placed on the eligibility for office of new citizens, such as the Cretans in Miletus, but these were not due to their earlier servile state.[66] *Adscripti* or οἱ προσγραφέντες were simply the newly enfranchised citizens in a city. In itself, the term had no association whatsoever with the new citizens' previous status, whether slave or free, but merely with their present condition in relation to the *politeuma* they had just entered.

If Livy's definition is an accurate reflection of Polybius' text, then the Achaean historian was telling only half the truth. *Adscripti Lacedaemoniis* was certainly what Spartans called the freed slaves who had been made citizens by tyrants, but it was also the designation for all newly-enfranchised citizens. We must not make the same mistake of identifying all the *adscripti* as ex-slaves, since Nabis had also given citizenship to his mercenaries. In addition, during the years of bloody turmoil between Cleomenes and Nabis it is not difficult to imagine that various leaders selectively rewarded mercenaries and others of non-Spartiate origin with citizenship, and that there was by the early 180s a sizeable group in the population with less than impeccable claims to Spartan citizenship who could be lumped together as those who owed their status to "the tyrants". Livy's (and Polybius') implication that all these new citizens were former slaves is sweeping and inaccurate. Some certainly were, but many were foreign mercenaries, as well as perhaps perioeci, foreign traders, and others, whose offspring (some by now adults) would have been included in the expulsion order.

Former slaves comprised only a segment of the mass of people stripped of their Spartan citizenship. And of those ex-slaves, how many, if any, were helots? The answer to this question will also solve the problem of whether Nabis liberated any helots. We are in complete ignorance as to the number of normal, chattel slaves owned by Spartans compared to the population of helots at all periods of Spartan history. Scholars have supposed that even at this late date helots so far outnumbered other slaves at Sparta that Polybius and, after him, Livy still followed fifth-century usage in calling them δοῦλοι and *serui*. However, the Platonic *Alcibiades*, from the later fourth century, already made allusion to the wealth of Spartans as shown by their possession of large numbers of slaves, among them helots (ἀνδραπόδων κτήσει τῶν τε ἄλλων καὶ τῶν εἰλωτικῶν), which presupposes that helots formed a particular sub-category among the slaves as a whole.[67] Admittedly, this is not compelling testimony for the existence of

---

[66] Launey 1950: 660-664; see also Bousquet and Gauthier 1994: 333.

[67] [Pl..] *Alcib.* 122d.

large numbers of chattel slaves at Sparta in the Hellenistic period. Nevertheless, on the specific point of Nabis' relations with helots, matters are a little less obscure.

Despite the common belief that Nabis enjoyed widespread public support, even from the helot population, his actions when preparing for the Roman onslaught betray his suspicion of disloyalty at both ends of society.[68] After gathering a massive army of 2,000 Cretan troops, 3,000 mercenaries, and 10,000 locals, including helots, he eliminated eighty of what Livy calls the *principes iuuentutis* and followed this with the brutal beating to death throughout all the city's districts of helots he accused of being about to desert to the Romans.[69] Nabis may have been justified in his suspicion, for Strabo says that the helots, whom he includes among the perioeci, were the first to go over to the Romans when Sparta was under a tyranny.[70] Only these two testimonia about the helots' attitude survive, but they are consistent, with Strabo's Ῥωμαίοις προσέθεντο paralleling Livy's *transfugere uoluisse*, and should not be lightly dismissed. This, all the evidence there is, shows helots deserting Nabis for the Romans, not the behavior to be expected if he had liberated helots in any significant proportions. It should be considered in the light of the fact that the Spartans' name for the new citizens does not imply any of them had originally been helots.

On the other side, apart from the universal assumption that "slave" is equivalent to "helot", is Pausanias. He baldly states that when the Spartans were far gone in civil war, Philopoemen expelled from the Peloponnese 300 of those most to blame for the unrest and sold 3000 of the helots.[71] Only Pausanias explicitly identifies the 3000 sold into slavery as helots. According to Livy, some of the *Lacedaemoniis adscripti* ordered to leave Laconia had scattered into the countryside where many of them were captured by pursuing Achaeans and sold.[72] Plutarch relates that Philopoemen re-settled in Achaea all those who had been made citizens by the tyrants except for 3000 who were unwilling to leave Laconia; these he sold

....

[68] E.g. Texier 1975: 84; Mendels 1979: 321: "The Perioikoi did not sympathize with Nabis as did the liberated Helotes."

[69] Liv. 34.27.2, 8-10.

[70] Strab. 8.5.5 (36), συνέβη δὲ καὶ τοὺς Ἐλευθερολάκωνες λαβεῖν τινα τάξιν πολιτείας, ἐπειδὴ Ῥωμαίοις προσέθεντο πρῶτοι οἵ τε ἄλλοι καὶ οἱ Εἵλωτες. On this passage see most recently, Kennell 1999: 192-194.

[71] Paus. 8.51.3, Λακεδαιμονίων δὲ τηνικαῦτα ἐς ἔμφυλον προηγμένων στάσιν, τριακοσίους μὲν τῆς στάσεως μάλιστα αἰτίους ἐξέβαλεν ἐκ Πελοποννήσου καὶ τῶν εἱλώτων τε ἀπέδοτο ὅσον τρισχιλίους.

[72] Liv. 38.34.5-7: decretum Tegeae in concilio communi Achaeorum de restituendis iis factum est; et mentione inlata externos auxiliares dimissos ac Lacedaemoniis adscriptos (ita enim uocabant qui ab tyrannis liberati erant) urbe excessise <et> in agros dilapsos, priusquam dimitteretur exercitus, ire praetorem cum expeditis et comprehendere id genus hominum et uendere iure praedae placuit. multi comprehensi uenierunt.

into slavery.[73] It is clear that Pausanias made the common mistake of identifying Polybius' ex-slaves as ex-helots, if indeed he derived his information directly from Polybius. That may be open to some doubt, for, as the analytical table (Table 4.1) shows, Pausanias' account of the post-Compasium settlement provides only a small fraction of the information Livy and Plutarch convey and what little it does contain is disordered and inaccurate. Pausanias' inaccuracy is most evident when he reports that 300 ringleaders were exiled, which is almost certainly a result of confusion between the massacre at Compasium, where according to Aristocrates Philopoemen killed 350 leading members of the anti-Achaean party, and the expulsion of Nabis' mercenaries from Sparta.[74] Pausanias is not a trustworthy authority.

Livy 38.34.5-7	Plut. *Philop.* 15.12d-f	Paus. 8.51.3
1. Exiles restored	Exiles restored	—
2. —	Walls destroyed	Walls destroyed
3. Report of mercenaries dismissed	—	Expelled 300 ringleaders from Peloponnesus
4. and of *Lacedaemonii adscripti* (freed slaves) scattering through country	Resettled ἀποδεδειγμένοι πολῖται in Achaea.	—
5. General sent after them with light-armed troops to capture and sell them	3000 did not want to move from Laconia	—
5a. A great number captured and sold	Philopoemen sold them	Sold 3000 of the helots
5b. Porticus at Megalopolis built with proceeds	Built a stoa in Megalopolis	—
6. Belbinatis returned to the original owners	Great amount of land restored to Megalopolis	—
7. *Agogê* abolished	*Agogê* abolished	*Agogê* abolished
8. —	Restored by Romans later	Restored by Romans later

TABLE 4.1 *Sources for the post-Compasium settlement*

....

[73] Plut. *Philop.* 16.5-6: ὅσοι δ᾽ ἦσαν ὑπὸ τῶν τυράννων ἀποδεδειγμένοι πολῖται τῆς Σπάρτης, μετῴκιζεν ἅπαντας ἀπάγων εἰς Ἀχαίαν πλὴν τρισχιλίων· τούτους δ᾽ ἀπειθοῦντας καὶ μὴ βουλομένους ἀπελθεῖν τῆς Λακεδαίμονος ἐπώλησεν.

[74] The number of deaths as reported by Aristocrates: Plut. *Philop.* 16.4.

A final indication that Nabis' new citizens did not include any sizeable number of helots is the attitude towards Philopoemen's settlement expressed before the Senate in 184 by the very persons whom he had reinstated at Sparta—the so-called "old exiles". Among the many grievances Philopoemen's ham-fisted treatment of his city's old enemy had engendered, even among the very people he had ostensibly invaded Laconia to support, was his forcible deportation of what Polybius calls τὸ πλῆθος and Livy the *plebs*.[75] That τὸ πλῆθος and the *plebs* were precisely the new citizens exiled after Compasium is clear from Livy's statement that they had been abducted into Achaea.[76] The conservative "old exiles," so called because they had been expelled in the decades before the multiple expulsions that had accompanied each change of government since Compasium, would hardly have been well disposed to any of the tyrant's policies, especially the wholesale incorporation of helots into the citizen body.[77] To remedy the present situation, a group of old exiles called for the enfranchisement of all those who were worthy of receiving citizenship—they surely did not intend to include ex-helots, who owed their citizenship to Nabis, the very ruler who had exiled at least some of them.[78] These considerations, combined with the intimation that there existed perhaps sizeable numbers of chattel slaves in Laconia in the Hellenistic period make it unlikely, in my view, that Nabis liberated any helots.

When Livy describes Nabis' execution of the disloyal helots, he calls them *ilotarum quidam iam inde antiquitus castellani, agreste genus*—"certain of the helots, a rural people, *castellani* from antiquity". Except for Kathleen Chrimes, no historian has attempted to exploit this passage to understand how helots lived in the later Hellenistic period. She took *castellani* to be a technical term and, relying on a contemporary inscription from Spain in which slaves who occupied a fortress were given land after their manumission, interpreted it as denoting the garrison of a fortress (*castellum*).[79] The helots of Hellenistic Laconia were in her view free men, called, as in the classical period, *neodamôdeis*, who were legally bound to guard the forts where they lived and farmed. Her interpretation has had no serious supporters; Walbank led the attack in his review by dismissing it altogether: "In Livy xxiv.27.9 *castellani* is Livy's explanation of Polybius' 'helots;' and we know from the *lex Rubria* that a *castellum* is virtually the same as a *pagus* or *vicus*: *castellani*, then, are *pagani*, country folk".[80] Since Walbank's devastating salvo, no one has taken

....

75 Polyb. 22.12.2; Liv. 39.33.6.
76 Liv. 39.33.6: abductam plebem in Achaiam et uenumdatam.
77 On the "old exiles", see Errington 1969: 174-180; Cartledge and Spawforth 1989: 80-82.
78 Polyb. 23.4.3: τοῖς ἀξίοις τῆς πολιτείας. See also Walbank 1979: 217-218.
79 Chrimes 1949: 38-42.
80 Walbank 1951.

Chrimes' approach seriously. This is unfortunate because, although her conclusion was faulty, her insight that *castellani* has a specific significance in a Laconian context still has merit.

In Chrimes' defense, it should be pointed out that Walbank was mistaken in thinking that "a *castellum* is virtually the same as a *pagus* or *vicus*". The *lex Rubria* itself shows that they are different entities, listed separately. In the section that lays down the procedures for settlement of claims for unpaid debts in Cisalpine Gaul, the localities where such actions might be laid are "any town, *municipium*, colony, *praefectura*, *forum*, village (*uicus*), *conciliabulum*, fortress (*castellum*), or territory".[81] A *uicus* was similar to a *castellum* in that they were each a type of small, rural community (*territorium*), but they were clearly not considered the same by the redactors of the *lex Rubria*. Similar catalogues of settlement types appear in the treaties Livy reports, where *castella* are always distinguished from *vici, oppida,* and *urbes*. For example, the Treaty of Apamea awarded to the Rhodians "the towns, villages (*uici*), fortresses (*castella*), and fields that face Pisidia".[82] In 188 King Antiochus was required to withdraw from "the cities, fields, villages (*uicis*), fortresses (*castellis*) on this side of the Taurus mountain".[83] Such lists can also be found in the epigraphical texts. A *senatus consultum* of 39 BC confirmed the rights of the people of Aphrodisias/Plasara to the enjoyment of all their οἰκοδομῶν, κωμῶν, χωρίων, ὀχυρωμάτων, ὁρῶν, προσόδων, where ὀχυρωμάτων is equivalent to *castellorum*.[84] *Castellani,* then, are not simply "country folk," but have something to do with *castella*, fortresses.

The Latin *castellanus* means "having to do with a fortress," and so can denote either the actual garrison of the fort itself or the civilian population who lived and worked the land around it. The key to deciding which of the two meanings the word has here in Livy lies in the wording of his source. Despite Chrimes' assumption that the words following *ilotarum quidam* cannot be derived from Polybius, Livy's sole source for this period, apparently because no Greek audience would need to be told who the helots were, there is good reason to believe that Polybius' text lies behind this definition too.[85] It is dangerous to impose modern ideas of superfluity on an ancient historian: though we might think that not a single person capable of reading Greek would have needed to be informed that the name of the river running beside

....

81 Bruns, *FIR*⁷ 97-101, no. 16, XXI: in eorum quo o(ppido) m(unicipio) c(olonia) p(raefectura) f(oro) u(eico) c(onciliabulo) c(astello) t(erritorio)ue.

82 Liv. 37.56.6: oppida, uici, castella, agri, qui ad Pisidiam uergunt.

83 Liv. 38.38.4: excedito urbibus agris uicis castellis cis Taurum montem.

84 Reynold 1982: 54, no. 8, lines 58-59: μεθ᾽ ὧν ἀγρῶν τόπων, οἰκοδομιῶν, κωμῶν, χωρίων, ὀχυρωμάτων, ὁρῶν, προσόδων.

85 Chrimes 1949: 38: "Livy's source–presumably here Roman."

Sparta is the Eurotas, Polybius in fact does precisely that in his sketch of the city's topography in book 2.[86] Unlike Latin, which only has *castellum*, Greek differentiates between a fortress proper, ὀχύρωμα, and the area including the fortress and its surrounding population, χωρίον.[87] For example, the στρατιῶται οἱ διαταγέντες εἰς τὸ χωρίον at a fort in Lycia made a dedication in 129 BC on behalf of their commander ἐπὶ τοῦ ὀχυρώμα[το]ς.[88] In the *sumpoliteia* between Smyrna and Magnesia ad Sipylum, the Smyrnaeans took possession of the stronghold Palaimagnesia, whose inhabitants (τοὺς οἰκοῦντας ἐν τῶι χω[ρ]ίωι) were to hand the keys of the fort over to a magistrate and accept a garrison.[89] Once again Polybius' usage is consistent with that of the inscriptions: he refers to fortresses both as ὀχυρώματα and χωρία.[90] On their advance into Laconia, the Macedonians under Doson drove the Spartan garrisons from the forts Cleomenes had constructed (ἐκ τῶν ἐποικοδομηθέντων χωρίων ὑπὸ Κλεομένους) and later forced the Spartans out of their fortified positions (ἐκ τῶν ὀχυρωμάτων) at the battle of Sellasia.[91] At the outset of the Social War in 221, the Aetolians seized a fort called Klarion (τὸ καλούμενον ὀχύρωμα Κλάριον), while far in the east Antiochus began a campaign against the rebel Molon by occupying two forts, one of which was called Brochoi (Βρόχοι προσαγορευόμενόν τι χωρίον). Polybius also refers to the civilian inhabitants of a fortress as οἱ κατοικοῦντες τὸ χωρίον.[92]

Behind Livy's *castellani*, I believe, lies a expression like οἱ τὰ χωρία κατοικοῦντες, "dwelling in χωρία". In other words, the helots lived in or near fortified settlements throughout Laconia, under the protection and watchful eye of the garrison stationed there. Whether this truly went as far back into antiquity as Livy claims is unclear. The participants in the Pylos Regional Archaeological Project discovered a more nucleated settlement pattern in the area under examination than was usual elsewhere in the archaic and classical periods, which they tentatively speculated might have been connected with helot communities, but they did not report seeing any signs

....

86 Polyb. 5.22.2, ὃς καλεῖται μὲν Εὐρώτας.
87 Robert 1970: 588-589 (= *OMS* VI, 638-639); Debord 1994: 53-61.
88 *TAM* V 528.
89 *I. Smyrna* 573 III (245 or 243 BC), lines 93-97. Cf. *SEG* 26.1306, line 5, where the inhabitants of a fortress are called τοὺς ἐγ Κυρβισσῶι κατοικοῦντες.
90 E.g. Polyb. 4.61.5 (fortress Ambrakos), ὁ γὰρ Ἀμβρακός ἐστιν μὲν χωρίον εὐκατεσκευασμένον καὶ προτειχίσμασιν καὶ τείχει; 4.65.6 (fortress Elaos), πρός τι χωρίον ὀχυρόν, ὃ καλεῖται μὲν Ἔλαος ἠσφάλισται δὲ τείχεσι καὶ ταῖς λοιπαῖς παρασκευαῖς; 4.83.3, παρέδοσαν τὸ φρούριον τῷ Φιλίππῳ, χωρίον οὐ μέγα μὲν ἠσφαλισμένον δὲ διαφερόντως; 5.20.4 (fortress Glympeis), παραγενόμενοι δὲ πρὸς Γλυμπεῖς χωρίον; 11.33.6, συνέβη διασωθέντα φυγεῖν εἴς τι χωρίον ὀχυρόν.
91 Polyb. 2.54, 69.9.
92 Polyb. 4.6.3; 5.20.5, 46.1.

of fortifications.[93] The frequent invasions of Laconia during the Hellenistic period (eight between Leuctra and Compasium) with their concomitant devastation would be reason enough for the Spartans to construct fortified settlements inside Laconia to guard the helots and their produce. Nabis had evidently made the building of forts part of his policy, as the treaty of 195 explicitly forbade him to erect any *oppidum* or *castellum* whatsoever in his own or foreign territory.[94]

One of these fortified helot settlements may perhaps have already been discovered. On the crown of the hill Agios Konstantinos, near the village of Voutianoi to the northeast of the Eurotas valley, lies a large fort with 22 towers and a circuit wall enclosing an area of about 6 hectares. The surface finds recorded by the Laconia Survey range in date from Neolithic to Hellenistic, and the construction itself seems to be of Greek rather than Roman or later date.[95] About 2 km to the northeast is the village of Palaiopyrgos, which is a good candidate for the site of ancient Sellasia.[96] Sellasia was the final fixed point in the large, elongated loop Agis IV described leading from the water course at Pallene, along Taygetus, over to the Malea peninsula, and then north, the land within which—essentially the Eurotas valley—he proposed to divide into equal *klêroi* for his revived Spartiate citizen body.[97] The fort at Agios Konstantinos, just within the northern boundary of this area and with a clear line-of-sight to Sparta, was ideally situated to safeguard the Spartan-owned estates northeast of the city and, when Cleomenes III put his predecessor's plan into force in 227, the *klêroi* and helots in the area. Moreover, a large amount of produce could be stored temporarily within its walls.[98] Doubtless other possible helot *choria*, like this fort, wait undiscovered throughout Laconia.

Finally, the end of helotage. Our single source, Strabo, says that the institution lasted at Sparta "until the Roman dominion" (μέχρι τῆς Ῥωμαίων ἐπικρατείας). Strabo uses this vague expression several other times in the course of his *Geography* and his meaning is clear in none of them.[99] For instance, he helpfully states that the Athenians kept their democracy "until the Roman dominion," and the Spartans, despite their decline, kept themselves independent "until the Roman dominion".[100] The other passage in which Strabo mentions helots does, fortunately, provide a

....

93 Harrison and Spencer 1998: 160-162. A large country house in northern Messenia near the village of Kopanaki, which was in use for about a hundred years from the second quarter of the sixth century BC, has been tentatively identified as belonging to a Spartiate whose land was worked by helots. The excavator also associated its destruction with the Messenian revolt in the 460s: Kaltsas 1983: 220-221.

94 Liv. 34.35.11.

95 Cavanagh et al. 1996: 325-328.

96 Cartledge 1979: 188.

97 Plut. *Agis* 8.1.

98 On fortresses as storehouses for agricultural produce, see Debord 1994: 60.

99 Strab. 5.1.1; 9.1.20; 9.2.37; 16.1.19.

100 Strab. 9.1.20, 2.37.

comfortable chronological context. In describing the founding of the League of Lacedaemonians, whose name he gets wrong, Strabo says it happened *that the Eleutherolaconians also got some sort of constitutional arrangement, since the perioeci, including the helots, had gone over first to the Romans, while Sparta was under a tyranny.*[101] From these two passages, some have maintained that a form of helotage lasted until the time of Gaius Julius Eurycles, the strongman installed in Sparta after Actium, but, as I and others have pointed out, Strabo is hardly likely to have characterized a *protégé* of Augustus as a tyrant, and the passage's larger context, as a brief aside within a longer account of the Spartan constitution until 146 and just after an allusion to the Spartans mistreating Roman generals because of being badly governed at the time, makes it certain that the tyrant meant is Nabis.[102] The Roman *epikrateia* therefore refers either to the establishment of Roman rule in 146 or the period when Rome's influence was predominant over Greek states in the earlier second century.

More interesting than the attempt to establish a specific date for the disappearance of Laconian helots is to assess Strabo's statement that the helots also received a sort of constitution along with other perioeci for transferring their loyalty first to the Romans. His Greek is clear and unambiguous: συνέβη δέ καὶ τοὺς Ἐλευθερολάκωνες λαβεῖν τινα τάξιν πολιτείας, ἐπειδὴ Ῥωμαίοις προσέθεντο πρῶτοι οἱ περίοικοι τυραννουμένης τῆς Σπάρτης, οἵ τε ἄλλοι καὶ οἱ Εἵλωτες. The phrase οἱ περίοικοι . . . οἵ τε ἄλλοι καὶ οἱ Εἵλωτες has a close parallel in Strabo's catalogue of peoples who live around the Mediterranean coast from Egypt to Pamphylia: καὶ οἱ μετ᾽ αὐτοὺς Αἰγύπτιοι καὶ Σύροι καὶ Κίλικες οἵ τε ἄλλοι καὶ οἱ Τραχεῖται λεγόμενοι, τελευταῖοι δὲ Πάμφυλοι ("and after them the Egyptians and Syrians and Cilicians, including the so-called Tracheiotai, and finally the Pamphylians").[103] On this point Strabo is not vague: the helots, being among the perioeci, received "a sort of constitution" as well. As Ducat correctly saw, this is a reference to liberation of the helots by the Romans as a reward for their actions during the campaign against Nabis, but he does not pursue the implications of Strabo's statement, namely that after 195 both perioeci and helots were grouped together under some very loose union or community of interest, which later evolved into the League of Lacedaemonians.[104] This small, but important piece of evidence sheds some light on the circumstances surrounding the

....

[101] Strab. 8.5.5.
[102] Chrimes 1949: 435; Bernhardt 1971: 96; Kennell 1999: 192-193; Cartledge and Spawforth 1989: 165-166; Ducat 1990: 195-197.
[103] Strab. 2.5.32.
[104] Ducat 1990: 193-199. On the foundation of the League of Lacedaemonians, see Kennell 1999: 193.

disappearance of helotage in Laconia. If Strabo is accepted, then we must entertain the possibility that some at least of the smaller sites in Laconia usually identified as perioecic settlements because Pausanias includes them among the members of the League of Lacedaemonians' successor the Eleutherolaconian League may actually have begun as fortified helot communities.[105] One possible candidate is the site at Agios Athanasios, which Curtius identified as the *komê* Selinous, 20 stades from ancient Geronthrai, where extensive ashlar walls have been found.[106]

Excavation at one of the smaller sites in Pausanias' catalogue might yield physical evidence of its prior existence as a helot settlement, although it is an open question what that evidence would need to be. For the voices of the helots in Hellenistic Laconia are thoroughly silenced. Almost certainly illiterate, they served a people without a living literature themselves; toiling in the country, they left no mark on the city-centered histories that have come down to us. They operated on the shadowy margins of a society famous for its obsession with secrecy. Finally, they lived in a particularly obscure period of Greek history, whose records have mostly vanished. There will never be a definitive picture of the helots in later Sparta, since the evidence is so scarce, even in Spartan terms. All aspects of any reconstruction, including this one, are open to challenge and reinterpretation. My aim in this paper has been to subject what little useful material there is to intense scrutiny and pursue the implications of that scrutiny as far as possible.

....

[105] Paus. 3.21.7.
[106] Cavanagh et al. 1996: 286. For a list of smaller sites, some clearly non-helot, see Shipley 1997: 261-263.

Bibliography

Bernhardt, R. 1971. *Imperium und Eleutheria*. Hamburg.

Bousquet, J., and P. Gauthier. 1994. "Inscriptions du Létôon de Xanthos." *Revue des études grecques* 107: 319-361.

Cartledge, P. 1979. *Sparta and Laconia: A Regional History 1300-362 BC*. London.

Cartledge, P., and A. Spawforth. 1989. *Hellenistic and Roman Sparta*. London.

Cavanagh, W., J. Crouwel, R. W. V. Catling and G. Shipley. 1996. *The Laconia Survey: Continuity and Change in a Greek Rural Landscape*. Vol. 2. *Archaeological Data*. (Annual of the British School at Athens. Supplementary Volume 27). London.

Chrimes, K. M. T. 1949. *Ancient Sparta: A Re-examination of the Evidence*. Manchester.

Daubies, M. 1971. "Cléomène III, les hilotes et Sellasie." *Historia* 20: 665-695.

Debord, P. 1994. "Le vocabulaire des ouvrages de défense." *Revue des études anciennes* 96: 53-61.

Ducat, J. 1990. *Les Hilotes*. (Bulletin de correspondance hellénique, Supplément 20). Athens and Paris.

Errington, R. M. 1969. *Philopoemen*. Oxford.

Furtwängler, A. 1985. Review of S. Grunauer-von Hoerschelmann. *Die Münzprägung der Lakedaimonier*. *Gnomon* 57: 637-641.

Grunauer-von Hoerschelmann, S. 1978. *Die Münzprägung der Lakedaimonier*. Berlin and New York.

Harrison, A. B., and N. Spencer 1998. "After the Palace: The Early 'History' of Messenia." In J. L. Davis (ed.), *Sandy Pylos: An Archaeological History from Nestor to Navarino*. Austin: 147-162.

Hodkinson, S. 2000. *Property and Wealth in Classical Sparta*. London.

Kaltsas, N. 1983. " Ἡ ἀρχαικὴ οἰκία στὸ Κοπανάκι τῆς Μεσσηνίας." Ἀρχαιολογικὴ ἐφημερίς: 207-237.

Kennell, N. 1985. *"The Public Institutions of Roman Sparta."* Unpublished Ph.D. thesis, University of Toronto.

_____. 1992. "*IG* V.1, 16 and the Gerousia of Roman Sparta." *Hesperia* 61: 193-202.

_____. 1995. *The Gymnasium of Virtue: Education and Culture in Ancient Sparta*. Chapel Hill.

_____. 1999. "From *Perioikoi* to *Poleis*: The Laconian Cities in the Late Hellenistic Period." In S. Hodkinson and A. Powell (eds.), *Sparta: New Perspectives*. London: 189-210.

Launey, M. 1950. *Recherches sur les armées hellénistiques*. (Bibliothèque des écoles françaises d'Athènes et de Rome 169). Paris.

Mendels, D. 1979. "Polybius, Nabis, and Equality." *Athenaeum* 57: 311-333.

Miller, F. D., Jr. 1995. *Nature, Justice, and Rights in Aristotle's Politics*. Oxford.

Oliva, P. 1971. *Sparta and Her Social Problems*. Amsterdam and Prague.

Papazoglou, F. 1993. "La *patrios politeia* et l'abolition de l'hilotie." *Ancient Society* 24: 5-25.

Reynolds, J. 1982. *Aphrodisias and Rome*. (Journal of Roman Studies Monographs 1). London.

Robert, L. 1970. Review of F. G. Maier, *Griechische Mauerbauinschriften*. *Gnomon* 42: 579-603. (Republished in *Opera minora selecta*. Vol. 6. Amsterdam, 1989: 629-653).

Shimron, B. 1972. *Late Sparta: The Spartan Revolution 243-146 B.C.* Buffalo.

Shipley, G. 1997. "'The Other Lakedaimonians': The Dependent Perioikic Poleis of Laconia and Messenia." In M. H. Hansen (ed.), *The Polis as an Urban Centre and as a Political Community*. (Acts of the Copenhagen Polis Centre 4). Copenhagen: 189-281.

Steinhauer, G. 1992. "An Illyrian Mercenary in Sparta under Nabis." In J. M. Sanders (ed.), ΦΙΛΟΛΑΚΩΝ: *Lakonian Studies in Honour of Hector Catling*. London: 239-245.

Texier, G. 1974. "Nabis et les hilotes." *Dialogues d'histoire ancienne* 1: 189-205.

_____. 1975. *Nabis*. (Centre de recherches d'histoire ancienne 14). Paris.

Walbank, F. W. 1951. Review of K. M. T. Chrimes, *Ancient Sparta*. *Classical Review* n.s. 1: 98-100.

_____. 1966. "The Spartan Ancestral Constitution in Polybius." In E. Badian (ed.), *Ancient Society and Institutions: Studies Presented to Victor Ehrenberg on his 75th Birthday*. Oxford: 303-312.

_____. 1979. *A Historical Commentary on Polybius*. Vol. 3. Oxford.

Part II
Ideologies

Five

The imaginary conquest of the Helots

Nino Luraghi

In a previous paper, I have questioned the idea that the Helots who worked the land of the Spartiates in Laconia and Messenia were the descendants of free populations who had occupied those areas before the Dorian conquest of Laconia and the Spartan conquest of Messenia, respectively, and had been enslaved en masse by the Spartans at the time of the conquest. This idea, with slight variations, can be fairly depicted as a *communis opinio* in modern scholarship. Only very few scholars separate conquest and enslavement, in this following in fact what most sources from the fourth century onwards say or imply, and fewer still have rejected the idea of the enslavement of the native population altogether.[1] Developing the insights of these few and building on the little that is known about the characteristics of Helotry in the classical period and on comparison with other slave systems, my previous contribution tried to show that mass enslavement of an indigenous population is an inherently unlikely explanation for the origins of Helotry.[2] The present contribution started as a discussion of the relevant ancient sources, in order to assess if and to what extent the *communis opinio* can be said to be based on their evidence, but it soon turned into an inquiry in ideology and the politics of memory. Since the connection between conquest and enslavement is a crucial point that has attracted discussion by ancient and modern historians, some early evidence on the Spartan conquest of Messenia that does not relate explicitly to the origins of Helotry will also be considered.

The ancient sources that deal directly or indirectly with the origins of Helotry and the Spartan conquest of Messenia have been discussed many, many times. However, most investigations are based on the assumption that, since all the sources

....

[1] Recently, only Jean Ducat; Ducat 1978: 44-45. But he has illustrious predecessors: see the refreshing remarks of Eduard Meyer (1937: 258-259).

[2] Luraghi 2002a.

109

reflect, in a more or less partial or distorted way, the same historical phenomenon, the goal of the student should be to highlight areas of consistency among sources and assess their relative trustworthiness in order to reconstruct real historical events or processes. Naturally, this involves devoting less attention to divergences than to convergences and discarding the less plausible or satisfactory details provided by the sources, a potentially dangerous process, when dealing with such a small corpus of evidence scattered over such a long period of time. The present paper will take a different approach. Rather than trying to reconstruct how Helotry really originated or how the Spartans really conquered Messenia, its aim will be to elucidate how these two events were conceived—imagined, in a neutral sense—at different points in time,[3] making sense of each source in its historical context rather than conflating it with the corpus. In order to prevent the later evidence from distorting the record, the sources will be scrutinized in their chronological order, without filling the gaps of the earlier sources with the fuller information provided by the later ones. In the best of cases, the result of such a process will be a history of perceptions and ideologies, rather than of structures and events. However, understanding the perceptions and ideologies that have left their mark in the sources, besides being a fruitful activity in its own right, is—or should be—an indispensable preliminary stage to any use of the sources for a reconstruction of events and structures.

1. Tyrtaeus and the Spartan conquest of Messene

Spartan expansion west of the Taygetos is documented much earlier than Helotry. Tyrtaeus, who composed his elegies probably in the mid seventh century or soon afterwards, thought that "spacious Messene, good to plough and good to plant", had been conquered thanks to king Theopompus, dear to the gods (fr. 5,1-3 W.[2]). This had happened two generations before Tyrtaeus, if the "fathers of our fathers" he refers to are to be taken literally. Without contesting this assumption, shared by most readers of Tyrtaeus, ancient and modern,[4] it may be useful to keep in mind that archaic lyric poetry was composed in order to be re-performable, mostly in a sympotic context, and therefore the textual "I" or "we" were normally not fixed in

---

[3] This approach has been championed particularly by Pierre Vidal-Naquet (1981: 223-248) and applied most extensively by J. Ducat (1990: 3-100); see his reflections, p. 6.

[4] It forms in fact the backbone of the chronology of the First and Second Messenian Wars in ancient historiography (Jacoby 1943: 114). Schwartz (1899: 429) suggested that the expression 'fathers of our fathers' could be taken in a more general way, to mean simply 'our ancestors'; see also Nafissi 1991: 37 n. 26.

time in a specific way, in order to be adaptable to the uttering person(s)[5]—although Tyrtaeus' poems, or some of them, could be an exception in terms of performative context and therefore also of generic rules.[6]

According to Tyrtaeus (fr. 5,7-8 W.[2]), after twenty years of fighting the enemies had "abandoned their rich fields and fled from the high Ithomaean mountains"; in other words, the Spartans had conquered their land and driven them away. This point is important, in view of later versions that implied that the defeated Messenians had remained in their region, to be reduced to the status of Helots in due course. But even more important is to determine precisely what Tyrtaeus thought that the fathers of the fathers led by Theopompus had conquered. Later authors, like Strabo (8.5.8) and Pausanias (4.1.4), explain that before the foundation of Epaminondas' Messene in 369 BCE, no city with that name had existed, while "Messene" in olden times had been the name of the whole region which in their own times was called "Messenia".[7] This made it possible for ancient and modern readers to embed Tyrtaeus' verses into a general representation of a "First Messenian War" which had brought to the Spartans control of the region,[8] a war that had ended with the Messenians surrounded and besieged in their fortress on Mount Ithome: the narrative that is found in the most comprehensive form in Pausanias. But none of this is really in Tyrtaeus, and it is not at all clear that "Messene" should have been for him the name of a region,[9] let alone that that region should have included the whole of later Messenia. The only other archaic

....

[5] On the meaning of the first person in archaic lyric, see Slings 2000: esp. 26-28. For a nice case of misunderstanding that involves Tyrtaeus, see Strab. 8.4.10, where Strabo discusses Tyrt. fr. 2 W.[2] taking the first person in the verses as a reference to the poet's biography and using the fragment as an argument against those who made Tyrtaeus an Athenian; Strabo's way of deducing historical information from these verses should be kept in mind whenever a later source is used as evidence on an early period based on the assumption that it could depend on Tyrtaeus.

[6] On the contexts in which archaic lyric poetry in general and Tyrtaeus' elegies in particular were performed, see Bowie 1986: 13-35, esp. 30-31, and 1990: 221-229, esp. 224-229.

[7] Ironically, it was in the fourth century and in the Hellenistic period that the name 'Messene' oscillated between indicating the Messenian polity, which included the lower Pamisos plain and most of the Akritas peninsula, and the main settlement of that polity, which was called Ithome at least until the end of the fourth century. See Roebuck 1941: 37, confirmed by *SEG* 43.135, on which see Matthaiou 2001: 221-227.

[8] With an important difference: as Jacoby (1943: 112) has correctly emphasized, all ancient sources say or imply that Messenia had been completely conquered by the Spartans as a result of the 'First Messenian War'. The notion that the Spartans conquered only part of Messenia, e.g. the Pamisos valley and the Stenyklaros plain, during this war, and completed their conquest during the 'Second Messenian War', appears only in modern research; it has been argued especially by Franz Kiechle (1959: esp. 65-70) and accepted e.g. by Clauss (1983: 20) and Cartledge (2002: 103).

[9] The epithets associated with it in Tyrt. fr. 5 W.[2] can refer to both cities and regions.

111

source where the name "Messene" appears is a passage in the *Odyssey* (21.13 ff), which relates the encounter of young Odysseus and Iphitos in Lakedaimon (in dative), at Messene (ἐν plus dative), in the house of Ortilochos, where Iphitos gave Odysseus the famous bow as a present to establish guest-friendship. Although "Messene" in this passage has sometimes been interpreted as referring to a region rather than to a city, it is clearly more natural to interpret the second place-name as a specification of the first, as indicating something smaller than a region, that is, presumably a city, to the extent that it makes sense to speak of cities for the eighth century, or possibly a smaller territorial unit. It would be strange if all the geographic information conveyed in these verses were that Ortilochos' place was somewhere south of the Neda and west of the Taygetus.[10]

In fairness to previous scholars, it must be emphasized that one reason for their readiness to accept Strabo's and Pausanias' views on the original meaning of the name "Messene" was the lack of archaeological evidence for an earlier settlement on the site of later Messene.[11] Now that new excavations have shown that a settlement existed at the foot of Mt. Ithome in the ninth and eighth centuries,[12] the case should be reconsidered. In the light of the new evidence, it seems preferable to think that Tyrtaeus' Messene was the Geometric settlement at Mt. Ithome with its territory, extending perhaps southwards on the western side of the Pamisus, possibly as far as the sea (see below). The later interpretation of the name in fact reflects an attempt at projecting back in the past a regional unity that was really a result of Spartan expansion. As a matter of fact, there is no reason to believe that the whole region west of the Taygetos ridge and south of the river Neda, the region that later became Messenia, had been united in any way between the end of the Bronze Age and the Spartan conquest.

Although the Homeric poems are notoriously difficult to fix in time, it is also worth pointing out that they seem to reflect, and retroject to the age of the heroes, a rather developed stage of the process of Spartan westward expansion. The Messene of the *Odyssey* is a part of Lakedaimon, Menelaus' kingdom, and it probably appears also, slightly disguised, in the mysterious city of Messe, mentioned in

....

[10] For the identification of this Messene as a place rather than a region, see Visser 1997: 485-486. His further suggestion that this place should be located in Laconia rests on no argument.

[11] Cf. e.g. Meyer 1978: 137.

[12] During the excavations started by Petros Themelis in 1987 at Mavromati, the site of Epaminondas' city, Geometric pottery has been found at various locations: around the later temple of Asklepios (see Themelis 1987: 87), close to the Klepsydra fountain in the modern village of Mavromati (Themelis 1988: 45) and to the *naiskos* of Artemis Orthia (Themelis 1991: 95). To this has to be added the fragment of a leg of a geometric bronze tripod, found on Mt. Ithome itself (Maaß 1978: 33-34, n. 57 and pl. 67).

the Lakedaimonian portion of the *Catalogue of Ships* (*Il.* 2.582), together with Sparte.[13] Furthermore, the six cities offered by Agamemnon to Achilles to convince him to return to the fight (*Il.* 9.149-53), insofar as it is possible to pinpoint them, were located along the gulf of Messenia,[14] while Homeric geography does not know of any independent entity between the kingdom of Pylos, roughly Triphylia, and Lakedaimon.[15] Interestingly, the only thing we learn about the Messenians from the *Odyssey*, apart from the fact that they were supposed to possess ships and have access to the sea (*Od.* 21.19),[16] is that they had a somewhat dubious reputation: Odysseus goes to Messene because Messenian raiders had stolen from Ithaca some cattle together with the herdsmen, while Iphitos was there looking for twelve mares of his that had been abducted. One wonders whether this should not be seen as the first trace of the Spartans' attempt at justifying in front of a broader audience their violent conquest of Messene.

Besides talking about the conquest of Messene, Tyrtaeus may have also mentioned further fights against the Messenians in his own times. The relevant text (fr. 23 W.²) comes from a very fragmentary papyrus, but it clearly mentions the Messenians, fighting, and "us", and the only verb in a finite form is in the future tense.[17] In fact, this would explain why later authors thought that Tyrtaeus had lived at the time of the "Second Messenian War" and fired up the Spartans with his poems.[18] Fifth-century authors' ignorance about a "Second Messenian War" should however suggest some caution.

It has often been thought that Tyrtaeus also mentioned Helotry, but the evidence for this assumption is anything but straightforward. Two famous fragments quoted by Pausanias (4.14.5), not adjoining but presumably coming from the same poem, describe the harsh plight of unspecified people compelled to give

....

13 Discussed in Visser 1997: 483-486; cf. Shipley 1997: 253. The possibility that Messe should be identified with Messene occurred already to the ancient readers of Homer (mentioned by Strab. 8.5.3). Tellingly, the only author who appears to know a location for Messe is the philo-Messenian Pausanias; his Messe of course is in Laconia (3.25.9).

14 See Hope Simpson 1966: 113-131, and Visser 1997: 492-501.

15 On the location of Pylos and the situation in southwestern Peloponnese in Homeric geography, see Giovannini 1969: 28-30 and Visser 1997: 508-531.

16 Probably for this reason it has been thought that the Messene of *Od.* 21.15 should be identified with Pherai, where Telemachus met Diocles, son of Orsilochos, on his way from Pylos to Sparta and back (*Od.* 3.486-488 = 15.185-188); however, even if one adheres to a strictly realistic reading of Homer's geography, there is no reason to exclude that Messene could have a harbor, presumably west of the mouth of the Pamisos or in the area of Kyparissia.

17 For the interpretation of this fragment see West 1974: 188.

18 Most explicitly Aristot. *Pol.* 5.1306b37-1307a2; Philochorus *FGrHist* 328 F 216; Diod. 8.27.1; but this is also implied by the story that made of Tyrtaeus an Athenian, on which see below. Tyrt. fr. 9 W² also mentions a battle against the Messenians, but without any chronological reference.

up half of the produce of the fields and to mourn at their masters' funerals (fr. 6 and 7 W.[2]). This has often been taken by modern scholars as a description of the conditions of the Helots;[19] however, Pausanias thought otherwise, since he quotes Tyrtaeus' verses to corroborate his statement that the Messenians had not been reduced to the status of Helots after the "First Messenian War" (cf. 4.14.4). On balance, Pausanias' use of this passage shows at the very least that Tyrtaeus did not call Helots the people he was talking about,[20] and probably also that later authors could not recognize Helotry in his description.[21] This is confirmed by a passage in Aelian (*VH* 6.1), also depending directly or indirectly on Tyrtaeus, where the conditions imposed on the Messenians are clearly not being interpreted as Helotry.[22]

If Tyrtaeus was not talking about Helots, whom was he talking about? Given the fact that these verses were used to buttress a particular position in a very sensitive controversy, one should probably be cautious in attributing to Tyrtaeus anything that is only in the surrounding sentences of Pausanias and not in the verses themselves. This means, in other words, that the assumption that the verses referred to the Messenians at all should not be regarded as a certainty, particularly since the conditions imposed to the Messenians after the first and the second war respectively were clearly an object of disagreement among later authors (see below), which would be surprising if among Tyrtaeus' verses there had been an unambiguous testimony on this point. The obligation to come to mourn at the masters' funerals finds an interesting parallel in the description of the conditions imposed by the Corinthian Bacchiads on the Megarians,[23] but in their case there is no hint of alienation of resources. Moreover, Tyrtaeus' verses, in which different words for "masters" recur twice,[24] seem to describe people held in a relation of personal dependence, rather than a submitted community; they recall to some extent the "shameful slavery" imposed by some Athenians on others according to Solon (fr. 36.13-15 W.[2]). If they do not refer to a condition imposed on some part of the population of Messene, which they might, they should probably be seen as

....

[19] See e.g. Lotze 1959: 28 and 32-33; Oliva 1971: 108-112; Link 1994: 1 n. 6; Hodkinson 2000: 126-127; Cartledge 2002: 303.

[20] As Ducat astutely points out (1990: 61 n. 21), if Tyrtaeus had mentioned by name the Helots later sources would certainly not have failed to refer to him.

[21] See Kiechle 1959: 61 and Ducat 1990: 60-61.

[22] For more detailed arguments in support of the interpretation presented here, see Luraghi 2002a.

[23] According to the Atthidographer Demon (*FGrHist* 327 F 19), writing probably in the late fourth century, the Megarians were compelled to go to Corinth to mourn at the funerals of the Bacchiads. The parallel with Tyrtaeus has been noticed by Bockisch (1985: 44-45) and is developed by Hans van Wees in this volume.

[24] Notice particularly δεσπόσυνοι (fr. 6.2 W.[2]), possibly a Doric word, cf. Plut. *Lyk.* 28.10 and *SGDI* 4334.

describing the plight of dependant labor force working for the Spartiates. Be this as it may, in the end the only thing that Tyrtaeus does say explicitly about the Messenians, in the very few verses that are preserved, is that they fled from their country in consequence of the war. He may have had a lot more to say, for all we can tell, but this can only be the object of speculation.

2. Seen from the West: Antiochus of Syracuse on Helotry

Ironically, the earliest version of the introduction of Helotry found in the sources happens to be a somewhat eccentric one, one that does connect it to the conquest of Messenia, but in a very peculiar way. According to Antiochus of Syracuse (*FGrHist* 555 F 13 *ap.* Strab. 6.3.2), the Spartans who did not take part in the Messenian war were enslaved and called Helots. In other words, the original Helots would have been former members of the citizen body who had lost their rights because they had failed to comply with their military duties—a very Spartan idea, although even for Spartan standards these conscientious objectors fell very low.[25] The text does not specify that the disenfranchised were Spartiates, but the development of the story, particularly the revolt planned by the Partheniai for the Hyakinthia, the Spartan festival of Apollo at Amyclae, seem to imply just this. If this is the case, Antiochus is the only ancient author who considers Helotry to have originated from internal differentiation within the Spartiates.[26]

Before discussing this view of the origins of Helotry—if this is what it is (see below)—it should be pointed out that Antiochus, like his contemporaries Herodotus and Thucydides, does not seem to distinguish between a first and a second Messenian war. As has often been observed, in assessing the relevance of his testimony it is necessary to keep in mind that what Antiochus was really talking about was the foundation of Taras in Southern Italy in the late eighth century. To an extent that is difficult to determine, his story is likely to have been concocted in order to make sense of the name Partheniai, traditionally considered to be the name of the group that sailed from Sparta to found the colony. Probably Partheniai was etymologized as "children of unmarried women", and the fathers' loss of citizen rights in Antiochus' story could be a way of explaining that name.

....

[25] As Vidal-Naquet's comparison with the τρέσαντες, the Spartans who lost their full political rights because of cowardice, makes clear (1981: 238 and 279; see also Moscati Castelnuovo 1991: 64-79, esp. 72-74).

[26] See Ducat 1990: 67. A process of internal differentiation is envisaged also in Plat. *Resp.* 8.547b-c, which however does not have to refer specifically to Spartan history; see Vidal-Naquet 1981: 240 and Ducat 1990: 75-76.

The connection between Partheniai and Helots was certainly less than flattering for the Tarentines: it made of them the offspring of slaves and severed any blood ties between them and the Spartans. It is difficult to resist the suspicion that this version of the foundation of Taras might not come from Taras at all, but rather be a hostile distortion of what the Tarentines thought of their forefathers.[27] After all, if the Partheniai had been sons of freeborn fathers who became enslaved, they should have simply become slaves, too:[28] the enslavement of their fathers is not indispensable to explain their name and their predicament, and therefore is likely to be a spurious element. As a matter of fact, the next version of the story, by Ephorus (*FGrHist* 70 F 216 *ap.* Strab. 6.3.3), corrects precisely this point, making of the Partheniai the offspring of the young Spartan warriors who were fighting in Messenia but were not bound by the oath sworn by their senior comrades at the beginning of the war, not to come home until victory was achieved.[29] A further reason to suspect that Antiochus' story might not reflect accurately what the Tarentines thought of their origin is the fact that Taras throughout its history had an untypically friendly and close relationship to its mother-city. Given that all foundation stories, being about the expulsion of a portion of the community, by their very nature involve a certain amount of conflict, one would rather expect the Tarentines to imagine a story in which that conflict was de-emphasized; after all, the name Partheniai could as well have had that very function.[30]

The idea that the fathers of the Partheniai did not take part in the war against the Messenians could reflect a precise historical context: the alliance between Taras and Rhegion in 473, at a time when Rhegion was particularly emphasizing its

[27] On this, I follow Nafissi 1999: 251-258. The hostility in Antiochus' story is surprisingly overlooked by most scholars, but it becomes clear if one compares it with Ephorus' version (*FGrHist* 70 F 216 = Strab. 6.3.3). Musti's view (1988: 156 and 158), according to which Antiochus found the servile origin in the tradition and did his best to tone it down, is not very convincing; Antiochus could well have passed over the servile origin of the colonists completely in silence, had he so wished: after all, Ephorus did just that (see below).

[28] As noted by Moscati Castelnuovo 1991: 69-70. It is rather puzzling that Antiochus should not say who the 'unmarried' mothers of the Partheniai were; in any case, the very name of the Partheniai will probably have prevented him from considering them bastard sons of the wives of the Spartans who were fighting in Messenia.

[29] Ephorus, who wrote a universal history from the return of the Heraclids, unsurprisingly has a version of the foundation of Taras that shows a much closer familiarity with Spartan history and institutions than Antiochus'; see now Lupi (2000: 172-176) who shows elegantly that Ephorus' version implies a rather precise knowledge of Spartan marriage customs. Furthermore, Ephorus clearly goes out of his way to clear every trace of blame on Partheniai or Spartans (Nafissi 1999: 254).

[30] The word *parthenios* is used in the *Iliad* to refer to Eudorus, one of the leaders of the Myrmidons, a son of the god Hermes and of the maiden Polymele, who after his birth married a mortal man, Echecles; Eudoros was then reared in the house of Polymele's father, Phylas (*Il.* 16.179-92).

Messenian ancestry.[31] If the foundation story of Taras was reworked in connection with the alliance, which seems an extremely attractive conjecture, then it becomes also easier to understand the origins of the hostile touch in Antiochus, that is, the genealogical connection between colonists and slaves, and especially, slaves who had been enslaved because they had not fought against the Messenians: Syracuse was a traditional enemy of Rhegion, and this enmity had been particularly fierce in the first quarter of the fifth century, while its relations to Taras may also have been less than friendly for most of the fifth century. Antiochus may have either added the sting himself[32] or perhaps even more likely received it from some earlier Syracusan elaboration.

However one interprets his testimony, the introduction of Helotry was obviously not what Antiochus was really interested in. Therefore, when he describes the treatment meted out to the fathers of the Partheniai, the possibility should not be excluded that what he really meant was something much simpler and less specific than normally thought, something along the lines of e.g. "they were made slaves, and called Helots, as slaves are called at Sparta".[33] Such a comment would make sense in the work of a western Greek historian, writing for an audience that was less familiar with Spartan institutions than a mainland audience could have been expected to be. Of course, if this is what the text means, than it does not deal with the origins of Helotry at all. But this cannot be ascertained, and in the end Antiochus' story is bound to generate in a modern interpreter the mixed feelings typical of a *lectio difficilior*.

3. The conquest of the Helots: emergence of a *vulgata*

With Thucydides, slightly later than Antiochus, we meet the first occurrence of what would later become the *vulgata* on the origins of Helotry. Relating the uprising against Sparta that exploded in Messenia after the earthquake in the sixties of the fifth century, Thucydides (1.101.2) says that the majority of the Helots who revolted were descendants of the "old Messenians", who had been enslaved in the past

....

[31] On the alliance between Rhegion and Taras in 473, see Hdt. 7.170.3 and Diod. 11.52 with Vallet 1958: 370-372. The idea that the alliance could have influenced the narrative of the foundation of Taras as found in Antiochus was first put forward by Georg Busolt (1893: 407 n. 1), and has been accepted by many other scholars: see Pais 1922: 124 n. 1; Ciaceri 1928: 225; Cordano 1995: 54. On the emphasis on Messenian heritage in early-fifth century Rhegion, see Luraghi 1994: 200-202.

[32] Antiochus' hostility to Taras: Nafissi 1995: 299-300 with further references.

[33] This has been suggested by Pierre Lévêque (1979: 114-119 at 115); *contra*, Ducat 1990: 7-8 and 67. Both possibilities are admitted by Musti (1988: 155 n. 7), who opts cautiously for seeing in Antiochus a reference to the introduction of Helotry. Garlan (1995: 101) leaves the problem open.

(Thucydides simply says τότε, probably meaning "in that well known occasion").[34] It is no accident that the first mention of the enslavement of the Messenians should appear in the context of the fifth-century revolt, given the central importance that the Messenian identity had for the rebels. Unfortunately, Thucydides' allusion to the enslavement is rather vague, and he does not explain whose descendants the other Helots were, who also took part in the uprising, nor does he say explicitly whether the revolt was confined to Messenia or raged in Laconia, too. However, in so far as it is possible to pinpoint anything, every single element in Thucydides or other early sources on the revolt refers to Messenia: Thucydides says that the perioikic town of Thouria, located east of the Pamisos, joined the revolt (1.101.2), Herodotus mentions the defeat of a Spartan army in Stenykleros (9.64.2),[35] Aristophanes (*Lys.* 1141) and the Old Oligarch (*Ath. Pol.* 3.11) speak of Messene and Messenians as the Spartans' foe. This justifies the assumption that the revolt was really confined to the Spartan territory west of the Taygetos. Evidence of unrest among the Helots in Laconia comes exclusively from later sources that, while admitting that the Messenians had been reduced to the condition of Helots, still treated Helots and Messenians as two different entities, and may therefore have deduced that the revolt had involved Laconia from the fact that Thucydides implied that not all the Helots who partook were of Messenian descent. But of course, Thucydides may as well have thought that not all the Helots living west of the Taygetos were descendants of the "old Messenians".[36]

The emerging of Messenian ethnicity in the Peloponnese was an extremely conspicuous phenomenon in fifth-century Greece. The Spartans were unable to crush the uprising and the rebels, after ten years of fighting, were allowed to evacuate their stronghold on Mt. Ithome and founded an independent community of Messenians in the West-Locrian city of Naupactus, whence they sent their troops to fight on the Athenian side during the Peloponnesian war. Their contribution to the Pylos campaign was particularly significant. They were not only very active, but very vocal, too: the famous statue of Victory by the sculptor Paionios of Mende, that stood on a tall pillar in front of the temple of Zeus at Olympia, one of the most prominent monuments in the sanctuary, was dedicated by them, probably during

....

34 See Ducat 1990: 132 and Whitby 1994: 116 n. 38. The interpretation of this passage is discussed in Luraghi 2002b.

35 Cf. also 9.35.2, where Ithome may be mentioned in conjunction with the revolt, if one accepts Paulmier's emendation of Ἰσθμῷ in Ἰθώμῃ; the rebels, at any rate, are called Messenians.

36 See Ducat 1990: 132-134. Whitby (1994: 115-116 n. 38) thinks that the participation of Laconian Helots is implied by Diod. 11.63.6-64.1 and Plut. *Cim.* 16.4, describing Archidamus' prompt reaction that saved Sparta from a direct attack. The interpretation of the revolt outlined here is argued in detail in Luraghi 2001a: 285-290.

the Peloponnesian war.[37] It would therefore be hardly surprising if the idea that (some of?) the Helots in Messenia were descendants of the formerly free local population had influenced general views of the origins of Helotry, producing an "ethnic" theory for the origins of the Helots in Laconia, too. The first traces of such a theory can be found in an admittedly problematic source, an entry from the medieval abridgment of a II c. CE lexicon (Harpokr. s.v. εἱλωτεύειν, with Hellan. *FGrHist* 4 F 188):

> To be a Helot: to be a slave; Isocrates in the *Panegyric*. The Helots, in fact, were slaves of the Spartans, but not by birth. Rather, they were the first among the inhabitants of the city of Helos to be conquered by the Spartans, as, among many others, Hellanicus witnesses in book I.

The text of the entry is somewhat confusing, to say the least. The sentence "the first among the inhabitants of Helos to be enslaved" should most probably be taken to mean that the inhabitants of Helos, once enslaved, became the first Helots, as suggested also by the description of the Helots as "slaves but not by birth", which of course is pure nonsense if applied to the Helots in general and can only be referred to the "first generation" of Helots. It is also possible, but much less likely, that the expression "the first inhabitants of Helos" was meant to differentiate them from people, *perioikoi* or Eleutherolakonians, who lived in Helos in later times.[38] It is difficult to say in which of his many works Hellanicus might have had a reason to discuss the origins of Helotry. The fact that he is quoted together with unspecified many others suggests that somewhere behind our garbled entry there was some fuller text, in which perhaps authors were listed who supported this view of the meaning of the name "Helots". Very probably only the name of Hellanicus has survived because he was the first of the list, that is, the oldest. The one thing that can be said for sure is that this passage implies that the name Helots derives from Helos, in southern Lakonia, and that this idea existed in the second half of the fifth century.

Obviously, such a view of the origin of Helotry results from an *a posteriori* process consisting in interpreting the name "Helots" as an ethnic and then looking for a more or less suitable place-name in Laconia to combine it with. It is important not to forget that this explanation of the name is fictitious: in purely linguistic

....

[37] Figueira 1999: 215, speaks of 'a virtual *blitzkrieg* of self-assertion by the Messenians spanning about a generation from *c.* 460'. On the Nike, see Hölscher 1974; the dedicatory inscription, mentioning Messenians and Naupactians, is *IvO* 259.

[38] A detailed discussion of this passage is found in Ducat 1990: 77, with further references. Helos was probably a perioikic settlement in the fifth century; see Shipley 1997: 252-253; on the status of Helos see also Kiechle 1963: 271-272.

terms, "Helots" cannot be the ethnic of "Helos", and this was clear already in antiquity.[39] Hellanicus' view has the appearance of a learned speculation. The question is, what prompted this learned speculation in the first place. It seems highly probable that the interpretation of the Laconian Helots as descendants of the formerly free citizens of Helos, conquered by the Spartans, may have been concocted—probably not at Sparta—as a parallel to the other view we find in Thucydides, and that probably goes back to the age of the revolt, the one that made Helots in Messenia the descendants of the "old Messenians". The fact that (some of?) the Helots of Messenia were recognized as descendants of an enslaved indigenous population may have drawn attention to the question of where the other Helots came from. In that perspective, it would have been natural to extend the same explanation to the Helots of Laconia, and of course the next step had to be to find a suitable native population; until more articulate reconstructions of the Dorian invasion of Laconia were formulated, such as those found in Ephorus and Theopompus, the most obvious thing to do was to look for a place-name that could be connected somehow to the name "Helots".

It is possible that up to that point, no "historical" explanation of the origin of Laconian Helots had existed, except perhaps Antiochus'—again, assuming that Antiochus was really talking about the origins of Helotry. After all, for the Spartiates it was not very important to know who the Helots had been before being turned into Helots; it was enough to know who they were *hic et nunc*, and this the Spartiates knew well enough: inferior beings, who embodied all the characteristics that the Spartiates despised. By way of a number of practices of ritualized contempt, the Spartiates tried to inculcate this concept in the Helots, while at the same time reassuring themselves of their superiority.[40] They may have had a vague notion that their domination over the Helots was a result of military superiority, a notion without a specific historical context (see below), but on the other hand, they probably had positive reasons to oppose the notion that the Helots were descended from formerly free ethnic communities (see below). In this connection, it is worth noting that not even in later sources is any alternative view of the origin of Laconian Helots to be found.

Before moving on to the fourth-century sources, one point has to be underlined. While there is no evidence that the idea of a region called "Messene" or "Messenia", comprising the whole of the Spartan territory west of the Taygetus, had

[39] Cf. Steph. Byz. s.v. *Helos* and Ducat 1990: 9, and see below on Theopompus' version of the ethnic of Helos.

[40] On such practices see Ducat 1974: 1451-1464, and 1990: 105-127. Cf. Figueira 1999: 221, who stresses the absence of ethnic symbolism in them.

existed at all during the archaic period, by the fifth century this idea was clearly emerging. It is implied by the tradition on the Dorian conquest and division of the southern Peloponnese, which is attested for the first time by Pindar in 462 and probably originated at Argos, perhaps in the early fifth century.[41] When Thucydides located Pylos in what had once been the Messenian land (4.3.2; 41.2), he was obviously assuming that more or less everything west of the Taygetos had been Messenian land. In this context, the name "Messene" apparently started to be used as the name of a region.[42] In due course, this shift in meaning would have its consequences for the way in which the Spartan conquest was imagined.

4. "Old Messenians" or new Messenians?

With the liberation of most of Messenia by Epaminondas in 369, both the original Spartan conquest of that region and the status of its inhabitants became hotly debated issues, tied as they were to conflicting claims, on the one hand the right of Sparta to control the region, on the other the right of the new Messenian polity to be recognized as legitimate.[43] The Spartan viewpoint on such issues is probably to be found in a speech written by the Athenian orator Isocrates, a speech in which the speaker purports to be the Spartan Archidamus, son of Agesilaus and future king of Sparta. In spite of its being fictitious, the speech, composed probably in the mid-sixties, is very likely to reflect the Spartan "party line", which was certainly known in Athens.[44] Isocrates' Archidamus had a very clear-cut view of how and why the Spartans had taken control of Messenia (always called "Messene" in the speech) and, indirectly, of the origin of the Helots living in Messenia. In his view, Messenia had come under Spartan control very early, because the Messenians had killed their Heraclid king, Cresphontes, and exiled his children; these fled to Sparta, also ruled by Heraclid kings, and entrusted their land to the Spartans, begging for revenge. The Spartans, after asking the oracle of Apollo, had accepted the gift and the task and conquered the land (*Archid.* 22-3). In short, their claim to Messenia was founded on the ancestral rights of the Heraclids, on Apollo's will, and on armed conquest, and was therefore as unimpeachable as their claim to Laconia itself

---

[41] The relevant sources are discussed in Luraghi 2001b.

[42] The first instance of this usage is Eur. fr. 1083 *ap.* Strab. 8.5.6, from the lost tragedy *Temenos*, which narrated the division (see Harder 1991: 133-134): Strabo uses 'Messenia', except when he introduces line 10 of the fragment, where his 'Messene' in highly likely to reflect Euripides' terminology.

[43] The recognition of Messene as a sovereign state was a stumbling block of attempts at renewing the common peace in the sixties; see Jehne 1994: 80-85 and 96-97. The sources on the foundation of the new Messene have been collected by Dipersia 1974: 54-61.

[44] See Jehne 1994: 11 n. 21 with further bibliography.

(*Archid.* 25). Clearly, this story cancels any Messenian claim to independence based on the story of the division of the Peloponnese among the Heraclids.

It is not clear how exactly Isocrates-Archidamus envisioned the Spartan conquest (*Archid.* 31). The idea that the siege of the Messenian stronghold that concluded the war (*Archid.* 23) lasted twenty years (*Archid.* 57) is obviously taken, directly or indirectly, from Tyrtaeus (fr. 5 W.²).[45] Isocrates' description of the long war includes more details that later sources would refer to the "First Messenian War", such as the fact that both sides turned to the oracle of Delphi, which recurs, with a different bias, in Pausanias' narrative of that war (4.12.1-4). On the other hand, the oracle's answer, explaining to the Spartans where they should seek help, might be considered an allusion to the tradition accoding to which during the "Second Messenian War" the Spartans had been told by the Delphic oracle to ask for a leader at Athens and the Athenians had sent Tyrtaeus, a tradition that was apparently known to Plato (*Laws* 1.629a-b) and is explicitly attested for the first time by Callisthenes (*FGrHist* 124 F 24).[46] But this is far from certain, and some uneasiness might be felt about assuming that Isocrates was mixing up things to this point.[47]

What happened to the Messenians after the war, Isocrates-Archidamus does not explain precisely, except for saying rather casually that the Spartans had conquered the land and expelled those who were guilty of murdering Cresphontes (*Archid.* 32). For Isocrates-Archidamus, the citizens of the new polity founded by the Thebans in 369 were not, as he says, "the true Messenians", that is, descendants of the people the Spartans had fought against, but rather Helots, former slaves of the Spartans (*Archid.* 28 and 87-8).[48] In other words, the Messenians were not there any more, and the Helots living in Messenia and forming, in the Spartan perspective, the citizen body of the new Messene were not the descendants of the free

....

[45] Note that because of the shift in meaning of the toponym 'Messene', fourth-century readers were bound to deduce from Tyrtaeus that the Spartans under king Theopompus had conquered Messenia, i.e. the region, rather than a settlement in that region.

[46] See Mazzarino 1966: 462. The story is also in Diod. 8.27, on which see Jacoby 1943: 114, lines 19-21. The version of the story found in Justin (3.5.5-6) and Pausanias (4.15.6), according to which Tyrtaeus was lame and the Athenians had sent him because they did not want to help the Spartans, is clearly an attempt at excusing Athens, and as such certainly a later concoction.

[47] Massimo Nafissi reminds me that oracles are endemic in traditions on the Heraclid conquest, and some oracle might well have been linked to the conquest of Messenia, too.

[48] The same view of the citizens of Epaminondas' Messene may be reflected in the proverbial expression δουλότερος Μεσσήνης (notice the form of the place-name: since the late third century BCE at the latest, 'Messene' was—again—the name of the city at the foot of Mt. Ithome, it did not indicate the region any more), later misunderstood by the paroemiographers and connected to the harsh conditions imposed on Helotized Messenians (Macarius 3.35, Zenobius 3.39). Unless, that is, the proverb really refers to the Messenians who revolted in the fifth century, which is possible.

Messenians of old. Therefore they had no legitimate right to the land the Thebans had given them. As Giulia Dipersia put it, the Spartan view voiced by Isocrates was meant to reduce the "Messenian question" to a conflict between slaves and masters, thereby projecting over the Thebans the image of the subverters of the traditional order and attracting to the Spartans the sympathy of the other Greeks.[49]

Who the Helots of Messenia really were, is a question on which one would very much like to have Archidamus' answer. However, the answer might be disappointing. As noted above, although the Spartiates were very careful to devise a collective identity for the Helots and impose it on them, they do not seem to have been interested in the question of where the Helots came from in the first place. On the contrary, the Spartans consistently refused to recognize the Messenian identity of the fifth-century rebels, even after they allowed them to leave Ithome, as shown by the clause of the treaty which allowed anybody to enslave any of the former rebels if caught in the Peloponnese.[50] Archidamus' position on the identity of the Helots living in Messenia confirms that considering the Helots an ethnic group was not something the Spartans were very fond of, and understandably so.[51] To the Greeks, an ethnic group, especially if Greek, had an implicit right to its own land and to its freedom, and of course the Spartans were not particularly prone to acknowledge such rights in the case of their own slaves.

Isocrates' speech is the only preserved text that comes from the immediate aftermath of the liberation of Messenia. The Theban-Messenian point of view can be reconstructed only tentatively and indirectly, based on later sources. Rather surprisingly, or perhaps not so surprisingly, the Theban "party line" seems to have agreed with the Spartans'—as identifiable based on the *Archidamos*—on a crucial point: the assumption that no Messenians were living in Messenia at the time of the liberation by the Thebans. Where the Theban-Messenian version of course sharply disagreed from the Spartan one, was in maintaining that the citizens of the new Messenian polity were indeed Messenians, the descendants of the "old Messenians" who had been exiled to various places at various points in time, and returned to their old fatherland, freed by Epaminondas. Or at least, this is what is found the sources such as Pausanias (4.26.5) and Plutarch's *Life of Pelopidas* (24.5),[52] who may be expected to reflect more or less closely the Theban-Messenian viewpoint. More importantly, this way of conceptualizing the foundation of the new Messene is

....

[49] Dipersia 1974: 58.

[50] See Thuc. 1.103.1 with Figueira 1999: 234-235.

[51] See Figueira 1999: 221-222.

[52] Cf. also Plut. *Ages.* 34.1. Plutarch depends largely on Callisthenes' *Hellenics*, a work composed in the late forties of the fourth century and characterized by a strong bias in favor of the Thebans; see Fuscagni 1975: 31-55.

implied by the text of the epigram that accompanied Epaminondas' statue at Thebes (Paus. 9.15.6): "By my counsels was Sparta shorn of her glory /and holy Messene received at last her children."[53] This last piece of evidence is not as decisive as one could think, however, since the inscription and the statue will hardly have survived the destruction of Thebes by Alexander in 335; in the form in which Pausanias saw it, this monument was probably later than the refoundation of the city by Cassander in 316.[54] At any rate, based on the available evidence the assumption that the Thebans and their allies depicted the foundation of the new independent Messenian polity as a return, not liberation, of the Messenians is extremely likely. As for the citizens of the new polity, whoever they were, wherever they came from, to be associated with former slaves would not have been very attractive for them. In the dawn of the new Messene, the supposed Messenian origin of the Helots west of the Taygetos seems to have been forgotten by all and everybody.

5. Systematizing the past: Ephorus and Theopompus

The mid and late fourth century was a very important period for the elaboration by Greek historians of more consistent and detailed views of the distant past. For us, this process of (re)construction is connected mainly with two figures, the historians Ephorus and Theopompus, both allegedly pupils of Isocrates.[55] The works of both are lost, but remarks by later authors show that they were regarded as highly authoritative and influential, both as models of style and historiographic technique, and as sources. Ephorus' *Universal history* in particular was to become the standard work of reference on archaic and classical Greek history for centuries to come. They both seem to have had very clear ideas about early Spartan history and the origins of Helotry.

Ephorus systematized the more recent part of the mythic past, after the return of the Heraclids to the Peloponnese, connecting different plots, narratives and local traditions and casting them into a consistent whole.[56] His views of the Spartan conquest of the Helots—as we can reconstruct them based on fragments and passages by other authors who used his work as their source—are to some extent the result of a development probably set in motion by the revolt after the earthquake, and certainly accelerated by the new Messenians' quest for their past, which

....

[53] Interesting observations on the text of the epigram in Dipersia 1974: 60.

[54] On Cassander's motives, see Bearzot 1997: 265-276; if her interpretation is correct, the statue seen by Pausanias could well date back to this moment.

[55] On the tradition that made Ephorus and Theopompus pupils of the Athenian orator, see Nicolai (1992) who explains it as the result of speculation based on similarities in style.

[56] See the interesting analysis of Ephorus *FGrHist* 70 T 8 *ap.* Diod. 4.1.2-3 by Parmeggiani 1999: 107-125.

started after the foundation of a free Messenian state in 369. At the same time, his narrative shows visible signs of an attempt to create a plausible early history of the Peloponnese based on parallels and inferences derived from later periods. According to Ephorus, the early histories of Laconia and Messenia had been remarkably similar. In both cases, the incoming Dorians were not so numerous as to fill the land they had conquered. In Laconia (*FGrHist* 70 F 117 *ap.* Strab. 8.5.4), after the Achaeans had left, the Heraclids Eurysthenes and Procles divided the region into six districts in which they founded six cities. They kept Sparta as their residence, assigned Amyklai to the man who had helped them get rid of the Achaeans, designated kings for the other four districts and gave the right of citizenship on an equal footing with the Dorians to whoever wanted to settle there.[57] A generation later, king Agis, the son of Eurysthenes, decided to tighten up Sparta's control on the region, imposing a tribute on the—non-Dorian or mostly non-Dorian—inhabitants of the five districts.[58] Most of them yielded, but the Heleioi, inhabitants of Helos, did not. Therefore the Spartans besieged and conquered them and reduced them into slavery at particular conditions: they could neither be freed nor sold outside the Spartan territory. This war came to be known as the war against the Helots—so ends Strabo's excerpt from Ephorus.[59] The concluding sentence seems to suggest that Ephorus, while calling the free inhabitants of Helos "Heleioi", accepted the connection between Helos and the name "Helots" established probably by Hellanicus. He may have thought, as Theopompus seems to have thought, too, that "Helots" was a twisted form of the correct ethnic of Helos. It should also be noted that Ephorus' story assumed an ethnic discontinuity not only between Spartiates and Helots, but also between Spartiates and *perioikoi*.[60]

In Messenia, things had started in a similar way. The Heraclid king Cresphontes divided the land into five districts and founded five cities, chose Stenykleros as his residence and sent kings to the other four cities, also giving

....

[57] This story may have something to do with the classic topos of the Spartan *oliganthrôpia*, as suggested by Figueira 1999: 217.

[58] Ephorus must have been mostly retrojecting conditions he was familiar with from his own time, and this reference should probably be connected to the mysterious *basilikos phoros* paid by the Lacedaemonians according to Plat. *Alcib. I* 123a, and perhaps also to Xenophon's statement (*Lac. Pol.* 15.3) that the Spartan kings owned choice land in perioikic territory. See Oliva 1971: 60-61 and Cartledge 2002: 155 (both skeptical); but cf. Cartledge 1987: 16.

[59] On the extension of the excerpt from Ephorus, see Jacoby's edition of this fragment and Hodkinson 2000: 117-118.

[60] This does not seem to have been the most common view: Herodotus' ethnic map of the Peloponnese (8.73) seems to exclude it, except in the case of the Dryopians of Asine, while Isocrates in the *Panathenaicus*, in the late forties of the fourth century, considers the *perioikoi* Dorians like the Spartiates (*Panath.* 178-179, on which see Ducat 1985: 99-100).

equality of rights to Dorians and non-Dorians, who in this case seem to have been indigenous, presumably Achaeans.[61] But since the Dorians resented his decision, Cresphontes tried to take it back, concentrating all the Dorians in Stenykleros (*FGrHist* 70 F 116 *ap.* Strab. 8.4.7). Nicolaus of Damascus' account, clearly based on Ephorus,[62] gives further details (*FGrHist* 90 F 31): Cresphontes tried to use the argument, that had been used in Lakedaimon, too, that it was not fair that the Dorian conquerors should share their privileges with the previous inhabitants, but he ended up dissatisfying both sides. The Dorians resented his initial overture to the locals and generally disliked his political course,[63] and finally decided to get rid of him and his offspring. Only one child escaped murder, little Aepytus, who was saved by his maternal grandfather king Cypselus of Arcadia and regained his father's throne. Comparison with fifth-century versions of the story shows that this Arcadian detour is probably a result of the friendly relations between Arcadians and Messenians after 369. Aepytus' return, however, did not put a stop to the conflicts between kings and their subjects in Messenia. Aepytus himself survived an attack, and conflicts between his successors and their subjects continued until finally the Spartans conquered the region and enslaved its inhabitants. The excerpt from Nicolaus (*FGrHist* 70 F 34) does not give a clear chronological framework for this concluding phase, so that one could see here an allusion to the enslavement of the Messenians as a result of the "First Messenian War". However, a passage in Diodorus' *Historical Library* (15.66.2), also drawing on Ephorus, completes the picture and makes it virtually certain that in Ephorus' view the Spartans had taken control of Messenia well before the murder of Teleclus and the "First Messenian War".[64] Accordingly, that war, caused by the rape of the Spartan maidens and the murder of king Teleclus by the Messenians, was in a sense a rebellion.

Unfortunately, it is not possible to say with certainty at which point, in Ephorus' reconstruction, the conquered Messenians were turned into Helots. The excerpt from Nicolaus seems to suggest that that happened as soon as the Spartans took control of the region, but one should probably not put too much weight on

....

[61] No source calls them such, but one does not see what other ethnic definition they could have had; cf. Diod. 15.66.2, where Orestes is king of Messenia (and Laconia).

[62] See already Niese 1891: 2-3.

[63] 'Were suspicious of his μετακόσμησις τῶν καθεστώτων', as Nicolaus puzzlingly puts it. It is possible that Ephorus already depicted Cresphontes as a demagogue, as did Pausanias (4.3.7), whose account is much more favorable to Cresphontes than Nicolaus' and eliminates any trace of conflict between Dorians and indigenous inhabitants.

[64] *pace* Stylianou 1998: 439, who does not consider Nicolaus *FGRHist* 90 F 34. Cf. the analysis of Diod. 15.66 by Jacoby 1930: 424-425 (*ad* 124 F 23-24).

this, since the enslavement is mentioned in the very last sentence of the excerpt, which may well be telescoping a longer process. In the passage from Diodorus, which covers more evenly the whole history of Messenia from Nestor to Epaminondas, a clear distinction is visible between the period when the Spartans were κύριοι of Messenia, after the descendants of Cresphontes lost the kingship (15.66.2), and the situation that obtained after the "First Messenian War", when the Messenians became slaves of the Spartans (15.66.3). Furthermore, in Ephorus' version of the story of the foundation of Taras, reported by Strabo (*FGrHist* 70 F 216 *ap.* Strab. 6.3.3), reference is made in passing to the fact that after the "First War" the Spartans apportioned the Messenian land among themselves. It seems more likely on the whole that in Ephorus' view the Messenians had been Helotized as a result of the "First Messenian War".[65]

Interestingly, Ephorus' version of the Spartan conquest of Messenia bears an important similarity to Isocrates', in that it presupposes a very early date for the Spartan takeover.[66] Of course, Ephorus had a much more precise reconstruction of the stages of this process, based in part on a more scrupulous use of Tyrtaeus' poems as evidence. One obvious result was assigning to the final conquest a significantly lower date than the one implied by Isocrates' rather confused hints. Moreover, Ephorus accepted the idea, introduced by Callisthenes and perhaps again based on Tyrtaeus, that there had been two Messenian wars, one in the age of king Theopompus, the other in Tyrtaeus' own times.[67] Later sources, though, more friendly to the Messenians, would down-date the conquest of the region to the "First War", while keeping Ephorus' separation of conquest and enslavement: in their perspective, as we will see in more detail in a moment, the enslavement was the consequence of the "Second Messenian War".

The other "Isocratean", Theopompus, seems to have discussed Helotry in the framework of a general reflection on the origins and development of slavery in the Greek world. In a retrospective excursus, probably in his *Philippic histories* (*FGrHist* 115 F 122 *ap.* Athen. 6.265b-c), Theopompus contended that the Chians had been the first among the Greeks to make use of purchased slaves. Thessalians and Spartans, according to Theopompus, did not acquire their slave populations by way of slave trade, but rather by enslaving Greeks who had formerly inhabited their territories, Perrhaebians and Magnesians and Achaians, respectively. Unlike

....

[65] See Kiechle 1959: 60.

[66] This has been noted already by Niese 1891: 6.

[67] Jacoby 1943: 113-114. The distinction between a first and a second war had probably been introduced by Callisthenes; see *FGrHist* 124 F 23 and Jacoby 1943: 118.

Spartans and Thessalians, the Chians did not enslave Greeks, but used barbarians.[68] This passage represents the earliest and only explicit instance of the theory that dominates modern scholarship on the origin of the Helots of Laconia, according to which they were the descendants of the pre-Dorian inhabitants of the region. It is important to underline that Theopompus is absolutely unique in making of the Helots the descendants of the Achaeans of Laconia. Ephorus, as we have just seen, distinguished both Helots and *perioikoi* from the Spartiates, but considered neither the ones nor the others indigenous.[69]

But apparently, Theopompus' views were more complex, and more similar to Ephorus',[70] than this fragment would lead one to think. In another passage, from his earlier work *Hellenics (FGrHist* 115 F 13 *ap.* Athen. 6.272a), describing, perhaps in conjunction with Cinadon's conspiracy,[71] the hard plight of the Helots, Theopompus specifies that they had been subject to the Spartans for a very long time and were in part Heleatai, who had formerly inhabited a place called Helos, in Laconia, and in part from Messene.[72] The strange form Ἐλεᾶται, which is not very obvious as an ethnic of a place called Ἕλος, is probably the product of an attempt at narrowing the gap between Ἕλος and εἵλωτες,[73] an attempt that underlines the nature of erudite construct of the whole connection Helots-Helos.

This second fragment poses some problems, both in itself and in relation to the first one. Certainly nobody would object to merging them to the extent of admitting that the enslaved Achaeans mentioned in the *Philippic histories* are the same as the Heleatai of the *Hellenics*. It is less clear whether the merging should be

---

68 See Vidal-Naquet 1981: 223-230. Chios and Sparta are singled out for having particularly many slaves already by Thucydides (8.40.2). On Thessaly, see Ducat 1994. Both Shrimpton (1991: 49-50) and Flower (1994: 81-82) suggest plausibly that Theopompus was critical of the enslavement of Greeks by the Spartans, and probably also of the latter's brutal treatment of the Helots (cf. Theop. *FGrHist* 115 F 13 discussed below).

69 Herodotus' map of ethnic groups in the Peloponnese (8.73) does not mention any non-Dorians living in Laconia, but this point should not be pressed too far, since it is perfectly possible that Herodotus simply ignored the Helots, *qua* slaves.

70 As noted by Ducat 1990: 69.

71 As suggested by Jacoby 1930: 357.

72 Quite puzzlingly, in both fragments Theopompus speaks in the present tense. If Jacoby was right in attributing the first fragment to Theopompus' *Philippic histories*, then the two fragments would reflect two different authorial presents, but even the earlier *Hellenics*, from which the second fragment comes, can hardly have been written earlier than 369, when Sparta lost control of Messenia. In other words, Theopompus' use of the present tense cannot be seen without qualification as an argument against the conclusion that the first fragment (*FGrHist* 115 F 122) refers to Helots both in Laconia and Messenia. Also noteworthy is the fact that Theopompus in F 13 does not speak simply of enslavement of the Messenians, but says that some Helots were 'from Messene'. Perhaps, he thought that the Helot population had been mixed up or relocated by the Spartans, so that some Helots 'from Messene' were still serving their Spartan masters in Laconia after the liberation of Messenia?

73 As suggested by Ducat 1978: 9 n. 16.

carried one step forward to include the Messenians. That Theopompus admitted an Achaean presence in early Messenia would not be too surprising. However, the fragment from the *Philippic histories* is to some extent focused on chronology, so it would be understandable if Theopompus had in mind at that point only the first Greeks Helotized by the Spartans, that is, the Helots of Laconia, all the more so since he speaks of enslavement of the Greeks who originally possessed the lands that Thessalians and Spartans have "now", and Messene was free at the time he was writing. In the end, it is probably safer to admit that we do not have any evidence of how Theopompus imagined the ethnic composition of Messenia at the time of the Spartan conquest.

After Theopompus, sources on the conquest of Messenia and the origins of Helotry are virtually non-existent for almost three centuries. From the Hellenistic period, which was certainly decisive for the construction of a Messenian past, and saw dramatic transformations in the Spartans' views of their past, too, no explicit evidence has survived to document how that crucial cluster of events was being conceptualized. The next evidence that is preserved dates to the late first century BCE and comes from the works of Diodorus Siculus, Pompeius Trogus, Nicolaus of Damascus, and Strabo. However, these authors mostly reflect—and, as we have seen, often explicitly refer to—the views of mainstream fourth century historiography, particularly of Ephorus, who clearly enjoyed a very high prestige in their age.[74] Therefore, first-century sources are on the whole more useful to reconstruct the views of earlier historians. To find an identifiably new stage in the development of ancient perceptions on the origins of Helotry we have to reach the second century CE.

6. Pausanias' views on Helots and Messenians

The second century CE was arguably a crucial phase for the Greeks' definition of their cultural identity, a process that involved massive engagement with their past by figures of the caliber of a Plutarch. Pausanias' *Periegesis* belongs fully in that cultural climate. His summaries of early Laconian and Messenian history represent by far the most comprehensive corpus of information on the subject in ancient literature. In his work, and only in his work, events and processes that are only alluded to in earlier sources appear as elements of a consistent narrative, together with a remarkable amount of information found in no earlier source. As a matter of fact, all detailed modern reconstructions of Spartan and Messenian history of the

....

[74] For Diodorus' use of Ephorus, particularly for the history of mainland Greece in book XV, see Stylianou 1998: 49-50. For Nicolaus, see Jacoby 1926: 233-234.

eighth and seventh centuries BCE, and especially all reconstructions of the Messenian wars, depend to a significant extent on Pausanias.[75] His texts are so much more detailed and consistent than anything else that has been preserved from antiquity that they have often dominated the interpretation of the earlier authors as well, deluding some scholars into recognizing in the fragmentary early evidence the elements of a *vulgata* and often distracting their attention from the surviving signs of conflicting views.

As it is often the case with post-classical authors, Pausanias has in the past been taken as a mere compiler, whose work mainly provided evidence on those of earlier lost historians. In the case of Messenia, Eduard Schwartz formulated the thesis, successively developed by Jacoby, that Pausanias abridged a regional history of Messenia dating to the early imperial age, without consulting the works of any earlier author and basically replicating the bias of his immediate source.[76] Recent scholarship has moved away from this reductive interpretation, and with good reason, since the Messenian narrative in Book 4 provides many telling examples of Pausanias' actively and creatively engaging with earlier sources and traditions, showing that his work cannot be seen as anything else than a carefully thought-out narrative, with a precise, if sometimes elusive, agenda.[77] In the absence of external evidence, Pausanias should therefore be treated as an author *sui iuris*, contemporary with his own age.[78] And of course, it is necessary to remember that in his age the political map of the southern Peloponnese had changed dramatically since the fourth century BCE.

Pausanias has answers to all the questions we have been discussing so far. On the origins of Laconian Helots, he accepts the connection with Helos, both in etymological and in historical terms, that is, he takes "Helots" as the ethnic of Helos (3.2.7 and 20.6) and says that the inhabitants of Helos were the first to be Helotized by the Spartans (3.20.6). To round things off, according to Pausanias the

....

[75] A particularly egregious example is Huxley 1962.

[76] Schwartz 1899, developed by Jacoby 1943, esp. 19-20.

[77] The Schwartz-Jacoby theory was challenged by Pearson 1962: 397-426. For an analysis of book IV as reflecting Pausanias' own intent, see Alcock 2001: 142-153. Of course, once the alleged local source is done away with, the pro-Messenian and anti-Spartan bias in Pausanias' book IV, easy to explain if it reflected the use of a local history of Messenia, becomes problematic. For some precious indications of Pausanias' agenda, which might help explain his antipathy for the Spartans, see Goldmann 1991, and Dalfen 1996.

[78] The last decades of the twentieth century witnessed a massive revival of Pausanian studies, triggered by the Italian edition and commentary in the series of the Fondazione Lorenzo Valla (see Domenico Musti's extensive introduction to the first volume, Musti and Torelli 1982: ix-lv), and by Christian Habicht's Sather Lectures (1985). Another milestone in this revival was the entretien the Fondation Hardt devoted to Pausanias in 1994 (Bingen 1996). Two very rich volumes have appeared very recently: Knoepfler and Piérart 2001; Alcock, Cherry and Elsner 2001.

Argives, Sparta's archenemies, had helped the Helots of Helos against the Spartans (3.2.7). However, Pausanias dates the conquest of the town much later than previous authors did, during the reign of king Alcamenes, the successor of Teleclus, while attributing the conquest of most of Laconia to Teleclus himself (3.2.6). In his view, up to that point the Dorians had occupied only Sparta itself, while the neighboring settlements were still inhabited by Achaeans, who were then expelled by the Dorians. Before embracing this view of the growth of the Spartan state, which might sound inherently plausible to a modern interpreter, it should be underlined that in Pausanias' times the former perioikic settlements were independent from Sparta; they had been separated from Sparta in 195 BCE, after Flamininus' war against Nabis, and later joined to form a league that took the name of League of the Eleutherolaconians, or Free Laconians, in the age of Augustus.[79] Pausanias' downdating of their conquest by the Spartans is perhaps more likely to reflect and retroject this situation than to preserve a genuine memory of early Spartan history—a memory, it should be remembered, that somehow would have escaped all earlier extant authors.

In Pausanias' chronology, Helotry would have been introduced in Laconia in the generation of the "First Messenian War", which he dates to the generation of the kings Alcamanes and Theopompus. In his prodigiously detailed narrative (4.7-13), that war ended, after Tyrtaeus' twenty years, with those Messenians who had guest-friends in other places, mostly in the Peloponnese, leaving their fatherland, and the others surrendering to the Spartans (4.14.1). Pausanias' description of the hard conditions of the surrender imposed on the Messenians by the Spartans is based on some verses of Tyrtaeus discussed at the beginning of this paper (4.14.4-5). One important element mentioned by Pausanias that is not found in Tyrtaeus' verses is the oath not to revolt against Sparta. This hard and humiliating plight was not yet Helotry, and Pausanias uses Tyrtaeus to make this point. Two generations after the first war, the fathers' fathers' war, the Messenians revolted under the leadership of their national hero, Aristomenes, and were defeated again after a long struggle (4.15-22). This time, exile brought them farther away, to southern Italy and Sicily, and those who stayed behind were finally reduced to the condition of Helots, or rather "merged with the Helots", as Pausanias says (4.16.1 and 24.5), while the Spartans divided the land among themselves.[80] These enslaved

....

[79] On the *perioikoi* after 195 BCE, see the groundbreaking contribution of Kennell 1999; on the extension of Spartan territory thereafter, see Shipley 2000.

[80] In another passage (3.20.6), Pausanias says that the enslaved Messenians came to be called Helots, although they were Dorians. This does not probably mean that Pausanias thought that Messenia was inhabited only by Dorians at the time of the Spartan conquest: in book IV, he tells how in Messenia the Dorians did not expel the previous inhabitants, that is, the Achaeans (4.3.6).

Messenians revolted against the Spartans after the earthquake, left the Peloponnese under a truce (4.24.5-7), and after further wanderings their descendants came back for the grande rentrée promoted by the Thebans in 369 (4.26.5). Thus, Pausanias separated the conquest of Messenia from the enslavement of the Messenians and their transformation into Helots. In a sense, in so doing he replicated the sequence of the Spartan subjugation that we found in Ephorus, except that Pausanias down-dated the first phase to the "First Messenian War" and the final enslavement to the "Second". He was certainly not the only ancient author to do so, and probably not the first. As we have seen, the idea that after the Spartan victory in the "First War" the Messenians had become dependant without being enslaved is found also in Aelian (*VH* 6.1), in a passage that reflects the same verses of Tyrtaeus quoted by Pausanias, but cannot depend on Pausanias himself. Unfortunately, it is impossible to locate in time the ultimate source of Aelian's passage, nor to say with any certainty if Pausanias depends on the same source.

7. The war on the Helots: a Spartan tradition?

Before moving towards a conclusion, a point should be emphasized. Of all the sources discussed so far, only a tiny minority can be connected tentatively with views held by the Spartans themselves. Nevertheless, these few bits and pieces suggest a reflection that could explain a central aspect of almost all the sources. Very much in keeping with classic Spartan ideology, Tyrtaeus' verses confirm that the Spartans liked to think that whatever they possessed, they had conquered with their strength and courage: their land in Laconia, under the leadership of the Heraclids, and their land in Messenia following their king Theopompus; the same concept, in a more articulate form, is attributed by Isocrates to Archidamus. These same Spartans, at least since the sixth century—but most scholars would date this much earlier—peacefully kept the Helots as a self-reproducing slave population and were fed by them, instead of acquiring new slaves by way of trade or, more like Spartans, of war. At the same time, Aristotle tells that every year the Spartan ephors upon entering their tenure declared war on the Helots (fr. 543 Gigon *ap.* Plut. *Lyc.* 28.7). The reason for this famously odd custom, according to Aristotle, was that the declaration allowed the Spartans to kill Helots, if appropriate, without incurring into ritual pollution. One wonders if the Spartans could not have simply purified themselves after killing a Helot, just like an Athenian would do for killing a slave;[81] was it because the Spartans were killing Helots much more frequently than other Greek

---

[81] See Fisher 1993: 63-64. For modern interpretations of Aristotle, see Link 1994: 8-9 with further references.

slave-owners killed their slaves? Perhaps, but perhaps the declaration of war could also serve a further function: it allowed the Spartans to conceptualize their domination on their slaves as a result of their military superiority, affirmed by an ongoing victorious war.

In a society like the classical Spartan one, so strongly based on the performance of public rituals, this sort of permanent state of war could have had a more explicit symbolic meaning than the memory of a war fought in the distant past by their ancestors. One wonders whether the strange expression "war against the Helots" that recurs in Ephorus (*FGrHist* 70 F 117 *ap.* Strab. 8.5.4)[82] might not be the trace of a misunderstanding, a Spartan institution transformed by later authors into an event that had happened once in the past, according to a pattern well-attested in Greek historiography, particularly but not only in the case of religious rituals (incidentally, the murder of Teleclus at Limnae could belong to the same category).[83]

8. Conclusions

Some interesting lines of continuity emerge from the sources. First of all, there does not seem to have been a Spartan tradition on the origins of Helotry, or perhaps more cautiously, there are no traces whatsoever of such a tradition, not even in works inspired by the lively reworking of Spartan tradition that took place in the late third century BCE, such as Plutarch's *Life of Lycurgus*.[84] From Tyrtaeus to Isocrates, the Spartans seem to have thought that they had conquered their land and evicted its previous occupants, particularly on the Messenian side. They apparently accepted no distinction between Helots west or east of the Taygetos: they were all their slaves; as one could say, to the Spartans a Helot was a Helot was a Helot.

From a more general perspective, an interesting point that deserves emphasizing is the separation and difference in quality between accounts of the origins of Laconian and Messenian Helots. The reflection on the origins of the latter cannot be separated from the reflection on the Spartan conquest of Messenia, and was obviously triggered by political conflicts, the revolt in the fifth century and then the birth of independent Messene in the fourth. Although neither Thucydides nor Ephorus are likely to reflect precisely what the Messenians themselves thought of their past,[85] their views on the enslavement of the old Messenians were certainly

....

[82] Cf. also ὁ εἰλωτικὸς πόλεμος in Plut. *mul. virt.* 8 (=*mor.* 247a).

[83] See Strab. 6.1.6 and 8.4.9, and Paus. 4.4.2-3; cf. now Leitao 1999.

[84] Plut. *Lyk.* 2.1, given its chronology, is probably simply a short allusion to the Helos story; see Ducat 1990: 70.

[85] Thucydides' perspective, that follows neither the Spartan nor the Messenian viewpoint but is on the whole more sympathetic to the former, has been investigated very convincingly by Figueira 1999: 213.

and deeply influenced by the claim to freedom staked by the Messenians of their times. Instead, all sources on the origins of Helotry in Laconia, with the problematic exception of Antiochus, accept the connection Helots-Helos, a connection that was obviously the result of erudite speculation; in other words, narratives on the origins of Laconian Helotry are more likely to have originated on the desk of some historian than to be a product however mediated of political conflicts.[86] In their attempt at explaining Laconian Helotry in ethnic terms, ancient historians were clearly applying to it an explanatory scheme developed for Messenian Helotry. Incidentally, this remarkable readiness to assume parallel developments in the early histories of Laconia and Messenia worked both ways, and finds its most accomplished expression in Ephorus' narrative of the two Doric kingdoms.

A further parallel between ancient views of the origins of Laconian and Messenian Helotry pertains to how the enslavement of the local populations came about. Most or all ancient authors saw the enslavement in both Laconia and Messenia as the result of defeat in war, but the defeated community, as far as it is possible to tell, was considered to have been already in a relation of more or less strict dependency from the conqueror at the time of the war.[87] Therefore, in both cases the war itself was a sort of rebellion: both the people of Helos and the Messenians were reduced to Helotry after they had rejected some less heavy imposition. It is difficult to say exactly where this idea came from. It is moderately pro-Spartan, in that it implies that somehow the would-be Helots had drawn the punishment upon themselves, but it was entrenched enough for a pro-Messenian author like Pausanias not to discard it outright. Even in this case, in all likelihood it was Messenia that set the pattern: in the fourth century, Plato seems to have seen an obvious association between Messenian Helots and revolt.[88] Incidentally, the connection between Helotry and revolt underlines an interesting fact: although the liberation of Messenia certainly triggered a certain amount of pro-Messenian reworking of the past, mainstream Greek historiography seems to have kept a moderately pro-Spartan stance. Fourth-century Messenians' views of their past remain rather obscure.

The idea of an incoming conquering group that appropriates the land of the indigenous inhabitants and enslaves them is nowhere explicitly attested in ancient

....

[86] This tentative conclusion keeps account of the possibility, suggested to me by Massimo Nafissi, that interest in the ethnic identity of the Helots of Laconia was triggered by the Athenians' attempt at destabilizing Laconia moving from Cythera during the Peloponnesian war (Thuc. 5.14).

[87] Even in Laconia, the perioikic cities, of which Helos was one, albeit receiving equality of rights with the Dorians of Sparta, accepted to obey them, according to Ephorus (*FGrHist* 70 F 117).

[88] See Plat. *Leg.* 6.777b-c and Ducat 1990: 83-89.

sources on Helotry.[89] Even in Theopompus' version, the only one that bears a significant resemblance to the modern *vulgata*, there was certainly a precise explanation for the fact that only the Achaeans of Helos had been enslaved. Thucydides' view of the enslavement of the Messenians may also have been similar to the modern *vulgata*, but his text is too laconic to decide either way, and there are strong reasons to think that even here, the ancient source might allude to a more complex process. In other words, what I called the modern *vulgata* on the conquest of the Helots, envisaging the origins of Helotry as a parallel process of conquest of the land and enslavement of its inhabitants by the Dorian Spartans, is not based on the ancient sources, but rather on an idiosyncratic selection of details taken from some of them. This does not mean that it is wrong, but only, that it cannot claim for itself the authority enjoyed among classicists by anything written in Greek.

More importantly, this investigation of sources draws attention to the fact that ancient ideas on the origins of Helotry did not exist in a scholarly vacuum. On the contrary, even though some of the texts that have been discussed are certainly to some extent the product of erudite speculation, they all show more or less clear signs of reacting to the cultural and political environment in which they were composed. In this perspective, the ancient sources themselves preserve all their importance as evidence: first and foremost, evidence not for the origins of Helotry and the early history of Laconia and Messenia, but rather, for the way in which the changing political map of the southern Peloponnese challenged subsequent generations of Greeks to rethink the crucial "time of the origins", compelling them to revise critically previous notions and adapt them to new viewpoints and new agendas.[90]

....

[89] That no ancient source explicitly states a direct connection between conquest and enslavement, and particularly between conquest by the Dorians and mass enslavement of the pre-Dorians, has been emphasized particularly by Ducat 1990: 69.

[90] Besides the debt to the participants in the Workshop at Harvard in 2001, this article owes a great deal to the careful reading and competent remarks of Susanne Ebbinghaus, Massimo Nafissi and Eric Robinson. While ultimate responsibility for the views expressed here is the author's, their help has done much to improve the present text.

Bibliography

Alcock, S. E. 2001. "The Peculiar Book IV and the Problem of the Messenian Past." In Alcock, Cherry and Elsner 2001: 142-153.

Alcock, S. E., J. F. Cherry and J. Elsner. (eds.). 2001. *Pausanias: Travel and Memory in Roman Greece.* Oxford and New York.

Bearzot, A. 1997. "Cassandro e la ricostruzione di Tebe: propaganda filellenica e interessi peloponnesiaci." In J. Bintliff (ed.), *Recent Developments in the History and Archaeology of Central Greece.* Oxford: 265-276.

Bingen, J. (ed.). 1996. *Pausanias historien.* (Entretiens de la Fondation Hardt 41). Geneva.

Bockisch, G. 1985. "Die Helotisierung der Messenier. Ein Interpretationsversuch zu Pausanias IV 14, 4f." In H. Kreißig and F. Kühnert (eds.), *Antike Abhängigkeitsformen in den griechischen Gebieten ohne Polisstruktur und den römischen Provinzen.* Berlin: 29-48.

Bowie, E. 1986. "Early Greek Elegy, Symposium and Public Festival." *Journal of Hellenic Studies* 106: 13-35.

_____. 1990."*Miles Ludens?* The Problem of Martial Exhortation in Early Greek Elegy." In O. Murray (ed.), *Sympotica: A Symposium on the Symposion.* Oxford : 221-229.

Busolt, G. 1893. *Griechische Geschichte bis zur Schlacht bei Chaironeia.* Vol. 1. Gotha.

Cartledge, P. 1987. *Agesilaos and the Crisis of Sparta.* Baltimore and London.

_____. 2002. *Sparta and Lakonia: A Regional History 1300 to 362 BC.* Second edition. London and New York.

Ciaceri, E. 1928. *Storia della Magna Grecia I.* Milano.

Clauss, M. 1983. *Sparta. Eine Einführung in seine Geschichte und Zivilisation.* München.

Cordano, F. 1995. "La forzata partenza dei fondatori di Taranto nell'attualità del V secolo a.C." In M. Sordi (ed.), *Coercizione e mobilità umana nel mondo antico.* (Contributi dell'istituto di storia antica 21). Milano: 51-59.

Dalfen, J. 1996. "Dinge, die Pausanias nicht sagt." In R. Faber and B. Seidensticker (eds.), *Worte, Bilder, Töne. Studien zur Antike und Antikenrezeption Bernhard Kytzler zu ehren*. Würzburg: 159-177.

Dipersia, G. 1974. "La nuova popolazione di Messene al tempo di Epaminonda." In M. Sordi (ed.), *Propaganda e persuasione occulta nell'antichità*. (Contributi dell'istituto di storia antica 2). Milan: 54-61.

Ducat, J. 1974. "Le mépris des Hilotes." *Annales (ESC)* 30: 1451-1464.

———. 1978. "Aspects de l'hilotisme." *Ancient Society* 9: 5-46.

———. 1985. "Isocrate et les Hilotes." In R. Braun (ed.), *Hommage à Jean Granarolo: philologie, littératures et histoire anciennes*. (Annales de la Faculté des lettres et sciences humaines de Nice 50). Nice: 95-101.

———. 1990. *Les Hilotes*. (Bulletin de correspondance hellénique, Supplément 20). Athens and Paris.

———. 1994. *Les Pénestes de Thessalie*. (Annales Littéraires de l'Université de Besançon 512). Paris.

Figueira, T. 1999. "The Evolution of the Messenian Identity." In S. Hodkinson and A. Powell (eds.), *Sparta: New Perspectives*. London: 211-244.

Fisher, N. R. E. 1993. *Slavery in Classical Greece*. London.

Flower, M. 1994. *Theopompus of Chios: History and Rhetoric in the Fourth Century BC*. Oxford.

Fuscagni, S. 1975. "Callistene di Olinto e la 'Vita di Pelopida' di Plutarco." In M. Sordi (ed.), *Storiografia e propaganda*. (Contributi dell'istituto di storia antica 3). Milan: 31-55.

Garlan, Y. 1995. *Les esclaves en Grèce ancienne*. Second edition. Paris.

Giovannini, A. 1969. *Étude historique sur les origines du Catalogue des vaisseaux*. Bern.

Goldmann, S. 1991. "Topoi des Gedenkens. Pausanias' Reise durch die griechische Gedächtnislandschaft." In A. Haverkamp and R. Lachmann (eds.), *Gedächtniskunst: Raum – Bild – Schrift. Studien zur Mnemotechnik*. Frankfurt: 145-164.

Habicht, C. 1985. *Pausanias' Guide to Ancient Greece*. Berkeley.

Harder, A. 1991. "Euripides' Temenos and Temenidai." In H. Hofmann and A. Harder (eds.), *Fragmenta dramatica. Beiträge zur Interpretation der griechischen Tragikerfragmente und ihrer Wirkungsgeschichte*. Göttingen: 117-135.

Hodkinson, S. 2000. *Property and Wealth in Classical Sparta*. London.

Hölscher, T. 1974. "Die Nike der Messenier und Naupaktier in Olympia." *Jahrbuch des Deutschen Archäologischen Instituts* 89: 70-111.

Hope Simpson, R. 1966. "The Seven Cities Offered by Agamemnon to Achilles." *Annual of the British School at Athens* 61: 113-131.

Huxley, G. L. 1962. *Early Sparta*. Cambridge, MA.

Jacoby, F. 1926. *Die Fragmente der griechischen Historiker* 2c. *Kommentar zu Nr. 64-105*. Berlin.

_____. 1930. *Die Fragmente der griechischen Historiker* 2d. *Kommentar zu Nr. 106-261*. Berlin.

_____. 1943. *Fragmente der griechischen Historiker* IIIa. *Kommentar, 265 Rhianos von Bene (Kreta)*. Leiden.

Jehne, M. 1994. *Koine Eirene*. Stuttgart.

Kennell, N. 1999. "From *perioikoi* to *poleis*." In S. Hodkinson and A. Powell (eds.), *Sparta: New Perspectives*. London: 189-210.

Kiechle, F. 1959. *Messenische Studien. Untersuchungen zur Geschichte der Messenischen Kriege und der Auswanderung der Messenier*. Kallmünz.

_____. 1963. *Lakonien und Sparta*. Munich.

Knoepfler, D., and M. Piérart (eds.). 2001. *Éditer, traduire, commenter Pausanias en l'an 2000*. Geneva.

Leitao, D. 1999. "Solon on the Beach: Some Pragmatic Functions of the *Limen* in Initiatory Myth and Ritual." In M. W. Padilla (ed.), *Rites of Passage in Ancient Greece: Literature, Religion, Society*. (Bucknell Review 43.1). Lewisburg: 247-277.

Lévêque, P. 1979. "Les dépendants du type hilote." In *Terre et paysans dépendants dans les sociétés antiques. Colloque international tenu à Besançon les 2 et 3 mai 1974*. Paris: 114-119.

Link, S. 1994. *Der Kosmos Sparta. Recht und Sitte in klassischer Zeit*. Darmstadt.

Lotze, D. 1959. Μεταξὺ ἐλευθέρων καὶ δούλων. *Studien zur Rechtsstellung unfreier Landbevölkerungen in Griechenland bis zum 4. Jahrhundert v. Chr*. Berlin.

Lupi, M. 2000. *L'ordine delle generazioni. Classi di età e costumi matrimoniali nell'antica Sparta*. Bari.

Luraghi, N. 1994. *Tirannidi arcaiche in Sicilia e Magna Grecia da Panezio di Leontini alla caduta dei Dinomenidi.* Florence.

_____. 2001a. "Der Erdbebenaufstand und die Entstehung der messenischen Identität." In D. Papenfuß and V. M. Strocka (eds.), *Gab es das griechische Wunder? Griechenland zwischen dem Ende des 6. und der Mitte des 5. Jahrhunderts v. Chr.* Mainz: 279-301.

_____. 2001b. "Die Dreiteilung der Peloponnes. Wandlungen eines Gründungsmythos." In H.-J. Gehrke (ed.), *Geschichtsbilder und Gründungsmythen.* Würzburg: 37-63.

_____. 2002a. "Helotic Slavery Reconsidered." In A. Powell and S. Hodkinson (eds.), *Sparta: Beyond the Mirage.* London: 229-250.

_____. 2002b. "Helots called Messenians? A Note on Thuc. 1.101.2." *Classical Quarterly* 52: 588-592.

Maaß, M. 1978. *Die geometrischen Dreifüße von Olympia.* (Olympische Forschungen 10). Berlin.

Matthaiou, A. 2001. "Δύο ἱστορικὲς ἐπιγραφὲς τῆς Μεσσήνης." In V. Mitsopoulos-Leon (ed.), *Forschungen in der Peloponnes.* (Österreichisches Archäologisches Institut, Sonderschriften 38). Athens: 221-231.

Mazzarino, S. 1966. *Il pensiero storico classico.* Vol. 1. Roma and Bari.

Meyer, Ernst. 1978. "Messenien." *Realenzyklopädie der classischen Altertumswissenscahft.* Suppl. 15: 136-289.

Meyer, Eduard. 1937. *Geschichte des Altertums.* Vol. 3. Second revised edition. Stuttgart.

Moscati Castelnuovo, L. 1991. "Iloti e fondazione di Taranto." *Latomus* 50: 64-79.

Musti, D. and M. Torelli (eds.). 1982. *Pausania. Guida della Grecia.* Vol. 1. *L'Attica.* Milan.

Musti, D. 1988. *Strabone e la Magna Grecia. Città e popoli dell'Italia antica.* Padova.

Nafissi, M. 1991. *La nascita del kosmos. Studi sulla storia e la società di Sparta.* Napoli.

_____. 1995. In E. Lippolis, S. Garraffo and M. Nafissi. *Culti greci in Occidente.* Vol. 1. *Taranto.* Taranto.

_____. 1999. "From Sparta to Taras: *nomima, ktiseis* and Relationships between Colony and Mother City." In S. Hodkinson and A. Powell (eds.), *Sparta: New Perspectives.* London: 251-258.

Nicolai, R. 1992. *La storiografia nell'educazione antica.* Pisa.

Niese, B. 1891. "Die ältere Geschichte Messeniens." *Hermes* 26: 1-32.

Oliva, P. 1971. *Sparta and her Social Problems.* Amsterdam and Prague.

Pais, E. 1922. *Italia antica.* Vol. 2. Bologna.

Parmeggiani, G. 1999. "Mito e *spatium historicum* nelle *Storie* di Eforo di Cuma." *Rivista storica dell'antichità* 29: 107-125.

Pearson, L. 1962. "The Pseudo-History of Messenia and its Authors." *Historia* 11: 397-426.

Roebuck, C. A. 1941. *A History of Messenia from 369 to 146 B.C.* Chicago.

Schwartz, E. 1899. "Tyrtaeos." *Hermes* 34: 428-468.

Shipley, G. 1997. "'The Other Lakedaimonians': The Dependent Perioikic Poleis of Laconia and Messenia." In M.H. Hansen (ed.), *The Polis as an Urban Centre and as a Political Community.* (Acts of the Copenhagen Polis Centre 4). Copenhagen: 189-281.

_____. 2000. "The Extent of Spartan Territory in the Late Classical and Hellenistic Periods." *Annual of the British School at Athens* 95: 367-390.

Shrimpton, G. 1991. *Theopompus the Historian.* Montreal.

Slings, S. R. 2000. *Symposium: Speech and Ideology. Two Hermeneutical Issues in Early Greek Lyric, with Special Reference to Mymnermus.* (Koninklijke Nederlandse Akademie van Wetenschappen, Medelingen van de Afdeling Letterkunde 63.1). Amsterdam.

Stylianou, P. J. 1998. *A Historical Commentary on Diodorus Siculus, Book 15.* Oxford.

Themelis, P. G. 1987. " 'Ανασκαφὴ Μεσσήνης." Πρακτικὰ τῆς ἐν 'Αθήναις ἀρχαιολογικῆς ἑταιρείας 1987 [1991]: 73-104.

_____. 1988. " 'Ανασκαφὴ Μεσσήνης." Πρακτικὰ τῆς ἐν 'Αθήναις ἀρχαιολογικῆς ἑταιρείας 1988 [1991]: 43-79.

_____. 1991. " 'Ανασκαφὴ Μεσσήνης." Πρακτικὰ τῆς ἐν 'Αθήναις ἀρχαιολογικῆς ἑταιρείας 1991 [1994]: 85-128.

Vallet, G. 1958. *Rhégion et Zancle. Histoire, commerce et civilisation des cités chalcidiennes du détroit de Messine.* (Bibliothèque des écoles françaises d'Athènes et de Rome 189). Paris.

Vidal-Naquet, P. 1981. *Le chasseur noir. Formes de pensée et formes de société dans le mond grec.* Paris.

Visser, E. 1997. *Homers Katalog der Schiffe.* Stuttgart and Leipzig.

West, M. L. 1974. *Studies in Greek Elegy and Iambus.* Berlin and New York.

Whitby, M. 1994. "Two Shadows: Images of Spartans and Helots." In A. Powell and S. Hodkinson (eds.), *The Shadow of Sparta.* London and New York: 87-126.

Six

The Dorianization of the Messenians*

Jonathan M. Hall

It is an axiom of recent scholarship that the primordial and essential identity proclaimed by an ethnic group may often be a recent and illusory fiction, forged in the context of—and in response to—precise historical circumstances, but this view was actually anticipated already in 1922 by Max Weber, who emphasized that *subjective* beliefs in common descent were at the heart of ethnic consciousness, regardless of "whether or not an objective blood relationship exists".[1] Operating on the assumption that *all* group identities—even in situations where a deep and pervasive historical continuity can be demonstrated—need to be continuously and actively reconstructed in changing circumstances rather than passively inherited within a system of intergenerational homeostasis, I here seek to account for the possible historical circumstances in which the Messenians gained, maintained and chartered cognizance both of their own identity and of their affiliation to a broader Dorian ethnocommunity.

For Pausanias, writing shortly after the middle of the second century of our era, the Dorian heritage of the Messenians was taken for granted. "The Messenians", he says, "were actually wandering outside the Peloponnese for three hundred years, in which time they clearly abandoned none of the customs of their homeland nor did they cease to speak the Doric dialect, but even in my own day preserve it more accurately than any of the other Peloponnesians" (4.27.11). Interestingly, this linguistic

....

* I am especially grateful to Nino Luraghi for providing me with useful suggestions and insights at various stages in the development and execution of this chapter. I should also like to thank both him and Sue Alcock for their original invitation to attend the workshop at which these ideas were first aired.

[1] Weber 1978: 389. Note that Weber is not here establishing a classificatory dichotomy between 'subjective ethnicity' and 'objective ethnicity', as Hall 1992 supposes. For a summary of theoretical definitions of ethnicity, see Hall 1997: 17-33, 2002: 9-19.

observation conforms with the findings of philologists, who not only assign the Messenian dialect to the *Doris severior* group—believed by many to comprise a more conservative stratum within the West Greek dialect group—but also consider Messenian to be one of the least innovative of all the West Greek dialects.[2] Further indications of just how rooted this Dorian heritage had become in the Messenian landscape are provided by the periegete's description of a ruined city named Dorion in the upper Pamisos Valley (4.33.7) and of a sacred grove, outside the city of Pharai, dedicated to Apollo Karneios (4.31.1)—a god whose festival was, according to Thoukydides (5.54.2), particularly sacred among the Dorians. Nor was there any reason for Pausanias to believe that the Messenians' affirmations of Dorian descent were recent: in describing events of the Second Messenian War, conventionally dated to the mid-seventh century,[3] he recounts how the Messenians accused their Lakonian aggressors of impiety, "since it was out of pure greed that they were attacking men who were kinsfolk (συγγενεῖς), showing no respect for the ancestral gods of the Dorians and Herakles above all" (4.8.2).

The simplest way of explaining why the Messenians of Pausanias' day should have considered themselves Dorians would be to invoke the ancient traditions that told how the Dorians had migrated south from their homeland in central Greece and conquered the Peloponnesian territories of the Argolid, Lakonia, Messenia and Korinthia, thus putting an end to the "Akhaian" dynasties portrayed in the Homeric epics.[4] For what it is worth, stylistic analysis of Dark Age II pottery from Messenia (ca. 975-800 BC) suggests a certain homogeneity with the contemporary styles of Lakonia as well as an association with a broader West Greek *koinê* that included Ithaka, Akhaia and Aitolia.[5] Similarly, the Messenian dialect, in addition to its affiliation to the West Greek dialect group, shares a number of specific

....

[2] *Doris severior* is the term designated by Ahrens (1843) for the group of West Greek dialects that assimilate the lengthened vowels created by the three compensatory lengthenings ('secondary vowels') with the pre-existing 'primary' long vowels; it includes the Theran, Kyrenean, Kretan, Lakonian, Herakleian and Messenian dialects. *Doris mitior*, instead, denotes those West Greek dialects that created new 'close' long vowels to represent 'secondary' vowels. See Bartonek (1972: 117) for the intermediate category of *Doris media*. Most believe *Doris mitior* to be more innovative with respect to *Doris severior*, though see Ruijgh (1986, 1989) who argues that the assimilation of primary and secondary vowels was a later phenomenon, and that therefore *Doris severior* and *Doris media* are more innovative than *Doris mitior*. For the innovation coefficients of the Messenian dialects, see Bartonek 1972: 91, 159, 185.

[3] For doubts about the historicity of the Second Messenian War, see Osborne 1996: 178; Luraghi 2001a: 280.

[4] For the traditions, see Vanschoonwinkel 1991: 335-366.

[5] Coulson 1986: 55, 71; cf. Coulson 1985: 66. These observations may need to be revised slightly with the full publication of the Pylos Regional Archaeological Project: see Davis et al. 1997: 452.

features with the dialect of Lakonia.[6] Yet, quite apart from the fact that the traditions associated with the coming of the Dorians would also require archaeological and linguistic correlations with the material culture and dialects of the Argolid which cannot be sustained, the historicity of those very traditions has itself come under increasing scrutiny. Supposed archaeological innovations (e.g. ironworking, the Protogeometric style of pottery, cremation, single burial in cist tombs and new types of weapons and jewellery), once thought to indicate the arrival in the Peloponnese of a new northern population, have now proved to be either anterior to the destructions of the Mycenaean palaces or first attested in areas such as Attika or Euboia which never claimed to be Dorian.[7] Similarly, the structural correspondences shared by the so-called "Doric" dialects of the Peloponnese assume less significance in light of the observation that no single shared linguistic innovation can be isolated that is not also found in at least one other non-Doric dialect, suggesting that the similarities may have derived from prolonged "lateral" contact rather than common descent from a single "proto-Doric" linguistic ancestor.[8] Even the literary tradition for the Dorian invasion—defended by some historians as the only reliable testimony for the migration[9]—appears, on closer examination, to be a composite amalgam of originally independent charter myths telling of separate ancestral leaders (Doros; Aigimios; the Herakleidai) and different homelands (Doris; Hestiaiotis) which can only have coalesced in the centuries after the supposed date of the invasion.[10]

There is, then, a growing realization among scholars that the legend of the Dorian invasion may be a charter myth, invented to legitimate a common Dorian ethnicity that was itself the product of the protohistoric, rather than prehistoric, period. The myth may have developed initially in Asia Minor, where Dorians coexisted alongside Ionians and Aiolians,[11] or—as I have attempted to argue elsewhere—in the context of Spartan conquests of the ninth and eighth centuries BC.[12] In the latter case, the apparent cultural similarities between Lakonia and Messenia in the tenth century need not be accidental, but neither need they be relevant to later, more

....

6 Bartonek 1972: 186. It should be noted, however, that characterizations of the Messenian dialect are, for the most part, based on inscriptions that postdate Epameinondas' (re)foundation of Messene in 369 BC: see further below.
7 For a summary: Hall 1997: 114-128, 2002: 75-76, 78-79.
8 E.g. López Eire 1978: 293, 296; Fernández Alvarez 1981: 39. See Hall 1997: 161-162, 2002: 78.
9 E.g. Brillante 1984; Musti 1985: 43-44.
10 See Hall 1997: 56-65.
11 So Ulf 1996, reviving a position previously held by Duncker 1881: 365; Beloch 1913: 82; and De Sanctis 1939: 78-79.
12 Hall 2002: 82-89.

subjective and self-conscious professions of identity. That is to say, the Dorianization of the Spartans did not necessarily have to entail the simultaneous Dorianization of neighbouring Messenians, and indeed there is no hint that the seventh-century Spartan poet Tyrtaios regarded the Messenians as Dorians. Granted, the omissions of a poet whose writings exist in only fragmentary form should not be overstated. On the other hand, since it is commonly held that much of Tyrtaios' poetry was composed against the backdrop of Spartan hostilities against the Messenians, it becomes difficult to understand why the Dorian ancestry of the Spartans should be emphasized if it were an inheritance common to both Spartans and Messenians. For example, Tyrtaios proclaims how "Zeus himself, the husband of fair-crowned Hera, gave this city (Sparta) to the Herakleidai, in whose company we (Dorians) left windy Erineos and arrived in the broad Peloponnese" (fr. 2 West), and elsewhere describes a battle-scene with "Pamphyloi, Hylleis and (Dymanes), separately, brandishing in their hands man-slaying spears of ash" (fr. 19 West).[13] The Hylleis, Dymanes and Pamphyloi were the distinctive *phulai* ("tribes" in the political, rather than ethnic, sense) in many Dorian cities and—like the reference to the Dorian-Heraklid foundation of Sparta—would seem to denote a distinctive quality about the Spartans that loses its force were it equally true of the Messenians.[14]

A *terminus ante quem* for the Dorianization of the Messenians is provided by Herodotos who, in his account of the battle line-up at Salamis in 480 BC, describes the Peloponnese as being inhabited by seven *ethnê*. Of these, two—the Arkadians and the Kynourians—are autochthonous; one, the Akhaians, is not autochthonous in the strict sense but had always lived in the Peloponnese, fleeing the territories of Lakonia and the Argolid and settling along the southern shore of the Korinthian Gulf at the time of the Dorian invasion. The four remaining populations are descended from immigrants: the settlers of Elis originated from Aitolia; the Paroreatai were formerly Lemnians; the cities of Hermione and Asine were populated by Dryopes; but the majority of cities—and certainly the most famous ones—were founded by the Dorians (8.73.1-2). The Messenians are not explicitly mentioned (save for the inhabitants of the perioikic community of Asine), but they should certainly be classified by default among the Dorian inhabitants of the Peloponnese.

The question of the Messenians' Dorian affiliations cannot be dissociated from the traditions relating to the origins of the Messenians themselves. These are recounted most fully in the fourth book of Pausanias' *Periegesis*, whose historiographical complexities are well known and need not be rehearsed in detail here.

....

[13] The name 'Dymanes' is a reasonable restoration for the lacuna that occurs at this point in the papyrus.

[14] For the Dorian *phulai*, see Roussel 1976: 221-229.

Suffice it to say that Pausanias' self-professed reliance upon the third-century prose-writer Myron of Priene and the poet Rhianos of Bene for his account of the Second Messenian War has suggested to some that the Messenian "history" that Pausanias recounts is in fact an invented tradition, coined after the (re)foundation of Messene in 369 BC to lend historical depth and legitimacy to a population whose enslavement to the Spartans throughout the Archaic and much of the Classical periods had robbed it of its own authentic history and identity.[15] Others have refused to believe that the Messenians' historical memory could have been entirely extinguished during the centuries of their servitude and suggest that Messenian identity was preserved through the transmission of mythical traditions and ritual practices, perhaps serving as a type of symbolic resistance to Spartan dominion.[16]

The *ethnikon* employed to denote the Messenians—"Messenioi" (Μεσσήνιοι) in Attic; "Messanioi" (Μεσσάνιοι) in its epichoric Doric form—and its relationship with the toponym "Messenia" (Μεσσηνία) are not quite as straightforward as might be assumed. The adjectival *i*-grade that appears between the root and the termination in "Messenia" might, by analogy with toponyms such as Aitolia, Akhaïa, Boiotia or Makedonia, have suggested that it belongs to the category of social nomenclature that Fritz Gschnitzer defines as "Stammesgemeinde"—i.e., where a region is named after the population group that inhabits it.[17] Yet if this were the case, we would expect the *ethnikon* to be "Messenoi" without the *i*-grade (cf. Aitoloi, Akhaioi, Boiotoi, Makedones). The fact that the adjectival *i*-grade does appear in the *ethnikon* should indicate instead that the Messenians are what Gschnitzer terms an "Ortsgemeinde"—that is, where a community takes its name from a central settlement ("Athenaioi" < "Athenai"; "Korinthioi" < "Korinthos"; "Lakedaimonioi" < "Lakedaimon") or, less commonly, a broader region ("Eleioi" < "Elis"; "Peloponnesioi" < "Peloponnesos").[18] Indeed, it is in this latter, regional sense that the *ethnikon* "Messenioi" is commonly understood, yet there is a

....

[15] See, however, Luraghi (2001a, 2002, and this volume) who questions the *opinio communis* that all Messenians were enslaved to Sparta at such an early date.

[16] For the sceptical view of Messenian history, see *inter alios* Grote 1869: 421-440; Niese 1891: 26-30; Jacoby 1943: 112-181; Pearson 1962; Asheri 1983: 29-30; Musti and Torelli 1991: xii-xxviii. *Contra* Shero 1938: 504; Treves 1944: 104; Kiechle 1959; Zunino 1997. For more reconciliatory positions (and discussion of the debate): Alcock 1999; Luraghi 2002: 46-8; cf. Figueira 1999; Alcock 2001.

[17] Gschnitzer 1955.

[18] Hansen (1996) defines the former as a 'city-ethnic' and the latter as a 'regional-ethnic'. For 'Lakedaimonioi' as a city-ethnic and not a regional-ethnic, see Hall 2000: 77-80.

problem. The toponym "Messenia" is attested relatively late in our sources: instead, the form that we find in both Homer (*Od.* 21.15) and Tyrtaios (fr. 5 West) is "Messene". Since it has generally been assumed that a city named Messene cannot have existed prior to Epameinondas' foundation at the foot of Mount Ithome, modern scholars—following Strabo (8.5.8) and Pausanias (4.1.4)—have tended to understand "Messene" as designating a region rather than a specific settlement.[19] Yet recent excavations, conducted by Petros Themelis, have revealed that the site of Messene-Mavromati was in fact already occupied in the Geometric period,[20] making it a reasonable guess that a settlement named Messene—whether that situated below Ithome, by whose name it may also have been known,[21] or elsewhere—existed from an early period.[22] The simplest solution, then, would be to suppose that the *ethnikon* of the Messenians follows the norm attested elsewhere in Greece—namely, that "Messenioi" is a city-ethnic derived from the toponym "Messene", and that "Messenia" is a *ktêtikon* also derived from the primary toponym (cf. "Korinthia" < "Korinthos").[23]

Nevertheless, this conclusion carries a further implication. Mogens Herman Hansen has observed that in the vast majority of documented cases, the attestation of a city-ethnic implies not only a geographical, but also a political, identity: in other words, it marks its bearers as simultaneously members of both an urban and a political community.[24] Now clearly it makes little sense to attribute a sense of political identity to those Messenians enslaved as Helots by the Spartans. Nor is it reasonable to suppose that Messenian perioikoi adopted the city-ethnic "Messenioi" when they already possessed city-ethnics of their own.[25] If, then, we find the city-ethnic "Messenioi" employed prior to the liberation of Messenia, we can only conclude that it was a designation employed by those free inhabitants of Messenia who formed a political community-in-waiting—that is, the Messenians who had fled Spartan occupation in various waves, settling (among other places)

....

[19] See Deshours 1993: 43.

[20] For recent bibliography on the excavations, see Luraghi 2001a: 299 n. 82.

[21] See Diod. 19.54.5 and Plut. *Pel.* 24.5 with Luraghi 2001a: 300 n. 88.

[22] Luraghi 2002: 48-50 and in this volume, 112.

[23] As elsewhere in the Greek world, 'Messene' would include not only the physical settlement of Messene but also its surrounding territory. It is, however, unlikely that Messene's territory embraced the whole of the region that constitutes the modern *nomos* of Messenia. For 'Messenioi' as a city-ethnic, see Hansen 1996: 195.

[24] Hansen 1996.

[25] E.g. the Aithaies and Thouriatai mentioned in Thuc. 1.101.2.

Rhegion in Southern Italy,[26] Zankle-Messina in Sicily,[27] Kyrenaika,[28] and—above all—Lokrian Naupaktos, where the Messenian population served as valued allies of the Athenians during the Peloponnesian War.[29] To the extent that these Messenians (i) were scattered throughout various host-communities among whom they constituted a minority, (ii) entertained a desire to return to Peloponnesian Messenia, and (iii) retained a collective memory of the homeland, articulated not least through the employment of a city-ethnic derived from their ancient birthplace, it is reasonable to describe them as a diaspora.[30]

This distinction between the Messenians of the diaspora ("Messenioi") and those who remained in Messenia to endure enslavement on their own territory (Helots) is one that is preserved in a number of authors. Thus, in his account of the revolt of the mid-460s BC, Diodoros writes:

> For at this time, the Lakedaimonians had been waging war for a considerable period of time against the Helots and the Messenians and had finally prevailed over both. They let [the Messenians] depart from Ithome under truce, as has been said, but they punished those Helots who were most involved in the revolt and enslaved the rest (11.84.8).[31]

Thomas Figueira has argued that Diodoros is mistaken in identifying Helots and Messenians as two separate groups, and reasonably enough prefers to privilege Thoukydides' account of the revolt in which all the insurgents on Ithome were allowed to leave the Peloponnese under truce and were only threatened with

....

[26] Paus. 4.23 has Rhegion already under the rule of the Messenian tyrant Anaxilas in 664 BC and notes that his great-grandfather, Alkidamidas, arrived in Rhegion from Messenia at the time of the First Messenian War (cf. Antiokhos of Syrakousai *FGrHist* 555 F9), but this conflicts with the early fifth-century dates provided for Anaxilas' reign by Hdt 7.164.1 and Thuc. 6.4.6. It is, then, generally believed that Alkidamidas arrived in Rhegion with Messenian refugees in the late-seventh or early-sixth century: see Pearson 1962: 421; Asheri 1983: 32; and, defending Pausanias through a recalibration of Olympiad dating, Shaw 1999: 275-281. Luraghi 1994: 193-197 doubts the existence of a true Messenian element at Rhegion.

[27] *SEG* 26.311-314; Hdt. 7.164.1; Thuc. 6.4.6; Diod. 15.66.5; Strab. 6.2.3; Paus. 4.23.1-10. For the numismatic evidence, Robinson 1946. See, however, Luraghi 1994: 200-201, 209 who is more sceptical.

[28] Diod. 14.34.3; Paus. 4.26.2-4.

[29] Thuc. 1.103.3; Diod. 11.84; Paus. 4.24.7.

[30] See Safran 1991; Cohen 1997. The term is most famously associated with Jewish and Armenian communities overseas. It is commonly believed that it was first used of Jewish communities outside Judaea (e.g. in the third-century BC Greek translation of *Deuteronomy* 28.25), though in fact it is used approximately a century earlier by Plato (*Leg.* 699a-d) where it describes the hypothetical Athenian community that would have existed overseas had the Athenians not decided to unite in self-defence against the Persian invasion in 480 BC.

[31] Cf. Plut. *Cim.* 17.2. For the chronology of the rebellion, see Luraghi 2001a: 280-285.

enslavement if they attempted to return (1.103.1).[32] In his view, Thoukydides describes the dependent population of Messenia as both Messenians and Helots— the former in contexts where they interact with Athenians and the latter in contexts that "involve their social and political status *vis-à-vis* the Spartiates and the Lakedaimonian state".[33]

It may be, however, that Thoukydides is here being credited with more subtlety than is warranted. In his account of the revolt, no part seems to be played by diasporic Messenians of communities such as Zankle-Messina (i.e. Diodoros' "Messenioi"); instead, the rebels are Helots joined by perioikic communities such as the Thouriatai and the Aithiaies (1.101.2).[34] I would like to suggest that while Diodoros may have erred in giving the name "Messenioi" to the rebels *before* their departure from Ithome,[35] the distinction that he draws between those who fled Messenia ("Messenioi") and those who remained (Helots) is in fact one preserved also by Thoukydides, even if it is not always expressed with the clarity for which one might have wished.[36] For example, in an authorial comment on the revolt, he notes: "Most of the helots were descendants of the old Messenians (παλαιῶν Μεσσηνίων) who were then enslaved, and it is for this reason that all are called Messenians" (1.101.2). At first sight, this appears to corroborate Figueira's belief that the dependent population of Messenia could be described as both Helots and Messenians. On the other hand, the fact that Thoukydides has to explain contemporary usage of the ethnonym simultaneously implies that the usage is technically erroneous. Furthermore, Thoukydides quite deliberately adopts the language of temporal disjuncture rather than continuity: the Helots *used to be* (ἐγένοντο) Messenians, but *then* (τότε) they were enslaved; for this reason they have all been called (ἐκλήθησαν) Messenians (*sc.* but they should more properly be termed Helots).[37] A similar temporal distinction recurs in Thoukydides' description of Pylos as being located "400 stades from Sparta and . . . in the land that *was once* Messenia" (4.3.2; cf. 4.41.2), while in his account of the Sicilian expedition he notes that the Athenians were accompanied by "those who *are now* called the Messenians, from Naupaktos and Pylos, which was at that time under Athenian occupation" (7.57.8)—in other words, the Messenians of

....

[32] Figueira 1999: 217.

[33] Figueira 1999: 216.

[34] See Luraghi 2002: 60. For the perioikic communities of Lakonia and Messenia, see Shipley 1997.

[35] Hdt. 9.35.2, 9.64.2 and [Xen.] *Ath.pol.* also use the term 'Messenioi' to refer to the rebels of Messenia, but—as Thuc. 1.101.2 notes (see below)—this need not represent an 'internal' classification and may be a product of claims forged among the Messenian diaspora.

[36] *Contra* Luraghi 2001a: 291.

[37] Cf. Paus. 4.24.6: 'On top of this disaster [a destructive earthquake], those of the Helots who *used to be* Messenians launched a rebellion on Mount Ithome'.

the diaspora.[38] Perhaps the most explicit formulation, however, of this distinction between Messenians of the diaspora and the dependent population of Messenia comes in Thoukydides' description of the failure of the Peace of Nikias:

Πύλον μέντοι ἠξίουν σφίσιν ἀποδοῦναι· εἰ δὲ μή, Μεσσηνίους γε καὶ τοὺς Εἵλωτας ἐξαγαγεῖν, ὥσπερ καὶ αὐτοὶ τοὺς ἀπὸ Θράκης, ᾿Αθηναίους δὲ φρουρεῖν τὸ χωρίον αὐτούς, εἰ βούλονται. Πολλάκις δὲ καὶ πολλῶν λόγων γενομένων ἐν τῷ θέρει τούτῳ ἔπεισαν τοὺς ᾿Αθηναίους ὥστε ἐξαγαγεῖν ἐκ Πύλου Μεσσηνίους καὶ τοὺς ἄλλους Εἵλωτάς τε καὶ ὅσοι ηὐτομολήκεσαν ἐκ τῆς Λακωνικῆς. (5.35.6-7).

Meanwhile they [the Lakedaimonians] thought that Pylos should be restored to them, but if not that the Athenians should withdraw the Messenians and Helots, just as they had withdrawn the troops from Thrake, and guard the place themselves if they really wanted to. And after many speeches on many occasions over that summer, they persuaded the Athenians to withdraw from Pylos the *Messenians* and the *others*—both the *Helots* and those who had deserted from Lakonia.[39]

In short, Thoukydides never describes the contemporary inhabitants of Messenia as Messenians unless some temporal qualifier is added.

That Messenians of the diaspora should describe themselves as "Messenioi" in the fifth century finds confirmation in epigraphical evidence. The inscription on the triangular base of the famous Nike, carved by Paionios of Mende and erected to the southeast of the Temple of Zeus at Olympia, declares that the statue was dedicated to Olympian Zeus out of the tithed spoils of the enemy by "the Messanioi and the Naupaktians"—that is to say, by those Messenians of the diaspora whom the Athenians installed ca. 460 BC in the West Lokrian town of Naupaktos together with the original inhabitants of the city.[40] A similar victory dedication of the

....

[38] Cf. Thuc. 4.41.2.

[39] In Figueira 1999: 217, the final part of this passage is translated 'they persuaded the Athenians to withdraw from Pylos the Messenians and the other helots and anyone who had run away from Lakonia.' I should note, however, that the author has shown me page proofs indicating his corrections to the manuscript at this point that were regrettably not incorporated in the final published version.

[40] For the inscription: *IvO* 259; ML 74; *SEG.* 28. 432. For the possible historical context of the victory commemorated by the dedication, see Hölscher 1974. Beloch (1914: 165 n. 2) believed that the inscription referred to two separate communities resident at Naupaktos, though Asheri (1983: 35) tentatively speculates that both designations refer to the same community (i.e. Messenian by origin but Naupaktian by enfranchisement). For an unpublished inscription referring to a treaty between Messenians and Naupaktians, see Mastrokostas 1964: 295, cited in Figueira 1999: 214.

"Messanioi" at Delphi can hardly have been commissioned by Helots on a day-pass to Phokis;[41] the early fifth-century ruler of Rhegion, Mikythos, describes himself as Ῥηγῖνος καὶ Μεσσήνιος (Rhegian and Messenian) on the dedications he offered at Olympia;[42] and the funerary stele of a certain Skoteas, buried at Athens, declares that he was a "Messanios".[43]

It is not, however, sufficient to demonstrate that Messenians of the diaspora called themselves "Messenioi". Rather, the case needs to be made that this ethnonym was not regularly employed by the resident population of Messenia prior to liberation. Two pieces of potentially contradictory evidence need to be considered. The first is the now near-universal belief that a *stele*, datable to the mid-sixth century and set up on the frontier between Lakonia and Arkadia, carried a treaty forbidding the Arkadians to enfranchise Messenian Helots who might flee across the border.[44] This would seemingly indicate that the Archaic population of Messenia was already named "Messenioi" in the sixth century, but in reality this "evidence" may be nothing more than a mirage of modern historiography. No trace of the *stele*—let alone concrete indications for its date—has ever come to light. It is known through a reference in Ploutarkhos' *Greek Questions* (repeated in the *Roman Questions* [*Mor.* 277c]), which seeks to provide an answer to the question, "Who are the *khrêstoi* among the Arkadians and Lakedaimonians?" Ploutarkhos writes:

> When the Lakedaimonians had come to terms with the Tegeates, they made a treaty and erected a common *stele* on the banks of the River Alpheios, on which it was written—among other things—that they should expel the Messenians from their land and not be able to make them *khrêstoi*. In interpreting this, Aristotle says that it was not possible to put someone to death for assistance lent to the pro-Spartan party among the Tegeates (*Mor.* 292b).

It is worth noting that it is not Aristotle (presumably Ploutarkhos' source here) who interprets the treaty's provisions as applying to the Helots of Messenia but rather the magisterial authority of Felix Jacoby, who opposed the term *khrêstoi* to the phrase ἄκρηστον ἦμεν ("to be unemployable" and, hence, "disenfranchised"?) in an inscription from Kretan Dreros.[45] Yet Aristotle is guilty of considerably more

....

[41] Daux 1937: 67-72; Jeffery 1990: 206 no. 8.

[42] *SEG* 28 431; cf. Paus. 5.26.4-5. See, however, Luraghi 1994: 226 who suggests that Mikythos here describes himself as a citizen of both Rhegion and Zankle-Messina rather than as a Rhegian citizen whose ethnic origins are Messenian.

[43] *IG* I² 1030.

[44] E.g. Leahy 1958: 163; Pritchett 1965: 125; Wade-Gery 1966: 297; Forrest 1968: 79; Ste. Croix 1972: 97; Cartledge 1979: 138-139.

[45] Jacoby 1944. The Dreros inscription is ML 2.

than a simple "misunderstanding" of the treaty if he can interpret the phrase "not make the Messenians *khrêstoi*" as a reference to internal political conflicts at Tegea,[46] and this should urge some caution on our part before jettisoning his explanation entirely.[47] In any case, given that this particular provision of the treaty (itself merely one of a series, according to Ploutarkhos) is evidently not cited directly from the inscription since it is rendered in the Attic, rather than Lakonian or Arkadian, dialect, we cannot be entirely certain that the term "Messenioi" was actually employed in the original treaty (if it ever existed), nor are there any compelling grounds—other than hypothetical reconstructions of Spartan-Tegean relations in the Archaic period—for assuming that such a treaty has to belong to the sixth century.[48] Furthermore, even if "Messenioi" was employed in an original sixth-century treaty, it need not refer to Helot refugees: David Asheri believes that the decree forbids the Tegeates from giving full citizen rights to already-settled groups of Messenians resident in Arkadia.[49] In this case, the ethnonym would refer to Messenians of the diaspora.

The second case is more complicated and involves two inscribed bronze spear butts—one dedicated at Olympia and reading "The Methanioi [captured and dedicated this] from the Lakedaimonians",[50] the other dedicated at the sanctuary of Apollo Korythos near Messenian Korone and reading "The Methanioi dedicated [this] from booty [captured from the] Athen[ians?]".[51] When the Korone spear butt was discovered, it was immediately associated with the already-known example from Olympia and both were interpreted as dedications by the small city-state of Methana in the Eastern Argolid. Lilian Jeffery, however, was troubled by the Korone dedication, seeing as it was offered in a local Messenian sanctuary at a considerable distance from the Argolid, and therefore suggested that in this case—but not in the case of the Olympian example—"Methanioi" was a local designation for the inhabitants of the Messenian perioikic town of Methone.[52] Robert Bauslaugh, by contrast, has argued that "Methanioi" is a local dialect form for

....

[46] E.g. Asheri 1983: 31: 'il giusto senso, già mal compreso al tempo di Aristotele . . .'

[47] See Braun 1994: 40-42.

[48] Moretti (1946: 101-103) prefers to date the treaty to the mid-fifth century, thus referring to the Helot revolt of the 460s BC; cf. Nafissi 1991: 141; Cawkwell 1993: 368-370; Luraghi 2001a: 288 n. 34. Braun (1994: 43-45) inclines towards a seventh-century date though admits that a date in the fifth century is entirely feasible. The reconstructions of Spartan and Tegean relations are ultimately based—sometimes rather fancifully—on Hdt. 1.66-68.

[49] Asheri 1983: 31. Kallisthenes (*FGrHist* 124 F23) referred to Arkadia as the second fatherland (δευτέρας πατρίδος) of Messenia.

[50] Roehl 1882, no. 46; *IvO* 247; *SGDI* no. 3369; Jeffery 1990: 182 no. 4.

[51] Versakis 1916: 88-89, 114-115; Jeffery 1990: 206 no. 3.

[52] Jeffery 1990: 177, 203-204.

"Messenioi".[53] Starting from Thoukydides' observation (4.41.2) that the Athenian general Demosthenes deployed a contingent of Messenian troops at Pylos on the grounds that they spoke the same dialect (ὁμόφωνοι) as the Spartans, he notes that Aristophanes frequently portrays Spartan dialect-speakers as uttering sibilants in place of Attic *theta*—for example, Ἀσαναῖοι (*Asanaioi*) for Attic Ἀθηναῖοι (*Athenaioi*).[54] A similar linguistic phenomenon may be detected in a treaty, probably to be dated to the later fifth century, which binds the Aitolian Erxadieis to follow "whithersoever the Spartans lead, both by land and sea" (κ]αὶ κὰ(θ) θάλα(θ)αν, rather than Attic καὶ κατὰ θάλατταν [θάλασσαν]).[55] In Bauslaugh's view, both the spear butt at Olympia and that at Korone represent dedications made by Messenian Helots in the wake of the revolt of the 460s against the Spartans and their Athenian allies, in which case we would have to accept that the Helots of Messenia regarded—and denominated—themselves as "Messenioi".

A number of objections may be levelled against this interpretation. The letter-forms of the inscriptions do not lend much assistance since our knowledge of the Archaic scripts for both Messenia and Methana is pitifully meagre, though it is worth noting that every letter form on the spear butts—especially, the more diagnostic characters such as *delta, epsilon, theta, kappa, lambda* and *pi*—can be matched with the (admittedly earlier) funerary stele of Androkles, discovered on the Methana peninsula.[56] The dialectal arguments, instead, are less compelling than they might appear. Firstly, the Greeks showed little interest in a properly linguistic analysis of dialects before the Hellenistic period, and even then the dialect groupings that were recognized did not conform exactly to the isoglosses identified by philologists today.[57] There is no reason to believe that Thoukydides was peculiar or exceptional in this regard and, in fact, in his account of how Demosthenes employed Messenians of Naupaktos in the vanguard of his campaign against the Ambrakiotes "because they spoke the Doric dialect" (3.112.4), it becomes clear that the Messenians are later described as ὁμόφωνοι not because of specific observable correspondences between the Lakonian and Messenian dialects, but because all the populations of western Greece spoke a broadly similar idiom.[58] Secondly, apart

....

[53] Bauslaugh 1990.

[54] Ar. *Lys.* 170, 980, 1244, 1250, 1300.

[55] *SEG* 26. 461. For the various dates ascribed to the treaty as well as interpretations concerning the identity of the Erxadieis, see Peek 1974; Cartledge 1976, 1978; Kelly 1978; Shipley 1997: 275 n. 53.

[56] *SEG* 11.391; Jeffery 1990: 181 no. 1.

[57] See Buck 1955: 14-15; Hainsworth 1967; Cassio 1984; Morpurgo Davies 1987; Hall 1995: 87-89, 1997: 174-177.

[58] Figueira (1999: 213) notes that later the Messenians join the Argives in singing the Doric Paian (Thuc. 7.44.6). For the employment of *homophônia* as a *topos* in Greek literature (and especially battle narratives), see Petrocelli 2001.

from the fact that the precise relationship between what we now read in the manuscripts of Aristophanes and what was actually heard on the Attic stage in the fifth century is poorly understood,[59] provisional acceptance that the Spartans pronounced aspirated dentals as sibilants does not automatically entail that they wrote sibilants as aspirated dentals. Thirdly, the spelling of θάλαθαν in the Spartan-Aitolian treaty is, as Bauslaugh admits,[60] unprecedented in the Lakonian dialect, but his appeals to other instances in both Doric and non-Doric dialects where *theta* is substituted for a sibilant (e.g. θεθμός (*thethmos*) for Attic θεσμός (*thesmos*), or πρόθθα (*proththa*) for Attic πρόσθα (*prostha*)[61] do not really establish a valid parallel since in all these other examples it is a question of the assimilation of a sibilant with a pre-existing aspirated dental—something that is evidently not the case with "Messenioi". In any case, the shift that Bauslaugh posits from the sibilant to *theta* is unattested in other Messenian inscriptions of the period. That the decision to inscribe the dedication on the base of the Olympia Nike in the Doric dialect was deliberate is indicated by the fact that Paionios' own signature is inscribed in the Ionic dialect. It would, then, be strange if the Messenians (named here "Messanioi" rather than "Methanioi") had employed a form of Doric that they did not actually speak.[62]

Finally, while we remain at a loss to provide a precise historical context in which troops from Argolic Methana might have scored a victory over the Spartans (and possibly the Athenians—if that is the correct restoration),[63] our knowledge of even relatively major events that occurred in the fifty or so years between the Persian Wars and the outbreak of the Peloponnesian War is hardly sufficient to exclude such a possibility. Jeffery's original unease about Methanians offering a dedication in a local Messenian sanctuary may have been occasioned by the assumption that Sparta exercised continuous and total control over the entire territory of Messenia. Yet there are grounds for supposing that this particular stretch of the Messenian coastline was not a centre of Helot habitation. Pausanias says that to the south of the sanctuary of

....

59 Harvey 1994: 44; Colvin 1995: 45.
60 Bauslaugh 1990: 664; cf. Cartledge 1976: 91.
61 Bauslaugh 1990: 663-664.
62 Interestingly, this is precisely the period in which Zankle-Messina began to issue coins with the Doric legend ΜΕΣΣΑΝΙΩΝ, despite having previously employed legends in the Khalkidian dialect: see Jeffery 1990: 243. Although Anaxilas of Rhegion was probably the first to promulgate an ideology of Messenian origins in the 490s BC in order to detach Rhegion and Zankle-Messina from the Khalkidian orbit (see Luraghi 1994: 200-203), it was evidently the middle decades of the fifth century that witnessed the critical stage in the construction of a Dorian consciousness among the Messenians of the diaspora.
63 The restoration is that of Jeffery 1990: 204. However, Versakis (1916: 114) restored the fragmentary inscription as Μεθάν[ιοι] ἀνέθε[ν] Ἀθάναι [ἐκ] λαΐδο[ς] (The Methanians dedicated [this] to Athena from the spoils), followed by Zunino 1997: 173. See Figueira 1999: 214.

Apollo Korythos lay Kolonides, whose population was originally Attic even if it learnt the Doric dialect and customs over time (4.34.8), and the city of New Asine (modern Koróni), supposedly granted by the Spartans to Dryopeans who had fled Argolic Asine (cf. 2.36.5; 3.7.4; 4.8.3). On the opposite (western) coast of the Akritas peninsula was Mothone, apparently settled with refugees from Argolic Nauplia (4.24.4; 4.27.8; 4.35.2). We cannot, then, rule out the possibility that dedicants from another Argolic city, Methana, might have made their way to a local Messenian sanctuary in a coastal region dominated by perioikic settlements.[64]

To sum up thus far, references in fifth-century literary accounts and inscriptions to "Messenioi" almost invariably denote Messenians resident overseas rather than in Messenia itself. Furthermore, it is these residents of the diasporic Messenian community who are described—and described themselves—as Dorian. This is clear from the Doric dialect employed on the joint Messenian and Naupaktian dedication at Olympia, but it is also evident from Thoukydides' enumeration of the contingents that fought in the Sicilian theatre of operations, where the Messenians of Naupaktos and those garrisoned by the Athenians at Pylos are mentioned immediately after the Dorians of Kerkyra and its metropolis, Korinth, and directly before the Dorians of Megara and its grand-daughter colony, Selinous (7.57.7-8). If it is really true that the Messenians of Tyrtaios' day were not necessarily considered Dorians (see above), then we would have to assume that this identity was forged among the Messenians of the diaspora—perhaps to neutralize the Spartans' own appeals to their Dorian superiority.[65] Certainly, it is scarcely credible that Herodotos derived his information for the Dorian ancestry of the Messenians (see above) from the dependent population of Messenia, given its subjugated and supposedly highly-policed condition,[66] and it is a more reasonable conjecture that his informants were either Messenians living in exile at Naupaktos or—perhaps more likely—their Athenian benefactors. This in turn, however, raises the possibility that the dependent population of Peloponnesian Messenia did not necessarily regard itself as Dorian—a possibility that finds some confirmation in the mythical traditions of Messenia.

If ancient authors are surprisingly reticent in the significance they attach to Epameinondas' establishment of Messene as capital of the newly liberated state of

....

[64] For a recent summary of the sanctuary of Apollo Korythos, together with its material connections to Sparta (a further indication of Korone's perioikic status), see Luraghi 2002: 50-3.

[65] For the rhetoric of Spartan (and Syrakousan) appeals to Dorian characteristics, see Alty 1982; Hornblower 1996: 61-80; Hall 1997: 37-38; Jones 1999: 30-31.

[66] The Spartans were famous for their periodic deportations of foreigners (e.g. Thuc 1.144; 2.39; Xen. *Lac.* 14.4; Pl. *Prt.* 342c; *Leg.* 950b). Given the fear they entertained during the Messenian Revolt of the 460s BC that the Athenians might eventually begin to sympathize with the plight of the Messenians (Thuc. 1.102.3), it is hard to believe that they practised a more open policy with regard to Messenia.

Messenia,[67] modern historians have perhaps tended to underestimate the immense difficulty with which this event must have been achieved. Presumably, claims had to be balanced between those liberated Helots who might have expected to take possession of the land they had formerly farmed for their Spartan masters and those returning Messenians of the diaspora who probably anticipated a handsome reward for having borne the brunt of the resistance against the Spartans and their allies during the Peloponnesian War. These conflicting claims find their reflex in our literary sources.[68] Diodoros (presumably following Ephoros) emphasizes the refoundation of Messene as a new home for those who had endured centuries of exile overseas:

> And so finally, and according to these circumstances, the Thebans founded Messene at the suggestion of Epameinondas, who gathered together Messenians from every direction and restored to them their ancient territory (15.66.6).[69]

Isokrates, by contrast, purports to present a Spartan viewpoint which privileges the liberation of the Helots over the repatriation of the diasporic Messenians. He has the Spartan king Arkhidamos complain:

> If they [the Thebans] were bringing back those who are really Messenians, they would still be committing wrong against us, but on seemingly nobler grounds. But now they are installing Helots next to us, so that the real danger is not that we shall wrongfully be deprived of our land but that we shall see it in the possession of our slaves (*Arch.* 28).[70]

What is interesting about this conflict of viewpoints is that it is almost precisely paralleled in Messenian traditions about the arrival of the first Dorians. When Pausanias comments that "the ancient Messenians were not dislodged by the Dorians but agreed to be ruled by Kresphontes and to divide up their land with the Dorians" (4.3.6), it is difficult not to recognize in his "ancient Messenians" (Μεσσηνίων τῶν ἀρχαίων . . . ὁ δῆμος) those "Messenians of old" (παλαιῶν Μεσσηνίων) whose enslavement on their own territory was described by Thoukydides (1.101.2), thus establishing in turn a correlation between the Dorian newcomers who arrived at the end of the Heroic Age and those Dorian Messenians of the diaspora who were repatriated by Epameinondas. Yet if Pausanias suggests a relatively pacific coexistence by

....

[67] Xenophon neglects entirely (and perhaps deliberately) to mention this event in the *Hellenika*.

[68] See generally Dipersia 1974; Asheri 1983: 37-38; Figueira 1999: 219-220; Luraghi 2002: 61-4.

[69] Cf. Plut. *Ages.* 34.1; *Pel.* 24.5; Nep. *Epam.* 8.5; *Pelop.* 4.3; Paus. 4.26-27.

[70] Cf. Alkidamas' support (ap. Schol. ad Arist. *Rh.* 1.13.1373b18) for the liberation of the helots on the grounds that nobody is a slave by nature. See Raaflaub, this volume.

the two groups, a more conflictual situation is presented by Ephoros (*FGrHist* 70 F116), who tells how Kresphontes originally intended to administer his kingdom through five cities—Stenyklaros, Pylos, Rhion, Mesola and Hyameitis—and to give to the Messenians the same political and judicial rights (ἰσονόμους) as were enjoyed by the Dorians, until the Dorians became annoyed at what they regarded as an inequitable settlement, thus forcing Kresphontes to change his mind and to gather all the Dorians together in Stenyklaros alone. Nikolaos of Damascus (*FGrHist* 90 F31) elaborates further and recounts how the conflict between the Dorians and the indigenous Messenians (ἐγχώριοι) over the equality of land divisions (ἰσόμοιρον) escalated to the point where the Dorians finally killed Kresphontes and all but one of his sons.

The myth of Kresphontes' murder was not itself a recent invention. It was in fact the subject of a Euripidean play which exists now only in a few fragments, though was probably first performed in the 420s BC, but in Euripides' version the perpetrator of the crime is Kresphontes' own brother, Polyphontes.[71] It is tempting, then, to suppose that the transfer of blame to the Dorians collectively was a later modification to the legend, forged in the context of the conflicts that arose when repatriated Messenians of the diaspora were settled alongside recently liberated farm labourers. Two other features of these stories may also point in the same direction. The first is the continued emphasis on the equality of shareholdings between the already resident Messenians and the newly arrived Dorians—a concern that tellingly reflects the provisions contained in the late sixth-century decree regulating the division of territory among former (ὑπαπροσθιδίον) and new (ἐπιΦοίκον) settlers at Naupaktos.[72] The second is the impression—given especially by Ephoros' account—that Dorians were outnumbered by the indigenous Messenians, perhaps by as many as four to one (on the basis of the five cities designated by Kresphontes). Since nothing is heard of Messenians at Rhegion after the expulsion of Anaxilas in the 460s (and the city was itself practically destroyed by Dionysios I in 387 BC) and since Naupaktos had been abandoned at the end of the Peloponnesian War, it is entirely possible that there were comparatively few Messenians to repatriate by 369 BC.[73]

If the Helots of Messenia were not always considered Dorians, what were they? Theopompos (*FGrHist* 115 F122) draws a parallel between the Spartans and the Thessalians in that "both equipped themselves with a slave force from the Hellenes

....

[71] Cf. Pearson 1962: 405; Luraghi 2001b: 51-52. For a text and translation of the surviving fragments of the *Kresphontes*: Harder 1985.

[72] ML 13. For similar provisions in a fourth-century inscription that purports to replicate the original founding-decree of Kyrene, see ML 5.

[73] Asheri 1983: 39.

who formerly occupied the land which they now hold—the former from the Akhaians, the Thessalians from the Perrhaiboi and Magnesians". Theopompos may be ascribing an Akhaian identity to the Helots of Lakonia only, though there is nothing to preclude a wider application to embrace the Helots of Messenia as well, and it would certainly not be unreasonable to suspect that the Spartans were reluctant to draw an ethnic distinction between two populations that effectively shared the same politico-juridical, social and economic status within the Lakedaimonian state.[74] That suspicion finds some support in Pausanias' testimony (4.34.6) that a coastal settlement near Korone was named Limen Akhaion ("Port of the Akhaians") and in Strabo's belief (8.4.1) that the whole of Messenia had originally belonged to the kingdom of the "Akhaian" king Menelaos. Perhaps the clearest indication, however, of Messenia's formerly Akhaian legacy is presented by those traditions that recount the tripartite division of the Peloponnese among the descendants of Herakles. The story is invariably associated with the arrival of the Dorians in the Peloponnese, though in fact concerns the territorial rights of their Heraklid leaders who were more properly Akhaian.[75]

Later versions of the story focus on the theme of deception. In Pausanias' account (4.3.5), it is decided that the territories of Argos, Sparta and Messene should be assigned to the Heraklids on the basis of seniority. Temenos, as the eldest, receives Argos, but a dispute then arises between Kresphontes, who is older than the two sons (Eurysthenes and Prokles) of the recently defunct Aristodemos, and Theras, who is older than Kresphontes and is serving as regent for the two orphans. Eventually it is decided to throw clay lots into a water pitcher to see which lot rises to the surface first, but Temenos gives a sun-baked—rather than kiln-fired—lot to the sons of Aristodemos which promptly dissolves in the pitcher. Consequently Kresphontes' lot rises to the surface and he chooses Messene. That this is a Messenian version of the tale is evident from the fact that Messenia is regarded as a more desirable territory than Lakonia (which is assigned by default to the sons of Aristodemos) and that the deceit practised to obtain this assignment for Kresphontes is not of his volition but engineered instead by Temenos.[76] What is not so immediately apparent is why the procedure to establish the relative seniority of

....

[74] Theopompos' opinion on the Akhaian origin of the helots has not, however, been accepted by all scholars: Meyer (1937: 258), Kahrstedt (1919) and Pareti (1920: 189) argued that they were ethnically indistinguishable from their Spartan masters. See Oliva 1971: 40-41.

[75] E.g. Hdt. 5.72.3; Paus. 7.1.5-7. See Hall 1997: 60, 2002: 80. For the distinction between the Dorians and Herakleidai, see Prinz 1979: 293; Musti 1985: 38; Piérart 1985: 278; Sakellariou 1990: 151; Vanschoonwinkel 1991: 360; Malkin 1994: 38-43; Ulf 1996: 252-264; Hall 1997: 59-62, 2002: 80-81.

[76] *Contra* Pearson 1962: 408.

Kresphontes and the sons of Aristodemos has to be so elaborate, and this suggests that the Messenian version transmitted by Pausanias is itself a response to an alternative tradition in which the story of the lot plays a greater role. That alternative version is the one recounted in the pseudo-Apollodoran *Bibliothekê* (2.8.4) where the cities are first arranged in a fixed order (Argos-Sparta-Messene) and then lots are thrown into a water pitcher regardless of the relative ages of the contestants. Since Kresphontes is anxious to secure Messenia as his realm he engages in trickery by casting a lot not of stone but of earth which dissolves in the pitcher, thus automatically assuring that Argos and Sparta are assigned first. Kresphontes' deceit in this version ultimately serves to undermine his title to Messenia,[77] thus betraying a non-Messenian, presumably Spartan perspective which is also evident in earlier versions of the tale, even if they do not specifically ascribe deceit to Kresphontes.[78] In Isokrates' *Arkhidamos*, Kresphontes obtains Messenia fairly but is then murdered by his subjects, prompting his sons to seek Spartan support for vengeance in return for ceding to them their hereditary kingdom—a clear aetiological justification for the Spartan annexation of Messenia.[79] Sparta also seems to be given priority in Pindar's brief notice of the division of the Peloponnese (*Pyth.* 5.69-72).[80]

There are, then, indications that the Spartans considered the Helots of Messenia to be Akhaians. At first sight it seems paradoxical that they should have attributed the same ethnic origins to a neighbouring servile population as to their own kings, but it may be that the Spartans were constrained by a relatively simple dualistic (Dorian-Akhaian) system of ethnic classification. The egalitarian tendencies of the Greeks (often more ideal than real) met a severe challenge in cases where one group exercised supremacy over another. In such situations, it was relatively common to ascribe the imbalance to ethnic differences between rulers and subjects,

....

[77] Luraghi (2001b: 47-49) correctly notes that trickery is often a laudable trait in heroes and need not carry negative connotations, but this also runs the risk of ignoring the victims of deceit. That Kresphontes' duplicitous victory *may* be a source of self-congratulation in Messenian eyes does not necessarily preclude the possibility that, from a Spartan or Argive perspective, it has resulted in ill-gotten gains to which the Messenians have no title.

[78] The partition of the Peloponnese among the Herakleidai appears to have been treated in both the *Temenos* and the *Temenidai* of Euripides, but it is not certain that Kresphontes' trick was being recounted this early—the *Temenidai* actually seems to have attributed deception to the sons of Aristodemos. See *POxy.* 2455 fr. 9, with the discussion by Luraghi 2001b: 40-41. The specific ruse to which Kresphontes resorted in the pseudo-Apollodoran version is known from other contexts (see Soph. *Aj.* 1283-1287) but, again, this does not prove that it was associated with Kresphontes already in the fifth century: see Kiechle 1966: 496-497.

[79] Pearson 1962: 404-405. A less specific account is presented in Pl. *Leg.* 3.683c-d.

[80] This may present some difficulty to the otherwise robustly-argued view of Luraghi (2001b) that the pro-Spartan variant, recounted by Isokrates, was a modification of an earlier version, coined in the mid-fifth century to legitimate Argive interests.

thus in a sense naturalizing the basis for dominion.[81] The kings of Sparta, to the extent that they exercised rule over Dorian subjects, could not themselves be Dorians—hence their appeals to an Akhaian-Heraklid heritage (see above). But by the same token, those who worked the fields of Messenia for Dorian absentee land-lords in Sparta also had to be thought of as non-Dorian Akhaians—albeit of a much lower status.[82]

Populations do not always have to accept the ethnic classification foisted upon them—particularly in cases where this identity is perceived to be negatively evaluated. In such situations, the population in question may try either to assimilate with the dominant group, or to develop new dimensions of comparison to bypass those by which it is disadvantaged, or else to redefine seemingly negative characteristics in a more positive light.[83] The first option was obviously unattainable; the second would certainly warrant further investigation; but it is the third option that seems to have been adopted by the Helots of Messenia. Instances of tomb-cult (i.e. post-Mycenaean cultic veneration at the site of Late Bronze Age tombs) occur with greater frequency in Messenia than in all other areas except Attika and the Argolid. More importantly, however, tomb-cult in Messenia is more persistent than anywhere else, continuing throughout the Archaic and Classical periods,[84] and it is tempting to interpret this practice as an "ancestralizing strategy" designed to forge a link to the Heroic "Akhaian" past and thus to consolidate a sense of Akhaian identity in the present.[85] Another possible instance of such ancestralizing strategies may be represented by Sanctuary ω-ω west of the Asklepieion at Messene. The evidence of votive offerings in this sanctuary suggests that cultic activity commenced in the seventh century BC and continued through to the first—thus spanning much of the period in which the inhabitants of Messenia were enslaved to Spartan masters.[86] At any rate, it is difficult to account for why remnants of an Akhaian identification should have survived the refoundation of Messene and the

....

[81] Cf. the Neleid ancestry of the Peisistratid tyrants of Athens, the rule of Akhaian-Heraklid leaders over the Aiolians of Thessaly, and the dominion of 'Greek' autocrats over supposedly 'non-Greek' populations in Makedon and Molossia. See Hall 2001: 168-169, 2002: 166.

[82] *Contra* Figueira 1999: 221: 'In the socialization by which the Spartiates endeavored to inculcate into the Helots their inferior status, it is noteworthy that elaborated *ethnic* symbolism was not included'.

[83] See Giles et al. 1977: 320-321; Hall 1997: 31.

[84] Antonaccio 1995: 70-102.

[85] For possible instances of ancestralizing appeals to the Akhaian past in the Argive Plain, see Hall 1997: 99-107, 138-142; in perioikic Lakonia, Hall 2000: 87-89.

[86] For recent bibliography on the excavation, see Luraghi 2001a: 299 n. 83. Elsewhere (2002: 55-56), Luraghi compares the iconography of the terracotta relief plaques found in the sanctuary with that of the so-called Lakonian hero-reliefs. For the possibly Akhaian connotations of the latter, see Hall 2000: 88.

repatriation of Dorian Messenians had it not served some practical function in the preceding centuries.

The connection that the legend of the Heraklid partition of the Peloponnese forged between Messene and the important cities of Sparta and Argos must have proved valuable in establishing the historical credentials of the newly liberated fledgeling state of Messene,[87] but it was difficult to harmonize this tradition with the Dorian identity professed by post-liberation Messenia—an identity that sought to occlude the previous centuries of subjugation during which the residents of Messenia had clung to a pre-Dorian Akhaian heritage which had itself been forged by others, notably the Argives and the Spartans.[88] What the liberated Messenians appear to have done is to have preserved the mythical association between Messene, Argos and Sparta by retrojecting it to a more distant past, prior to the arrival of either the Akhaians or the Dorians. Thus, Pausanias (4.2.4) tells how Perieres, the son of Aiolos and the founder of a new dynasty in Messenia, married Gorgophone, daughter of the Argolic hero Perseus, and that Gorgophone herself had previously been married to the Spartan hero Oibalos—in pseudo-Apollodoros' account (1.9.5), Perieres is himself originally of Spartan descent. But even this association is simply a replication of a network of contacts between Messenia, Lakonia and the Argolid that, according to Pausanias (4.1.1-2), had existed several generations earlier when Messenia was first named by the eponymous Messene, daughter of the Argive hero Triopas and wife of Polykaon, son of the Spartan *Urvater* Lelex.[89] The figure of Messene (who was probably originally differentiated from the homonymous nymph of Sicilian Zankle-Messina)[90] features prominently in the myths of independent Messenia, and the multiplicity of roles assigned to her—as both founder and queen of Messenia, as initiator of the cult of Zeus Ithomatas and as the first host of the Andanian Mysteries—would seem to betray an urgent need on the part of liberated Messenia to equip itself with charter myths and founder heroes/heroines that were satisfied by resorting to the time-honoured (but hardly very original) practice of eponymous attribution.[91] Certainly, if we are prepared to trust Pausanias' confession that he was heavily dependent upon post-Leuktra sources in his account of Messenian history, then we should also take him at his

．．．．．．．．．．．．．．

[87] Cf. Asheri 1983: 30: 'Uno dei primi desiderata del governo filo-tebano locale fu per forza di cose l'identità nazionale'.

[88] For a parallel reticence on the part of Pausanias concerning Messenia's history under Spartan rule, see Alcock 2001: 143-145. For the originally non-Messenian origins of the myth of the tripartite division of the Peloponnese among Akhaian Heraklids, see Luraghi 2001b.

[89] For Triopas' connection with Argos, see Paus. 2.16.1. For Lelex as first king of Lakonia: 3.1.1.

[90] Deshours 1993: 47-49; Figueira 1999: 231.

[91] See Deshours 1993: 47, who nevertheless proceeds to argue that the -*ênê* suffix is prehellenic and that the figure of the eponymous Messene predates Epameninondas' foundation of the city.

word when he says that he could find no mention of the eponymous Messene, or the children she had by Polykaon, in such epic and genealogical poems as the *Eoiai*, the *Naupaktia*, or the works of Kinaithon and Asios; only the *Great Eoiai* presented an account of Polykaon, but here his partner was not Messene but Euaikhme, daughter of Herakles' son Hyllos (4.2.1).[92]

There was nothing primordial or inevitable about the Dorian identity professed by the Messenians of Pausanias' day. There is no evidence that the Messenians were thought of—or thought of themselves—as Dorians at an early date and indeed some indications that they may have subscribed to a general pre-Dorian or "Akhaian" heritage. Rather, the Dorianization of the Messenians was effected in two stages: firstly, among the Dorians of the diaspora as a counterclaim to the Dorian legacy that was being proclaimed so vigorously by the Spartans in the fifth century; and secondly, as a result of mythopoeic developments in the post-liberation traditions of Messenia in which the Akhaian component of Messenian identity was, if not entirely eradicated,[93] at least neutralized and bypassed by rooting Messenia's origins—and its role within the Peloponnese—in the earliest phases of human history. I have previously had occasion to remark that the archaizing tendencies exhibited by the dialect of post-liberation Messenia are some-what unexpected given that the city recruited not only freed Helots but also Messenians of the diaspora (whose dialects are unlikely to have remained uninflu-enced by the linguistic idioms of their host communities) and even non-Messenians, and I tentatively hypothesized that the Messenians adopted a type of "katharevousa" (or purified dialect) in order to equip themselves with a linguistic authenticity that they felt was otherwise lacking.[94] I hope here to have sketched a plausible discursive context in which that linguistic event could have occurred.

....

[92] Figueira 1999: 231 argues that Messene was discussed by Hellanikos, on the basis of Schol. Eur. Or. 932. It is evident that the Scholiast to Euripides made use of Hellanikos' genealogy, though that cannot exclude the possibility that Messene (who is not specifically mentioned by Hellanikos) is a later addition: see the stemmata in Hall 1997: 82-83.

[93] One of the post-liberation *phylai* at Messene took its name from Kresphontes; the other four were also named after Heraklids. See Jones 1987: 146-148; Luraghi 2001b: 57.

[94] Hall 1995: 91, 1997: 180.

Bibliography

Ahrens, H. 1843. *De Graecae Linguae Dialectis*, Vol. 2. Göttingen.

Alcock, S. E. 1999. "The Pseudo-History of Messenia Unplugged." *Transactions of the American Philological Association* 129: 333-341.

_____. 2001. "The Peculiar Book IV and the Problem of the Messenian Past." In S. E. Alcock, J. F. Cherry and J. Elsner (eds.), *Pausanias: Travel and Memory in Roman Greece.* Oxford and New York: 142-153.

Alty, J. 1982. "Dorians and Ionians." *Journal of Hellenic Studies* 102: 1-14.

Antonaccio, C. M. 1995. *An Archaeology of Ancestors: Tomb Cult and Hero Cult in Early Greece.* Lanham.

Asheri, D. 1983. "La diaspora e il ritorno dei Messeni." In E. Gabba (ed.), *Tria Corda. Scritti in onore di Arnaldo Momigliano.* Como: 27-42.

Bartonek, A. 1972. *Classification of the West Greek Dialects at the Time About 350 BC.* Prague.

Bauslaugh, R. A. 1990. "Messenian Dialect and Dedications of the 'Methanioi.'" *Hesperia* 59: 661-668.

Beloch, K. J. 1913. *Griechische Geschichte*, Vol. 1.2. Second edition. Strasbourg.

_____. 1914. *Griechische Geschichte*, Vol. 2.1. Second edition. Strasbourg.

Braun, T. 1994. "ΧΡΗΣΤΟΥΣ ΠΟΙΕΙΝ." *Classical Quarterly* 44: 40-5.

Brillante, C. 1984. "L'invasione dorica oggi." *Quaderni urbinati di cultura classica* 16: 173-185.

Buck, C. D. 1955. *The Greek Dialects: Grammar, Selected Inscriptions, Glossary.* Revised edition. Chicago.

Cartledge, P. 1976. "A New 5th-Century Spartan Treaty." *Liverpool Classical Monthly* 1: 87-92.

_____. 1978. "The New 5th-Century Spartan Treaty Again." *Liverpool Classical Monthly* 3: 189-190.

_____. 1979. *Sparta and Lakonia: A Regional History 1300-362 BC.* London.

Cassio, A. C. 1984. "Il 'carattere' dei dialetti greci e l'opposizione Ioni-Dori: testimonianze antiche e teorie di età romantica." *Annali dell'Istituto Orientale di Napoli. Sezione linguistica* 6: 113-136.

Cawkwell, G. L. 1993. "Sparta and her Allies in the Fifth Century." *Classical Quarterly* 43: 364-376.

Cohen, R. 1997. *Global Diasporas: An Introduction.* Seattle.

Colvin, S. 1995. "Aristophanes: Dialect and Textual Criticism." *Mnemosyne* 48: 34-47.

Coulson, W. D. E. 1985. "The Dark Age Pottery of Sparta." *Annual of the British School at Athens* 80: 29-84.

_____. 1986. *The Dark Age Pottery of Messenia.* (Studies in Mediterranean Archaeology 43). Göteborg.

Daux, G. 1937. "Inscriptions et monuments archaïques de Delphes." *Bulletin de correspondance hellénique* 61: 57-78.

Davis, J. L., S. E. Alcock, J. Bennet, Y. G. Lolos and C. W. Shelmerdine 1997. "The Pylos Regional Archaeological Project. Part I: Overview and the Archaeological Survey." *Hesperia* 66: 391-494.

De Sanctis, G. 1939. *Storia di Grecia dalle origini alla fine del secolo V.* Vol. 1. Florence.

Deshours, N. 1993. "La légende et le culte de Messènè ou comment forger l'identité d'une cité." *Revue des études anciennes* 106: 39-60.

Dipersia, G. 1974. "La nuova popolazione di Messene al tempo di Epaminonda." In M. Sordi (ed.), *Propaganda e persuasione occulta nell'antichità.* (Contributi dell'istituto di storia antica 2). Milan: 54-61.

Duncker, M. 1881. *Geschichte des Alterthums.* Vol. 5. Third edition. Leipzig.

Fernández Alvarez, M. P. 1981. *El Argólico occidental y oriental en las inscripciones de los siglos VII, VI y V a.C.* Salamanca.

Figueira, T. J. 1999. "The Evolution of the Messenian Identity." In S. Hodkinson and A. Powell (eds.), *Sparta. New Perspectives.* London: 211-244.

Forrest, W. G. 1968. *A History of Sparta, 950-192 BC.* London.

Giles, R. B. and D. Taylor 1977. "Towards a Theory of Language in Ethnic Group Relations." In H. Giles (ed.), *Language, Ethnicity and Intergroup Relations.* London: 307-348.

Grote, G. 1869. *A History of Greece.* Vol. 2. Second edition. London.

Gschnitzer, F. 1955. "Stammes- und Ortsgemeinden im alten Griechenland." *Wiener Studien* 68: 120-144.

Hainsworth, J. B. 1967. "Greek Views of Greek Dialectology." *Transactions of the Philological Society* 65: 62-76.

Hall, E. 1992. "When is a Myth not a Myth? Bernal's 'Ancient Model'." *Arethusa* 25: 181-201.

Hall, J. M. 1995. "The Role of Language in Greek Ethnicities." *Proceedings of the Cambridge Philological Society* 41: 83-100.

_____. 1997. *Ethnic Identity in Greek Antiquity.* Cambridge.

_____. 2000. "Sparta, Lakedaimon and the Nature of Perioikic Dependency." In P. Flensted-Jensen (ed.), *Further Studies in the Ancient Greek Polis.* (Historia Einzelschriften 138). Stuttgart: 73-89.

_____. 2001. "Contested Ethnicities: Perceptions of Macedonia within Evolving Definitions of Greek Edentity." In I. Malkin (ed.), *Ancient Perceptions of Greek Ethnicity.* Washington D.C.: 159-186.

_____. 2002. *Hellenicity: Between Ethnicity and Culture.* Chicago.

Hansen, M. H. 1996. "City-Ethnics as Evidence for *Polis* Identity." In M.H. Hansen and K. Raaflaub (eds.), *More Studies in the Ancient Greek Polis.* (Historia Einzelschriften 108). Stuttgart: 169-196.

Harder, A. 1985. *Euripides' Kresphontes and Archelaos. Introduction, Text and Commentary.* (Mnemosyne, Supplement 87). Leiden.

Harvey, D. 1994. "Lacomica: Aristophanes and the Spartans." In A. Powell and S. Hodkinson (eds.), *The Shadow of Sparta.* London: 35-58.

Hölscher, T. 1974. "Die Nike der Messenier und Naupaktier in Olympia." *Jahrbuch des Deutschen Archäologischen Instituts* 89: 70-111.

Hornblower, S. 1996. *A Commentary on Thucydides.* Vol. 2. Oxford.

Jacoby, F. 1943. *Die Fragmente der griechischen Historiker.* Vol. IIIA: *Geschichte von Städten und Völkern (Horographie und Ethnographie): Kommentar zu Nr. 262-296.* Leiden.

_____. 1944. "ΧΡΗΣΤΟΥΣ ΠΟΙΕΙΝ (Aristotle fr. 592 R.)." *Classical Quarterly* 38: 15-16.

Jeffery, L. H. 1990. *The Local Scripts of Archaic Greece. A Study of the Origin of the Greek Alphabet and its Development from the Eighth to the Fifth Centuries BC.* Revised edition by A. Johnston. Oxford.

Jones, N. F. 1987. *Public Organization in Ancient Greece: A Documentary Study.* (Memoirs of the American Philosophical Society 176). Philadelphia.

Jones, C. P. 1999. *Kinship Diplomacy in the Ancient World.* Cambridge, MA.

Kahrstedt, U. 1919. "Die spartanische Agrarwirtschaft." *Hermes* 54: 279-294.

Kelly, D. H. 1978. "The New Spartan Treaty." *Liverpool Classical Monthly* 3: 133-141.

Kiechle, F. 1959. *Messenische Studien. Untersuchungen zur Geschichte der Messenischen Kriege und der Auswanderung der Messenier.* Kallmünz.

———. 1966. "Die Ausprägung der Sage von der Rückkehr der Herakliden. Ein Beitrag zur Bestimmung des ethnischen Standorts der Messenier" *Helikon* 6: 493-517.

Leahy, D. M. 1958. "The Spartan Defeat at Orchomenus." *Phoenix* 12: 141-165.

López Eire, A. 1978. "El retorno de los Heraclidas." *Zephyrus* 28-29: 287-297.

Luraghi, N. 1994. *Tirannidi arcaiche in Sicilia e Magna Grecia da Panezio di Leontini alla caduta dei Dinomenidi.* Florence.

———. 2001a. "Der Erdbebenaufstand und die Entstehung der messenischen Identität." In D. Papenfuß and V. M. Strocka (eds.), *Gab es das Griechische Wunder? Griechenland zwischen dem Ende des 6. und der Mitte des 5. Jahrhunderts v.Chr.* Mainz: 279-301.

———. 2001b. "Die Dreiteilung der Peloponnes. Wandlungen eines Gründungsmythos" In H.-J. Gehrke (ed.), *Geschichtsbilder und Gründungsmythen.* Würzburg: 37-63.

———. 2002. "Becoming Messenian." *Journal of Hellenic Studies* 122: 45-69.

Malkin, I. 1994. *Myth and Territory in the Spartan Mediterranean.* Cambridge.

Mastrokostas, E. 1964. "Ναύπακτος." Ἀρχαιολογικὸν Δελτίον 19B: 295.

Meyer, E. 1937. *Geschichte des Altertums*, Vol. 3. Second edition. Stuttgart.

Moretti, L. 1946. "Sparta alla metà del VI sec. I. La guerra contro Tegea." *Rivista di filologia e d'istruzione classica* 24: 87-103.

Morpurgo Davies, A. 1987. "The Greek Notion of Dialect." *Verbum* 10: 7-28.

Musti, D. 1985. "Continuità e discontinuità tra Achei e Dori nelle tradizioni storiche." In D. Musti (ed.), *Le origini dei Greci: Dori e mondo egeo.* Rome: 37-71.

Musti, D., and M. Torelli (eds.). 1991. *Pausania. Guida della Grecia.* Vol. 4. *La Messenia.* Milan.

Nafissi, M. 1991. *La nascita del kosmos. Studi sulla storia e la società di Sparta.* Naples.

Niese, B. 1891. "Die ältere Geschichte Messeniens." *Hermes* 26: 1-32.

Oliva, P. 1971. *Sparta and her Social Problems.* Amsterdam and Prague.

Osborne, R. 1996. *Greece in the Making, 1200-479 BC.* London.

Pareti, L. 1920. *Storia di Sparta arcaica.* Vol. 1. Florence.

Pearson, L. 1962. "The Pseudo-History of Messenia and its Authors." *Historia* 11: 397-426.

Peek, W. 1974. "Ein neuer spartanischer Staatsvertrag." *Abhandlungen der Sächsischen Akademie der Wissenschaften zu Leipzig. Philologisch-Historische Klasse* 65: 3-15.

Petrocelli, C. 2001. "Le parole e le armi: omofonia/omoglossia in guerra." *Quaderni di storia* 54: 69-97.

Piérart, M. 1985. "Le tradizioni epiche e il loro rapporto con la questione dorica: Argo e l'Argolide." In D. Musti (ed.), *Le origini dei Greci: Dori e mondo egeo*. Rome: 277-292.

Prinz, F. 1979. *Gründungsmythen und Sagenchronologie*. Munich.

Pritchett, W. K. 1965. *Studies in Ancient Greek Topography*. Vol. 1. Berkeley and Los Angeles.

Robinson, E. S. G. 1946. "Rhegion, Zankle, Messana and the Samians." *Journal of Hellenic Studies* 66: 13-21.

Roehl, H. 1882. *Inscriptiones Graecae Antiquissimae*. Berlin.

Roussel, D. 1976. *Tribu et cité: études sur les groupes sociaux dans les cités grecques aux époques archaïque et classique*. Paris.

Ruijgh, C. J. 1986. Review of M.P. Fernández Alvarez, *El Argolico occidental y oriental. Mnemosyne* 39: 452-459.

_____. 1989. Review of J. Méndez Dosuna, *Los dialectos del Noroeste. Mnemosyne* 42: 155-163.

Safran, W. 1991. "Diasporas in Modern Societies: Myths of Homeland and Return." *Diaspora* 1: 83-99.

Sakellariou, M. B. 1990. *Between Memory and Oblivion: The Transmission of Early Greek Historical Traditions*. (Meletemata 12). Athens.

Shaw, P.-J. 1999. "Olympiad Chronography and 'Early' Spartan History." In S. Hodkinson and A. Powell (eds.), *Sparta: New Perspectives*. London: 273-309.

Shero, L. R. 1938. "Aristomenes the Messenian." *Transactions of the American Philological Association* 69: 500-531.

Shipley, G. 1997. "'The Other Lakedaimonians': The Dependent Perioikic Poleis of Laconia and Messenia." In M. H. Hansen (ed.), *The Polis as an Urban Centre and as a Political Community*. (Acts of the Copenhagen Polis Centre 4). Copenhagen: 189-281.

Ste. Croix, G. E. M. de. 1972. *The Origins of the Peloponnesian War.* London.

Treves, P. 1944. "The Problem of a History of Messenia." *Journal of Hellenic Studies* 64: 102-106.

Ulf, C. 1996. "Griechische Ethnogenese versus Wanderungen von Stämmern und Stammstaaten." In C. Ulf (ed.), *Wege zur Genese griechischer Identität: die Bedeutung der früharchaischen Zeit.* Berlin: 240-280.

Vanschoonwinkel, J. 1991. *L'Égée et la Mediterranée orientale à la fin du IIe millénaire: temoignages archéologiques et sources écrites.* Louvain-la-Neuve and Providence.

Versakis, P. 1916. "Τὸ ἱερὸν τοῦ Κορύνθου Ἀπόλλονος." Ἀρχαιολογικὸν Δελτίον 2: 65-118.

Wade-Gery, H. T. 1966. "The Rhianos-Hypothesis." In E. Badian (ed.), *Ancient Society and Institutions: Studies Presented to Victor Ehrenberg on his 75th Birthday.* Oxford: 289-302.

Weber, M. 1978. *Economy and Society.* Translated by E. Fischoff et al. Berkeley, Los Angeles and London.

Zunino, M.L. 1997. *Hiera Messeniaka. La storia religiosa della Messenia dall'età micenea all'età ellenistica.* Udine.

Seven

Freedom for the Messenians? A note on the impact of slavery and helotage on the Greek concept of freedom

Kurt A. Raaflaub

1

In 371 the Thebans defeated a Spartan army at Leuctra and destroyed the myth of Spartan invincibility.[1] In the winter of 370/69 Epameinondas led an army of Thebans and allies into Lakonia, devastated parts of the country, and almost launched an attack against Sparta itself. During this campaign, the Theban leader separated Messenia from the Lakedaimonian state and proclaimed it an independent *polis,* centered in a newly founded town, Messene. This town was located at the foot of Mt. Ithome, site of a sanctuary of Zeus, which had long been a Messenian refuge and the center of long-lasting resistance against Sparta during the well-known revolt of the 460s.[2] It was populated not only by former helots, who had farmed the estates of their Spartan masters, but also by descendants of Messenians who had left their country during earlier conflicts with Sparta and formed a Messenian diaspora in various places of the Mediterranean, whether authentic or not.[3]

The creation of this new state, at the expense of Sparta, long the predominant military power in Greece, was a sensational event. One of its consequences was the emergence of a Messenian version of Messenian history or perhaps rather, of a Messenian mythology concerning the early Messenian wars. It was celebrated by various authors in works of formal Messenian history, *Messêniaka.* Much of this

....

[1] I thank the editors for inviting me to contribute this chapter. I keep references to a minimum; the problem I intend to discuss here has not received much attention in scholarship.

[2] For the events of 370/69, see Roebuck 1941: ch. 2; Buckler 1980: 70-87; Demand 1990: 110-111; Hamilton 1991: 215-231. On the revolt of the 460s, see below n. 21.

[3] See, e.g., Asheri 1983.

tradition found its way into the account of Pausanias which therefore needs to be considered with great critical caution.[4]

Probably around the time of Messene's foundation, Alkidamas, a sophist and rhetorician, pupil of Gorgias, published an oration, presumably intended as a showpiece for recitation and teaching, in which he apparently recommended to the Spartans to liberate the Messenians. This "Messenian oration," about which we know nothing otherwise, became famous because Alkidamas made in it a bold statement about the natural equality of slaves and free men: "God has set all men free; nature has made no man a slave." Later in the fourth century, a comic playwright, Philemon, reiterated the universality of this principle: "Even if a man be a slave, he has the same flesh; no one was ever a slave by nature, though chance enslaves the body." In his *Politics,* Aristotle, who vigorously opposed this view, refers to it: "Some hold that slave-ownership is unnatural. It is only by *nomos* (convention) that one is a slave and another free, for in nature there is no difference. Neither, then, is it just, for it is based on force."[5]

If Alkidamas indeed published his speech, whatever its purpose, in the historical context of the creation of an independent Messenia, the liberation of the helots and thus of slaves here had a political connotation. The sentence that survives, however, is entirely unpolitical; it is part of a debate about a social and ethical problem, namely the question of whether or not slavery was reconcilable with laws of nature; if not, as Alkidamas postulated here, that is, if it contradicted nature, it was based entirely on human convention, power, and force, and as such theoretically and ethically unjustifiable. This debate was rooted in two strands of thought. On the one hand, it was related to discussions about the validity of other traditional social distinctions, such as elite vs. non-elite and Greek vs. barbarian, which were challenged vigorously in sophistic treatises of the late fifth century.[6] On the other hand, it was connected with the problem of whether the inferiority of slaves, observable in real life, was based on natural disposition, even on birth, or on the impact of conditioning by the institution itself; the latter idea, in turn, had a long history, visible in the emergence of a typology of slave behavior that is reflected already in the *Odyssey* and accentuated in the last third of the fifth century by

....

[4] On this and the development of a "Messenian" identity, see recently Alcock 1999, 2001; Figueira 1999; Luraghi 2001, 2002a.

[5] Alkidamas: Schol. Arist. *Rhet.* 1373b 6; Avezzù 1982: no. 3 (p. 36) with commentary on pp. 82-83. Isocrates' *Archidamus* is a similar piece, representing the Spartan perspective. Philemon: fr. 95 Kock (not considered authentic by Kassel and Austin in *Poetae Comici Graeci,* vol. VII [concordance and p. 317]). Arist. *Pol.* 1253b 20. The translations are taken from Guthrie 1969: 159-160. For discussion, see, e.g., ibid., 155-163; further bibliog. on this issue is listed in Schütrumpf 1991: 234-235.

[6] Esp. Lykophron 83 B4 Diels-Kranz; Antiphon 87 B44 B1-2 Diels-Kranz.

medical or anthropological theories postulating a direct connection between, on the one hand, climate, fertility of the country, or a community's constitution, and on the other, human physiology, character, and intelligence. Such discussions are echoed in Herodotus and Euripides.[7] Insofar as they touch upon political issues, however, they are concerned only with free persons and societies; the debate about slavery is limited entirely to social and anthropological aspects.

Until recently, the case of the helots (whether Lakonian or Messenian) was seen not as unique (because the status of slave populations in other parts of Greece, especially in Thessaly and Crete, was considered closely comparable already in antiquity) but as extraordinary, to be distinguished sharply from other forms of slavery (especially "chattel slavery") that were common in large parts of Greece. The helots belonged, to use an ancient label, among various categories of dependent labor "between slaves and free" (*metaxy doulôn kai eleutherôn*), while chattel slaves were simply *douloi*.[8] To some extent, this distinction is still valid, but some of the presuppositions that determine such categorizations are in the course of being changed quite radically. The comprehensive reassessment of the development of Spartan society and institutions, carried on in patient and painstaking work on many aspects and details by Stephen Hodkinson and several other scholars over the last twenty years, has caught up with the helots as well. Due mostly to pathbreaking studies by Jean Ducat, Thomas Figueira and, most incisively, Nino Luraghi, a different reality and development of helotage and a new understanding of Messenian identity and history are beginning to emerge.[9] I for one find the thrust and initial results of such recent work exciting and convincing. I summarize here the suggestions that seem most important for my present study.

However we imagine the Spartans to have conquered (and possibly reconquered) Messenia in the eighth and seventh centuries,[10] the stories we read in Pausanias and other late sources most likely contain very little authentic material, and helotage very probably was not the result of that conquest. Rather, this peculiar slave system, as we know it from the fifth and early fourth centuries, may well have emerged as the result of a conscious regulation and homogenization of various forms of dependent labor that co-existed in Archaic Sparta and in each case were

....

[7] *Od.* 17.320-323; 24.249-253; see Raaflaub 1985: 31-32. Theories: esp. Hippocr. *Airs, Waters, Places;* echoes in Herodotus: Thomas 2000: ch. 2 and pp. 103-114; Euripides: Nestle 1901: 348-361; Synodinou 1977.

[8] Pollux, *Onomastikon* 3.83; Lotze 1959; Finley 1982: chs. 7-9.

[9] Ducat 1990; Figueira 1999; Luraghi 2001, 2002a, 2002b, and this volume. More generally on Sparta: Hodkinson 2000 (listing important earlier articles on pp. 462-463); see also, e.g., Nafissi 1991; Thommen 1996.

[10] For detailed discussion, see recently Meier 1998: pt. 2; Luraghi, this volume.

paralleled in many other communities of Greece. This reform should probably be dated to the first part of the sixth century and connected with other reforms that produced the Spartan *kosmos* known from the classical period. The explanation of the helots' origin as war captives, reflected in their name, is part of the foundation myth of the Spartan polity. Some forms of collective identity arose among those slaves in part because of their shared living and working conditions and in part (and perhaps considerably later) as the result of rituals of inferiority and alterity imposed on them by their Spartan masters.

Material and cult evidence suggests that the entire region controlled by Sparta was culturally homogeneous, "Lakonian"; a distinctly "Messenian" identity is unlikely to have survived, if it ever existed at the time of the original conquest. Such an identity might rather have developed among some of the perioikic towns in Messenia, one of which seems to have been located at the foot of Mt. Ithome, on the site of Epameinondas' Messene. This identity broke powerfully into the open during the "earthquake revolt" of the 460s, when helots and *perioikoi* of at least two towns fought an extended war of resistance at Ithome against the Spartans and thwarted all their efforts at bringing them under control again. The survivors were finally evacuated under a truce and settled by the Athenians in Naupaktos. While the Spartans (and other Greeks adopting their perspective) considered this only and entirely a slave revolt,[11] the evacuees themselves maintained their newly found "Messenian" identity and developed it further. The myth of their Messenian origin and their claim to Messenia as their native land are parts of this new identity; they must thus be considered political rather than historical: the results of specific developments beginning in the 460s and greatly enhanced, of course, by the foundation of Messene a century later.

From at least the 450s, when the survivors of Mt. Ithome were settled in Naupaktos on the Corinthian gulf, and perhaps earlier, Messenian refugees thus lived outside of Messenia in a diaspora that formed communities with their own "Messenian" identity. This identity, it seems, was shared by both former *perioikoi* and former helots. Later tradition suppressed the memory of the role the *perioikoi* had played in all this—a crucial role in several respects, as Luraghi has suggested convincingly—just as late fifth- and early fourth-century writers on Sparta left them mostly out of the picture.[12] Rather, ancient writers on Messenian matters focused almost exclusively on the contrast and conflict between Spartiates and helots. The latter's identity could be, and was, perceived and described in

....

[11] See below n. 41 and, for detailed discussion, Ducat 1990: esp. pp. 137-142; Figueira 1999.

[12] Xenophon's *Lak. Pol.* is an obvious example. On the role of *perioikoi*, see Luraghi 2001: 297-301; on its suppression, ibid., 293.

conflicting ways: they were seen as slaves, in some ways even representing the most radical form of slavery, because they enabled their Spartan masters to be more absolutely free than most other free Greeks,[13] but also as a collectivity with common ethnic traits and a common past and common claims. Moreover, the "Messenians" of Naupaktos participated actively in Athens' war against Sparta and were used to some extent as instruments to undermine Spartan control over Messenia.[14]

For all these reasons, this was an exceptional case, in which the slave population of a specific Greek polis was an issue of intense public interest and even concern to many contemporaries. It was well known that these slaves or enslaved Messenians had fought a long and bitter war against the Spartans—once or perhaps several times. Hence there could be no doubt about their own awareness of the value of freedom and their yearning for freedom. Moreover, in this case the existence of slavery could have prompted—and, as Alkidamas' Messenian speech seems to indicate, did in fact prompt—among other, free Greeks a demand for their liberation. Here, then, the experience of slavery could have resulted in the articulation of a concept of liberty, both among the slaves and the free.

It is the purpose of this chapter to examine this possibility. For the result may help us answer the important and more general question of whether the social experience of slavery could have produced in contemporaries an awareness of the value of freedom that was sufficiently explicit and marked to prompt them to develop a true and conscious concept of freedom. For the contrast between slave and free, and thus presumably an awareness of the potential or real misery of slavery and the corresponding value of freedom must have existed at least minimally in many slave-owning societies.[15] Among the Archaic Greeks this found expression in individual images focusing on the suffering caused by slavery and in the evolution of a contrasting typology of slave and free, mentioned earlier. This too was hardly unique. But only the Greeks, it seems, raised their consciousness of the value of freedom to a level that enabled them to create an explicit concept of freedom with a differentiated terminology and political emphasis.

Currently available evidence suggests that both the concept and terminology, reflecting political consciousness, emerged, and were prompted by, the confrontation of the Greek *poleis* with an eastern territorial state and authoritarian monarchy in the Persian Wars of the early fifth century.[16] At least the opposite of freedom, however, "slavery" or "servitude" (*doulosynê*), seems to have been conceptualized politically a

---

[13] See Kritias 88 B37 Diels-Kranz; Plut. *Lyc.* 28.

[14] For details, see Ducat 1990: 135-137.

[15] Patterson 1991: chs. 1-2 shows, however, that this must not be taken for granted.

[16] See Raaflaub 1985: ch. 3.

good century earlier, when the citizens of some poleis were facing the threat or reality of "enslavement" by a tyrant.[17] The question is thus justified whether the positive concept too was already in existence long before the Persian Wars even if it did not leave a trace in the extant evidence. If so, we need to ask what prompted the development of this concept and whether the experience of slavery as such could have offered a sufficient impulse. In his widely acclaimed book on *Freedom in the Making of Western Culture,* Orlando Patterson gives to this question a very strongly positive answer. In my own earlier book on *The Discovery of Freedom,* I came to a negative conclusion.[18] Perhaps the helots can help us clarify the issue.

Now clearly, by the time the helots entered the brightly lit stage of history, in their revolt of the 460s, the Greeks had already developed a political concept of freedom and begun to use it extensively in political argumentation and propaganda, both locally and "internationally." Supposedly 35,000 helots (and thousands of *perioikoi*) participated in some capacity or other in the battle of Plataea in 479 and perhaps even observed the victory celebration with the Spartan king's sacrifice to Zeus Eleutherios (the god of freedom).[19] Luraghi points out that many of these same helots and *perioikoi* may have been among the rebels of Mt. Ithome—the self-proclaimed "Messenians"—only little more than a decade later, and suggests that "the possibility of a connection between the idea of political freedom, prompted by the Persian War experience, and the earthquake revolt is more than merely an audacious hypothesis."[20] If so, unrest must have been brewing among helots and, apparently, *perioikoi,* and the earthquake, as the extant descriptions suggest, merely offered an unexpected and highly welcome opportunity to start the revolt.[21]

At any rate, the fact alone that a concept of freedom already existed and was used intensively makes it all the more likely that it would have been applied to the helots' struggle against the Spartans if contemporaries had been used to connecting the phenomenon of slavery consciously with the idea of freedom. This likelihood would seem even greater—and might in fact falsify our examination—if the helots were indeed seen already at the time of the "earthquake revolt" not only as slaves but also as members of an ethnically distinct unit that had its own history, derived specific claims from it, and was fighting for its collective and communal independence. This seems more likely from the mid-fifth century onward—when the

....

[17] Raaflaub 1985: 54-70.

[18] Patterson 1991: ch. 3; Raaflaub 1985: ch. 2.

[19] Helots at Plataea: Hdt. 9.10.1, 28.2, 29.1; for discussion, Welwei 1974: 120-141, esp. pp. 120-126; Hunt 1997, 1998: 33-39. Zeus Eleutherios: Raaflaub 1985: 126-128.

[20] Luraghi 2001: 301.

[21] For a careful evaluation of the sources and reconstruction of the events, see Ducat 1990: 131-135; Luraghi 2001 (with earlier bibliog.).

"Messenians" formed their own community in Naupaktos, side-by-side with, but separate from, the Naupaktians—and even then only in specific situations and under specific conditions.[22] If, on the contrary, the helot issue did not automatically trigger conscious concerns about liberty, or such concerns were consistently ignored, this might strengthen the conclusion that the slave-free contrast was traditionally viewed at a low level of consciousness or assigned low significance.

It is important to clarify what the issue is here. I am obviously talking of outside observers, that is, other Greeks who themselves were free. As pointed out before, it is absolutely clear what the Spartans thought about the "Messenian" rebellion, and there can be little doubt about what the helots among the "Messenians" fighting the Spartans thought about the freedom they hoped to achieve. The question is to what extent their hopes mattered to the outside world. By focusing on the perspective of the free, my approach differs starkly from that of Patterson who pays much attention to the point of view of the slaves themselves and considers it crucial for the formation of freedom consciousness in society at large. My reason—and at the same time my thesis—is that slavery as such was able to trigger high consciousness of the value of liberty in a society only if the free, and especially those among them who mattered because they controlled power and set the tone in the community, adopted such consciousness themselves and integrated it into their value system. This did not happen on the basis of consciousness among the slaves themselves or of sympathy with the fate of the slaves among the free, however strongly and sincerely such sentiments may have been felt or even expressed by however many individuals. It happened, I suggest, only if the freemen or citizens themselves were exposed to the threat of loss of liberty in a traumatic and broad or extended experience[23] or if, for whatever reasons, slavery as such became widely objectionable.

2

Before I examine the evidence concerning the helots, I need to substantiate my disagreement with some of Patterson's arguments. I should say at the outset that I find his book most impressive and very important. The amount of new insight it offers, even in fields far removed from his own, is truly remarkable. I am neither a comparative sociologist nor an anthropologist; I am interested in social and political history, and my expertise is essentially limited to ancient Greece and Rome. I am thus not able to join the discussion on Patterson's level of theoretical and

....

[22] For details, see Figueira 1999; Luraghi 2002a.

[23] If such an experience was temporary or limited, passed quickly, or was overcome with relative ease, it might have failed to achieve a deep and lasting impact on collective consciousness. Such may have been the result of Solon's sweeping elimination of debt bondage (as I suggest in Raaflaub 1985: 54-70).

comparative sophistication and breadth. What I can do is to question and examine some of his assumptions, approaches, and conclusions in an area that is of crucial importance both to the argument of his book and to my own work: early Greece.

Scholars interested in the beginnings and evolution of freedom can choose between various approaches; those Patterson and I have selected for our studies lie at the extremes of the spectrum. Patterson's is, naturally, based on sociology and anthropology. It is, to some extent, speculative and imaginative, intending to (re)construct a social history of freedom. Patterson looks at the situations and experiences of various categories of persons in ancient societies, especially slaves, and asks how such persons might have reacted to certain conditions, what changes in consciousness might have occurred among them, and whether these reactions or changes might have prompted awareness of the value of freedom—whether or not the ancient peoples themselves used "freedom" or related words to describe this experience. This approach makes it possible to identify or postulate the existence of "freedom consciousness" long before the corresponding terminology existed—at all or at least in substantial or socially and historically effective forms. Terminological developments here offer useful confirmation but are not essential to the argument.

My own approach is more strictly historical, developed precisely for the study of the history of concepts ("Begriffsgeschichte").[24] It assumes that ideas and concepts that were significant in a given time and society will be reflected in this society's language. Developments in terminology thus offer important clues to changes in societal experiences and attitudes; absence of words is as illuminating as is their presence, and the full range of relations between terms as well as variations in a broader "conceptual field" need to be taken seriously.[25] One should therefore be reluctant to assume a high level of consciousness of a given value in a society that does not have a corresponding word to express it. From this perspective, it is significant, for instance, that a noun existed in Archaic Greece for the condition of slavery (*douleia, doulosynê*) but apparently not for that of freedom (*eleutheria*), and that other concepts, such as justice and equality, were expressed by nouns long before freedom was.

I will illustrate the difference between the two approaches with two examples, one unrelated, the other related to the present study. The Greek god Dionysos and the Roman god Liber were both connected with growth and fertility, vines and

---

[24] See Richter 1986.

[25] It does seem significant, for example, that *doulos*, slave, stood in opposition not only to *eleutheros*, free, but also to *despotês*, master. Extant evidence suggests that the latter, but apparently not the former, was applied to the dynamics in the relationship between a tyrant and his subjects in the polis. We should try to understand and explain this rather than assuming that, of course, tyranny prompted in the "enslaved" citizens a strong consciousness of the value of freedom; see Raaflaub 1985: 65-68 and ch. III.2.

wine. In connection with the latter, they were believed to "liberate" their worshippers from the sense of oppression by all kinds of bonds, whether personal, psychological, or social. Each deity received a major sanctuary at the end of the Archaic period: Dionysos in Athens in the late sixth century, Liber in Rome in the early fifth. Liber is etymologically linked with *libertas,* freedom, and the Athenian Dionysos' association with a village named Eleutherai might similarly have evoked *eleutheria.* Much later generations took these links literally and celebrated the deities as real liberators. Yet it is clear that this was a secondary association. *Liber* and *eleutheros* are both derived from an Indo-European root (**leudh-*) denoting growth. *Eleutheroi* and *liberi* could thus describe the descent group and those belonging to the group, the insiders, as opposed to those not belonging to it, the outsiders. Since the latter included slaves, the two adjectives eventually came to mean "free." Clearly, therefore, both words had their primary function in the sphere of fertility, and this applies to the two gods as well. In the case of Liber, this is still obvious in his cult (which he shared with his consort Libera and Ceres). Among Dionysos' many bynames that of Lyaios (he who "loosens") is prominent, that of Eleutherios (the god of freedom), well attested for other gods, is conspicuously absent. Hence it was the verb *luein* ("to loosen") that was used to describe the god's service to his worshippers. This verb in turn seems conceptually close to "saving" (*sôizein*): the god who loosens from bondage is also the "savior," and the concept of "being saved and surviving" (*sôtêria*) is enormously important in Archaic Greece. To those using the sociological approach, these differences will seem insignificant: they will interpret the "loosening" function of the gods in question as an indication of freedom consciousness and a yearning for emancipation from bondage especially among the non-elite classes who worshipped these gods. To those favoring the historical approach, the differences matter greatly, not least by providing negative evidence; they might conclude that there may well have existed among the non-elite masses in archaic Greece and Rome (whether free or unfree) a desire for such emancipation but this desire was apparently not expressed by the word freedom, at least not in this particular context. Hence, whatever the reason, words related to *eleutheria* and *libertas* were apparently not yet used *ad libitum* or metaphorically. We should thus not assume, without explicit evidence, that these terms had assumed great significance in their societies around that time.[26]

The other example is directly pertinent in our present context. Patterson states, in the third chapter he devotes to Greek freedom, "Freedom, as a social value, was already well in existence by the end of the sixth century." In fact, he maintains, all

....

[26] For a more detailed discussion, see Raaflaub 2000: 255-260; the opposite view is represented by Connor 1989; Wiseman 1998. On the concept of *sôtêria,* see Raaflaub 1985: 41-43.

three categories of freedom into which he divides the concept (see below) had already been invented, at least in primitive forms. In this chapter, which deals with the experience and impact of the Persian Wars, his purpose is to examine "the means by which the language of freedom became fully attached to these three values, whatever they may have been called and however conceived at the end of the sixth century." The experience of this war "was also the occasion for the imprinting of the language of freedom on the preexisting reality" of various elements of freedom (82-83). I find this difficult to accept. If the language and terminology of freedom were only at this point "attached to" or "imprinted upon" values that were up to that time perceived and described differently, it seems more logical to conclude that the value of freedom did not exist previously in a form or on a level of consciousness that prompted expression and formulation. Moreover, it would seem important to define and take seriously, on the one hand, what values *were* formulated expressly and thus *did* exist previously and, on the other hand, why important experiences that *we* perceive as conducive to freedom consciousness were apparently not described as such by Archaic Greeks. Citing my own argument, Patterson concludes that the "internal threat of tyrannies, combined with the external threat of invasion . . . and the need to avoid both, led to what Raaflaub calls a 'breakthrough' toward their own notion of freedom among the aristocrats. For the aristocrats, freedom meant power and political equality, *among their class equals*" (80-81, Patterson's emphasis).[27] The well-documented fact that Archaic aristocrats vied above all for power and leadership and, in their conflicts with tyrants, discovered the value of equality, prompts me to draw a rather different conclusion. In that period, I suggest, the concepts of equality and power sharing predominated in the elite's political consciousness, and freedom (which is not attested in any political context in the sixth century) had not yet entered political consciousness at all. This leaves open the question of whether it had done so in the personal or private realm, but Patterson's context here clearly is political.

So much for methodology and approaches. Patterson's main thesis is twofold. (1) Freedom "was generated from the experience of slavery. People came to value freedom, to construct it as a powerful shared vision of life, as a result of their experience of, and response to, slavery or its recombinant form, serfdom, in their roles as masters, slaves, and nonslaves" (xiii). "Freedom began its career as a social value in the desperate yearning of the slave to negate what, for him or her, and for nonslaves, was a peculiarly inhuman condition" (9; cf. 48 and often). (2) Women "played a decisive role in the Western social invention of *personal* freedom" (xv).

....

[27] This does not represent my view. My conclusion is, to the contrary, that freedom never was an aristocratic concept; see Raaflaub 1985: 112-118, 332-333.

"Freedom began its long journey in the Western consciousness of a woman's value. It was women who first lived in terror of enslavement, and hence it was women who first came to value its absence, both those who were never captured but lived in dread of it and, even more, those who were captured and lived in hope of being redeemed . . ." (51).

Now Patterson is well aware that in later stages of the development, when there emerged two different but related forms of freedom, which he calls "civic" and "sovereignal" (3-4), this value became a men's and a communal or civic issue, although there too, he insists, the experience of slavery was fundamental and indispensable (chaps. 4-5). I will focus here on his argument supporting the emergence of the first form: personal freedom (chap. 3), because it bears directly on reactions to the helot experience.

The first of Patterson's two theses is certainly correct in a general and basic way: it is indeed the experience of and response to slavery that lies at the origin of the creation of freedom as a value and concept. But, I would object, what was decisive in this process was not the experience of the slaves themselves, nor that of women, but the perception and reaction of the free men in their society. The feelings of the slaves themselves, the fears of women enslaved or dreading this fate, and the yearnings, however formulated, of these categories of persons would have been insufficient to create a socially effective and accepted value and concept. If the development had ended there, it would have remained an evolutionary dead-end in the history of freedom, like so many others that Patterson describes acutely in his book (chaps. 1-2). Hence I am doubtful as well about his second thesis that women played a decisive role in the "making of freedom", attractive though the idea is at first sight.

The first focal point of Patterson's examination is the world of Homer and Hesiod. In this world, he argues, men were rarely enslaved (if defeated in war, they died, out of necessity or for the sake of honor), and if they were they had virtually no chance to be freed and returned to their own society. Hence accommodation in their master's household (*oikos*) was their only and best option. Women, by contrast, were frequently enslaved after military defeat of their community. They were not burdened by their men's obsession with the warrior's honor; hence integration as wives into their master's family and thus redemption from slavery were distinct possibilities. Women thus empathized with the fate of slaves and realized the value and desirability of freedom. Patterson sees this confirmed by the fact that in Homer virtually all references to slavery and all but one of the few references to the experience of freedom or its loss concern women (50-55).

This picture is correct in many ways but significantly incomplete. First, men too were enslaved, less as the result of war (although ransoming of male prisoners of war is attested) than of piracy. Hence male slaves are rarely mentioned in the

179

Iliad but they form a major part of the story in the *Odyssey.* For example, two of three men who help Odysseus regain control over his *oikos* by defeating the suitors are slaves, and in Odysseus' own fictitious life story the risk of the freeman's enslavement and the possibility of his liberation from slavery is a prominent feature.[28]

Second, Odysseus rewards the two faithful slave-herdsmen not by explicitly liberating them but by promoting them within his *oikos* and moving them as closely as possible to his own and his son's position: they will receive a wife and a house next to his own and be like brothers of Telemachos.[29] This, of course, de facto presupposes non-slave status, but will they be free? This, at any rate, is not what matters. In a world of undeveloped statehood, security, prosperity, and influence can be found only by being attached to a powerful master's *oikos*, not by being independent outside of such an *oikos*. Promotion within the hierarchy of dependence on a master is thus preferable to complete independence. Typically, in this society the worst fate is not that of the slave but that of the day laborer (*thês*) who has no protector and is exposed to the whims and abuse of those who employ him and of anybody else who is more powerful than he is.[30]

Third, the same, I suggest, is true for women. Briseis is an exceptional case: a spear-won woman who might have become the wife of her captor, Achilles, a highly prominent elite leader. Something similar probably happened quite often on the level of the common soldiers but the normal fate of war captives was slavery and exploitation, illustrated by many examples, including the twelve servant women in Odysseus' household who, whether voluntarily or out of necessity, play along with the suitors and share their fate after the master's return.[31] To describe the war captives turned into wives as freed slaves, however, is hardly adequate. Homer's world does not operate with sharply defined legal statuses. The *Odyssey* distinguishes numerous categories among the servants in an elite household, but by function rather than legal status (and *doulos* is relatively rare among them).[32] In other words, by becoming the leader's wife, a woman like Briseis might not explicitly be set free but rise within the leader's household to the highest position available to a woman. This, I think, is closely comparable to what happens to the two herdsmen in Odysseus' *oikos*.

This does not mean, of course, that the misery of a slave's life was not real or not clearly perceived by slaves and free alike. It just means that the slaves might not

....

[28] See esp. *Od.* 14.199-359; on various aspects of slavery in "Homer's world," see esp. Lencman 1966; Gschnitzer 1976; Wickert-Micknat 1983.

[29] *Od.* 21.214-216; cf. 14.62-66.

[30] *Od.* 18.356-375; 11.489-491; cf. *Il.* 21.441-452. On all this and the larger context, see Finley 1977: esp. pp. 58-59; Raaflaub 1985: 36-46, 1997: 631, 638-639.

[31] Briseis: *Il.* 19.287-300. Women: *Od.* 22.417-425, 457-473.

[32] Ramming 1973; Gschnitzer 1976.

necessarily have perceived freedom as the best alternative available to them. What Patterson says of Eumaios, that there was no chance for him to return as a free man to his native community, is exactly true for Briseis whose parents apparently had died earlier, who had lost her brothers and city in one of Achilles' raids, and who could not possibly yearn for restoration to her former life.[33] For both women and men, accommodation and promotion within the new power structure in which they found themselves may have been their best hope.

Fourth, what we hear in the epics on these matters is never a woman's own voice and rarely the voice attributed to her by the (male) narrator; in most cases, it is the men who talk and think about the women's enslavement. The conversation between Hektor and Andromache illustrates this vividly: she worries about his death that will make her a widow and her son an orphan; he describes in detail the suffering that, after his death and the fall of Troy, enslavement will cause for her.[34] In other words, whatever the women may have thought and said, slavery was a concern the men shared with them. Since, at least in war, enslavement was not a realistic outcome for themselves, they visualized it through the experiences (real, threatened, or imagined) of the persons who were closest and dearest to them. Hence, if slavery was conducive to creating freedom consciousness in the freemen themselves, opportunities were certainly not lacking. This was prevented from happening by factors on which Patterson and I are in full agreement: to the men who mattered in this society, other issues and values were far more important than the slaves' experiences and even the fate of their womenfolk. To these men themselves, freedom was but a remote condition of their status and aspirations.[35]

Finally, Patterson's claim that women were instrumental in fostering freedom consciousness is not supported well by his additional arguments. That women made up more than half of the population (55) would be relevant only if women's views were able to impose themselves on men's values (and this was not determined by sheer numbers). Everything we know about early Homeric and Hesiodic society argues against this—as much as men may have loved women and been considerate of their feelings. For the same reason, it is not relevant to this particular argument that women may have been "less oppressed" in Homeric and Archaic society than they were in democratic Athens, and that they may have asserted themselves in personal relations with husbands, lovers, and sons, as many certainly did at all times, even in democratic Athens. Telemachos knows how to remind his mother, Penelope, of her place in the hierarchy: the formula, "This is men's business!" which he and

....

[33] *Il.* 19.291-294.
[34] *Il.* 6.407-465.
[35] Raaflaub 1985: 38-41.

others use on appropriate occasions in the epics,[36] illustrates the crucial point. Unless men accepted as "their business" what women told them, the latter's feelings had little effect beyond the walls of their homes. On the communal level, peer pressure and tradition would overrule individual sentiment. In the end, what Patterson surmises about women's assertiveness as the cause of men's freedom consciousness, illustrated by Hesiod's misogyny and Archilochos' love poem (60–63), is highly imaginative but lacks any explicit confirmation in the sources.

Nor do I find the following scenario compelling: "When the average woman of sixth- and even fifth-century Greece saw a slave and paused to reflect on her or his condition, her musings must have run along the lines of 'There but for the grace of the gods go I.' By empathizing with the slave end of the master-slave relation, then, women became more conscious of freedom by the ever present experience of power-lessness, natal alienation, and dishonor." In other words, since women were "excluded from the public household" and had no means of wresting concessions from the elite, they inevitably empathized with the slave condition (78). How oppressed women really were, and in what ways, is much debated. Moreover, evidence from the classical period suggests that they knew how to cope with their masters and were capable of creating their own space and network of relations. Unlike the slaves, very many of whom were not born as such, the women's condition was not the result of a sudden, catastrophic change in their lives. Rather, they were used to this condition, which had prevailed for generations, and took it as a given. I consider it a priori more likely that they would decidedly empathize and identify with the master end of the master-slave relation. Despite the restrictions placed on them, they belonged to the master class and were *astai*, citizen women, and as such held a crucially important position in the *oikos* and the community.[37] I do not see, therefore, why free women, despite their inferior status, should have been in a substantially different position from free men when it came to deriving freedom consciousness from the observation of the slave condition—except of course that they were not able to draw from such consciousness political consequences.[38]

In sum, support for the thesis that the experience of slavery as such was the source of freedom consciousness and the foundation of an explicit concept of freedom seems less strong and clear than Patterson puts it. This is in part because in the early Archaic period, illustrated by Homer and Hesiod, slavery was but one category of

....

[36] *Od.* 1.356-359; *Il.* 6.490-493. On the position of women in "Homeric society," see the summary in Raaflaub 1997: 639-641 (with bibliog.).

[37] *Astai:* Cynthia Patterson 1986. For bibliography on the women's condition in classical Athens (and a brief summary of the debate), see Raaflaub 1998: 32-36.

[38] I should mention that Patterson devotes an entire chapter (7) to "A Woman's Song: The Female Force and the Ideology of Freedom in Greek Tragedy and Society."

personal dependence and not sharply defined only by reference to lack of freedom, and because freedom was not the only and not necessarily the best alternative available and imaginable to slaves or dependent persons. This changed gradually, as "chattel slavery," supplied by slave trade and of foreign origin, became more predominant, and even more so, when other forms of personal dependence were abolished. At around the same time, in the late seventh and early sixth centuries, at least in Athens and probably far beyond, communities were confronted with a serious crisis, caused by the rapid spreading of debt bondage and its consequences, that was concerned directly with the loss of freedom of increasing numbers of citizens. In the same period, entire communities came under the power of tyrants and, as contemporaries put it, were "enslaved" by them. Finally, by the middle of the sixth century, the Greeks living on the western coast of Anatolia and, by the early fifth century, those in mainland Greece as well experienced an entirely new threat and reality: the subjection and "enslavement" of formerly free poleis by the authoritarian regimes of Eastern empires, the Lydians and especially the Persians.

These were the situations in which the free men of the polis were forced to consider "enslavement" as a serious threat they could not ignore: a threat partly to themselves, partly to communal peace, partly to the survival of the entire community as they had known it. In these situations the men who mattered in the community and who previously had found other issues (status, power and influence, justice, or equality) more important than freedom, realized the significance of freedom for themselves and for their community. Now freedom consciousness could and eventually did break through; now the men incorporated freedom into their own value system. Because this happened on the communal and political level, and this new value was embraced by the free, freedom quickly became a potent, explicitly formulated, and differentiated value concept. Slavery, I conclude, did lie at the roots of the concept, as a necessary but much more distant and much less sufficient condition than Patterson suggests.

3

We are now ready to return to the helots of Sparta. Virtually all the evidence available to us concerns reactions, at various times, to problems and tensions within the Spartan state by one other polis, Athens, or by Athenian writers.[39] The first of these occasions is the "earthquake revolt." Details and chronology are unclear and much debated. Two issues, however, seem fairly certain. One is that, like other allies of Sparta, the Athenians had no qualms in supporting Sparta against the rebels, perhaps even twice. What may have been debated, before the large Athenian hoplite

....

[39] For a broader survey of Greek views on helotage, see Klees 1991-1992.

contingent set out, was certainly not which side was more deserving of support but whether it was advisable to support Sparta at all—at a time when relations between the former allies were less than harmonious and influential leaders were advocating a change from collaboration to confrontation with Sparta anyway.[40] In other words, the very polis, which claimed proudly to have saved the liberty of the Hellenes in the Persian Wars, always to have helped selflessly those who were oppressed and in danger, and thus to deserve preeminence and leadership in its growing sphere of influence, seems not to have viewed the cause of the helot rebels with sympathy or considered it to be anything but what the Spartans declared it to be: the revolt of slaves against their masters.[41]

The second issue that is fairly certain is that at some point, apparently at a later stage when the rebels were besieged on Mt. Ithome, the Spartans dismissed the Athenians under less than honorable circumstances. This unexpected turn of events caused angry and hostile reactions in Athens, discredited Kimon and accelerated his fall, and gave decisive support to those who favored a political realignment and confrontation with Sparta. What precisely caused the Spartans to make a decision that was certain to have grave consequences is unknown. The only explanation provided in the sources, that they feared the Athenians might change sides and aid the rebels, has been considered unlikely, perhaps spun out of the fact that the Athenians later in fact did support the refugees from Mt. Ithome, settling them in Naupaktos. However that may be, the Spartans must have had serious reasons to act as they did. They may have discovered only belatedly that even the hoplites and elite officers of the Athenians were ideologically infected by the "freedom virus," and considered it dangerous to keep them around for too long. They may have heard about the democratic reform enacted under the leadership of Ephialtes (if it really took place while the army was away) and become suspicious of the Athenians at that point. The Athenians themselves may have become less enthusiastic about supporting the Spartans, having for the first time gained direct and intimate insight into the conditions prevailing in Sparta's domain and perhaps having discovered only late that among the rebels were not only slaves but also large numbers of *perioikoi*—which changed the complexion of the affair considerably.[42]

Whether any of this is correct remains unknowable. What matters is that there is not a shred of evidence about a tradition surviving in Athens that the hoplites sent to Sparta under Kimon did in fact empathize with or support the rebels. Nor

....

[40] Plut. *Kim.* 16.9-10; see, e.g., Fornara and Samons 1991: 126-129.

[41] Made abundantly clear by the condition in the truce, that the rebels should never set foot in the Peloponnese again; "if any of them was caught there in the future, he should be the slave of whoever caught him" (Thuc. 1.103.1); cf. Luraghi 2001: 293. Athenian self-presentation: Raaflaub 1985: ch. V.1.

[42] Thuc. 1.102.3. For discussion, see Fornara and Samons 1991: 127-128; Luraghi 2001: 287-288.

did whatever they saw and learned about the helots and their conditions in Messenia cause the Athenians to take a more active stance in this matter in later years, not even when they supported the "Messenians" in Naupaktos and collaborated with them. In 432, shortly before the outbreak of the Peloponnesian War, the Spartans sent several embassies to Athens with demands that might have avoided the war. The last of these demands was, in Thucydides' formulation, "Sparta wants peace. Peace is still possible if you will give the Hellenes their autonomy" (Thuc. 1.139.3, cf. 140.3). They referred, of course, to the Athenian allies, most of whom had long become subjects in the empire and for whose liberation the Spartans and their allies were about to go to war.[43] The Athenians, after intensive debates, responded, upon Pericles' recommendation, that "we will give their autonomy to the poleis if they had it at the time that we made the treaty and when the Spartans also allow their own poleis to be autonomous not as is advantageous to the Spartans but to themselves as they want it" (1.144.2 with 145). Whom did Pericles mean by "the Spartans' own poleis"? One might be tempted to think of the perioikic towns in Lakonia and Messenia but this is excluded by Pericles' use of the same word for the Athenian allies; hence it must allude to Sparta's allies in the "Peloponnesian League" and to the view, widespread at the time, that Sparta was promoting oligarchy in its sphere of influence and thus depriving its allies of constitutional autonomy, just as Athens' opponents claimed was the case with democracy in the Athenian empire. We conclude, not surprisingly but importantly in our present context, that the Athenians in these diplomatic exchanges did not mention the issue of the helots nor, for that matter, that of the status of the *perioikoi*. Both were considered domestic affairs of the Spartans, too delicate and dangerous to be interfered with. This implies, I think, the recognition or at least acceptance of the Spartan view that the helots were slaves—the contrasting claims of the "Messenians" in Naupaktos notwithstanding. Slaves were slaves, and no Greek polis would have dared to tell another to let its slaves go, out of principle and fear of making itself vulnerable to the same demand.

To some extent, this changed during the war. In 425 Kleon won his surprise victory at Pylos and Sphakteria. The Athenians established a fortified camp at Pylos and used it to undermine Spartan control of Messenia. In these efforts "Messenian" contingents from Naupaktos played a significant role: speaking the native language and knowing the land and customs, they could operate with relative ease "behind the enemy lines" and serve as perfect undercover agents. The success of this operation, not least in enticing helots to defect, was considerable but, for various reasons, perhaps far from sensational, although it did contribute to increasing Spartan willingness to

....

[43] Thuc. 2.8.4-5; Raaflaub 1985: ch. V.3.

conclude a peace treaty.[44] As part of the agreements of the Peace of Nikias, Sparta insisted on the removal of the "Messenians" from Pylos, but the Athenians brought them back already in 419/18. In 413 Demosthenes created a second fortified refuge in southern Lakonia, "so that the helots might have a place to which they could desert, and so that raiding parties, as at Pylos, might have a base from which to operate." The Spartans reciprocated when they occupied Dekeleia in Attica in 413, apparently with more success: supposedly, more than 20,000 Athenian slaves defected.[45] What matters here is that both sides confined themselves to attempts to induce slave defection and thereby to weaken the enemy economically. Neither side made any general proclamation concerning the liberation of slaves. Nor, apparently, did the Athenians, despite their collaboration with the "Messenians" from Naupaktos, who claimed polis status and were recognized as allies, think of the possibility of proclaiming as one of their goals the liberation of Messenia from Spartan rule, as Epameinondas did half a century later. The helots, it seems, were still considered Spartan slaves and nothing more; the Messenian identity, ideology, and related claims advanced by the free "Messenians" perhaps were too recent and too obviously partisan to be generally acceptable and easily usable as a tool of a political offense. As Simon Hornblower puts it, "It seems that the weapon of the *bellum servile* had yet to be thought of."[46]

In a general way, all this is confirmed by a clause in the treaty of the Peace of Nikias in 421: "If the slave force rises up, the Athenians shall support the Spartans with all their strength according to their ability" (Thuc. 5.23.3, tr. Rhodes). All commentators point out that this is a one-sided clause, not balanced by a corresponding obligation of Sparta to support Athens in case of a slave revolt. The structural difference and volatility of the Spartan slave system was thus well known and publicly acknowledged but this did not

---

[44] Actions from Pylos: Thuc. 4.41.2-3 (partly resuming 4.3.3), mentioning acts of brigandage, defection of helots as a result but apparently not a primary goal of the action, and Spartan fear of a helot revolt; see also 55.1; 80.2-4. Willingness for peace: Thuc. 5.14.3: "The helots were deserting, and there was always an expectation that even those who remained, relying on those outside, would take revolutionary action in view of their present circumstances, as they had before" (tr. P. J. Rhodes). On the general impact, see Gomme 1956; Hornblower 1996; Rhodes 1998: all at 4.41.2-3.

[45] Thuc. 5.35.6, 56; 7.26.2, 27.5.

[46] Hornblower 1983: 133-134 (cf. 1996: 197). I quote the preceding sentences: "Why Athens did not do more to *promote* servile insurrection in the war is a mystery: she could certainly have won it very quickly if she had. But the facts are clear: what Athens does is to establish bases *to which* (*autose*, vii.26.2) helots could desert; she does little actively to bring about such desertion." For Spartan insistence during the Peace of Nikias that the "Messenians" and helots who had recently defected be removed from Pylos even before the fort was returned to Sparta, see Thuc. 5.35.6-7. In Sicily, the Athenians seem to have taken the first steps in the direction of encouraging slave revolt (Polyain. 1.43.1), and Kritias apparently pursued it more radically later in the war in Thessaly (Xen. *Hell.* 2.3.36).

make a difference. Again, the Spartan perspective prevailed, that of the "Messenians" was ignored: slaves were slaves and as such their masters' and nobody else's concern.

The evidence thus speaks very clearly. The general and traditional views about slavery remained unchanged even in the case of the helots and even when several factors might have encouraged a new assessment. The case of the helots was acknowledged to be different from that of other slaves. Former helots, now forming a free polis of "Messenians," were promoting claims to a national identity, a history of former independence, and a homeland, with potentially far-reaching effects on Sparta's occupation of Messenia and exploitation of the helots. "Freedom" had long been discovered as a crucial political concept and in the last third of the fifth century was at the center of an intense propaganda war in which both Athenians and Spartans claimed to be "liberators of the Hellenes." Despite all this, to our knowledge, nobody associated the fate and condition of the helots even remotely with the idea that they should be freed, and the Athenians—in our view foolishly—failed to develop this idea into a successful military and ideological strategy against Sparta.

This corresponds to another fact, pointed out earlier. Even the scanty evidence that survives about sophistic ideas indicates that already in the fifth century some of them challenged, on the basis of the law of nature (*phusis*), the justification of the value attached to some traditional social or ethnic distinctions: elite versus commoners, Greeks versus barbarians; none of them, before Alkidamas, seems to have extended this to challenging, in principle, the justification of slavery.[47]

I am fully aware that the case of the helots is special in several ways—although perhaps less special than was long thought. The results of a case study focusing on how people thought of them and reacted to their situation in the fifth century, and in the context of foreign policy and diplomacy, can obviously not be used as evidence directly illuminating the thoughts and reactions to slavery of free Greeks several centuries earlier. But these results certainly fail to refute—and thus offer at least indirect support for—the conclusions I reached in my 1985 book, based on the examination of terminology and social conditions in Archaic Greece. Overall, then, I continue to believe that the existence and observation of slavery as such would have been insufficient to elicit freedom consciousness among the free on a level and in an intensity that would have been capable of triggering a conscious and explicit conceptualization of freedom.

---

[47] Synodinou (1977) claims that Euripides did; I remain doubtful but cannot argue for this here. Klees (1991-1992: 1.45-50) emphasizes, rightly, that the rejection of the enslavement of Greeks by Greeks, voiced by Greek authors from the late fifth century, apparently was not applied to the helots and that Epameinondas freed the Messenians not for humanitarian reasons but in order to weaken Sparta.

Bibliography

Alcock, S. E. 1999. "The Pseudo-History of Messenia Unplugged." *Transactions of the American Philological Association* 129: 333-341.

_____. 2001. "The Peculiar Book IV and the Problem of the Messenian Past." In S. E. Alcock, J. F. Cherry, and J. Elsner (eds.), *Pausanias: Travel and Memory in Roman Greece.* Oxford and New York: 142-153.

Asheri, D. 1983. "La diaspora e il ritorno dei Messeni." In E. Gabba (ed.), *Tria corda. Scritti in onore di Arnaldo Momigliano.* Como: 27-42.

Avezzù, G. (ed.). 1982. *Alcidamante: Orazioni e frammenti. Testo, traduzione e note.* Rome.

Buckler, J. 1980. *The Theban Hegemony, 371-362 BC.* Cambridge, MA.

Connor, W. R. 1989. "City Dionysia and Athenian Democracy." *Classica & Mediaevalia* 40: 7-32. (Reprinted in W. R. Connor, M. H. Hansen, K. Raaflaub and B. Strauss, *Aspects of Athenian Democracy,* Copenhagen 1990: 7-32).

Demand, N. H. 1990. *Urban Relocation in Archaic and Classical Greece: Flight and Consolidation.* Norman, OK.

Ducat, J. 1990. *Les Hilotes.* (Bulletin de correspondance hellénique, Supplément 20). Athens and Paris.

Figueira, T. J. 1999. "The Evolution of the Messenian Identity." In Hodkinson and Powell 1999: 211-244.

Finley, M. I. 1977. *The World of Odysseus.* Second edition. London.

_____. 1982. *Economy and Society in Ancient Greece.* Ed. by B. D. Shaw and R. P. Saller. New York.

Fornara, C. W., and L. J. Samons II. 1991. *Athens from Cleisthenes to Pericles.* Berkeley and Los Angeles.

Gomme, A. W. 1956. *A Historical Commentary on Thucydides.* Vol. 3. *The Ten Years' War, Books IV-V.24.* Oxford.

Gschnitzer, F. 1976. *Studien zur griechischen Terminologie der Sklaverei.* Vol. 2. *Untersuchungen zur älteren, insbesondere der homerischen Sklaven-terminologie.* (Forschungen zur antiken Sklaverei 7). Wiesbaden.

Guthrie, W. K. C. 1969. *Greek Philosophy.* Vol. 3. Cambridge.

Hamilton, C. D. 1991. *Agesilaus and the Failure of Spartan Hegemony.* Ithaca, NY.

Hodkinson, S. 2000. *Property and Wealth in Classical Sparta.* London and Swansea.

Hodkinson, S. and A. Powell (eds.). 1999. *Sparta: New Perspectives.* London and Swansea.

Hornblower, S. 1983. *The Greek World 479-323 BC.* London.

_____. 1996. *A Commentary on Thucydides.* Vol. 2. *Books IV-V.24.* Oxford.

Hunt, P. 1997. "Helots at the Battle of Plataea." *Historia* 46: 129-144.

_____. 1998. *Slaves, Warfare, and Ideology in the Greek Historians.* Cambridge.

Klees, H. 1991-1992. "Zur Beurteilung der Helotie im historischen und politischen Denken der Griechen im 5. und 4. Jh. v. Chr." *Laverna* 2: 27-52; 3: 1-31.

Lencman, J. A. 1966. *Die Sklaverei im mykenischen und homerischen Griechenland.* Wiesbaden.

Lotze, D. 1959. Μεταξὺ ἐλευθέρων καὶ δούλων. *Studien zur Rechtsstellung unfreier Landbevölkerungen in Griechenland bis zum 4. Jahrhundert v. Chr.* Berlin.

Luraghi, N. 2001. "Der Erdbebenaufstand und die Entstehung der messenischen Identität." In D. Papenfuß and V. M. Strocka (eds.), *Gab es das griechische Wunder? Griechenland zwischen dem Ende des 6. und der Mitte des 5. Jahrhunderts v. Chr.* Mainz: 279-301.

_____. 2002a. "Becoming Messenian." *Journal of Hellenic Studies* 122: 45-69.

_____. 2002b. "Helotic Slavery Reconsidered." In A. Powell and S. Hodkinson (eds.), *Sparta: Beyond the Mirage.* London: 229-250.

Meier, M. 1998. *Aristokraten und Damoden. Untersuchungen zur inneren Entwicklung Spartas im 7. Jahrhundert v. Chr. und zur politischen Funktion der Dichtung des Tyrtaios.* Stuttgart.

Nafissi, M. 1991. *La nascita del kosmos. Studi sulla storia e la società di Sparta.* Naples.

Nestle, W. 1901. *Euripides, der Dichter der griechischen Aufklärung.* Stuttgart.

Patterson, C. 1986. "*Hai Attikai:* The Other Athenians." *Helios* 13: 49-67.

Patterson, O. 1991. *Freedom.* Vol. 1. *Freedom in the Making of Western Culture.* New York.

Raaflaub, K. 1985. *Die Entdeckung der Freiheit.* (Vestigia 37). Munich. Revised English edition forthcoming: Chicago 2003.

_____. 1997. "Homeric Society." In I. Morris and B. Powell (eds.), *A New Companion to Homer*. Leiden: 625-649.

_____. 1998. "The Transformation of Athens in the Fifth Century." In D. Boedeker and K. A. Raaflaub (eds.), *Democracy, Empire, and the Arts in Fifth-Century Athens*. Cambridge, MA: 15-41.

_____. 2000. "Zeus Eleutherios, Dionysos the Liberator, and the Athenian Tyrannicides." In P. Flensted-Jensen, T. H. Nielsen, and L. Rubinstein (eds.), *Polis & Politics: Studies in Ancient Greek History Presented to M. H. Hansen*. Copenhagen: 249-275.

Ramming, G. 1973. "Die Dienerschaft in der Odyssee." Diss. Univ. of Erlangen.

Rhodes, P. J. 1998. *Thucydides, History IV.1-V.24, Edited with Translation and Commentary*. Warminster.

Richter, M. 1986. "Conceptual History (Begriffsgeschichte) and Political Theory." *Political Theory* 14: 604-637.

Roebuck, C. A. 1941. *A History of Messenia from 369 to 146 B.C.* Chicago.

Schütrumpf, E. 1991. *Aristoteles, Politik, Buch I, übersetzt und erläutert*. Berlin.

Synodinou, K. 1977. *On the Concept of Slavery in Euripides*. Ioannina.

Thomas, R. 2000. *Herodotus in Context: Ethnography, Science and the Art of Persuasion*. Cambridge.

Thommen, L. 1996. *Lakedaimonion Politeia. Die Entstehung der spartanischen Verfassung*. (Historia Einzelschriften 103). Stuttgart.

Welwei, K.-W. 1974. *Unfreie im antiken Kriegsdienst*. Vol. 1. Wiesbaden.

Wickert-Micknat, G. 1983. *Unfreiheit im Zeitalter der homerischen Epen*. (Forschungen zur antiken Sklaverei 16). Wiesbaden.

Wiseman, T. P. 1998. "Two Plays for the Liberalia." In T. P. Wiseman, *Roman Drama and Roman History*. Exeter: 35-51, 181-186.

Part III

Structures

Eight

The demography of the Spartan Helots

Thomas J. Figueira

The size of the Helot population under Spartan control in the classical period has not often been the focus of separate studies, although it has been an issue very often addressed in general appreciations of Spartan society and political history. Until recently, the estimates of Helot numbers have had an impressionistic coloration, serving to shed light on their authors' appreciation of the basic qualities of Spartan life and the structures of Laconian society rather than investigating this subject in its own terms. I shall attempt to show, however, that it is feasible to situate within useful limits the carrying capacity of the Laconian agrarian system for various social classes.

The nature of ancient demographic studies and Sparta

Demographic research about Greek *poleis* labors under a heavy load of evidentiary disability.[1] We lack the detailed data about births, baptisms, marriages, and deaths provided by administrative records for later European history.[2] There are indeed isolated exceptions. Demographic studies of fourth-century Athens have profited from examination of lists of members of the Council of the Five Hundred, rosters of young men receiving ephebic training, and other enumerations of quantifiable civic groups.[3] Inscribed casualty lists from the fifth century comprise another, albeit largely unexploited, resource.[4] In contrast, our evidence for most other times and places is primarily literary, and of two types. They may be called the "summary" and the "military" categories.

....

[1] Note Hansen 1988, but with the observations of Golden 1987.
[2] For recent overviews on ancient population studies, see Golden 2000; Scheidel 2001.
[3] Hansen 1986 (note Golden 1987), 1988, 1989, 1994; Rhodes 1980, 1981, 1984,; Ruschenbusch 1979, 1981a, 1981b, 1982, 1983, 1984a, 1984b, 1985, 1988a, 1988c; Sekunda 1992.
[4] Cf. Bradeen 1964, 1969, 1974: 3-34. Note Figueira 1991: 211-212.

In instances from the former category, an ancient authority will state the size of a specific demographic segment or a total population. As an apposite example *vis-à-vis* servile groups like the Helots, I would note the notorious passage in Athenaeus that provides us with slave numbers in excess of 400,000 for each of the cities of Athens, Corinth, and Aigina (6.103.272C-D; cf. Westermann 1941; Sallares 1991: 50-55). Athenaeus' sources help to illustrate the quality of the information contributing to such figures. For Corinth, the important west Greek historian Timaeus is cited (*FGrHist* 566 F 5), and for Aigina the constitutional treatise on that city attributed to Aristotle (fr. 475 Gigon; cf. *Schol.* Pind. *Ol.* 8.30i). For Athens, a census conducted by Demetrios of Phaleron (probably in 317/16) is the original source cited by the intermediary Ktesikles (*FGrHist* 245 F 1). This composite citation nicely combines three modes of demographic testimonia: descriptive historiography, constitutional historiography, and documentary historiography. And all three figures strain credulity beyond its breaking point. Through the process of transmission and homogenization, whatever was originally valid has been distorted or prejudiced, and is only to be restored through conjecture (e.g. Figueira 1981: 22-52; Canfora 1982: 36-45). We happen to lack any similar ancient summary for the number of Laconian Helots, in large part because their place in Spartan society did not activate even these limited modes of commentary. Nonetheless, if the *daimones* of evidence survival had so graced us, it is most unclear not only to what degree such a figure could be credited, but also whether its point of reference could even now be determined.

Figures for troop and ship mobilizations comprise the second class of evidence. Naturally they need considerable massaging in order to render population totals. The relevant classes of individuals serving have to be determined relative to the sum of adult male citizens, who in turn must be defined in relation to the total for adult males. A model life table, ideally, or some other reckoning of the likely proportion of adult males to the entire population, must then be applied (note, e.g., Coale and Demeny 1966: 782-783). Examples of this type of data are the figures for the mobilization of Spartan troops that provided one basis for my article in 1986. For Sparta, this line of analysis has a venerable history, extending back into the nineteenth century. I reproduce here my table from 1986, with some additions and corrections, as Table 8.1. Its basic conclusions have not, to the best of my knowledge, been systematically challenged.[5]

....

[5] Valzania 1996 does offer a type of contestation, accompanied by a limited citation of scholarship and an unusual selection of the ancient evidence in order to dismiss some attested figures. He specifically denies the sharp declines after the earthquake and between Mantineia and Leuktra, opting for a constant strength of 2,000 Spartiates! Cf. Valzania 1996: 34, 45, 47.

Context	Spartan Army	*Morai*	Spartiates (20-49)	Perioeci (20-49)[*]	Spartiate Decline
1. Plataia (479)	10,000 (20-49)	9400 (20-49)	5000	5000	NA
2. First Army Reorganization (455-446)	8004-8196 (20-49) (300 Hippeis, 600 Skiritai)	7104-7296 (20-49)	3055 (?)	4541 (+ 600 Skiritai)	39% (1. to 2.)
3a. Pylos (425)	7320 (20-49)	6720 (20-49)	2755	3965 (+ 600 Skiritai)	45% (2. to 3a.)
3b. Pylos Adjusted for Perioeci	7704-7896 (20-49)	7104-7296 (20-49)	2755	4349-4541 (+ 600 Skiritai)	45% (2. to 3b.)
4a. Mantineia (418)	7744 (20-54)	6144 (20-54)	2251	3239 (+ 600 Skiritai)	18% (3b. to 4a.)
4b. Mantineia Adjusted	7744 (20-54)	6144 (20-54)	2086-2141	3349-3404 (+ 600 Skiritai)	25% (3b. to 4b.)
5. Nemea River (394)	6600 (20-54)	5400 (20-54)	<1833	2991 (+600 Skiritai?)	12% (4b. to 5)
6. Leuktra (371)	4000-5000	3456 (20-54)	938	2150 (+600 Skiritai?)	51% (5. to 6.)
7. Post-Leuktra	4000-5000		876+		7%> (6. to 7.)

[*]This column estimates only the number of Perioecic hoplites.

TABLE 8.1 *The decline of Spartan manpower*

The number of Helots under Spartan control has long been a matter of scholarly interest. It was the essence of the Spartan social order that the Helots supported the class of full citizens or Spartiates, so that their numerical strength conditioned the size and prosperity of the civic body. Moreover, the measures taken to control the Helots strongly influenced Spartan life. The Spartans themselves negotiated terms for Attic assistance in the event of a Helot revolt in their alliance with Athens of 421 (Thuc. 5.23.3), and these terms may recapitulate provisions in place as early as the Hellenic League of 481 (Figueira 1993: 107, 294). Thucydides said that the design of Spartan institutions was predicated on security *vis-à-vis* the Helots, and outlined a Spartan atrocity to underline his point (4.80.2-4). Plato in the *Laws* referred, perhaps inaccurately, to Spartan anxieties over Helot unrest circumscribing their response at a critical moment, specifically the Persian incursion of 490 (698E; note Dušanic 1997). Aristotle vividly described the Helots as lying in ambush for the Spartans (*Pol.* 1269a37-b5). And Critias discussed a series of precautions taken by the Spartiates in daily life because of perceptions of danger from the Helots (fr. 37 DK [Lib. *Or.* 25.63]).

To gauge the magnitude and impact of Spartan fear of Helot unrest, scholars have attempted for many years to establish their numbers. Yet great care must be exercised in this line of speculation, because identification of the precise triggers for heightened levels of Spartan anxiety is a more complex issue than usually recognized, for such perceptions were profoundly ideologized.[6] Furthermore, perceived change in demographic proportions rather than absolute numbers may cause tension, as seen recently in Kosovo and Macedonia, where popular perceptions of the birthrate of Albanian speakers have profoundly and negatively influenced the politically dominant Slavs. For Sparta, it is noteworthy that our evidence for Spartan anxiety over the Helot threat derives from the period after the earthquake of c. 465, an event that altered the proportion between the exploited and exploiting social components (see below, pp. 224-7).

Unfortunately, our two categories of ancient demographic evidence are bound to serve us poorly in gauging the population of Spartan Helots. As a dependent group, the Helots were unlikely to generate the conventional type of literary reference. Nonetheless, several passages have been customarily cited for our question of Helot numbers. First, Thucydides observes that the people of the island of Chios had the most slaves except for the Spartans (Thuc. 8.40.2; cf. Theopompus *FGrHist* 115 F122a-b; Athen. 6.88-89, 265B-266F). That surely implies that the Spartan Helot population exceeded slave numbers not only at late fifth-century Athens, but also at other maritime centers such as Corinth, Aigina, and Samos.[7] Hence, Thucydides could intuitively place Helot numbers in a sequence of populations, the amounts of which can unfortunately no longer be determined. Second, Herodotus gives a number that might (marginally) count in either of our categories. Each Spartiate serving as a heavy infantryman mobilized for the campaign that led to the battle of Plataia was accompanied by seven Helots (9.28.2). That amounted to 35,000 Helots with 5,000 Spartiate hoplites. Third, in his discussion of the Spartan manpower crisis, Aristotle remarks that Spartan territory could support 1,500 cavalry and 30,000 infantry (*Pol.* 1270a29-31). That observation

----

[6] Talbert 1989 is particularly wrong-headed, especially in its dismissal of Helot resistance during the Peloponnesian War (cf. Figueira 1986: 196-198, 1999; Cartledge 1991 and this volume, pp. 21-3). Cf. also Roobaert 1977; Baltrusch 2001.

[7] Note Jameson 1992: 138-140. There is no reason to believe that Thucydides was referring to the density of slave population measured against the free population (cf. Finley 1959: 151, 163; *HCT* 5.86-87). That interpretation is not only unsupported by the text, but would also be an unusual way for a fifth-century observer to view the issue. It does remain uncertain whether the Chians had more slaves than the Athenians when Attic slave numbers peaked during the Pentakontaeteia. By winter 412/11, however, Athenian slave numbers were reduced through impoverishment, defection, military action, and manumission (cf. Thuc. 7.27.5).

naturally reflects on the carrying capacity of whatever segment of Spartan territory Aristotle was considering. Suffice it to emphasize again that even such valuable comments as these stand removed by several interpretative stages from actual estimates of a population for the inhabitants of *Lakônikê* and, specifically, for the Helots.

In the earliest scholarship, informed speculation mainly prevailed concerning the number of the Helots. This quality has persisted in more recent, cursory considerations. I say this not to belittle—since thoughtful and learned historians have been at work—but chiefly to rein in expectations. I list some earlier estimates in Table 8.2. Their wide range is noteworthy.[8] An investigative approach, emerging somewhat later, bypassed the absence of ancient evidence by focusing on the agrarian assets of the Spartans available to support the Helots and on modern economic and demographic parallels. This methodology was pioneered by Karl Julius Beloch in his groundbreaking monograph of 1886 (note Gallo 1990). After

Authority	Estimate	Relevant date	Spartiates: Helots
Manso 1800: 127-140	312,000-800,000	479	>1:14
Müller 1839(2): 44-45	224,000	479	1:7
Beloch 1886: 146-148*	175,000	c. 400	
Guiraud 1893: 412	220,000		1:7
Grundy 1908: 81	375,000	c. 480	1:15
Cavaignac 1912: 272-274	140,000	5th century	1:7
Kahrstedt 1919: 291	180,000		
Jardé 1925: 109-112	240,000-320,000	5th century	1:10
Busolt-Swoboda *GSK* 1926: 641-642			1:20
Coleman-Norton 1941: 63	250,000	c. 600	1:10
Ehrenberg 1960: 31	140,000-200,000	371	1:16-29
Cartledge 1987: 174	175,000-200,000		
Talbert 1989: 23	170,000-224,000		

*Beloch offers alternative minimum figures both of 100,000 based on Helot numbers exceeding Chian, Athenian, and Corinthian slave totals and of 60,000 based on an emended deployment of the Spartiates at Plateia and Herodotus' ratio of 7 helots to 1 Spartiate.

TABLE 8.2 *Estimates of Helot numbers*

....

[8] Oliva 1971: 53 n. 3 has a helpful conspectus of authorities.

refinement, this line of analysis could exploit data from modern Greek censuses, surveys on land usage, and research on the Greek and Mediterranean agrarian economy (see Gallo 1984: 7-22).

Moreover, unusually, in the case of Sparta, this methodology could be enriched by a quantitative appreciation of the actual processes of the Laconian economy, because the sort of speculative investigation of alimentation common for other *poleis* could in the case of Sparta be supplemented by data on the movement of products. Spartan subsistence was dominated by fixed or stereotypical transfers of output. The nature and scale of these movements of goods can be read backward to illuminate their implications for the nature of the underlying classes that sustained or were sustained by them. Moreover, our purpose in positing values for variables such as grain production per hectare and food consumption per capita is not predominantly to offer suppositions about lost data, although we may strive for the most accurate quantitative estimates. Rather we utilize the best hypotheses for the economic data to enable well designed "thought experiments" that test theories about the nature of the relevant social processes (such as a *klêros* system involving either sharecropping or fixed rents).

Our procedure is complicated by debates over the nature of Spartan property holding. Investigation is more straightforward for those who, like myself, accept the historicity of an archaic redistribution of a critical mass of real properties (the *politikê khôra* of Polyb. 6.45.3; cf. Plut. *Lyc.* 8.3; Plato *Laws* 684D) and the existence of a period during which *klêroi* were not exclusively transmitted by conventional, partible inheritance.[9] Analysis is more problematical, however, for those who see the tradition of the equality of the *klêroi* as solely a late ideological construct (Ducat 1983; cf. Papazoglou 1993). Even then, we would not be authorized to ignore the traditional figures on the number of *klêroi*, the level of rents, and the scale of mess dues. Their full ramifications would still deserve investigation in deference to the heuristic function of these figures in indigenous Spartan quantitative thinking about social relations. That conceptual status would truly be manifest, if it were the intention of the Hellenistic reformers to recreate a system of *klêroi* predicated on these amounts (cf., e.g., Plut. *Agis* 8.2). If these aspects of the system of *klêroi*, however, are to be condemned as merely Hellenistic constructs, the same details must consequently also be credited as Hellenistic appreciations, albeit intuitive, of the design parameters of various agrarian orders that may have been possible in *Lakônikê*.

....

[9] Figueira (forthcoming) will speak to this complex of problems.

Some recent treatments

There have been three significant recent discussions with a bearing on the linked issues of the Spartan agricultural economy and the number of the Helots: my own article in 1984, a study of Michael Jameson in 1992, and sections of a book of 2000 by Stephen Hodkinson.[10]

My earlier synthesis and reconsiderations

In my article in 1984, I took my departure from the rents in kind paid by the Helots to their Spartiate masters (Plut. *Lyc.* 8.7; cf. Myron *FGrHist* 106 F 2). These included 82 *medimnoi* of barley each year, which I estimated to equal c. 2,493 kilograms (kg) of barley by weight, to which I added a sixth to account for grain to be reserved for seed for the next harvest. That gave me an amount of 2,992 kg of barley for the annual rent and associated seed grain from each *klêros* or allotment. These figures for the weight of barley per *medimnos* and for the weight relationship of barley to wheat have been largely confirmed by the recently published Attic grain law of 374/73 (Figueira 1984: 92-94 [esp. n. 14]; cf. *SEG* 36.146.21-25; Stroud 1998: 54-55). For the productivity of *klêros*-land in barley, I adopted a range of yield of 750 kg to 900 kg for a hectare (ha = 10,000 square meters), having based myself on ancient and modern analogies (Figueira 1984: 99-100). Thus I reasoned that the rent-producing land of each *klêros* was c. 3.3-4.0 ha, which I doubled to allow for alternate year fallowing. To my resultant units of 6.6-8.0 ha (for producing the *klêros* rents in grain), I next added 0.6 hectares for grape production to allow for payment of the monthly mess dues in wine of each *klêros*-holder (Plut. *Lyc.* 12.3; Dicaearchus fr. 72 Wehrli). So my rent-producing *klêros* land was c. 7.2-8.6 hectares.

One Spartan tradition going back to Tyrtaeus puts the rents of the Helots at 50% of their production (fr. 6 W; Paus. 4.14.4-5; Ael. *VH* 6.1). Such an even split of output or assets between an invader and his victim is a feature of Dark Age raiding (*Il.* 18.509-512; 22.114-121). Furthermore, a 50% maximum rent is common in share-cropping arrangements (Figueira 1984: 103-104; Hodkinson 1992). Naturally, the question arises about the currency of this rule during the classical period, when fixed rents were in place (according to the Peripatetic authors of constitutional treatises on Sparta). Some have chosen to take the fixed rent and the levy of 50% as alternative traditions or as separate arrangements that were perhaps employed successively (see, most recently, Hodkinson 2000: 125-131). In that case,

....

[10] Earlier examples of this type of analysis are more useful on other features of the Laconian economy. Note Kahrstedt 1919; Lotze 1971; Buckler 1977.

however, it would be passing strange if the simpler 50% rule superseded the more specific amounts.

I would instead suggest that the fixed rents were a specification of the 50% levy and the fixed rents and the 50% levy were necessarily simultaneous provisions in the late archaic and classical periods (note Paus. 4.14.4-5).[11] The Helots of each *klêros* paid fixed rents that were envisaged as 50% of the "normal" production of the allotments. Using calculations comparable to those for splitting agricultural holdings in active cultivation and fallow, the *klêroi* were configured to yield the requisite rents from a 50/50 division. Moreover, in exigent conditions, the *klêros*-holder had to be content with 50% of actual production. This very arrangement is attested from classical Attic land leases in order to compensate for enemy incursions (*IG* II² 2492.12-14; *SEG* 21.644.11-16). Plutarch *Moralia* 239D-E, which also appears to derive from a Spartan *politeia*, envisages just this arrangement, a fixed rent resting on an ancient tradition.[12] Here a prohibition against exceeding the *apophora* was enforced by religious sanction (ἐπάρατον).

There are a number of further considerations that support this reconstruction. First of all, the combination of the two stipulations was practically helpful whenever land had to be assigned to a *klêros*-holder or a *klêros* had to be reconfigured. The *klêros* could not in fact comprise a fixed amount of land—let alone, a discrete, unified block—for that would require periodic wider redistribution to accommodate the creation of any new allotments.[13] Instead, it was merely any set of nearby parcels for which 50% of the likely output met the criteria for rent payment, such as 82 *medimnoi* of barley.[14] Second, a fixed rent was administratively easier, because the *klêros*-holder need not concern himself with concealment of production in normal years (unlike someone supervising a sharecropping arrangement). Furthermore, since the stipulations added two ceilings to the income from the *klêros* for its holder, both a fixed amount and 50% of the crop, the incentives for a Spartiate to manage his *klêros* in the conventional manner of Greek landholders were greatly lessened. That inhibition promoted the Spartiate's concentration on

---

[11] See the commentary on Paus. 4.14.4-15 of van Wees (this volume, pp. 36-7) and Luraghi 2002a: 235-236.

[12] *Moralia* 239E (*Instituta Laconica* 41): οἱ δὲ εἵλωτες αὐτοῖς εἰργάζοντο τὴν γῆν ἀποφορὰν τὴν ἄνωθεν ἱσταμένην τελοῦντες. ἐπάρατον δ' ἦν πλείονός τινα μισθῶσαι, ἵν' ἐκεῖνοι μὲν κερδαίνοντες ἡδέως ὑπηρετῶσιν, αὐτοὶ δὲ μὴ πλέον ἐπιζητῶσιν. Note also here, however, the defensive and propagandistic tendency.

[13] The incremental settlement of the area of the Laconia Survey which started after 600 (especially regarding the south-eastern sector) would be consistent with this practice. See Catling 2002: 157-161, 224-225; cf. pp. 233-237.

[14] As many *klêroi* experienced later fission and consolidation in the fifth and fourth centuries, these underlying assignments of various sub-rents to portions of the *klêroi* may have demarcated Helot responsibilities to *klêros*-holders. Cf. Hodkinson 2000: 126.

political and military communal activities (cf. Plut. *Ages.* 26.6-9; *Mor.* 213F-214).[15] Spartiates were non-khrêmatistic and non-oikonomic *klêros*-holders in their own terms and non-opportunistic or non-optimizing property holders in ours. Third, high fixed rents and relative stability of the configuration of a *klêros* offered strong incentives to the Helots to meet or exceed the expected output, because they appropriated that addition, while protecting themselves against their masters' displeasure (itself a punitive incentive). Finally, we shall discover below that a system of simple 50/50 sharecropping is hard to reconcile with the actual resource base of *Lakônikê*.

Consequently, if 50% is a default rent for the *klêros*, my calculation of the rent-producing part of the allotment had to be doubled to produce an estimate for a minimum size of the *klêros* that is consistent with any amount of rent in kind. Total minimum size of each *klêros* would be 14.4-17.2 ha. Unsurprisingly, the *klêroi* were larger than the size of ordinary Greek family farms (3.6-5.4 ha), even those supporting the families of hoplites (Burford Cooper 1977-78: 168-172; Gallant 1991: 82-87; Jameson 1992: 137; Isager and Skydsgaard 1992: 77-80).

There are five aspects of this reconstruction that I might now reconsider. First, I am now more tempted by the possibility that the measures of volume in this Plutarch passage are Aiginetic measures and not Attic, comparable to the citation of the mess dues in the same work (*Lyc.* 12.3). I would still note that such a stipulation does make it difficult to accommodate the system on the ground, because each *klêros* would require significantly more land. That revision would entail reworking all my calculations to account for rents about 50% higher in barley. Secondly, I would shift the seed grain into the portion of the output from the *klêros* that was retained by the Helots. Thirdly, I would emphasize more forcefully that there were rents levied in olives or in olive oil from each allotment, and that mess dues, calculated in terms of oil, were contributed by each Spartiate. These amounts, however, happened not to have been transmitted by the Peripatetic authors of constitutional works on Sparta.

Next, I would clarify the likely role of the production of wine grapes for the *klêros* and its rents. As I have noted above, our only figure involving wine is the monthly contribution to the mess. This contribution is likely to have been a larger share of the rent in wine than were the contributions in grain, because more wine than grain was probably consumed in the company of messmates than without them. In addition, it is less likely that the Spartiates split wine production equally with their Helots despite

....

[15] Again Plut. *Mor.* 239D-E (*Inst. Lac.* 41) transmits a useful summary of the idea: Ἐν δὲ τι τῶν καλῶν καὶ μακαρίων ἐδόκει παρεσκευακέναι τοῖς πολίταις ὁ Λυκοῦργος ἀφθονίαν σχολῆς· τέχνης μὲν γὰρ ἅψασθαι βαναύσου τὸ παράπαν οὐκ ἐξῆν· χρηματισμοῦ δὲ συναγωγὴν ἔχοντος ἐργώδη καὶ πραγματείας οὐδ' ὁτιοῦν ἔδει διὰ τὸ κομιδῇ τὸν πλοῦτον ἄζηλον πεποιηκέναι καὶ ἄτιμον.

the rule of 50% rent. Thus, it is unclear whether we ought to double the size of the acreage for vines of the *klêros*. In my actual calculations in 1984, this discrepancy was offset by using only the mess dues for estimating the size of the *klêros* and not a doubled or higher amount (to allow for Helot retention of one half the wine production). Wine is a high value agricultural product for its volume. Thus, wherever the value of farm output is to be transported over distances, stored, and perhaps redistributed, the prominence of wine,[16] just as in the mess dues, may indicate that the social processes at work transcend the simple conveyance of calories from producers to consumers.

To sum up, the cumulative force of these reconsiderations (of which the first is the most significant) might be to displace upward the range of the size of the *klêros* toward 18 to 21 hectares.

Finally, I would bring out more explicitly the implication of attributing a single particular yield in cereals to many thousands of hectares of agricultural land in *Lakônikê*, when so very broad a range of productivity may be justified. The crudity of that mode of estimation vitiates our incorporating an allowance for the attrition through mishandling, waste, spoilage, damage by vermin, and misappropriation, i.e., the effects that occur at each stage between harvesting and consumption. Rather than cloak our speculations about the Spartan agrarian system with a spurious exactitude, we are better advised to choose a "realizable output" per hectare that is sufficiently below the highest conceivable yields to include the wastage that ensued in subsequent processing.[17]

Later work on grain production in Greece and specifically Messenia has been divided on outputs for production per hectare, but has tended to stress the practice of alternate year fallowing. A study by Sanders (1984) has argued persuasively for higher yields for Melos (while correcting Wagstaff *et. al.* 1982), but there has been a tendency to downplay the relevance of Melos because of the fertility of its volcanic soils. The predominant trend, however, also based on comparative evidence, opts for lower yields, so that the force of my conclusions would be strengthened rather than diminished (Ruschenbusch 1988b; Sallares 1991: 372-389; Garnsey 1988: 10-14, 95-96, 1992, 1999: 26-28). Many high figures, however, do exist from the early twentieth century.[18] If we adopt a lower yield of barley for each hectare of, for

....

16 Appalachian farmers often arrogated the right to convert grain into more easily transported whiskey in defiance of the U.S. tax law, partly in order to overcome the challenges set by geography and a primitive transportation system. Concomitantly, the Spartans may have imposed high rents in wine on the Helots to simplify their problems of manipulating agricultural output.

17 Occasional years of high yield should not distort our estimates: there was not only considerable interannual variation because of climatic conditions, but also significant local variability from year to year (as G. Shipley reminds me *per litt.* [5/5/02]).

18 Note Gallant (1991: 75-78) who observes: " . . . I suspect ancient yields might well have been higher" (p. 78).

example, 650 kg per hectare, our range for the size of the *klêros* might find its upper limit at 24 hectares. That seems an outer possibility. Messenia was an especially fertile region and, in general, the *klêroi* occupied the best land in *Lakônikê*.[19]

At this point, I could have crudely estimated the number of Helots for any number of equal *klêroi*, so long as I observed the rule that the rents were fixed and could not exceed 50%, and that seed grain (at least a sixth) was subject to provision. The non-rent-producing land committed to grain would support about 8 people at *bare* total subsistence, which I take to be around 250 kg of wheat or its equivalent a year (Figueira 1984: 91-92, 107). Therefore, 6,000 such allotments would support 48,000 persons, and 9,000, 72,000 people. Adopting Aiginetic measures in place of Attic measures brings the number of people supported for each *klêros* to around 12 and for 9,000 *klêroi* 108,000. We ought to bear in mind this range of magnitude when we later consider the number of Helots more intently.

In point of fact, in my article in 1984, I did not take this approach. In the first place, it was clear that the Spartiate population had fallen from its high point by the period (450-370) for which I was investigating the operation of the messes (see pp. 224-7 below). That meant not only an aggregation of property, but also the likelihood that the procedure for the transmission of that property was evolving and land unit sizes were differentiating. More important, however, was my intention to illustrate the way in which the highly articulated material transfers in the Spartan social order tended to intertwine the economic and demographic destinies of citizen and dependent to an unusual degree.

Nevertheless, in 1984, I was compelled to focus on the allotments in Messenia and their Helot inhabitants. The *Laconia Survey* (Cavanagh et al. 1996, 2002) and the *Pylos Regional Archaeological Project* (*PRAP*) lay well in the future (Davis *et al.* 1997; Zangger *et al.* 1997; Davis 1998; Alcock 2002). Yet the *Minnesota Messenia Expedition* (*MME*) provided some valuable material on ecology and settlement patterns (McDonald and Rapp 1972; Rapp and Aschenbrenner 1978). Accordingly, I joined my estimates for the output and size of *klêroi* with the figure of 6,000 that I took to be not only a traditional number for a sub-unit of the *klêroi*, but one that also roughly fit the relative areas available for allotment in Messenia and Laconia (1984: 101-102). The total area of Messenia was 2,872 square kilometers (km^2), of which 1,276 km^2 was cultivated in 1960 (or 44%, well above the average for Greece). My figures for labor inputs for cereal farming were taken from modern Greek surveys, where the effects of modern mechanization could be discounted (cf. Gallant 1991: 75-76).

....

[19] *Lakônikê*: Strab. 8.5.6 C366. Messenia: Tyrtaeus fr. 5 W; Eur. fr. 1083 N; [Plato] *Alcib.* 122D; Paus. 4.4.3. See Roebuck 1945: 150-151. Lakonia: Polyb. 5.19.7 (Helos plain). See Jameson 1992: 137.

Out of the modern total for cultivated land, I had to subtract the land exploited by Perioecic settlements (Figueira 1984: 102-103). My results for the extent of arable land are outlined in Table 8.3.[20] Without the invaluable recent work of Graham Shipley (1992, 1996a, 1996b, 1997, 2000) and Jacqueline Christien (1982-83, 1989a, 1989b, 1992a, 1992b, 1998) on the topography of *Lakônikê* and in particular Perioecic sites, I was quite dependent on Niese 1906. In my review in 1984 Perioecic settlements comprised about 28% of Messenia.

Any such procedure of estimation can forward no great claim to precision. In the appendix, I assign each commune in modern Messenia either to *klêros*-land or non-*klêros*-land. Shipley's synthesis (1996) has reinforced the Perioecic status of

	0.74 mt/ha	0.9 mt/ha
1. Perioecic Land	351 km²	351 km²
a. Known cultivation: 226 km²		
b. Est. cultivation: 125 km²		
2. Rent Producing *klêros*-land:	516 km²	432 km²
3. Helot Supporting *klêros*-land:	409 km²	492 km²
4. Barley product of line 3:	15,375 mt	22,230 mt
wheat equivalent of line 3:	9,949 mt	14,450 mt
5. Helots sustained by line 4:	39,976	57,800
6. Man-days to farm lines 2 & 3:	2,513,950	2,513,950
7. Male man-days for lines 2 & 3:	1,759,550	1,759,550
8. Man-units avail. from line 5:	22,786	32,946
9. Male man-units from line 5:	11,860	17,149
10. Man-days/166 day year (1438 hrs):	3,782,476	5,469,036
11. Male man-days/166 day year:	1,968,760	2,846,739
12. Man-days/120 day year:	2,737,320	3,953,520
13. Male man-days/120 day year:	1,423,200	2,057,880

TABLE 8.3 *The agricultural economy of Messenia (mt = metric ton)*

....

[20] Although it was approached by a different methodology, I should note in comparison Roebuck's estimate of 789 km² available for all cereal cultivation in liberated Messenia and 875 km² for total cultivated area (1945: 156-157).

most of the candidates from the earlier literature.[21] Of the more doubtful examples, changing our mind on the status of Leuktron and Pephnos will not throw off our estimate.[22] Their position on the western littoral of the Tainaron peninsula between the probable Perioecic communities of Kardamyle and Thalamai makes the existence of *klêroi* in their vicinity unlikely.

The status of the next group of sites, including Abia, Alagonia and Gerenia to the north is, however, more questionable.[23] Some classical remains and pottery notwithstanding, refoundation or discontinuity cannot be definitely excluded. A similar reaction stands for the next group to the north, the two communities that lay to the south of the Nedon River, Pherai and Kalamai. Pherai was probably a Perioecic town.[24] Kalamai is attested by Pausanias as a Dark Age/archaic Messenian community (4.31.3) and was a Hellenistic Messenian town (Polyb. 5.92.4).[25] Doubtful location confuses the issue: it was either at modern Sóla, *MME* #140 (Perivolákia), primarily a Mycenaean site, or at Yiánnitsa, *MME* #537, where there are significant traces of classical and Hellenistic settlement. This area probably lay in one of the five traditional regions of Messenia, the Mesola (Strab. 8.4.5, 7). Unfortunately, we cannot ascertain whether Pherai and its environs approximated Thouria and its setting, that is, a Perioecic town amid *klêros*-land, or whether the Nedon River marked a more decisive boundary, below which there lay only Perioecic communities between Pherai and Kardamyle. One indication of the

....

[21] Of the 13 possible perioecic communities with which I dealt, Shipley 1997 classifies as contemporaneously-attested *poleis*: Aithaia (Shipley #18 = *MME* #136), Asine (19 = 512), Aulon (20 = 601), Thouria (21 = 137), and possibly Methone (36 = 412). Among Hellenistic/Roman *poleis* that are attested as archaic/classical settlements, he places Thalamai (33 = 150) and Kardamyle (34 = 147). Archaeological remains generally support their status as perioecic communities. Christien (1992: 154-163) prefers a different site for Aithaia, equating it with Aipeia/Korone, but a location at Rizómilo/Nichoria (*MME* #100) is problematical. It is hard to reconstruct the effect for our estimate of this placement, which would exchange one good agricultural site for another. Shipley has provided me with a tentative, reconsidered classification (*per litt.* 5/5/02). Definite: Asine, Mothone (Methone); probable: Aithaia, Thouria; possible: Aulon, Kardamyle, Korone, Kyparissos, Pharai/Pherai, Thalamai.

[22] Shipley classifies Leuktron = Leuktra (48 = 148) as a retrospectively attested *polis* (1996: 190, 239), and Pephnos as an unconfirmed *polis* (122 = 549); cf. Shipley 2000: 385-386, 387.

[23] Shipley classifies them as *poleis* attested in post-classical sources: Alagonia (38 = 548), Abia (55 = 144), and Gerenia (57 = 146). More recently, Shipley classes these sites as places that "cannot be shown to have existed as a settlement in Ar(chaic)/Cl(assical) times" (*per litt.* 5/5/02).

[24] Pharai = Pherai (79 = 142) is classed by Shipley as an early or legendary *polis*, but this status is probably a trick of the survival of our evidence, if Pharai is modern Kalamata (with remains dating back to the archaic period). Note Xen. *Hell.* 4.8.7, cf. Nepos *Conon* 1.1 (coloniam Lacedaemoniorum); Steph. Byz. *Eth.* 658; note also the heroic oecist in Paus. 4.30.2.

[25] Shipley classifies under "legendary or early *poleis* (and possible) *poleis*" (1997: 263 for #102). His more recent classification (*per litt.* 5/5/02) denies the presence of an "Archaic/Classical settlement."

presence of *klêroi* might be the loss of the region north of Gerenia to newly founded Messene (cf. Shipley 2000: 385-386).[26]

To be factored into our judgment is the tradition that the mid-eighth-century Spartan king Teleklos founded three towns, Ekheiai, Poiaessa, and Tragion, from the temple of Athena Nedousia (Strab. 8.4.4). These could be mythological names for some of the archaeologically or textually attested and possibly Perioecic sites in this area. Yet the tradition could also represent a later archaic "charter" myth, in which Messenian rebellion, hostility, or sacrileges against Athena Nedousia were intended to justify the creation of *klêroi* here. Hence it cannot be ruled out that southeastern Messenia provided some additional land for *klêroi*.

Nonetheless, in 1984, following Niese (1906: 124), I had not addressed the possibility that Kyparissos was a Perioecic site. Shipley has now marshaled the evidence, placing Kyparissos/Kyparissiai in his grouping of attested archaic/classical settlements whose *polis*-identity is established in the Hellenistic or Roman period.[27] Kyparissia may be equated with modern Kástro Kyparissías (*MME* #70), a placement with which most of the citations are consistent, although the strong association with Nestor and Pylos may indicate translocation.[28] Yet, there is also a strong association of Kyparissia with Triphylia.[29] Accordingly, the Kyparissioi may have inhabited a district stretching north to the Neda river and Triphylia (Polyb. 5.92.5), possibly encompassing Aulon, and south toward Pylos. Such a determination might have far-reaching ramifications for habitation patterns in northwest Messenia. Not only does Kástro Kyparissías have considerable agricultural land (c. 1,600 ha within a 2.8 km. radius), but a number of other known sites in its district (*MME* #69, #200, #409) might also be conceivably considered Perioecic. Thus, our belief in a Perioecic Kyparissia raises the possibility that a considerable amount of the land in this region should be subtracted from that available for accommodating *klêroi*.

When this analysis, however, is combined with my closer review of modern Greek communities in the appendix, only slight changes to our view of the classification of

....

[26] Christien (1998: 437-439) puts the new border further south. Yet the Boiotian character of Leuktron, Kharadra (= Pephnos?), and Thalamai (Strab. 8.4.4), and the Argive oecist of Oitylos (Paus. 3.25.10), are better interpreted as indicative of the heroic pedigrees fabricated as precedents that preceded an archaic reception by Sparta of immigrants from central Greece and the Argolid as Perioeci.

[27] *IG* V.1 1421 = *SIG*³ 952 = *SEG* 11.1026, 22.314; *SEG* 11.1025; Shipley 1997: 242-243 on #35. Shipley's more recent classification (*per litt.* 5/5/02) lists Kyparissos as a possible perioecic *polis*.

[28] Hom. *Il.* 2.593; Diod. 15.77.4; Strab. 8.4.1-2, 6 (citing Homer); Paus. 4.36.7; also Scylax *Periplus* 45; Ptol. *Geog.* 3.14.31; Plin. *NH* 4.5.15; Steph Byz. s.v. Κυπαρισσήεις, *Eth.* 395.3-5 (citing Homer).

[29] Strab. 8.3.22-25; Steph. Byz. s.v. Κυπαρισσία, *Eth.* 395.1-2.

Messenian land results. Non-*klêros*-land appears to have constituted at least 28% of Messenia (with 33% standing as an upper limit).

Returning to my earlier calculations, there were two important conclusions that emerged. First, it was clear that so much grain was extracted from the allotments in rents that very large numbers of Helots could not be supported at subsistence from the land committed to grain cultivation. This conclusion not only arises out of the assumption that around 50% of production went to pay rents. It was also implied by my investigation of the land left for the subsistence of the Helots after the land needed to pay the rents and the land held by Perioecic communities was subtracted. My analysis implied a global Helot population between 60,000 and 87,000, when a possible c. 3,000 Laconian *klêroi* and their Helots were factored into the estimate. That ceiling for the number of Helots did, however, appear low intuitively. Thus I posited recirculation of food from the Spartiates back to the Helots, in part mediated by the messes, as one mechanism for supporting a higher Helot population.[30] Such circulatory regimes using incentives among servile agriculturalists can be paralleled.[31] Any inclination to adjust the size of the *klêros* upward or to lower the output in barley of *klêros*-land has the impact of intensifying these effects. I have been disappointed in some scholarly reaction to this hypothesis.

Let me note first the discussion of J. Ducat (1990: 61-62). He compares the daily siege rations for the Spartans on Sphakteria of 2 *khoinikes* of *alphita* and 2 *kotylai* of wine that were agreed upon with the Athenians in 425 (Thuc. 4.16.1), and objects that the mess ration of *alphita* only exceeds the siege ration by 20%. I had been less impressed with this disparity in discussing the same comparison (1984: 88), but it is important here to make my position more explicit.

First, the regime for food provision at Pylos was to provide the total intake of food, while only a single, albeit the main, meal of the day was consumed in the mess. Second, the meal in the mess was supplemented by cheese, figs, *opsônion*, meat from hunting, olives and olive oil, and other edible contributions, while the siege ration included only a portion of meat (probably small, as the amount is unspecified by Thucydides). Third, Ducat did not offer an explanation for the mess dues in wine, which are quite remarkably 220-240% of the Pylos siege ration in wine. As noted above, wine was a particularly convenient means for conveying or redistributing value in a barter economy, centering on natural goods (see Figueira 2002).

....

[30] Compare Scheidel (this volume, pp. 241-5) where a "simplified model" for Helot numbers posits recirculation along with higher yields and higher arable totals as means to account for higher estimates for the Helot population.

[31] For positive and negative incentives in the *antebellum* south, see Fogel and Engerman 1974: 144-157, 239-243. On Louisiana sugar plantations, slaves grew corn for their own advantage, selling it to their masters, who used it for the slave rations of the plantation (McDonald 1993: 279-282).

Fourth, I emphasized the extraordinary total value of the mess dues, when expressed in terms of wheat, equaling at least c. 1280 kg, that is, enough economic output to support 5 people at bare subsistence. Furthermore, a mess of 15 Spartiates contributed annually an immense store of foodstuffs, equivalent in economic value to at least 20 metric tons of wheat. Truly it mattered not to a Helot whether he carried away a *kotylê* of *alphita* or the wine, figs, cheese, olives, vegetables, and meat from the mess contributions that could be traded for barley and wheat (cf. 1984: 91-96). Finally, the mess dues were indeed not the only source for grain and other products for redistribution. After each Spartiate had tendered his mess dues, he still possessed 44 *medimnoi* of barley from each intact *klêros*, not to mention other agricultural output that cannot now be quantified (Figueira 1984: 98-99). Any portions of this rent not consumed in a Spartiate *oikos* constituted a large supply from which to pay wages and offer emoluments in kind during recirculation to the Helots.

Even were we, however, to accept the validity of Ducat's comparison of unlike alimentary regimes and downplay the assets for redistribution other than mess contributions in grain, it would still not entirely vitiate my earlier hypothesis of recirculation. Even on Ducat's reckoning, 0.25 *medimnos* individually or 3.75 *medimnoi* for a whole mess of 15 Spartiates would be available monthly from surplus grain, enough to support 6 additional Helots at their Pylos rations, and (in Ducat's view) a maximum of 2,000 Helots in all. That last estimate is erroneous even on its own terms. The actual adult Spartan manpower of 8,000 c. 480 is roughly compatible with the traditional and conventional number of *klêroi* of 9,000 (Hdt. 7.234.2; Figueira 1986: 167-170). Eight thousand mess members gives us 3,200 more Helots supportable under Ducat's conditions, a number that comprises a substantial increment of additional adult males to the entire servile population and to the dependent labor force.

Nevertheless, arguing over the amount of additional Helots sustainable from recirculation can be misleading, if we suppose that increasing that total population was the chief goal of such a process instead of its beneficial byproduct. A servile redistributive system operates in the realm of marginal decision-making. No Helot *oikos* was ever faced with the option of supporting one or more additional family members for the next year in return for any one action. Rather, some Helots were daily confronted with the chance for some extra food in return for an acquiescent demeanor, adherence to specific orders, undertaking or executing some task more efficiently, or some act of pro-Spartiate initiative. From the totality of Helot decisions, contingent on the pleasure of their masters, more resources were available to sustain their lives. Their quality of daily life was radically conditioned by such choices because of the magnitude of the transfers of their production to their

Spartiate masters. Does this incessant grind of agonizing over compliance or passive resistance not truly lie at the heart of "le mépris des Hilotes?"[32]

Misreading the social texture, scaling, and complexity of food recirculation as a technique for controlling a dependent labor force also affects the comments of H.W. Singor (1993: 45-46). Recirculation through the messes influenced precisely those male Helots who interacted most intensely with the Spartiates, those who came into the "field of effect" of the *syssitia*. Hence, Singor's caricature of my view, in which there is conjured up a fantasy of mule trains back and forth over Taygetos, is an unnecessary complication.[33] Nor were recirculation through the Spartiate *oikos* or recirculation through the messes ever exclusive mechanisms, either in practice or in my piece of 1984. Nonetheless, it was significant that some considerable recirculation was probably enacted in the public space of the messes rather than in the private space of an *oikos* at Sparta or on the *klêros*. In the messes, such material exchange was pervaded by class-to-class psychological affects rather than shaped by a behavioral dynamic transacted by individual masters and their individual dependents. That context for performance not only restricted any managerial tendencies for the Spartiate, but also inhibited his development of a mode of personal paternalism over "his" Helots.

Moreover, the hypothesis of redistribution not only helped account for a larger Helot population and illuminated one mode by which the Helots were conditioned to their role of dependency, but it also dramatized the fragile equilibrium of the whole system. As my elaboration of the labor inputs necessary to farm the *klêroi* suggested, the productivity of the *klêroi* was probably vulnerable to any significant subtraction of manpower (Figueira 1984: 104-106).[34] For lower levels of productivity such as might prevail under wartime conditions, the flight or rebellion of male Helots brought the Spartan rural economy below the level of necessary inputs (cf. Gallant 1991: 75-76). This factor is probably implicated in the sharp decline of Spartiate numbers in the years after the Attic occupation of Pylos (Figueira 1986: 192-197). Many Spartiates then lost their ability to pay their mess contributions. The same cause accounts for an echo of this initial decline in the fourth century, when possible family limitation in the late fifth century seems to have had a marked delayed effect (Figueira 1986: 202-206).

One approach that has not been suggested previously but which would affect my earlier estimate of Helot numbers would be to hypothesize that some Helots

---

[32] Note Figueira 1984: 108 for its discussion of Athen. 14.74.2 657C with Theopompos *FGrHist* 105 F 22. Here a Thasian offer of delicacies to Agesilaos and the Spartiates is refused as illicit, while such an offer was properly made to the Helots, who might more appropriately be corrupted by such fare.

[33] Note my earlier specific rejection of this approach: Figueira 1984: 95-96 n. 25.

[34] On such constraints, see now the discussion in Halstead and Jones 1989: 47-50.

were supported by non-*klêros* land. This option can be admitted on our theory that the core territory of the Spartan villages was not subjected to redistribution during the seventh or early sixth centuries. That hypothesis may be invoked to explain the persistence of a Spartan aristocracy that had carried over intact, into the regime of *homoioi*, an early archaic steep hierarchy of landholdings (see Figueira forthcoming). Larger estates in this core area may have always been tilled by dependent workers who originated in the weaker communities of the upper Eurotas valley and its watershed that had been absorbed by the Spartans or who derived from more vulnerable groups among the Spartans themselves. Smaller estates in these core holdings had originally been cultivated by their owners. After the consolidation of the system of *klêroi*, *syssitia*, and *agôgê*, however, even these former smallholders needed to induce either poorer Perioeci or (more to our point here) Helots from the *klêroi* to work in their place.[35] How much the acceptance of this surmise might shift upward the range for Helot numbers is uncertain, but an additional 20% of the Laconian Helots would number 4,000-5,780 people in my earlier reconstruction.

Comments of M. H. Jameson

In a paper delivered in 1990 and published in 1992, Michael Jameson drew attention to several features of the rural economy of Sparta that have a bearing on the issue of Helot numbers.

1. He compared the output of the *klêros* to the 200 *medimnoi* production of the zeugite census class at Athens, the class from which the bulk of the Athenian phalanx was raised (Jameson 1992: 137). This comparison, however, would perhaps be better made with the next census class, that of the Attic *hippeis*, whose estates produced 300 measures of wet and dry agricultural product annually. If the Helots' rent was in Aiginetic measures and constituted 50% of production, the normative *klêros* produced at least 246 dry measures and 12 wet measures of wine (specifically for paying the mess dues). That gives a total of 258 measures, without considering all the production of olive oil, whatever wine production was not paid over in dues, and other products tendered in rent. Certainly, this analogy reminds us that one of the outstanding features of the "Lycurgan" order was its blending of aristocratic warfare patterns with a hoplite polity. The more elite quality of Spartan full citizenship demanded a notably broader base in agrarian and human assets than comparable institutional orders elsewhere.

....

[35] Yet the preserved economic hierarchy of the core territory was not static. The western zone of the Laconia Survey on the margins of the Eurotas plain experienced sixth century settlement on land to which earlier claim was probably laid by elite Spartiates and so presumably outside the system of *klêroi*. Helots and poorer Perioeci may have provided the workforce. See Shipley 1996b: 332-335, 355-377, 380-389; Catling 2002: 166-167, 180.

2. Jameson also revisited the issue of the land available for Spartan *klêroi*, focusing on the Eurotas valley and the Helos plain in Laconia. He concluded that no more than 21,000 hectares were available, which allowed for 2,000 10.8 hectare *klêroi*, his lower limit (cf. Wagstaff 1982: 48-64). Above, we have found that lower limit unrealistically low. At his upper limit for *klêros* size, which was 18 hectares, Jameson notes that only 1,200 *klêroi* could be accommodated in Laconia. Jameson graciously sent me a draft of a part of his research some years before this paper's delivery, so that I commented on some of his calculations in 1984 (n. 48, p. 102). At that time, I estimated that his appraisal of the arable land in the Eurotas valley and Helos plains would support 1,221 to 1,456 *klêroi*. Jameson also criticized Paul Cartledge for offering figures between 50,000 and 75,000 hectares for the land available for *klêroi* in Laconia (Cartledge 1987: 174-174). Although Jameson was not offering exhaustive discussion here, my fairness to both parties compels me to observe that Jameson is actually criticizing a long tradition of discussion on the topic, one that included such prominent representatives as Jardé (1925: 112-113), Kahrstedt (1919: 280-281), and Bölte (1929: 1339-1340; cf. Figueira 1984: 102; Hodkinson 2000: 132, table 1). With Cartledge, I believe that there were probably more than 1,500 *klêroi* in Laconia at the height of Spartan population between 480 and 465. Mobilization figures seem to support this conjecture.

Nevertheless, Jameson's investigation of the topography does suggest several observations about the Laconian *klêroi*. The existence of *klêros*-land outside the Helos plain should be envisaged. Shipley has drawn attention specifically to the plain around Kyparissia (1992: 219-220). There may well also have been encroachments of *klêros*-land in the vicinity of the Perioecic communities of the Eurotas valley like Pellana, Geronthrai, and Khrysapha, a doubtful case as Perioecic.[36] At Khrysapha, the Laconia Survey confirms a wave of sixth-century occupations. Moreover, some land near Sparta itself may have been distributed in *klêroi* because it belonged to Spartans excluded from the creation of the class of *homoioi*, just like the Partheniai dispatched as colonists to Taras.

Moreover, Laconian *klêroi* had probably undergone some evolution in their composition. It may be that subdivision, along with the creation of new *klêroi*, had occurred as Spartiate and Helot numbers had increased over the sixth century. More marginal farming land may have been incorporated into existing *klêroi*, with teams of Helot families conducting their operations in several proximate locales. In fact, it may make sense to envisage the Helots themselves as the motor of these changes, attempting to increase their production so that more was left after their payment of the fixed rents. Concealment of production doubtless played some role in this

....

[36] Shipley 1992: 216-228, 1996b: 423-438; Catling 2002: 164-166, 178-180, 224-225, 235-237, 244-248.

process. If we suppose that the 50% calculation was not constraining in non-exigent periods, and that *klêroi* were only examined at intervals for their output (as I have hypothesized above), the resultant periods of stable occupation were probably long enough to justify more intensive cultivation practices. The Spartans could be seen as periodically identifying and appropriating the advances of longer duration made by Helot farmers.

Therefore, we cannot speak dogmatically about the pattern of Helot settlement in *Lakônikê* (Laconia and Messenia). We can easily envisage that the Spartans would have acted to break up existing Dark Age settlements, like Nichoria in lower Messenia, for security reasons (cf. Lukermann and Moody 1978: 92-95; McDonald and Coulson 1983: 326; Spencer 1998). Scattered farmsteads constituting *klêroi* would then become more prevalent in these locales. And, in the Helos plain, there does seem to be evidence for more nucleation in the Hellenistic period, after the breakdown of the earlier socio-economic order (cf. Shipley 2000: 382-383). Elsewhere, however, the process of creating new *klêroi* as the Spartans exploited the expansion of cultivated area by increasing numbers of Helots would be consistent with more nucleated settlements. Such settlements would be autonomously shaped by the Helots consistent with the forces militating in favor of such conglomeration in other areas of rural Greece.[37] This hypothesis would be consonant with the good evidence for nucleation along with low density of occupation in the Pylos region found by *PRAP*.[38] Archaic Spartan agrarian "policy" was limited to simple interventions to carve out new *klêroi* as necessary through inspections (made at harvest times?) in a manner appropriate to the primitive administrative and managerial techniques that prevailed (cf. Hdt. 2.109.1-2).

3. Jameson recognized that Aristotle's observation about the carrying capacity of Spartan territory is problematical for his understanding of the limitations of the arable land available within Laconia (117,536 ha in modern Lakonia and Kynouria

....

[37] There may be some unappreciated literary evidence for such nucleation in a fragment of the *Philolakôn* of Stephanos, a poet of New Comedy (fr. 1, *PCG* 7.614-615 [Athen. 11.469b]; cf. T 1-3): {Σ.} τούτῳ προέπιεν ὁ βασιλεὺς κώμην τινά./ {Β.} καινόν τι τοῦτο γέγονε νῦν ποτήριον;/ {Σ.} κώμη μὲν οὖν ἐστι περὶ τὴν Θυορίαν./ {Β.} εἰς τὰς Ῥοδιακὰς ὅλος ἀπηνέχθην ἐγώ / καὶ τοὺς ἐφήβους, Σωσία, τοὺς δυσχερεῖς. While various candidates, including Philip II, Pyrrhos, and Alexander the Molossian, have been suggested for the king in line 1, surely there is a more economical hypothesis. A play about a Laconizer mentioning a grant of a *kômê* 'village' near Thouria in Messenia suggests a Spartan king. The context may be that an early Hellenistic Spartan king intends to reconquer southeastern Messenia so that he can reduce to dependency the formerly Helot communities in its vicinity, enabling him to make land grants (not traditional *klêroi*) to his supporters. Compare the foundation by an Athenian of Kolonides (Paus. 4.34.8). The *kômê* in question could derive from a nucleated Helot settlement.

[38] Note especially the sites of Romanou *Romanou* and Romanou *Glyfadaki* in survey area VI. See Davis et al. 1997: 454-469; Harrison and Spencer 1998: 158-162; Alcock 2002: 192-196.

in 1961). He countered by applying Aristotle's estimate of 1,500 cavalry and 30,000 heavy infantry to *Lakônikê* prior to 371, when the Spartans held all Messenia as well (Jameson 1992: 137-138 [n. 14]).

While not an impossible inference, since Aristotle does refer implicitly to the battle of Leuktra in this passage, this conjecture does seem a little incongruous when the refounding of Messene would have preceded the earliest forerunner of the *Politics* by a considerable lapse of time. At the time of the Persian wars, Sparta had at least 16,000 Spartiate and Perioecic hoplites (18 or older). Adult male Perioeci of non-hoplite rank may have numbered as many as 30,000, a good number of whom would have been hoplites in almost any other city-state than Sparta. After all, a figure of 30,000 Perioecic allotments is found in the "constitutional" tradition (Plut. *Lyc.* 8.3; cf. *Agis* 8.1; note Lotze 1993/94). Messenia alone could perhaps support, solely from agriculture, 60,000 male and female Perioeci at bare subsistence (Figueira 1986: 182-183). Thus it hardly makes for a striking point if Aristotle observed that all of *Lakônikê*, as constituted before Leuktra, could have produced 30,000 men of hoplitic rank under a different, more egalitarian social order and with a conventional Greek economy (cf. Polyb. 2.38.3).

Accordingly, our question is better formulated in these terms: could Aristotle, with some allowance for exaggeration, have believed that Laconia itself, along with the Spartan-held parts of the Arcadian borderlands, Messenia, and Kynouria (for which, see Shipley 2000; also Magnetto 1994), still had this demographic potential (31,500 of hoplite census) at the time of the composition of the *Politics*? If he did, he perhaps placed a high evaluation on the fertility of *Lakônikê* and on the aggregate income from non-agricultural sources. Yet, a legislator starting completely afresh could probably carve out at least 19,000 minimum hoplitic farms producing 150 *medimnoi* of barley out of Laconia and Kynouria alone, without considering non-cereal and non-agricultural income and without adding the production of the Spartan-controlled areas of Arcadia and Messenia.[39]

Comments of Stephen Hodkinson

Finally, let us consider Stephen Hodkinson's recent contributions, which build on his piece published in 1992. I call attention to several of his conclusions that are particularly relevant to the subject of Helot numbers.

1. Hodkinson discusses the issue of the arable land available for the *klêroi* both in Laconia and Messenia (2000: 131-145). Using the 1971 census, he has carefully explored the amount of cultivated land in modern Greek communities that might

---

[39] Note van Wees 2000 for a spirited argument on behalf of the thesis that hoplites at Athens were recruited from more prosperous *thetes*, in which he uses 150 *medimnoi*. as an important threshold level.

have been available for ancient *klêroi*. Noteworthy is his emphasis on the need to include the arable land in the Helos plain that now belongs to the Eparchia Epidaurou Limiras (2000: 141; cf. *NSS* 1978: 1.218). The significant result is to restore the land available in Laconia for *klêroi* up from Jameson's c. 21,000 ha toward Bölte's level of 50,000 ha.[40] His result for Messenia is in line with earlier work that opted for around 90,000 ha, but is welcome confirmation indeed. Although Hodkinson is not comfortable with ancient figures about the number of *klêroi*, I would recall that one traditional split of the received total of 9,000 *klêroi* into groups of 6,000 and 3,000 is nicely accommodated by his understanding of the geography. Hodkinson offers various figures for the size of citizen estates (2000: 382-385). These are a mean landholding size of 20.77 ha for 6,500 households, or, alternatively, the combination of an elite holding of 44.62 ha for 585 households and for 5915 households an ordinary Spartiate estate of 18.41 ha (in the range that I posited in 1984).

2. Let us turn to his estimate of Helot numbers (2000: 385-395). Hodkinson begins his estimate of the population of the Helots from the 35,000 Helots taken on the Plataia campaign, which he reduces by 5,000 for the Helot batmen regularly accompanying their masters on campaign, so leaving 30,000 Helot farmers. That distinction looks artificial to me, and I would probably collapse this category into his reduction that is made to account for young males. For him, that implies 45,000 adult male Helot farmers between 20 and 60, by applying the two-thirds levy to the Plataian mobilization, and 52,000 of all ages. With 20% unmarried males, the remaining 41,600 Helot family units give a total Helot population of 187,000 by applying a multiplier of 4.5. He believes that this reconstruction is consistent with a Helot land holding of 3.25 ha for each family. Thus, these Helot land holdings must occupy 135,200 ha, or virtually all the arable land available for *klêroi* in *Lakônikê* (in Hodkinson's view). Alternatively, Hodkinson offers the 7 to 1 ratio of the Plataia campaign as the Spartan perception of Helot numbers *vis-à-vis* themselves. Hence 8,000 Spartiates give ca. 56,000, and, subtracting batmen and youths, a sum of 36,000 Helot families and 162,000 Helots. This yields an average farm of 3.75 ha.

....

[40] One reservation, however, concerns the argument that the Malea fortification of the Athenians during the Peloponnesian War (Thuc. 7.26.2) necessitates the existence of *klêroi* in the vicinity of Neapolis on the southern end of the peninsula (Shipley 1997: 203; Hodkinson 2000: 141). The modest population of potential Helot defectors from an out of the way, small district could not have justified such a base on their own account. A strongpoint there was well placed, however, to receive runaways by boat from throughout the Laconian Gulf, while it accommodated raiders in a spot conveniently distant from Spartan bases.

This reconstruction is useful in my view because it illuminates the upper limits of a feasible Helot population. Its 3.25 ha average holdings would produce in barley between 1056 and 1463 kg, if we apply respectively a low output of 0.65 metric ton (mt) and a high output of 0.9 mt per ha and crop in alternate years. A 50/50 share-cropping arrangement will leave the Helots between 528 and 732 kg of barley each year. These incomes in barley are equivalent to between 323 and 476 kg of wheat. These outputs will not have supported Helot families, even if we adopt high incomes from non-agricultural sources. A population of 187,000 needs at least 46,750 mt of wheat equivalent to survive, or the output of a little below 100,000 ha of barley (at 0.75 mt per ha; 79,915 ha at 0.9 mt per ha); 200,000, with alternate-year fallow; 400,000 with 50/50 sharecropping. I shall not repeat my calculations to discuss Stephen Hodkinson's lower alternative (36,000 Helot families), but note that it differs from his higher estimate by a reduction of 13% in any of our calculations. This reconstruction demands either much more fertile land than *Lakônikê* could offer or a very high and unrealistic output from sources other than annual crops.

This Helot population seems too high in absolute terms for the agricultural base of *Lakônikê*, but that is not the only difficulty with this interpretation. A large contributing factor to its unfeasibility lies in the conjecture of 50/50 sharecropping without recirculation of food. That arrangement draws off far more output from the Helots than does the hypothesis of a system of fixed rents and an exigent exaction of 50% of production. That is because the achievement of higher levels of productivity for individual units of grain-producing land does not yield benefits in the short or middle term to the Helot farmers. Moreover, the hypothesis of fixed-rent *klêroi* suggests a much more workable system when the number of Spartiates had fallen below the level of 8,000 or 9,000 (the scenario imposed by conventional reconstructions of Spartiate demography). On the assumption that each *klêros*-fragment was to pay its set share of the fixed rent, handed down from an earlier intact *klêros*, the demographic decline of the Spartiates removed the pressure of marking off new *klêroi* so that any increases in production were retained by the Helots for their own subsistence. In contrast, 50/50 sharecropping is immune to such amelio-ration, as it does not correlate with changes in Spartiate numbers.

Simple sharecropping on a 50/50 basis shares the drawbacks of all reconstruc-tions that do not incorporate a cycling of foodstuffs back to the Helots, whether through the messes or by individual Spartiate dispensation. The Spartiate class was never large enough to consume all the food that would have been extracted from the *klêroi* through 50/50 sharecropping. Unless redistribution is posited, the entire surplus of rent left over after Spartiate consumption must be imagined to have exited a closed *klêros* system either to other groups within *Lakônikê* (e.g. the Perioeci) or to consumers outside *Lakônikê*. While there is no impediment to visualizing such flows in principle, their scale—on the basis of estimates offered below for recirculation—would be surprising *prima facie* and because of the silence of our sources. In the absence of recirculation too few Helots are left behind to satisfy traditional estimates of their numbers and, more significantly, to account for the 35,000 males mentioned by Herodotus. Admitting the necessity for redistribution not only changes the reasoning by which the population of Helots is estimated, but it calls into doubt the supposition of a 50/50 sharecropping system. Recirculation mediated by individual Spartiates is in practice variable rate sharecropping.

Summation

After this welter of figures and estimates, one may well ask what firm basis is left for estimating the number of Spartan Helots. Our answer is that the work of the last several decades has marked out considerable common ground. Five important premises are these.

1. Estimates for the size of the ordinary Spartiate *klêros* seem to be settling around 18 hectares.[41] Accordingly, the *klêroi* were larger than average ordinary Greek farms or even than the estates for most non-Spartan hoplites elsewhere, but much smaller than the large establishments once envisaged by authorities such as Jardé and Kahrstedt.

2. The amount of arable land available for *klêroi* probably lay between 115,000 and 145,000 hectares, a range that is once again much lower than that prevailing in an important portion of the earlier scholarship (see the appendix for discussion of the agricultural land of Messenia).

3. Further investigation of our topic seems to generate new constraints for the Spartan agrarian system to operate within, such as limitations on available land or lower cereal yields. While it is possible to mitigate the impact of such parameters in our modeling of the problem (as the arguments above suggest), there has been no breakthrough in recent scholarship in the opposite direction, that is, on behalf of hypothesizing significant new sources for output for Spartan agriculture. One might concede that some latitude to our calculations is provided by hypothesizing Helots working on non-*klêros* land, but that is not only conjectural but also relatively modest in its impact. Therefore, any emerging impression envisages Spartan landholding as characterized by both a fragile equilibrium and a prodigality in its use of resources.

....

[41] Cf. Catling 2002: 161-163, 193-195, where some sites within the study area of the Laconia Survey may imply farmsteads controlling estates of 10-20 ha. I hasten to add, however, that *klêroi* need not have been contiguous estates of any certain size, but merely obligations of groups of Helots exploiting assets that yielded rents of an appropriate scale.

4. High multiples of Helots to Spartiates seem increasingly improbable. While earlier scholars were comfortable with ratios of 10 to 1 or higher, the proportion of 7 to 1 implied by the mobilization for Plataia now seems a high upper limit. There remain, however, significant differences about the aggregates to which any such ratio may be applied.

5. Consequently, the very high numbers sometimes offered for the Spartan Helots that once appeared everywhere in accounts of Sparta appear more and more unlikely.

A new synthesis

What then is the likely range for the population of Spartan Helots? Let us consider a paradigmatic *klêros* c. 480-479 on the basis of our previous discussion. I emphasize that recirculation of food paid in rents back again to the Helots must be a factor in this economic context of low productivity. We shall use the amount of 0.9 mt of barley as the yield for each hectare. This is high, especially as it will be viewed as a "realizable output", but it is a ceiling for Helot numbers that is being sought. Moreover, the scale of the rents might have motivated more intensive cultivation that would raise the disposable resources (Halstead 1987: 85-86). If the rent in grain and wine were paid in Aiginetic measures, it would total 3,740 kg of barley (2880 of wheat equivalent). This rent and yield would fit a *klêros* of 17.4 hectares.[42] An amount equivalent to the rent is left for the Helots, but seed grain for rent and the residuum must be taken from it, let us say at 1:6, leaving 2506 kg of barley. This sum of barley will be considered equivalent to 1930 kg of wheat.[43] That would support 7.7 people at bare subsistence (250 kg of wheat equivalent per annum).

If we raise the total food consumption of these persons to 310 kg of wheat equivalent per year (to align with the common daily ration of one *khoinix* of wheat), we shall have to posit 462 kg of wheat equivalent as redistributed from the rent (or 16% of the rent in grain). Further, we might assign the Helots a total annual consumption of all goods of 360 kg of wheat equivalent in order to bring our Helots in line with nineteenth- and twentieth-century subsistence agriculturalists. We could do that by positing an additional 50 kg per capita of non-cereal production. That would give the Helots only a tiny output on the *klêros* outside of production of grain and grapes of 7%.

....

[42] C. 3740 kg of barley @ 900 kg per ha requires 4.2 ha. At alternate year fallowing, 8.4 ha is needed for rent-producing land. On the supposition of a 50% *klêros* rent, that amount is doubled again to make 16.8 ha. We shall again add 0.6 ha as a minimum for grape production.

[43] Using a ratio of 1 kg of *alphita* = 0.77 kg of wheat, which is halfway between my earlier ratio of 0.72 kg and the 0.82 kg of Foxhall and Forbes 1982: 75-81.

Yet, there would have been in point of fact significant non-cereal production, including olive cultivation and animal husbandry (Hodkinson 2000: 133-134, 151-152).[44] Moreover, in this reckoning the 7.7 Helots on each *klêros* would be generating 801 kg of wheat equivalent per capita per annum (although only consuming 360 kg of wheat equivalent). That level of productivity appears too high (cf. Clark and Haswell 1970: 77-78). Accordingly, 7.7 Helots on each *klêros* or 69,300 for 9,000 *klêroi* is too few. By setting our parameters for production high, we have paradoxically given our cohort of Helots too high a bar of productivity to achieve. If we raise the amount of recirculated grain to 37% of the rents (1066 kg of wheat equivalent) our Helots for each *klêros* could be 9.7. And if we posited that 20% of Helot economic output was in goods other than grain and grapes, we might reach c. 13 Helots for each *klêros*. Our assumption would have to be that this additional output had only a slight effect on the size of our paradigmatic *klêros* through inter-cropping, domestic production, and exploitation of marginal land. These c. 13 Helots would be consuming 350 kg of wheat equivalent and producing c. 693 kg of wheat equivalent per capita.[45]

Nine thousand *klêroi* would give us 117,000 Helots.[46] The upper range of my crude estimation of 7-11 Helots per *klêros* provided 99,000 Helots. My earlier reconstruction of Messenian agriculture suggests 86,700 Helots in *Lakônikê*, without factoring in redistribution and non-cereal/grape production. Utilizing more pessimistic parameters for productivity in barley per hectare, or for the area available for cultivation, in *Lakônikê* will create much lower populations. For example, a cogent case can be constructed for a Helot population as low as 75,000.[47] Admittedly, it is hard to imagine that 30-35,000 members of such a population could have been marched off toward central Greece in 479 for the Plataia campaign. Yet it should be stressed that 75,000 Helots *in toto* is not at all an unreasonable number in isolation of the literary texts, considering ancient agricultural techniques, the available arable land in Laconia and Messenia, and the omnipotent fact of the whole issue, namely that a large Spartiate class had to be supported by rent without any input of its labor.

....

[44] Nichoria, likely to have been an eighth-century site affected by Spartan domination over Lower Messenia, exhibits a pattern of intensive raising of livestock, among which cattle are notably prominent; see Sloan and Duncan 1978: 76-77; Stein and Rapp 1978: 256.

[45] That is a considerable level of output for subsistence agriculturalists. Clearly, however, we could manipulate redistribution, lower consumption, and reduce non-cereal output to lower per capita output to a certain degree.

[46] Roebuck (1945: 162-165) estimates a population of 90,000 (upper limit of 112,500) for free Messenia.

[47] Note the low numbers posited for the Bronze Age kingdom: McDonald and Rapp 1972: 128, 141, 254-256; Carothers and McDonald 1979.

Nonetheless, 9000 *klêroi* of 17.4 hectares would need 156,600 hectares, an amount that seems too large an area of cultivated territory compared to the best estimates. To bring down the amount of land required, we may well be forced to admit that income in kind flowed to the Helots from non-*klêros* land, as has been hypothesized above. That device might help to reduce the total needed below the 145,000 hectares that appear a reasonable upper-limit for the *klêros*-land of *Lakônikê*. Alternatively, we could surmise some mixture of higher yields, higher work incentives outside the *klêroi*, and higher non-agricultural income to generate smaller average *klêroi*, enough to offset the 11,000 or more hectares that cannot be found on the ground.

An attraction of breaching the 100,000 barrier for Helot numbers is that it enables us to utilize the 35,000 Helots marching toward Plataia to postulate something significant about Spartan demography (cf. Hdt. 9.10.1, 28.2, 29.1). First, we must reject that this was a "military" muster in any sense, unlike the two-thirds levy that appears in Spartan mobilization contexts.[48] There were unlikely to have been rolls of the Helots preserved in any administrative archive. Secondly, we must reject that there were seven Helot families, or seven adult males on each *klêros*. Such numbers could not be fed in a period in which the adult male Spartiates numbered at least 8,000. Since Sparta had only the most primitive governmental apparatus, the best way to envisage the levy of Helots for Plataia is as a security measure. With the possibility of Persian raids on *Lakônikê* not entirely excluded, the mass of Helots could not be left behind as potential dissidents.

Herodotus did indeed repeatedly emphasize this proportion of seven Helots to each Spartiate.[49] Yet the force of his initial phrasing has not received proper recognition:

....

[48] Hunt 1997 is ill-judged in its revival of the hypothesis (Cornelius 1973) that the Helots provided the bulk of the Spartan phalanx, which was fronted by the 5,000 Spartiates. It would take a lengthy presentation to untangle all its improbabilities. Let me outline some counter-arguments instead: 1) the presence of Helot dead does not entail activity in the phalanx; service as skirmishers and flank guards would be sufficient (ἐφύλασσον in Hdt. 9.28.2 has this technical sense; cf. 9.85.1); 2) the Helots are not functionally differentiated from the other *psiloi makhimoi* in 9.29.1-2; 3) one rank is too shallow a Spartiate frontage, especially when the area of lethality of the phalanx is remembered; 4) the engagement of the second and third ranks in active fighting made light-armed troops this far forward very risky (Cornelius suggested a deeper phalanx); 5) this mass of Helots to the Spartiate rear without a rearguard posed a safety risk to their masters; 6) the Helots ought not be thought to have usurped the Perioecic role as comprising the rear ranks of the Spartan phalanx; 7) Helot training and social conditioning ill suited them for this role; 8) Helots later fought with the promise of emancipation or after emancipation and they served in separate units; 9) there remain doubts over the feasibility of a 5 km. front for any hoplite army and its practicality on the ground at Plataia.

[49] Hdt. 9.10.1: καὶ ἑπτὰ περὶ ἕκαστον [Spartiate] τάξαντες τῶν εἱλώτων; 9.28.2: περὶ ἄνδρα ἕκαστον [Spartiate] ἑπτὰ τεταγμένοι; 9.29.1: πλὴν τῶν ἑπτὰ περὶ ἕκαστον [Spartiate] τεταγμένων Σπαρτιήτῃσι; 9.29.1: ὡς ἐόντων ἑπτὰ περὶ ἕκαστον ἄνδρα [Spartiate].

καὶ ἑπτὰ περὶ ἕκαστον [Spartiate] τάξαντες τῶν εἱλώτων (9.10.1).[50] This usage might well connote that each Spartiate was ordered to bring seven Helots with him, much as a financial levy might be apportioned, because other explanations of the participle τάξαντες here seem less satisfactory.[51] Herodotus believed the Spartiates were largely successful in fulfilling this requirement. We have no reason to doubt him, but also no warrant to assume the total of 35,000 is as "hard" a figure as the number of 5,000 for mobilized Spartiates, or that the total of 35,000 rests on anything independent of the tradition about the very terms of the muster.

To continue, let us posit *exempli gratia* that our 35,000 Helots were the males between 15 and 65 years of age, minus 10% or 3,500 left behind to maintain the *klêroi*, who were in turn assisted by boys, very old men, and women. The entire Helot population might then number 118,000, using a model life table (Coale and Demeny 1966, stable population, mortality level 4). Thus, our range for the Helot population in *Lakônikê* c. 480-479, when the Spartans were themselves close to their apogee in numbers, is 75,000 to 118,000, perhaps 3-5 times the number of the Spartiates.

Helot population in perspective

Other Peloponnesian *poleis*, such as Argos, Sikyon, and Epidauros, possessed groups with secondary civic statuses and dependent populations that approximated the Spartan pattern.[52] An important difference, however, was that the other exploitative systems benefited a sociopolitical elite, not the entire civic body. These dispositions gave way to more consolidated socio-political orders under various influences: hoplite military tactics, reactions to prevailing aristocratic leadership, the emergence of tyrannies, and the monetization of the local economy. In contrast, Sparta developed a unique type of civic or hoplitic dependent relations. An important factor in Sparta's divergent development was certainly the scale of its institution of servile labor, both on the basis of Helot numbers and because of the large territory necessarily occupied by *klêroi*. The scale of Helotage moved agrarian dependency to the central point in the social structure. The conquest of Messenia shifted Laconian

················

[50] Legrand (1954: 15) recognizes a problem that he addresses by emending καὶ to κατ' or excising on the grounds of omission from some manuscript traditions.

[51] Powell (1977: 351) opts for a rare non-military connotation of τάσσω in this passage (9.10.1). Yet Powell's other comparable examples can be seen as metaphorical or extended usage based on the military (75 examples) and administrative (33) senses of τάσσω (cf. 3.68.5; 8.98.1; 7.36.3). Another passage (3.91.4: . . . ἐς τὠυτὸ τεταγμένοι . . .), speaking of a classification for tribute payment, points us toward a better solution. The deployments of τάσσω relating to the Helots belong to the significant financial/taxational connotation (13 instances) where levies or fines are imposed (e.g., 2.65.5; 2.109.2; 3.89.1; 3.90.1; 6.42.2 *ter*; 6.79.1 [Kleomenes at Sepeia]).

[52] E.g. Pollux *Onom.* 3.83. See Lotze 1959: 53-56; van Wees, this volume, pp. 38-54,64.

dependency above a crucial threshold not otherwise met in the Peloponnesus. This conclusion would be reinforced, if we were indeed compelled to envisage (as suggested above) the Laconian *klêroi* as incrementally encompassing, during the late archaic period and early fifth century, less fertile or less contiguous land at the margins of the Helos plain, in the Eurotas valley, and on Cape Malea.

Therefore the status of Messenia and its population was at all times critically important for the status of Helotage. Some features of Messenian ecology were constants throughout the Spartan hegemony. First, Messenia was comparatively fertile. Second, the high density of Bronze Age settlement transformed the environment so dramatically that the very topography of later Messenia probably offered a ready-made template for human exploitation (even absent the possible reception of oral traditions about land resource utilization). In this light, the legacy of the massive cultivation of olive trees by the Mycenaeans is particularly relevant (McDonald and Coulson 1983: 424-425; Zangger *et al.* 1997: 592-593). Thirdly, Iron Age Messenia was relatively secure from extra-regional intervention behind mountainous terrain in its sea-girt corner of the Peloponnesus, until the Athenians mastered and put to use large-scale amphibious, flotilla naval warfare in the fifth century.

The conquest period

Sparta, as the chief political power in Laconia, benefited from the salient differences existing between that region and Messenia. Early archaic Laconia was relatively more densely populated. The *polis* structure was established early at Sparta, and hoplite warfare became a subject of precocious experimentation. While Laconian dependence may have had a complex aetiology, any eighth-century Messenian conquests were achieved through raiding that stimulated flight by some indigenous inhabitants and harried those remaining into surrendering a part of their output. Depopulation was always a powerful tool for archaic Spartan "imperialism," since it removed the most resistant and engendered compliance in those remaining by allowing the acquiescent to divide a proportionately larger, accessible resource base.[53] The evidence from Nichoria seems to demonstrate Dark Age II (975-850) interaction with Laconia.[54] By Dark Age III (800-750), raiding from Laconia may already have reduced the size of

....

[53] Compare Luraghi this volume, pp. 110-5 and van Wees this volume, pp. 34-7; cf. Bockisch 1985. Our view differs in that Spartan expansionism conditioned or even modulated Messenian depopulation. The hypothesis that the assemblage of the demographic components of classical Messenia was a complex evolution may reconcile the insights won from both approaches, seeing them as valid about distinct elements of the classical population. See Raaflaub this volume, pp. 171-2, who notes the importance of "homogenization of various forms of dependent labor."

[54] Witness the shared motifs between Dark Age II pottery at Nichoria and sherds from Sparta and Amyklai (Coulson 1983a: 78-9, 111).

the community at Nichoria, while the boundary between the Dark Age III and Late Geometric (early archaic in a historical perspective) saw the termination of the village (McDonald and Coulson 1983: 326-328; Coulson 1983b: 332).

Down to the middle or late seventh century, Messenian communities were probably dependent on the Spartans globally, without individual *klêroi*, although the advantages of this dependency perhaps accrued disproportionately to the Spartan elite (as elsewhere in the early archaic period). I would date the principle of the one-half tribute burden to these earliest conquests. The annual declaration of war on the Helots by the Spartan ephors also derived from this period (Aris. fr. 543 Gigon with Plut. *Lyc.* 28.4), when the arrival of raiding parties offered a choice to their victims of tendering "gifts" or resistance.[55] The *krypteia* began its reinstitutionalization in this period. Given the primitive character of the governmental apparatus, the *krypteia* was an important administrative mechanism over Messenia. Clearly, this whole dispensation was fragile, not only because of the existence of non-compliant Messenians, but also because growth in Messenian numbers endangered the status quo. The poems of Tyrtaeus portray this dispensation under challenge.

The significantly greater task of subduing all Messenia could not, however, be consummated without the thorough implementation of a hoplite polity, a painful evolution also reflected in Tyrtaean poetry. This challenge brought to acute significance the issue of division of spoils. I would hypothesize that the distribution of shares in a colony became a model for the creation of the system of *klêroi* and *syssitia* involving the entire citizen body. That reorganization affected conquered, Helot-tilled land, but left the core of civic property in Laconia with its hierarchy of holdings intact. Under prevailing administrative and military conditions, incremental expansion was possible with or without reduction to servile status of the conquered. So extensive an incorporation, however, as all Messenia with all its population *in situ*, however, was probably infeasible, so that its pacification in the second half of the seventh century involved another depopulation. Once again, the relict population, whether it became Perioecic or was Helotized, was a partial beneficiary along with the Spartiates of any reduction in regional inhabitants. Non-compliant Messenians had an escape route in colonial Greece, where settlers were needed, a phenomenon clearly attested at Rhegion and much dramatized by the later *Messeniaka* (local histories written from the standpoint of liberated and [re]founded Messene). That alternative may have simplified Spartan policy, as it provided a viable alternative to death or subjugation for some Messenians.

....

[55] For an independent, parallel exploration of similar insights, see Link (forthcoming). Contrast Luraghi this volume, pp. 132-3. Note also Bockisch 1985: 33-34.

The consolidation period

The scale of the Spartan conquest decoupled a usage of hoplite tactics from the pressure for political inclusivity that was the rule elsewhere. Yet the system of *klêroi*, rents, and messes labored under massive disabilities in the form of disincentives to productivity and a lack of coordination between asset holding and managerial behavior. Its heyday was the later archaic period. At first, a low population put little pressure on agricultural resources. Isocrates reports a tradition that the Spartans originally numbered 2,000 when they occupied Laconia (12.255). Such a tradition cannot derive from a mythic Dorian invasion, but might rather transmit an archaic Spartan contention that an appropriate social dispensation, one true to mythological precedent, ought to include a civic body of this size.

If the early archaic Spartiates (prior to 600) did indeed at some point number 2,000, that tradition would help substantiate the conjecture, reasonable in its own terms, that Spartiate and Helot numbers grew in conjunction during the sixth century (contrast Figueira 1986: 181-182). Any rigidities within procedures for assigning *klêroi* or tensions over their transmission were mitigated by availability of unoccupied land for distribution. The powerful inducement of allowing young Helot males to marry and to form households early promoted the formation of new *klêroi* and lowered restiveness among the dependent population. Internal colonization mixed the Helots, creating the single identity that is attested in the fifth century (Figueira 1999: 223-225). During this period, the demographic morale of the Spartans is clear in their willingness to suffer casualties in the duel of champions with the Argives, to undertake a distant expedition to Naxos and Samos, and to send out colonists under Dorieus (see Figueira 1986: 170-175).

The early fifth century

By the period of 479 and thereafter, the number of *klêroi* and thereby Spartiates was reaching the carrying capacity of *Lakônikê*. The received figure of 9,000 for the number of *klêroi*, rather than being a design feature from an omniscient legislator, is merely a reflection in tradition of a detail from the system at its height. If my discussion of the land and agricultural output is broadly correct, the 5,000 Spartiates who marched off to Plataia would imply a total male population of a little over 10,000, the number offered by Aristotle as a traditional maximum (*Pol.* 1270a36-38). Spartan numbers may indeed have risen further in the 14 years between Plataia and the Great Earthquake. It might have been becoming more difficult simply to assign *klêroi* to every Spartiate at will, although there could have been land held in reserve in the Thyreatis and other regions of ongoing occupation for this purpose (Figueira 1993: 299-308). Toward the end of this period, Pausanias began his intrigues with the Helots, which I interpret not only as a reaction to the emergent military challenge from the Athenians, but also as an attempt at a redefinition of social mobility.[56] Assuredly, any confrontation with Athens required many triremes manned by Perioecic and Helot rowers.

The later fifth and early fourth centuries

The Great Earthquake of 465 changed the socio-economic order of *Lakônikê* dramatically, because it lowered the number of Spartiates significantly (Table 8.1).[57] It struck Sparta and Laconia more directly than Messenia, so that the proportionate reduction in the number of Spartiates was probably much greater than any immediate fall in numbers of the Helots. Secondarily, the earthquake led to a great Helot revolt that killed many Spartiates and subtracted from the Helot workforce. The difficult in subduing the Helot rebels short of reaching terms for their withdrawal indicates that thousands of Helot fighters remained under arms to the end. The emigration of these and their dependents marked still another of the depopulations that characterized the history of Messenia during the Spartan hegemony. In principle, fewer Spartiates meant more numerous and more affluent Helots. Not only was the pool of resources for recirculation increased, but the marginal costs of policing Helot adherence to the norms of dependency (including scrupulous rent payment) were also heightened, so that concealment of production became more viable. The earthquake and revolt also meant more economic differentiation among the Spartiates. The ensuing period appears to have opened an era of more intense social competition among non-aristocratic Spartiates.[58] It was also a period when the Messenian civic identity was constructed, both within and without Messenia, although a substratum of earlier rural populism doubtless underlay the later ideological structures.[59]

....

[56] Thuc. 1.132.4; Nepos *Paus.* 3.6; cf. Aris. *Pol.* 1307a1-5. Note Figueira 1999: 224-225.

[57] The considerable reduction of the number of sites in the study area of the Laconia Survey during the mid-fifth century indicates the scale of the upheaval, and suggests that valuable workers were relocating to more productive locations. See Catling 2002: 175-178, 248-252.

[58] The large building at Kopanaki in the Soulima valley of northern Messenia, initially mistaken for a Roman villa, may instead be an establishment designed for a mode of industrial or plantation agriculture c. 450/25 (for which Catling 1996: 34 n. 13) and be indicative as well that a threshold in property concentration and entrepreneurial/managerial engagement had been passed. See Kaltsas 1983; Harrison and Spencer 1998: 161-162; Alcock 2002: 195-196; Hodkinson this volume, p.271. A date earlier in the century might lead us to hypothesize a royal estate.

[59] See Figueira 1999; also Christien 1998: 454-459; Luraghi 2001: 293-301; Luraghi 2002b. See also Alcock 1999 for the role of tomb cult in this process, and Coulson 1983b: 334-336 for the classical tomb cult at Nichoria.

Thus *Lakônikê* emerged from the late 450s with a lower population owing to the earthquake, the rebellion, and emigration. There was, however, a differential effect on various social components: the Spartiates were most depleted through catastrophic and combatant mortality; the Helots were next affected through hostilities, flight, and defection, and the Perioeci perhaps experienced the least demographic impact.[60] Yet even they were reduced through the earthquake affecting the nearest to Sparta of their towns, through the defection of two of their towns, Aithaia and Thouria, and through military casualties. The relative change in the balance of demographic components seems to have elicited from the Spartans bipolar responses. The Helot population was recognized as a potential political asset. I have suggested that the Helots rewarded by the Spartans, as reported in Thuc. 4.80.3-4, had earned their recognition in service during the hostilities of 465-446 before the Thirty Years Peace. These manumissions were followed later in the century by the Brasideioi, by the Neodamodeis (Willetts 1954 for references), and by the Helots who were mobilized to serve as rowers on Spartan warships (cf. Myron *FGrHist* 106 F 1; Xen. *Hell.* 7.1.12; cf. 5.1.11, 16, 24). Military service, however, also had the effect for Sparta of relieving it of many members of a repressed and, accordingly, distrusted social stratum.

Therefore, regarding the Helots as a demographic resource for warfare was counterbalanced by the fear of the Helots, so eloquently discussed by Thucydides. In the aftermath of the Athenian and Messenian raids from Pylos, he comments upon Spartan counteractions with these remarks (4.80.2-4):

καὶ ἅμα τῶν εἱλώτων βουλομένοις ἦν ἐπὶ προφάσει ἐκπέμψαι, μή τι πρὸς τὰ παρόντα τῆς Πύλου ἐχομένης νεωτερίσωσιν· ἐπεὶ καὶ τόδε ἔπραξαν φοβούμενοι αὐτῶν τὴν νεότητα καὶ τὸ πλῆθος - αἰεὶ γὰρ τὰ πολλὰ Λακεδαιμονίοις πρὸς τοὺς εἵλωτας τῆς φυλακῆς πέρι μάλιστα καθειστήκει· προεῖπον αὐτῶν ὅσοι ἀξιοῦσιν ἐν τοῖς πολέμοις γεγενῆσθαι σφίσιν ἄριστοι, κρίνεσθαι, ὡς ἐλευθερώσοντες, πεῖραν ποιούμενοι καὶ ἡγούμενοι τούτους σφίσιν ὑπὸ φρονήματος, οἵπερ καὶ ἠξίωσαν πρῶτος ἕκαστος ἐλευθεροῦσθαι, μάλιστα ἂν καὶ ἐπιθέσθαι. καὶ προκρίναντες ἐς δισχιλίους, οἱ μὲν ἐστεφανώσαντό τε καὶ τὰ ἱερὰ περιῆλθον ὡς ἠλευθερωμένοι, οἱ δὲ οὐ πολλῷ ὕστερον ἠφάνισάν τε αὐτοὺς καὶ οὐδεὶς ᾔσθετο ὅτῳ τρόπῳ ἕκαστος διεφθάρη.

Here a key phrase, τὴν νεότητα, which ought to mean 'males of an age for military service,' is not textually certain, but likely in interpretation (cf. Hdt. 9.12.2 with

[60] Yet many of the 20,000 direct casualties of the earthquake were Perioeci (cf. Diod. 11.63.1). See Figueira 1986: 177-178.

Figueira 1984: 101-102 n. 47).[61] After the losses of Helots to warfare, flight, and Spartan assassination, a new generation of Helots had reached manhood during the Thirty Years Peace and the first years of the Archidamian War. Not only was the global *plêthos* 'multitude' of the Helots disturbing, but a "baby boom" of potential rebels was also especially threatening.

Moreover, to believe Thucydides, the here-mentioned liberated Helot benefactors, who had been singled out for honors for their earlier services, had been subjected to an effective covert attrition at the hands of the Spartiates. In the context of this period of trial after the disaster at Pylos, however, Sparta's need for its Brasideioi, freed Helots enlisted to accompany Brasidas to Thrace, and later the Neodamodeis was too acute to permit any systematic mistreatment, however secret. Nonetheless, the Spartans did exhibit a willingness to keep soldiers of Helot extraction occupied on distant campaigns (in accordance with the sentiments attributed to them here) and, at least initially, were uncertain where they, with their families, were to be accommodated.

Not only was the proportionately larger Helot population of the period 455-371 paradoxically both an asset and a liability simultaneously, it was also both superfluous and insufficient at the same time. We have just noted the ability of the Spartan government in these years to redress the imbalance between free and servile Laconians by freeing and elevating favored Helots to the status of Perioeci. Yet, it is also clear that there was a significant reduction in the number of *homoioi* in the 420s and 410s, owing not only to losses on campaign, but also to their incapacity to tender their mess dues. While some of this shortfall in income from the *klêroi* is to be attributed to direct damage from raids, whether by Attic flotillas or from forays mounted from Pylos and Cape Malea, the flight of Helot workers was a more decisive factor. That is why at several junctures Thucydides emphasizes Helot flight in his descriptions of the Spartan predicament after the debacle on Sphakteria (4.41.3; 5.14.3, 35.7; cf. 4.56.1-2; 56.2-3).

Just as the earthquake triggered intensified social competition among Spartiates, the vicissitudes of the war seem to have created a competition over Helot labor, in which Spartiates lost workers to flight and conscription differentially. The winners moved upward socially; the losers became *hypomeiones,* 'Inferiors'. Let me note one scenario to aid in accounting for this phenomenon. We have supposed that some Messenian *klêroi* had been gradually established in the sixth century through internal colonization. These new *klêroi* benefited persons with less access

....

[61] Both νεότητα and σκαιότητα have manuscript authority, and a paleographical judgment cannot be made between the two alternatives. Gomme seems prudent to note that τὸ πλῆθος makes better sense with τὴν νεότητα (*HCT* 3.547). Hornblower (1996: 264-265) agrees, but complicates the issue with the translation "youthful vigour". Thompson 1987 is helpful for its discussion of the textual issues. His attempt to defend σκαιότης as Spartan conceptualization (inspired by the suppression of the great revolt) of Helot persistence as stupidity misreads the past and present contexts.

to other assets like private property, such as younger sons. These lineages were the least able to endure economic vicissitudes in the late fifth century, when Messenia was more vulnerable to Attic attack and Helot flight (Figueira 1986: 203)

The result for *Lakônikê* of the Spartan demographic crisis of the late fifth and early fourth centuries was still another depopulation. Xenophon describes *Lakônikê* in general as typified by *erêmia* 'depopulation' (*Hell.* 6.5.23, 25). Messenia had a low population even after the refoundation of Messene as a *polis* and the repatriation of thousands who claimed Messenian extraction. At the summons of Epameinondas, these claimants had gathered from Italy, Sicily, and Libya (Paus. 4.26.3, cf. 27.2; Plut. *Ages.* 34.1, *Pelop.* 24.9; cf. Dipersia 1974). The Sicilian contingent clearly drew on the refugee community at Tyndaris that included many naturalized "Messenians" (Diod. 14.78.5). Volunteer settlers were also enlisted to constitute πολλοὺς . . . οἰκήτορας 'many . . . settlers' (Diod. 15.66.1). The impressive fortifications of refounded Messene surrounded ample open spaces, intended to be built upon in a comprehensive urban program (cf. Themelis 1993: 36-37, 1994; Morizot 1994), and also protected agricultural land (Alcock 1998: 180-182). Furthermore, the palynological evidence is instructive. Cultivation of olive trees in the area of Pylos only reached its post-Helladic apogee after Messene had been refounded (Zangger et al. 1997: 594; Yazvenko 1998). The new community was militarily weak, dependent on Arcadian and Boiotian aid against even an enfeebled Sparta. In conjunction, these circumstances indicate that there were no longer all that many Helots living in pre-liberation Messenia (see also Luraghi, this volume, pp. 121-4). The demographic state of the region mirrored the fate of the Spartiate class, although the Perioeci and Helots in Messenia experienced a less dramatic decline.

The interdependence of Helot and Spartiate conjoined the demographic fates of the two groups in a way different from that of the classes within other classical *poleis*. The more we probe Sparta's version of the "peculiar institution" of *douleia*, the more that we seem to come to appreciate these departures. To note just two of those which have emerged from the foregoing sketch, I would first choose the way in which successive, reconfigured Spartan social and political orders were punctuated by episodes of depopulation (at least, in Messenia), and, second, how the formulaic character of material interaction between Spartiates and Helots begins in sharp definition, but ends in an indeterminacy in which the same population can be at once too many and too few, an asset and a liability.[62]

....

[62] I should like to thank the other participants in the conference *Helots and their Masters*, and especially the organizers, Professors Nino Luraghi and Susan E. Alcock, for their invitation, hospitality, and intellectual encouragement and assistance with this paper. I also express my gratitude to Professor Graham Shipley of the University of Leicester, who was kind enough to read this piece in draft and offer me criticisms and suggestions.

Appendix

Using the material collected in *MME* 1, *NSS* 1978, and various other topographical aids, I attempted to assign all the communities of the modern Nomos of Messenia to the categories of *klêros*-land and non-*klêros*-land. The vast majority of the latter category is composed of the territory of Perioecic communities, although some territory in the valley of the Neda or lying to its north or northeast probably lay completely outside *Lakônikê*. Such a classification labors under that customary disability of investigation of the ancient rural economy. Even though we possess extensive survey work on Messenia, attested or hypothetical ancient sites fall far short of demonstrating a cultivation of the territory of many modern communes. I shall not claim that this classification represents the final word on the subject, hoping that scholars with active field experience with Messenian topography will offer corrections. The census of 1971 states the extent of all the enumerated agricultural holdings in Messenia to have been c. 119,977 ha. It is hardly surprising, granted the movement from agricultural labor to other modes of production, that this total is reduced from 1951. My interest was less with the total of arable land in 1971, but in assigning it to, or withholding it from, the *klêroi*. This distribution is 72% *klêros*-land and 28% non-*klêros*-land. The strongest reservations in our analysis concerned communities in southeast Messenia (marked with an asterisk below) that were only doubtfully perioecic (cf. pp. 134-6 with ns. 21-6). This adjustment might add c. 2% to the amount of *klêros*-land.

Inasmuch as modern Messenia is characterized by a commercial agricultural economy that includes significant viticulture and olive cultivation, a determination of the extent of land producing annual crops is not likely to be indicative of ancient conditions (c. 31,634 ha). Because non-*klêros*-land is for the most part more elevated, less fertile, and more marginal, proportionately more of it is devoted to grain cultivation (for example) than vineyards and olive groves in contemporary Messenia. If one considers the proportions of the *klêros*-land and non-*klêros*-land as suggested by acreage of annual crops, the division becomes 67% and 33%. This 67% may represent a lower limit for the proportion of *klêros*-land in ancient Messenia.

Eparchy of Kalamata:
Non-*klêros*-land: Ágrilos, Aíthaia, Alagonía, Altomirá, Áno Ámfía, Ánthia, Arfará (25%), Artemisía, Avía*, Áyios Nikólaos, Áyios Níkon, Elaiochóri, Exochóri, Faraí, Kalamáta (50%), Káto Dholí*, Káto Vérga*, Kámbos*, Kardhamíli, Kariovoúni, Karvéli, Kastanéa, Kéndro, Ladhá, Lanádha, Mikrí Mandínia*, Nédhousa, Neochóri, Nomitsí, Pídhima, Pigádhia, Pírgos, Piyés, Plátsa, Polianí, Proástio, Prosílio, Rínglia, Saïdhóna, Sotiriánika*, Stamatinoú, Stavropiyí*, Thalámai, Trachíla, Tséria, Velanidhiá.

Klêros-land: Áyios Flóros, Alónia, Ammos, Anemómilos, Andikálamos, Arfará (75%), Ariochóri, Áris, Aspróchoma, Aspropouliá, Kalamáta (50%), Léïka, Mikrománi, Miléa, Platí, Sperchóyia, Thouría, Vromóvrisi.

Eparchy of Messini:
Non-*klêros*-land: Péfko.

Klêros-land: Agriliá, Agrilóvouno, Amfithéa, Análipsi, Andhroúsa, Andhanía, Áno Mélpia, Áno Voútena, Anthoúsa, Aristodhímion, Aristoménis, Arsinóï, Avramioú, Dhasochóri, Dhesíla, Dhiavolítsi, Dhiódhia, Dhraïna, Ellinoklisiá, Éva, Fília, Ichalía, Iléktra, Kalamará, Kalívia, Kallíróï, Kaloyerórachi, Karnásion, Karteróli, Káto Mélpia, Katsaroú, Kefalinoú, Kefalóvrisi, Kendrikó, Klíma, Konstandíni, Koromiléa, Koutífari, Lámbaina, Levkochóra, Likótrafo, Loutró, Mádhena, Magoúla, Málta, Mándhra, Mandzári, Mánesi, Manganiakó, Mavromáti (Ithómis), Mavromáti (Pamísou), Meligalá, Merópi, Messíni, Míla, Neochóri (Aristoménous), Neochóri (Ithómis), Paliókastro, Parapoúngi, Pilalístra, Piperítsa, Platanóvrisi, Políchni, Polílofos, Poulítsi, Soláki, Rematiá, Siámou, Skála, Spitáli, Steníklaros, Stréfi, Tríkorfo, Tríodhos, Tsoukaléïka, Valíra, Velíka, Zerbísia, Zevgolatió.

Eparchy of Pylia:
Non-*klêros*-land: Adhrianí, Akritochóri, Charokopió, Chrisokelariá, Chomatádha, Evangelismós, Falánthi, Finikoús, Iámia, Kainoúryio Chorió, Kallithéa, Kapláni, Kómbi, Koróni, Lachanádha, Longá, Mesochóri, Methóni, Milítsa, Néa Koróni, Pídhasos, Vasilítsi, Vounária.

Klêros-land: Achladhochóri, Ambelókipi, Chandhrinoú, Charavyí, Chatzí, Dára, Dhrosiá, Glifádha, Íklena, Kakórema, Kalochóri, Karpofóra, Kastánia, Kinigoú, Kókkino, Korifásion, Koukounára, Kourtáki, Kremmídhia, Likísa, Maniáki, Maryéli, Mathía, Mesopótamos, Metamórfosi, Milióti, Mirsinochóri, Nerómilos, Panipéri, Papaflésa, Papoúlia, Pelekanádha, Petalídhi, Petrítsi, Píla, Pylos, Romanoú, Romíri, Soulinári, Viachópoulo, Vlási.

Eparchy of Triphylia:

Non-*klêros*-land: Agalianí, Ambelióna, Armeníï, Avlón, Áyios Sóstis, Elaía, Kakalétri, Kalítsena, Kaló Neró, Kariés, Koúvela, Kyparissia, Mírou, Mouriatádha, Nédha, Pétra, Platánia, Pródhromos, Ráches, Sidherókastro, Skliroú, Spiliá, Stásimo, Stasió, Vanádha, Vríses, Xirókambos.

Klêros-land: Aëtós, Agriliá, Ambelófito, Amfithéa, Áno Dhórion, Áno Kopanáki, Artíki, Chalazóni, Chalkiá, Chóra, Chrisochóri, Christiánou, Dhórion, Dhrosopiyí, Exochikó, Farakládha, Filiatrá, Flesiás, Flóka, Gargaliáni, Glikorízi, Kaloyerési, Kamári, Kefalóvrisi, Kókla, Krionéri, Landzounátou, Levki, Likoudhési, Máli, Málthi, Marathópoli, Metaxádha, Monastíri, Mouzáki, Palió Loutró, Perdhikonéri, Pírgos, Pláti, Polithéa, Psári, Raftópoulo, Rodhiá, Selá, Sírrizo, Sitochóri, Tripília, Válta, Vasilikó.

Bibliography

Alcock, S. E. 1998. "Liberation and Conquest: Hellenistic and Roman Messenia." In Davis 1998: 179-191.

———. 1999. "The Pseudo-History of Messenia Unplugged." *Transactions of the American Philological Association* 129: 333-341.

———. 2002. "A Simple Case of Exploitation? The Helots of Messenia." In P. Cartledge, E. E. Cohen, and L. Foxhall (eds.), *Money, Labour and Land: Approaches to the Economies of Ancient Greece.* London and New York: 185-199.

Baltrusch, E. 2001. "Mythos oder Wirklichkeit? Die Helotengefahr und der Peloponnesische Bund." *Historische Zeitschrift* 272: 1-24.

Beloch, J. 1886. *Die Bevölkerung der Griechisch-Römischen Welt.* Leipzig.

Bockisch, G. 1985. "Die Helotisierung der Messenier: Ein Interpretationsversuch zu Pausanias IV 14, 4f." In H. Kreissig and F. Kühnert (eds.), *Antike Abhängigkeitsformen in den griechischen Gebieten ohne Polisstruktur und den römischen Provinzen.* Berlin: 29-48.

Bölte, F. 1929. "Sparta: C. Geographie." *Realenzyklopädie der classischen Altertumswissenschaft.* 2.3: 1294-1373.

Bradeen, D. W. 1964. "Athenian Casualty Lists." *Hesperia* 33: 16-62.

———. 1969. "The Athenian Casualty Lists." *Classical Quarterly* 19: 145-169.

———. 1974. *The Athenian Agora. Volume XVII. Inscriptions: The Funerary Monuments.* Princeton.

Buckler, J. 1977. "Land and Money in the Spartan Economy—A Hypothesis." *Research in Economic History* 2: 249-279.

Burford Cooper, A. 1977/78. "The Family Farm in Ancient Greece." *Classical Journal* 73: 163-175.

Canfora, L. 1982. "Il soggetto passivo della *polis* classica." *Opus* 1: 33-48.

Carothers, J., and W. A. McDonald. 1979. "Size and Distribution of the Population in Late Bronze Age Messenia: Some Statistical Approaches." *Journal of Field Archaeology* 6: 433-454.

Cartledge, P. 1987. *Agesilaos and the Crisis of Sparta.* London.

———. 1991. "Richard Talbert's Revision of the Spartan-Helot Struggle: A Reply." *Historia* 40: 379-381.

Catling, R. W. V. 1996. "The Archaic and Classical Pottery." In Cavanagh et al. 1996: 33-89.

_____. 2002. "The Survey Area from the Early Iron Age to the Classical Period (c. 1050-c. 300 BC)." In Cavanagh et al. 2002: 151-256.

Cavaignac, E. 1912. "La population du Péloponnèse aux Ve et IVe siècles." *Klio* 12: 261-280.

Cavanagh, W., J. Crouwel, R. W. V. Catling and G. Shipley. 1996. *The Laconia Survey: Continuity and Change in a Greek Rural Landscape.* Vol. 2. *Archaeological Data.* (Annual of the British School at Athens, Supplementary Volume 27). London.

_____. 2002. *The Laconia Survey: Continuity and Change in a Greek Rural Landscape.* Vol. 1. *Methodology and Interpretation.* London.

Christien, J. 1982-83. "La Laconie orientale: topographie antique et problèmes historiques." *Peloponnesiaka* 9: 58-76.

_____. 1989a. "Promenades en Laconie." *Dialogues d'histoire ancienne* 15: 75-105.

_____. 1989b. "Les liaisons entre Sparte et son territoire malgré l'encadrement montagneux." In J.-F. Bergier (ed.), *Montagnes, Fleuves, Forêts dans l'histoire. Barrières ou lignes de convergence?* St. Katharinen: 17-44.

_____. 1992a. "L'étranger à Sparte." In R. Lonis (ed.), *L'étranger dans le monde grec.* Nancy: 147-167.

_____. 1992b. "De Sparte à la côte orientale du Péloponnèse." In M. Piérart (ed.), *Polydipsion Argos. Argos de la fin des palais mycéniens à la constitution de l'État classique.* (Bulletin de correspondance hellénique, Supplément 22). Athens and Paris: 157-171.

_____. 1998. "Sparte et le Péloponnèse après 369 B.C." In Πρακτικὰ τοῦ Ε' διέθνους συνεδρίου Πελοποννησιακῶν σπουδῶν ("Αργος-Ναύπλιον 6-10 Σεπτεμβρίου 1995). Athens: 433-467.

Coale, A. J., and P. Demeny. 1966. *Regional Model Life Tables and Stable Populations.* Princeton.

Coleman-Norton, P. R. (ed.). 1941. *The Greek Political Experience: Studies in Honour of William Kelly Prentice.* Princeton.

Cornelius, F. 1973. "Pausanias." *Historia* 22: 502-504.

Coulson, W. D. E. 1983a. "The Pottery." In McDonald, Coulson, and Rosser 1983: 61-259.

_____. 1983b. "The Site and Environs." In McDonald, Coulson, and Rosser 1983: 332-339.

Davis, J. L. (ed.). 1998. *Sandy Pylos: An Archaeological History from Nestor to Navarino*. Austin.

Davis, J. L., S. E. Alcock, J. Bennet, Y. G. Lolos, and C. W. Shelmerdine. 1997. "The Pylos Regional Archaeological Project, Part I: Overview and the Archaeological Survey." *Hesperia* 66: 391-494.

Dipersia, G. 1974. "La nuova popolazione di Messene al tempo di Epaminonda." In M. Sordi (ed.), *Propaganda e persuasione occulta nell'antichità*. (Contributi dell'istituto di storia antica 2). Milan: 54-61.

Ducat, J. 1983. "Le citoyen et le sol à Sparte à l'époque classique." In *Hommages à Maurice Bordes. Annales de la Faculté des lettres et sciences humaines de Nice* 45: 143-166.

_____. 1990. *Les Hilotes*. (Bulletin de correspondance hellénique, Supplément 20). Athens and Paris.

Dušanic, S. 1997. "Platon, la question messénienne et les guerres contre les Barbares." In P. Brulé and J. Oulhen (eds.), *Esclavage, guerre, économie en Grèce ancienne: Hommages à Yvon Garlan*. Rennes: 75-86.

Ehrenberg, V. 1960. *The Greek State*. Oxford.

Figueira, T. J. 1981. *Aegina*. New York.

_____. 1984. "Mess Contributions and Subsistence at Sparta." *Transactions of the American Philological Association* 114: 84-109.

_____. 1986. "Population Patterns in Late Archaic and Classical Sparta." *Transactions of the American Philological Association* 116: 165-213.

_____. 1991. *Athens and Aigina in the Age of Imperial Colonization*. Baltimore.

_____. 1993. *Excursions in Epichoric History: Aiginetan Essays*. Lanham.

_____. 1999. "The Evolution of the Messenian Identity." In S. Hodkinson and A. Powell (eds.), *Sparta: New Perspectives*. London and Swansea: 211-244.

_____. 2002. "Iron Money and the Ideology of Consumption in Laconia." In S. Hodkinson and A. Powell (eds.), *Sparta: Beyond the Mirage*. London and Swansea: 137-170.

_____. Forthcoming. "The Nature of the Spartan *Klêros*." In T.J. Figueira (ed.), *Sparta: Structures, Ideologies, and Personae*. London and Swansea.

Finley, M. I. 1959. "Was Greek Civilization Based on Slave Labour?" *Historia* 8: 145-164.

Fogel, R. W., and S. L. Engerman. 1974. *Time on the Cross: The Economics of American Negro Slavery.* Boston and Toronto.

Foxhall, L., and H. A. Forbes. 1982. "*Sitometreia*: The Role of Grain as a Staple Food in Classical Antiquity." *Chiron* 12: 41-90.

Gallant, T. W. 1991. *Risk and Survival in Ancient Greece.* Stanford.

Gallo, L. 1984. *Alimentazione e demografia della Grecia antica.* Salerno.

_____. 1990. "Beloch e la demografia antica." In L. Polverini (ed.), *Aspetti della storiografia di Giulio Beloch.* Naples: 113-168.

Garnsey, P. 1988. *Famine and Food Supply in the Graeco-Roman World.* Cambridge.

_____. 1992. "The Yield of the Land in Ancient Greece." In B. Wells (ed.), *Agriculture in Ancient Greece.* Stockholm: 147-153. (Reprinted in *Cities, Peasants and Food in Classical Antiquity.* Cambridge 1998: 201-213).

_____. 1999. *Food and Society in Classical Antiquity.* Cambridge.

Golden, M. 1987. Review of Hansen 1986. *Phoenix* 41: 443-46.

_____. 2000. "A Decade of Demography. Recent Trends in the Study of Greek and Roman Populations." In P. Flensted-Jensen, T. H. Nielsen, and L. Rubinstein (eds.), *Polis & Politics: Studies in Ancient Greek History Presented to M. H. Hansen.* Copenhagen: 23-40.

Grundy, G. B. 1908. "The Population and Policy of Sparta in the Fifth Century." *Journal of Hellenic Studies* 28: 77-96.

Guiraud, P. 1893. *La propriété foncière en Grèce.* Paris.

Halstead, P. 1987. "Traditional and Ancient Rural Economy in Mediterranean Europe: Plus Ça Change?" *Journal of Hellenic Studies* 107: 77-87.

Halstead, P., and G. Jones. 1989. "Agrarian Ecology in the Greek Islands: Time Stress, Scale and Risk." *Journal of Hellenic Studies* 109: 41-55.

Hansen, M. H. 1986. *Demography and Democracy: The Number of Athenian Citizens in the Fourth Century B.C.* Herning.

_____. 1988. "Demography and Democracy Once Again." *Zeitschrift für Papyrologie und Epigraphik* 75: 189-193.

_____. 1989. "Demography and Democracy—A Reply to Eberhard Ruschenbusch." *Ancient History Bulletin* 3: 40-44.

_____. 1994. "The Number of Athenian Citizens *secundum* Sekunda." *Echos du monde classique* 13: 299-310.

Harrison, A.B., and N. Spencer. 1998. "After the Palace: The Early 'History' of Messenia." In Davis 1998: 147-162.

HCT = A. W. Gomme, A. Andrewes, and K. J. Dover, *A Historical Commentary on Thucydides.* Oxford: 1945-1981.

Hodkinson, S. 1992. "Sharecropping and Sparta's Exploitation of the Helots." In J. M. Sanders (ed.), Φιλολάκων: *Lakonian Studies in Honor of Hector Catling.* London: 123-134.

_____. 2000. *Property and Wealth in Classical Sparta.* London and Swansea.

Hornblower, S. 1996. *A Commentary on Thucydides.* Vol. 2. *Books IV-V. 24.* Oxford.

Hunt, P. 1997. "Helots at the Battle of Plataea." *Historia* 46: 129-144.

Isager, S., and J. E. Skydsgaard. 1992. *Ancient Greek Agriculture: An Introduction.* London and New York.

Jameson, M. H. 1992. "Agricultural Labor in Ancient Greece." In B. Wells (ed.), *Agriculture in Ancient Greece.* Stockholm : 135-146.

Jardé, A. 1925. *Les céréales dans l'antiquité grecque.* Vol. 1. *La production.* Paris.

Kahrstedt, U. 1919 "Die spartanische Agrarwirtschaft," *Hermes* 54: 279-294.

Kaltsas, N. 1983. " Ἡ ἀρκαικὴ οἰκία στὸ Κοπανάκι τῆς Μεσσηνίας." Ἀρχαιολογικὴ ἐφημερίς: 207-237.

Legrand, P.-E. 1954. *Hérodote. Histoires: Livre IX.* Paris.

Link, S. Forthcoming. "Snatching and Keeping. The Motif of Taking in Spartan Culture." In T. J. Figueira (ed.), *Sparta: Structures, Ideologies, and Personae.* London and Swansea.

Lotze, D. 1959. Μεταξὺ ἐλευθέρων καὶ δούλων. *Studien zur Rechtsstellung unfreier Landbevölkerungen in Griechenland bis zum 4. Jahrhundert v. Chr.* Berlin.

_____. 1971. "Zu einigen Aspekten der spartanischen Agrarsystem." *Jahrbuch für Wirtschaftsgeschichte* 2: 63-76.

_____. 1993/94. "Bürger zweiter Klasse: Spartas Periöken: Ihre Stellung und Funktion im Staat der Lakedaimonier." *Akademie gemeinnütziger Wissenschaften zu Erfurt. Sitzungsberichte der Geisteswissenschaftlichen Klasse* 2: 37-51.

Lukermann, F. E., and J. Moody. "Nichoria and Vicinity: Settlements and Circulation." In Rapp and Aschenbrenner 1978: 78-107.

Luraghi, N. 2001. "Der Erdbebenaufstand und die Entstehung der messenischen Identität." In D. Papenfuß and V.M. Strocka (eds.), *Gab es das Griechische Wunder? Griechenland zwischen dem Ende des 6. und der Mitte des 5. Jahrhunderts v. Chr.* Mainz: 279-301.

————. 2002a. "Helotic Slavery Reconsidered." In A. Powell and S. Hodkinson (eds.), *Sparta: Beyond the Mirage.* London and Swansea: 227-248.

————. 2002b. "Becoming Messenian." *Journal of Hellenic Studies* 122: 45-69.

Magnetto, A. 1994. "L'intervento di Filippo II nel Peloponneso e l'iscrizione *Syll.*³ 665." In S. Alessandrì (ed.), ᾽Ἱστορίη: *Studi offerti dagli allievi a Giuseppe Nenci in occasione del suo settantesimo compleanno.* Lecce: 283-308.

Manso, J. C. T. 1800-1805. *Sparta.* Three volumes. Leipzig.

McDonald, R. A. 1993. "Independent Economic Production by Slaves on Antebellum Louisiana Sugar Plantations." In I. Berlin and P. D. Morgan (eds.), *Cultivation and Culture: Labor and the Shaping of Slave Life in the Americas.* Charlottesville and London: 275-299.

McDonald, W. A., and W. D. E. Coulson. 1983. "The Dark Age at Nichoria." In McDonald, Coulson, and Rosser 1983: 316-329.

McDonald, W. A., and G. R. Rapp (eds.). 1972. *The Minnesota Messenia Expedition: Reconstructing a Bronze Age Environment.* Minneapolis.

McDonald, W. A., W. D. E. Coulson and J. Rosser. 1983. *Excavations at Nichoria.* Vol. 3. *Dark Age and Byzantine Occupation.* Minneapolis.

Morizot, Y. 1994. "Le hiéron de Messéné." *Bulletin de correspondance hellénique* 118: 399-405.

Müller, C. O. 1839. *The History and Antiquities of the Doric Race.* Second edition. London.

Niese, B. 1906. "Neue Beiträge zur Geschichte und Landeskunde Lakedämons." *Nachrichten von der königlichen Gesellschaft der Wissenschaften zu Göttingen, Phil.-Hist. Kl.*: 101-142.

NSS = National Statistical Service of Greece (= Ἐθνικὴ στατιστικὴ ὑπερηρεσία τῆς Ἑλλάδος) *Results of the Agricultural and Livestock Census of March 14, 1971* (= Ἀποτελέσματα ἀπογραφῆς γεωργίας καὶ κτηνοτροφίας τῆς 14ης Μαρτίου 1971). Volume 1. Athens 1978.

Oliva, P. 1971. *Sparta and Her Social Problems.* Amsterdam and Prague.

Papazoglou, F. 1993. "Sur le charactère communitaire de la propriété du sol et de l'hilotie à Sparte: À propos d'une thèse de J. Ducat." *Ziva Antika* 43: 31-46.

Powell, J. E. 1977. *A Lexicon to Herodotus.* Second edition. Hildesheim.

Rapp, G., and S. E. Aschenbrenner. 1978. *Excavations at Nichoria.* Vol. 1. *Site, Environs, and Techniques.* Minneapolis.

Rhodes, P. J. 1980. "Ephebi, Bouleutae and the Population of Athens." *Zeitschrift für Papyrologie und Epigraphik* 38: 191-201.

_____. 1981. "More Members Serving Twice in the Athenian Boule." *Zeitschrift für Papyrologie und Epigraphik* 41: 101-102.

_____. 1984. "Members Serving Twice in the Athenian Boule and the Population of Athens Again." *Zeitschrift für Papyrologie und Epigraphik* 57: 200-202.

Roebuck, C. A. 1945. "A Note on Messenian Economy and Population." *Classical Philology* 40: 149-165.

Roobaert, A. 1977. "Le danger hilote?" *Ktema* 2: 141-155.

Ruschenbusch, E. 1979. "Der soziale Herkunft der Epheben um 330." *Zeitschrift für Papyrologie und Epigraphik* 35: 173-176.

_____. 1981a. "Epheben, Buleuten und die Bürgerzahl von Athen um 330 v.Chr." *Zeitschrift für Papyrologie und Epigraphik* 41: 103-105.

_____. 1981b. "Noch einmal die Bürgerzahl Athens um 330 v.Chr." *Zeitschrift für Papyrologie und Epigraphik* 44: 110-112.

_____. 1982. "Die Diaitetenliste *IG* II/III² 1927. Zugleich ein Beitrag zur sozialen Herkunft der Schiedsrichter und zur Demographie Athens." *Zeitschrift für Papyrologie und Epigraphik* 49: 267-281.

_____. 1983. "Ein weiteres unbeachtetes Zeugnis zur Bürgerzahl Athens im 4. Jh.v.Chr." *Zeitschrift für Papyrologie und Epigraphik* 50: 202.

_____. 1984a. "Die Diaiteteninschrift vom Jahre 371 v.Chr. *IG* II² 143 frg. a, b, c, d und *Hesperia* 7 (1938) 278ff. Nr.13 (= H)." *Zeitschrift für Papyrologie und Epigraphik* 54: 247-252.

_____. 1984b. "Zum letzten Mal: Die Bürgerzahl Athens im 4. Jh.v.Chr." *Zeitschrift für Papyrologie und Epigraphik* 54: 253-270.

_____. 1985. "Die Sozialstruktur der Bürgerschaft Athens im 4. Jh.v.Chr." *Zeitschrift für Papyrologie und Epigraphik* 59: 249-251.

_____. 1988a. "Demography and Democracy. Doch noch einmal die Bürgerzahl Athens im 4. Jh.v.Chr." *Zeitschrift für Papyrologie und Epigraphik* 72: 139-140.

_____. 1988b. "Getreideerträge in Griechenland in der Zeit von 1921 bis 1938 n. Chr. Als Maßstab für die Antike." *Zeitschrift für Papyrologie und Epigraphik* 72: 141-153.

_____. 1988c. "Stellungnahme." *Zeitschrift für Papyrologie und Epigraphik* 75: 194-198.

Sallares, R. 1991. *The Ecology of the Ancient Greek World.* London.

Sanders, G. D. R. 1984. "Reassessing Ancient Populations." *Annual of the British School at Athens* 79: 251-262.

Scheidel, W. 2001. "Progress and Problems in Ancient Demography." In W. Scheidel (ed.), *Debating Roman Demography.* Leiden: 1-81.

Sekunda, N. 1992. "Athenian Demographic and Military Strength 338-322 B.C." *Annual of the British School at Athens* 87: 311-355.

Shipley, G. 1992. "*Perioikos:* The Discovery of Classical Lakonia." In J.M. Sanders (ed.), Φιλολάκων: *Lakonian Studies in Honour of Hector Catling.* London: 211-226.

_____. 1996a. "Archaeological Sites in Laconia and Thyreatis." In Cavanagh et al. 1996: 235-313.

_____. 1996b. "Site Catalogue of the Survey." In Cavanagh et al. 1996: 315-438.

_____. 1997. "'The Other Lacedaimonians': The Dependent Perioikic *Poleis* of Laconia and Messenia." In M. H. Hansen (ed.), *The Polis as an Urban Centre and as a Political Community.* (Acts of the Copenhagen Polis Centre 4). Copenhagen: 189-281.

_____. 2000. "The Extent of Spartan Territory in the Late Classical and Hellenistic Periods." *Annual of the British School at Athens* 95: 367-390.

Singor, H. W. 1993. "Spartan Land Lots and Helot Rents." In H. Sancisi-Weerdenburg et al. (eds.), *De agricultura: In memoriam Pieter Willem de Neeve.* Amsterdam: 31-60.

Sloan, R. E., and M. A. Duncan. 1978. "Zooarchaeology of Nichoria." In Rapp and Aschenbrenner 1978: 60-77.

Spencer, N. 1998. "Nichoria: An Early Iron Age Village in Messenia." In Davis 1998: 167-170.

Stein, J., and G. Rapp. 1978. "Archaeological Geology of the Site." In Rapp and Aschenbrenner 1978: 234-257.

Stroud, R. S. 1998. *The Athenian Grain-Tax Law of 374/3 B.C.* (Hesperia, Supplement 29). Princeton.

Talbert, R. J. 1989. "The Role of the Helots in the Class Struggle at Sparta." *Historia* 38: 22-40.

Themelis, P. G. 1993. "Damophon of Messene: New Evidence." In K. A. Sheedy (ed.), *Archaeology in the Peloponnese.* Oxford: 1-37.

_____. 1994. "Artemis Ortheia at Messene: The Epigraphical and Archaeological Evidence." In R. Hägg (ed.), *Ancient Cult Practice from Epigraphical Evidence.* Stockholm: 101-122.

Thompson, W. E. 1987. "The Corruption of Thucydides 4.80.3." *Ancient History Bulletin* 1: 61-64.

Valzania, S. 1996. "L'esercito Spartano nel periodo dell'egemonia: dimensioni e compiti strategici" *Quaderni di storia* 43: 19-69.

van Wees, H. 2000. "The Myth of the Middle-class Army: Military and Social Status in Ancient Athens." In T. Bekker-Nielsen and L. Hannestad (eds.), *War as a Cultural and Social Force: Essays on Warfare in Antiquity.* Copenhagen: 45-71.

Wagstaff, J. M. 1982. *The Development of Rural Settlements. A Study of the Helos Plain in Southern Greece.* Amersham.

Wagstaff, M., S. Augustson, and C. Gamble. 1982. "Alternative Subsistence Strategies." In C. Renfrew and M. Wagstaff (eds.), *An Island Polity: An Archaeology of Exploitation in Melos.* Cambridge: 172-180.

Westermann, W.L. 1941. "Athenaeus and the Slaves of Athens." *Athenian Studies Presented to W.S. Ferguson.* (Harvard Studies in Classical Philology, Supplement 1). Cambridge, MA: 451-70.

Willetts, R. F. 1954. "The *Neodamodeis.*" *Classical Philology* 49: 27-32

Yazvenko, S. 1998. "From Pollen to Plants." In Davis 1998: 14-20.

Zangger, E., M. E. Timpson, S. B. Yazvenko, F. Kuhnke, and J. Knauss. 1997. "The Pylos Regional Archaeological Project. Part II: Landscape Evolution and Site Preservation." *Hesperia* 66: 549-641.

Nine

Helot numbers: a simplified model

Walter Scheidel

The actual size of the Helot population at any particular point of Spartan history will forever remain unknown. The best we can hope for is a rough estimate of the number of Helots the *klêroi* of Lakonia and Messenia could have supported alongside a given number of Spartiates and their families. In the absence of ancient statistics, parametric models of production and consumption enable us define the boundaries of the possible and arguably even of the probable. This approach helps avoid or minimise many of the pitfalls of more inductive reconstructions that are necessarily premissed on the reliability of information gleaned from ancient literary texts. These hazards are much in evidence in Figueira's complex and sophisticated edifice of interlocking arguments concerning the number and average size of Spartiate *klêroi*, the extent of the recirculation of rents back to the primary producers, and additional variables. In its bid to accommodate and draw on the largest possible number of ancient testimonia that can be shown to be mutually reconcilable, the resulting reconstruction of Helot demography is inevitably rendered vulnerable to criticisms of its various underlying assumptions. What if there were no standardised *klêroi* in the fifth century BC after all? How can we determine the ratio of agrarian to domestic Helots? In the following, I follow a different route by deliberately eliminating as many variables and premises as possible and by drawing on the smallest feasible amount of ancient evidence and probabilistic postulates. In a second step, individual data or assumptions may then be "plugged into" this simple model in order to assess their inherent plausibility. To some extent, at least, this procedure should inure my estimates to old controversies about the utility of certain pieces of evidence and provide an independently derived framework or template for further discussion.

On this occasion, I will limit my analysis to the conditions during the supposed apogee of the Spartan system in the early fifth century BC. The key questions are straightforward: how much food could have been produced on land owned by Spartans, and how many citizens and Helots could it have supported? Both of these questions may be addressed without considering extrinsic problems such as rent quotas (one-half with or without seed grain?), the share of rents ultimately retained by the Helots, and the percentage of Helots not residing on *klêroi*.[1] Instead, only two assumptions are required, regarding the likely levels of production and consumption. In order to account for the uncertainties surrounding either variable, I will employ ranges rather than notional averages and compute results for every single combination of different ranges. This method not only serves to minimise the degree to which aprioristic assumptions pre-determine the outcome but also highlights the very considerable width of the band of probability.

In keeping with Figueira's work and other previous studies, the average yield of barley can be put at low, intermediate and high rates of 650, 775, and 900 kg per ha per harvest, respectively.[2] In order to convert these gross figures into estimates of net availability, we need to subtract seed (at one-sixth of the harvest) and spoilage, conservatively set at 10 per cent although much higher percentages are in fact attested even today.[3] For the sake of simplicity, biennial fallow is posited throughout (but see below).[4] I follow Figueira in estimating the total amount of arable land available for *klêroi* at between 115,000 and 145,000 hectares.[5] The resultant range of projections is set out in Table 9.1.

Arable	Yield (in kg/ha)		
(in ha)	650	775	900
115,000	28.03	33.42	38.81
	(18.69)	(22.28)	(25.86)
145,000	32.63	42.14	48.94
	(21.75)	(28.09)	(32.63)

* The figures in parentheses are based on a higher spoilage rate of 40%.

TABLE 9.1 *Annual total of consumable barley produced on* klêroi *in Lakonia and Messenia (in million kg)**

While partial suppression of biennial fallow would raise consumable yields, rates of spoilage in excess of 10% would cause them to drop. Both conditions are likely to have applied simultaneously but would tend to cancel each other out.

....

[1] For rent quotas and seed grain, see Figueira in this volume, p. 199-200; for recirculation, p. 207; for Helots in Spartan households, see Hodkinson 1997.

[2] For 650 and 900 kg/ha, see Figueira in this volume, p. 00. Garnsey 1998: 204 reckons with 770 kg/ha for barley in classical Attica. My intermediate estimate of 775kg/ha splits the difference between Figueira's low and high rates.

[3] For a 1:6 seed/yield ratio, see Garnsey 1998: 204. In the modern world, spoilage affects 40% of all agricultural output, according to recent estimates by the FAO.

[4] This traditional view is being increasingly challenged by proponents of the "New Model" of ancient Greek agriculture who envision more intensive mixed farming without universal fallow. For the debate, see, e.g., Halstead 1987; Hodkinson 1988; Gallant 1991: 34-59; Isager and Skydsgaard 1992: 108-114; Cartledge 1993; Morris 1994: 363-365; Garnsey 1998: 206-211.

[5] See Figueira in this volume, p. 216. Hodkinson (2000: 383) reckons with 135,000 ha.

Thus, by accommodating the possibilities of more intensive cultivation and more serious spoilage, the ranges in Table 9.1 provide a sufficiently robust basis for estimates of carrying capacity. However, food transfers between Spartan and Perioecic households represent another potential confounding variable which cannot be properly quantified. If Spartans converted grain rents into goods and services provided by Perioeci, the amount of barley available for Spartan and Helot consumption would have been correspondingly smaller. This factor, together with the possibility that not all cultivable land was actually put to good use, means that the estimates in Tables 9.1-4 should best be understood as probable *maxima* rather than realistic averages.

Average dietary requirements for Helots probably fell in a range between a minimal intake of 2,000 calories per day and a more adequate diet of 2,500 calories per day.[6] In an impoverished and exploited Mediterranean population such as the Helots, cereals must have accounted for a large share of total caloric intake: if barley satisfied 70% of the Helot's energy needs, net per capita consumption stood at between 193 and 241 kg/year.[7]

Notwithstanding our considerable ignorance about ancient age structures, a total of adult male Spartans of 8,000 to 9,000 may reasonably be thought to imply the existence of 6,000 to 6,800 men between ages 20 and 50, a figure that seems compatible with the reported turnout of 5,000 Spartan citizen soldiers at Plataea in 479 BC.[8] The application of a conventional model life table yields a total Spartan population of around 30,000 (or, to be spuriously precise, of between 27,880 and 31,365).[9] At 2,500 calories/day, they would dispose of 6.72 to 7.56 million kg of barley per year, and of 10.08 to 11.34 million kg/year at $1^{1}/_{2}$ times that intake. (Not all of this barley had to be actually consumed by Spartans; some may have been exchanged for other foodstuffs or left to spoil.) In my simplified model, the remaining consumable grain was absorbed by Helots, either on the *klêroi* or in Spartan households (Table 9.2). As shown in Table 9.3, the estimated maximum size of the Helot population is contingent on four separate variables, viz., land yields, total acreage, citizen consumption, and Helot diet. Again relying on a conventional model life table, the number of adult male Helots can be extrapolated accordingly. (I should repeat that my reconstruction is concerned with the peak period of the Spartan citizenry: fewer rentiers might translate to higher rates of recirculation and therefore larger Helot numbers.)

....

[6] For average intakes around 2,000 cals/day in developing countries, see Clark and Haswell 1970. Foxhall and Forbes (1982) envision 2,583 cals/day for ancient Greek farmers.

[7] Cf. Gallant 1991: 68 (65-70%); Foxhall and Forbes 1982; Garnsey 1999: 19 (70-75%).

[8] For 8-9,000 Spartan men, see Figueira in this volume, p. 208. Scheidel 2001 explores the questionable relevance of model life tables for ancient populations.

[9] Model West Males Level 4 (r=0; e_0=25.3) (Coale and Demeny 1983: 108).

Arable	Yield (in kg/ha)		
(in ha)	650	775	900
115,000	16.69-21.31	22.08-26.7	27.47-32.09
145,000	21.29-25.91	30.8-35.42	37.6-42.22

Table 9.2 *Annual total amount of barley available for Helot consumption (in million kg)*

Arable/Intake	Yield (in kg/ha)		
(in ha/cals)	650	775	900
115,000/2000	86,477-110,415	114,404-138,342	142,332-166,269
115,000/2500	69,253-88,423	91,618-110,788	113,983-133,153
145,000/2000	110,311-134,249	159,585-183,523	194,819-218,756
145,000/2500	88,340-107,510	127,801-146,971	156,017-175,187

Table 9.3 *Total number of Helots according to different estimates of carrying capacity*

Arable/Intake	Yield (in kg/ha)		
(in ha/cals)	650	775	900
115,000/2000	24,512-31,297	32,428-39,213	40,344-47,129
115,000/2500	19,630-25,063	25,969-31,403	32,308-37,742
145,000/2000	31,268-38,053	45,234-52,020	55,221-62,006
145,000/2500	25,040-30,474	36,225-41,659	44,223-49,657

Table 9.4 *Total number of adult male Helots aged 20 to 50 according to Table 9.3 and Model West Males Level 4 (r=0)*

The share of able-bodied individuals in the adult male Helot population is difficult to ascertain. The ranges plotted in Fig. 9.1 are based on the optimistic assumption that no more than 10% of Helots in that age group were physically incapable of participating in military campaigns. However, estimates of Disability Adjusted Life Expectancy (DALE) in the Third World today point to substantially higher levels of infirmity in high-mortality populations.[10] All we can say is that a higher

....

[10] In the most advanced western countries today, 7-8% of the average life is spent disabled, compared to up to 30% in the worst-off countries of Subsaharan Africa. Hansen (1985: 20) guesses that (at least) 20% of Athenian adults may have been unfit for military service. Figueira (1991: 208)—rightly in my view—cautions against this "liberal classification of disability" with regard to formal exemption from any form of military service. Even so, more demanding undertakings (such as a march from Messenia to Plataea: see in the text below) may well have been beyond the physical capacity of a significant number of sick or malnourished (but at other times able-bodied) Helots.

disability rate could be offset by more generously defined age limits for Helot military support service, such as from 15 to 60 years as envisaged by Figueira.[11] In the end, the estimates in Fig. 9.1 cannot be wide of the mark.

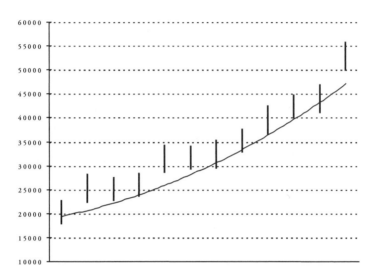

FIGURE 9.1 *Number of able-bodied adult male helots (aged 20 to 50) according to different estimates of carrying capacity (see Table 9.4)*

More than anything else, Figure 9.1 underscores the dramatic spread of estimates derived from a small number of underlying variables. The highest total of 55,800 exceeds the lowest figure of 17,700 by 215%. Even the trend line extends from about 20,000 to over 45,000, compared to a composite mean of approximately 30,000 for all ranges combined. These findings are a powerful reminder of the fragility of population estimates from carrying capacity and of the hazards of settling for streamlined "averages" that obscure the true margins of error.

Yet even a range of different estimates as wide as this one can help us gain a better perspective on ancient testimonia. Herodotus' ratio of seven Helots per Spartiate implies the presence of 35,000 Helots at Plataea.[12] Only one in three of the ranges in Fig. 9.1 consistently exceeds this threshold whereas half of them fail to reach it at all. In other words, the most optimistic assessment of crop yields must be coupled with the most pessimistic assumptions about consumption levels (for

....

[11] See Figueira in this volume, p. 220.
[12] Hdt. 9.10.1, 9.28.2, 9.29.1. See Figueira in this volume, p. 219.

both Spartans and Helots) to salvage the notion that as many as 35,000 Helots could indeed have accompanied the Spartan hoplites to Boeotia. Although this scenario cannot be ruled out, it is hardly the most economical or plausible option. In any case, there is no good reason to allow Herodotus' claim to constrict modern estimates of Helot numbers: more often than not, casual numerical references in this or other ancient authors cannot bear much weight.[13] This is true not only for patently fantastical figures such as the ancient estimates for Greek slave populations mentioned by Figueira but may well also hold for seemingly innocuous specimens.[14] Aristotle's assertion that Sparta's territory could have supported 1,500 cavalry and 30,000 hoplites is an obvious example.[15] How could he tell? He did not even pretend to report an actual number, merely a potential total. Was Aristotle an ancient Beloch, multiplying acreage with yields and dividing the result by caloric needs in order to establish some maximal carrying capacity? Hansen concludes in his study of Athenian population size that "thirty thousand is obviously a conventional figure and of little or no value whenever it is found." He adduces sources according to which the Athenian citizen body numbered 30,000, 30,000 Athenians attended the *ekklesia* and the theatre of Dionysios seated 30,000, and notes that Menander took 30,000 to be the normal population of a polis.[16]

This is not to say that individual numerical references are necessarily worthless. As it happens, two pieces of information on which Figueira builds his reconstruction are readily compatible with my model projections. If 8,000 to 9,000 Spartan households had each received 82 *medimnoi* of barley, and depending on whether this amount had equalled 2,493 or 3,740 kg,[17] rents would have totalled between 20 and 33.7 million kg/year, compared to between 18.7 and 32.6 million kg/year (i.e., one-half of gross harvest) in my own model. What matters here is that it is perfectly possible *but unnecessary* to assume that the Helots handed over one-half of the harvest and that Spartans were entitled to 82 *medimnoi* in order to estimate Helot numbers. Rather, the model provides independent criteria by which to judge the plausibility of ancient testimonia without circuitously implicating the same texts in the designing of that standard. Given the doubtful quality of several of the key testimonia, this is surely the safest route to take.

....

[13] For Herodotus' use of numbers, see Fehling 1990. Cf. Dreizehnter 1978 on the use of multiples of 7. Hunt (1998: 33-37) interprets Herodotus' seven-to-one ratio as a schematic multiplier based on the depth of the phalanx.

[14] See Figueira in this volume, p. 194.

[15] Aristot. *Pol.* 1270a29-31; see Figueira in this volume, p. 196-7.

[16] Hansen 1985: 26. Cf. also the reference to 30,000 Perioecic allotments in Plut. *Lyc.* 8.3 cited by Figueira in this volume, p. 213. For a similar preference for the figure 30,000 in a different context, compare Scheidel 1996.

[17] See Figueira in this volume, pp. 215, 199, and 201 for the volume of the *medimnos* in question.

Bibliography

Cartledge, P. A. 1993. "Classical Greek Agriculture: Recent Work and Alternative Views." *Journal of Peasant Studies* 21: 127-136.

Clark, C., and M. Haswell. 1970. *The Economics of Subsistence Agriculture.* London.

Coale, A. J., P. Demeny, and B. Vaughan. 1983. *Regional Model Life Tables and Stable Populations.* Second edition. New York.

Dreizehnter, A. 1978. *Die rhetorische Zahl: Quellenkritische Untersuchungen anhand der Zahlen 70 und 700.* Munich.

Fehling, D. 1990. *Herodotus and his "Source": Citation, Invention, and Narrative Art.* Leeds.

Figueira, T. J. 1991. *Athens and Aegina in the Age of Imperial Colonization.* Baltimore and London.

Foxhall, L., and H. A. Forbes. 1982. "*Sitometreia*: The Role of Grain as a Staple Food in Classical Antiquity." *Chiron* 12: 41-90.

Gallant, T. W. 1991. *Risk and Survival in Ancient Greece: Reconstructing the Rural Domestic Economy.* Stanford.

Garnsey, P. 1998. *Cities, Peasants and Food in Classical Antiquity: Essays in Social and Economic History.* Edited by W. Scheidel. Cambridge.

_____. 1999. *Food and Society in Classical Antiquity.* Cambridge.

Halstead, P. 1987. "Traditional and Ancient Rural Economy in Mediterranean Europe: plus ça change?" *Journal of Hellenic Studies* 107: 77-87.

Hansen, M. H. 1985. *Demography and Democracy: The Number of Athenian Citizens in the Fourth Century B.C.* Herning.

Hodkinson, S. 1988. "Animal Husbandry in the Greek Polis." In C. R. Whittaker (ed.), *Pastoral Economies in Classical Antiquity.* Cambridge: 35-74.

_____. 1997. "Servile and Free Dependants of the Classical Spartan '*oikos*'." In M. Moggi and G. Cordiano (eds.), *Schiavi e dipendenti nell'ambito dell'"oikos" e della "familia".* Pisa: 45-71.

_____. 2000. *Property and Wealth in Classical Sparta.* London and Swansea.

Hunt, P. 1998. *Slaves, Warfare, and Ideology in the Greek Historians.* Cambridge.

Isager, S., and J. E. Skydsgaard. 1992. *Ancient Greek Agriculture: An Introduction.* London and New York.

Morris, I. 1994. "The Athenian Economy Twenty Years after *The Ancient Economy.*" *Classical Philology* 89: 351-366.

Scheidel, W. 1996. "Finances, Figures and Fiction." *Classical Quarterly* 46: 222-238.

_____. 2001. "Roman Age Structure: Evidence and Models." *Journal of Roman Studies* 91: 1-26.

Ten

Spartiates, helots and the direction of the agrarian economy: towards an understanding of helotage in comparative perspective

Stephen Hodkinson

This paper is a first step in a project designed to study Sparta in comparative historical perspective, ancient to modern.[1] Modern thought has often followed ancient Greek and Roman sources in portraying Sparta as an exceptional society, somewhat different from other Greek poleis, and indeed from most other civilised human societies. In recent years my work has increasingly been concerned to deconstruct that image as it relates to Greek antiquity, to explore the complex manner in which Spartan institutions and practices were frequently both distinctive and yet reflected, and sometimes even exemplified, trends observable in elsewhere in the Greek world. For the study of helotage, the value of examining Spartan institutions in broader Greek context is amply demonstrated by the paper in this volume by Hans van Wees. My project is designed to develop such a comparative approach one stage further by viewing Spartan customs and institutions in the context of comparable practices in societies beyond the ancient Greek world. In this paper I shall explore some ways in which the operation of helotage may be profitably studied against the backdrop of systems of unfree labour in other historical times and places from antiquity to the modern world.

I should emphasise that the writing of this paper falls at an early stage of my comparative research. I shall not attempt to provide a definitive location of helotage within the wide range of unfree statuses in world history. My paper is, rather, a

....

[1] I am grateful to Sue Alcock, Richard Catling and Nino Luraghi for allowing me to read their important forthcoming work in advance of publication, to Peter Gatrell for advice on comparative reading on Russian serfdom, and to the participants in the Harvard conference for their supportive reception of the original version of this paper. This article was written during my tenure of an award under the Research Leave scheme of the UK Arts and Humanities Research Board.

starting-point for future research, a preliminary investigation of certain potential insights to be derived from comparative study, based upon an outline reading into certain major servile systems in the historical past. Its primary aim is to address the broad question: in what ways might the history and sociology of other systems of unfree labour help to illuminate the character of helotage and of relations between the helots and their masters? Given, in particular, the paucity of the ancient evidence for helot-Spartiate relations—the lack of historical detail highlighted by Sue Alcock in her introduction to this volume—to what extent can comparative study help us to map out some plausible broad contours for the operation of helotage, even if much of the detailed topography must necessarily remain obscure? For the purposes of this initial investigation I shall focus on Spartiate-helot relationships within the key area of the agrarian economy.

Comparative approaches

As has been emphasised in a number of studies, such as Mark Golden's salutary article (1992) on the uses of cross-cultural comparison in ancient social history, the enterprise of comparative history, and especially the methodology of comparison between unfree labour in antiquity and in more recent periods, is by no means straightforward. Although extensive theoretical discussion would be inappropriate in this volume, whose primary subject is the substantive relationship between helots and their masters, some brief remarks are appropriate by way of introduction to the comparative approach taken in my own substantive discussion.

I will start by indicating one kind of comparative approach which is *not* particularly fruitful for my purposes, an approach that I would broadly characterise as "globalising". The prime example is the longstanding debate about how the helots should be defined in terms of modern legal or sociological definitions of servile status. There has been considerable debate, in particular, about whether helotage should be categorised as a form of slavery or a form of serfdom—with the modern definition of serfdom in Article 1 of the UN Supplementary Convention of 1956 being invoked by Geoffrey de Ste. Croix as alleged proof of the helots' classification as "state serfs".[2] It is not my intention to dismiss entirely the exercise of definition; but the problem with such definitions for the purpose of comparative study is that they have only

....

[2] Classification of helotage as a form of slavery: e.g. Oliva 1971, "undeveloped slavery"; Lotze 1959, "Kollektivsklaverei". Definition as "state serfs": e.g. Ste. Croix 1981: 147, 149; Cartledge 1987: 172, 1988: 39. Ste. Croix's invocation (1981: 135-136) of the 1956 *UN Supplementary Convention on the Abolition of Slavery, the Slave Trade and Practices similar to Slavery* is followed by Cartledge in both works cited. For criticism of the definition of helots as serfs, Finley 1973: 65 with 189 n.5. Other classifications have been suggested, such as "intercommunal servitude" (Garlan 1988: 93-98).

limited value in illuminating the actual operation and condition of helotage.[3] The restricted range of categories (slavery-serfdom-debt bondage or slavery-serfdom-wage labour) employed in most modern classificatory schemes means that some considerable compression of actuality is inherent in the very act of classification.[4] Even Ste. Croix—in the midst of a long discussion of the classification of different types of unfree labour—concedes that, "Actually, we know of no precise parallels to the condition of the Helots . . . and a certain amount of oversimplification is involved by forcing it into any general category".[5] Moreover, even if the classification of helots were unproblematic, status is on its own a poor guide to economic and social reality.[6] As many students of slavery and serfdom have emphasised, persons of identical servile status can enjoy vastly different lifestyles or socio-economic conditions, even within a single society, let alone between different societies.[7]

Conversely, there is often considerable overlap between the practical conditions of different categories of unfree labour, especially between different societies (Engerman 1996: esp. 19-21). Within the realm of the agrarian economy, various forms of coerced labour have been exploited by ruling elites for both subsistence and market-orientated farming. The character of relationships between landowners and these different unfree labour forces is often affected by common variables; and, although examination of these variables may often reveal key differences between different forms of exploitation, at other times comparable conditions can be seen to apply. For example, as we shall see in more detail below, one important variable in many systems of unfree labour is the extent of labour obligations owed to the landowner. On this subject one can legitimately draw a contrast between most

....

[3] Note Ducat's criticism (1994: 116) of the similar approach of the ancient sources: "leur façon de réfléchir était le plus souvent globalisante, et visait beaucoup plus à définir un esclavage de type hilotique qu'à dresser le catalogue des spécificités de chacun des statuts relevant de ce type".

[4] The statement of Greenidge (1958: 24), quoted approvingly by Ste. Croix, that serfdom "is a status intermediate between slavery and complete freedom" reads uncannily like Aristophanes of Byzantion's inadequate classification of the helots, Penestai and a number of other groups as "between free people and slaves" (*ap.* Pollux, *Onomastikon* 3.83).

[5] Ste. Croix 1981: 149. Despite this admission, he then continues, "but for convenience I shall treat them as the 'State serfs' they undoubtedly were"—a dogmatic approach that reads like classification for its own sake.

[6] Cf. the comments of Biezunska-Malowist and Malowist 1989: 18-19; and of Bush 1996b: 1, 16-17. Cf. also Finley's criticism of the consequences of modern attempts at classification: "So the helots become serfs and the slaves with a *peculium* are discussed in the first instance as slaves, when, economically and in terms of the structure and functioning of society, they were mostly self-employed craftsmen, pawnbrokers, moneylenders and shopkeepers" (1973: 65).

[7] A few, very selective examples: by ancient historians, Bradley 1987: 15-16; Finley 1973: 64-65; by students of modern servile systems, Bush 1996c; Hoch 1996: 320; and the title of Lovejoy 2000: "Transformations in Slavery". Cf. the remarks of Annequin 1985: 664, on heterogeneity of historical forms of slavery.

systems of serfdom—in which serfs typically exercised some control over their labour, working only part-time for their lords with several days a week to farm their own lands—and some systems of agrarian slavery, in which the slaves worked full-time for their masters, being allocated little more than garden plots and little time to cultivate them. In other slave systems, however, such as in pre-colonial West Africa and in much of the Caribbean, the slaves' access to land and to time for its cultivation was often far closer to that enjoyed by most serfs.[8] The existence of common variables and, in certain circumstances, of overlapping conditions applying to different categories of unfree labour reinforces my argument that legal or sociological classification is not a fruitful starting-point for the comparative study of Spartiate-helot agrarian relations. As Michael Bush has observed, in summarising the conclusions of a recent comparative volume on serfdom and slavery (1996b: 1): "Both serfdom and slavery were defined by law . . . But what does this reveal about their true nature? . . . The conclusion is: very little . . . the character and condition of both were determined in reality by a wide range of other factors".

In contrast to the unhelpfulness of globalising approaches, a more promising comparative approach to an understanding of helotage is, I suggest, through the investigation of *specific* aspects or problems which can legitimately be viewed in broader historical perspective. A good example of such a "specific" comparative approach is Paul Cartledge's article "Rebels and *Sambos* in classical Greece: a comparative view" (Cartledge 2001, first published 1985), in which he successfully employed comparative insights from Eugene Genovese's study of slave revolts, *From Rebellion to Revolution* (Genovese 1979), to explain the capacity of the Messenian helots to revolt, in contrast to chattel slaves elsewhere in Greece. Similarly, my comparative essay takes as its subject another major aspect of helotage: the character of Spartiate-helot relationships within the agrarian economies of Lakonia and Messenia during their respective periods of domination by Sparta. Its specific focus is the social relations of production between Spartiates and helots, especially the degree of Spartiate direction of helot farming, and the implications for the helots' experience of servitude.

In line with my criticisms of the limitations of classificatory approaches to the comparative study of helotage, my own comparative study will purposely draw upon insights from diverse systems and types of unfree agrarian labour at different historical times and places. In this initial study, I will concentrate mainly upon three major agrarian servile systems from the modern world (serfdom in rural Russia; slavery in the U.S. South; and slavery in pre-colonial Africa). I shall also refer, at appropriate

....

[8] E.g. M. G. Smith 1955; Hill 1985: 37-38; Lovejoy 2000: 187-188; Kolchin 1993: 153.

points, to contemporary servile populations from Greek antiquity, especially the Penestai of Thessaly; and on occasion to certain systems of dependent agrarian labour in which the exploited labour force is legally free.[9] My study will focus upon certain key variables which have been shown to possess widespread significance for the character of social relations of production across these different types and systems of agrarian labour. The patterns and conclusions indicated, both positively and negatively, by comparative study of these variables will be used as context for assessing the limited and partial ancient literary and archaeological evidence, for drawing out implications, and for suggesting fresh insights into the nature of Spartiate-helot agrarian relations. On occasion, where there is a sufficient degree of similarity to conditions in another servile system, those correspondences will be used to supplement the exiguous ancient evidence by developing, with all due caution, plausible hypotheses regarding the character of helot servitude.[10]

The scope of my approach, consequently, differs from the kind of cross-cultural comparison currently most favoured by anthropologists: namely, comparison within a region or culture area. It also differs in scope from the approach adopted in many previous comparative studies by historians of ancient slavery, certainly in those focused upon agrarian labour, which have most frequently restricted their comparisons to ancient chattel-slave systems judged to have operated modes of exploitation directly comparable with the slave systems of the modern New World.[11] My focus on diverse examples of servile exploitation also necessarily implies the illumination of helotage by means of difference as well as by similarity. In terms of method, my approach shares something in common with each of the three types of comparative history identified in an influential article by Skocpol and Somers (1980)—macro-causal analysis; the

....

[9] Pertinent comparisons between free and unfree agrarian populations are appropriate on occasions when their conditions of exploitation are affected by similar variables. There have also often been respects regarding the practical conditions of agrarian life in which "he [the serf] closely resembled the free peasant" (Bush 1996c: 206) or in which "the difference between slave and free was only one of degree" (Klein and Lovejoy 1979: 188). For a defence against criticisms (Cartledge 1993: 132, 1998: 13) of my previous study (Hodkinson 1992), in which I illuminated Spartiate-helot share-cropping arrangements through comparative evidence for systems of dependent tenancy, see now Hodkinson 2000: 116-117; cf. also Alcock 2002b: 199 n.9. Attested within systems of servile labour (e.g. M. F. Smith 1954: 38), as well as within those involving legally "free" tenants, sharecropping is a good example of a topic for which comparative study embracing systems of both free and unfree dependent labour is highly appropriate.

[10] For both these sources of comparative insight, see, briefly, Annequin (1985: 640); and also the comments of Golden (1992: 311): "Of course, reports on other cultures cannot in themselves replace missing data from Greece and Rome, but they can be very useful all the same in . . . developing hypotheses, in identifying patterns from scattered scraps, in refuting generalisations."

[11] Cf. Martin 1980; Biezunska-Malowist and Malowist 1989: 18, 23. Cf. also the works cited by Golden 1992: 312 n.9.

parallel demonstration of theory; and the contrast of contexts—though it also differs with each in certain important respects. It shares with macro-causal analysis the method of breaking individual cases down into sets of variables and an interest in generalisation, though not its use of quantitative techniques or its de-emphasis upon specificity. Although not aimed at the demonstration of theory, my approach shares an interest in extracting parallel insights, where appropriate, from diverse historical cases. It also shares—as noted above—an awareness of contrast and difference between specific historical cases, although it does not eschew the formulation of explanatory generalisations through comparative analysis.

In his article on the methodology of comparative approaches to the history of slavery, Jacques Annequin has posed the question: "une réflexion comparative doit-elle se fonder sur des ressemblances factuelles ou sur des convergences de problématiques?" (1985: 641-642). Although not impervious to the value, in appropriate context, of factual resemblances between helotage and other systems of unfree agrarian labour, the primary concentration of my own "réflexion comparative" will be upon "des convergences de problématiques", the issues and variables common to diverse systems of exploitation which permit pertinent comparative study across historical time and space.

The agrarian economy: social relations of production and the helot experience

One of the main puzzles concerning helot farming, and indeed of helot life more generally, is how it actually worked on the ground. It is clear that, from the viewpoint of the Spartiate masters, the essential function of the vast majority of the helot population was to cultivate the Spartiates' landholdings and to deliver sufficient produce to enable them to sustain their position as a citizen elite with a near full-time devotion to civic and military affairs. It is equally clear that the Spartiates were rentier landowners who lived not on their estates but in Sparta itself. What is less clear, however, is the extent to which Spartiate masters took steps to intervene actively in directing and controlling the process of agricultural production or, alternatively, left the practical planning and management of farming to the helots themselves. The question of the control of helot labour, of the social relations of production between Spartiates and helots, is important for our understanding of more than just helot agriculture, since comparative evidence suggests that the location of control over the productive process will have had a potentially profound effect on the fundamental conditions of helot life, including the nature of local helot communities.[12] The issues concerned are ones currently under debate in the

....

[12] See the comments of Cooper 1979, in the context of African slavery.

study of diverse servile systems in human history, as scholars have become increasingly sensitive to the capacities of unfree peoples to develop, within their experience of servitude, various forms of (semi-)autonomous activity, organisation and culture.[13] Direct insight from the ancient sources into Spartiate intervention in the agricultural process is confined to one brief passage in Xenophon's account of the conspiracy of Kinadon around 398 BC (*Hell.* 3.3.5). Kinadon is depicted as taking a potential recruit to the conspiracy out from the streets of Sparta to the Spartiates' estates, where he pointed out on each estate a single enemy, the master, surrounded by many potential allies to the conspiracy. The implication is that helots who farmed estates close to Sparta may have experienced a fair degree of intervention and direction from their Spartiate masters. This single episode, located at a particular historical moment, is, however, a slender basis upon which to found an overall judgement regarding agrarian life throughout the entire 1,400 km² of helot-farmed territory within Lakonia and Messenia over a period of several centuries.[14]

Indeed, comparative evidence from various types of agricultural labour systems suggests that, even within a common framework of exploitation, we should expect considerable variation in the degree of Spartiate intervention. For example, M. G. Smith's study of the system of slavery maintained by the Fulani aristocracy of Zaria province (northern Nigeria) around 1900 notes different levels of intervention, with some slaves farming their owner's fields through communal work under a slave overseer, whilst in other cases the slaves enjoyed desultory supervision, as long as they performed the required labour or provided rent in kind (M. G. Smith 1955: 103-104). Similar variations in the degrees of autonomy permitted to slave cultivators have been noted within slavery in Thailand (Turton 1980: 278-279). James Scott's classic study of peasant rebellions and subsistence in Southeast Asia also identified a spectrum of landlord-cultivator relationships, ranging from those in which there was a considerable degree of landlord involvement in agricultural decision-making, and in provision of seed and necessary equipment, to relationships in which the landlord provided nothing beyond the land and a demand for rent (1976: 174-176). Such variations in the degree of intervention by master or landowner, observed in diverse systems of dependent labour exploitation, have been found to correlate with a number of key variables. Although none, on its own, is necessarily decisive, collectively they constitute a set of interacting contributory factors that are worth examining in an attempt to illuminate the social relations of production between Spartiates and helots.

....

[13] E.g. Hoch 1986: 91-159, 1996: 311-322; Kolchin 1987: 195-357, 1993: 133-168; Moon 1999, esp. 156-281. In studies of U.S. slavery the debate was sparked off by Stanley Elkins' controversial thesis (1976, originally published in 1959) regarding the "Sambo" character of black slaves.

[14] The figure of 1,400 km² derives from the calculations in Hodkinson 2000: 131-145.

The character of economic exploitation

One relevant factor is the character of the economic exploitation of the dependent farming population, the nature of the obligations demanded by the master or landowner. Historically, there have been two main methods of exploitation. One method has been to demand labour services, with the cultivators being compelled to spend much of their time working the owner's landholdings. Often under this arrangement, the cultivators have been allocated some (varying) amount of land for their own use. The other method has been for the owner to require the payment of dues, with the farming population being compelled to render tribute in kind (or, increasingly in the modern world, in cash) from the produce of the owner's estates. Comparative evidence indicates that obligations in the form of dues are typically associated with lower levels of intervention than when labour services are required (cf. Bush 1996c: 213-215). Within modern Russian serfdom, for example, "labour obligations (*barshchina*) required much greater supervision than dues (*obrok*) paid two or three times a year" (Moon 1999: 205; cf. Kolchin 1987: 63-64). Similarly, as Paul Lovejoy has noted, the system of plantation slavery practised in the Savanna region of Africa in the nineteenth century "included a variety of work regimes and management strategies", ranging from cases in which slaves provided labour services, working "in a regimented fashion on the fields of the master under an overseer" to less regimented arrangements in which "slaves lived in their own villages and were subject to fixed payments" (Lovejoy 2000: 212; cf. Mason 1973: 465-466). Although the associations are not hard-and-fast, and there can be other factors involved, the requirement for labour services tends to correlate with a higher, and the demand for dues with a lower, degree of production for the market (Cooper 1979: 115; Kolchin 1987: 65; Moon 1999: 70-71).

Our evidence for helotage suggests that the Spartiates extracted dues in kind rather than labour services.[15] This would fit well with the basic aims of agrarian production in Lakonia and Messenia. Although we should not think of Spartiates as completely divorced from market production, the primary function of their comparatively modest-sized landholdings—with a mean size of a mere 20 ha per citizen household—was to provide the subsistence needs of Spartiate families and the mess contributions required of their adult males.[16] This intimation that the subsistence-orientated aims of production favoured a lesser degree of Spartiate

....

[15] Ancient evidence: Tyrtaios *fr.* 6, West; Myron, *FGrHist* 106F2, *ap.* Athen. 657d; *Instituta Laconica* no.41, *ap.* Plut. *Mor.* 239e; Plut. *Lyk.* 8.4; 24.3 (probably also *Instituta Laconica* no.22, *ap.* Plut. *Mor.* 238e-f; Herakleides Lembos *fr.* 373.12, Dilts = Aristotelian *Lak. Pol. fr.* 611.12, Rose). Modern discussion: Hodkinson 1992, 2000: 85-90, 125-127.

[16] On the character of Spartiate agricultural production and the size of estates, Hodkinson 2000: 132-135, 382-385.

intervention is reinforced by comparison with the comparable contemporary servile population of the Penestai in Thessaly. In contrast to the helots, who delivered produce to their Spartiate masters, the large numbers of Penestai who worked the extensive landholdings of the wealthiest Thessalian aristocratic families appear to have lived under conditions of greater control in which they themselves were the recipients of monthly handouts from their owners.[17] As Moon (1999: 73) has pointed out, this latter system represents the logical extreme of a system of labour obligations, as is indicated by its similarity to the monthly distributions of rations to slaves mentioned in Hesiod's *Works and Days* (line 767). However, we should be careful not to exaggerate the lack of intervention implied by the nature of the helots' obligations. As the quotation above from Paul Lovejoy indicates, the dues required in the cases cited in the previous paragraph were in the form of fixed payments. The nature of the payments made by the helots is a matter of contro-versy. Later sources write of a fixed payment, but these references almost certainly relate to new conditions introduced by the third-century revolution. In archaic and classical times the helots' dues were probably organised on a sharecropping basis, comprising a proportional share of the produce (Hodkinson 1992, 2000: 125-131). This arrangement would have provided a greater incentive for Spartiate masters to intervene in helot farming, since they would gain directly from any consequent increase in agricultural production. This incentive may have been intensified by the fact that Spartiates themselves were compelled, on pain of loss of citizenship, to make monthly contributions of specified foodstuffs (barley flour, wine, cheese and figs) to their common messes. Consequently, they had to ensure that helot farming arrangements were geared towards the production of sufficient quantities of these particular foodstuffs, although the need for special pressure on this point would have been lessened by the fact that the foodstuffs in question were mainly staples required anyway by the helots for their own subsistence.

Relationship to the land

Another relevant factor is the relationship of the farming population to the land-holdings they worked, the extent to which they enjoyed practical fixity of tenure, whether *de iure* or simply *de facto*. This factor is clearly directly connected to the capacity of the master or landowner to intervene in the agricultural process by moving his labour force around to suit his interests. Here the practices of certain

....

[17] Theokritos 16.34-35; Scholion (*Oxoniensis Bodleianus Holkhamensis* 88) on Aristoph. *Wasps* 1274; *Etymologicum Gudianum*, s.v. Εἵλωτες, as interpreted by Ducat 1994: 46-48, 90-91. The evidence of Theokritos appears to derive from that of Simonides at the end of the sixth century. For the different picture presented by the third-century writer Archemachos, see below.

landowners with regard to peasant sharecropping tenants are particularly instructive. In the region of Tuscany in post-unification Italy, for example, tenants' rights were weak. The landlord's control was ensured by terms of contract which specified that the labour capacity and subsistence needs of the tenant's family should match the size and labour requirements of the holding. To achieve this balance landlords were able to disperse members of their tenants' families elsewhere or order the adoption of living-in help, could give or withhold permission for marriage, and could vet the appointment of new household heads (Gill 1983: 147). Such a high level of intervention in the (dis)placement of the agricultural labour force is also common in systems of slave labour. The potential of the master to separate slave families—man from woman, children from parents—has often been noted as the most poignant example of the potential powerlessness of slaves to ensure some element of continuity in their position (e.g. Bradley 1987: 52-70). Within the plantation slavery of the antebellum U.S. South, for example, children could be taken away into domestic service, and slaves of all ages were frequently sold, hired or loaned to other owners, or moved to other plantations. It has been estimated that, due largely to the strength of the interregional slave trade, "in the upper South about one first marriage in three was broken by forced separation and close to half of all children were separated from at least one parent", (Kolchin 1993: 125-126, drawing upon the work of Tadman 1989). The fact that a common occasion of sale was the death of the owner highlights the fundamental insecurity of the slave's link to the land that s/he cultivated.

Such an extreme degree of insecurity has not, however, been universal, even for slaves. In the lower U.S. South, for example, although owners' rights were no less strong, in practice slaves experienced much less disruption than in the upper South, owing to the region's position as net importer of slaves (Kolchin 1993: 126). Within other servile systems the security of farmers' attachment to the land has been increased by other factors. For example, within the Islamic society of the north African Savanna, although masters retained the legal right of sale, in practice public opinion against the sale of those born into slavery or living *en famille* exercised considerable restraint on their actions (Hill 1985: 37-38; Lovejoy 2000: 213).[18] Similarly, within Russian serfdom, noble landowners had by the early eighteenth century acquired the legal right to move their serfs between estates, convert them to domestic duties, and even buy and sell them separately from the land (Moon 1999: 67); and a few landowners did exercise these rights. On most estates, however,

---

[18] Cooper (1979: 118-119) argues that the lower frequency of sales of second-generation slaves was also a reflection of a different balance of power *vis-à-vis* their masters in comparison with first-generation slaves.

decisions regarding the relationship of serf households to the land were shared between the landowner's estate manager or steward and serf functionaries elected by their own village communes.[19] The outcome was a generic fixity of tenure at communal level, although there was a tendency towards greater instability of tenure at the level of individual households. The essence of Russian serfdom was that the serfs were peasants legally bound to the land. Commune members were secure, as a collectivity, from arbitrary removal from the local farming territory. However, since many communes were collectively responsible for meeting the demands of the landowner for labour services or dues, they themselves frequently intervened to ensure that the amount of land farmed by their member households matched their size and economic potential. Allocations of land were made to newly formed households and to those increasing in size, if necessary by taking land off households that had become smaller. Many communes also practised a periodic redistribution of land to take account of changes in household size. The instability of tenure potentially generated by these practices was, however, limited by the prevailing "complex household" structure of most serf households (embracing an "extended family" of two or more related married couples or a married couple with their children and one or more other relatives), especially those practising *post-mortem* division of inheritance, which helped to smooth out fluctuations in the size of each of its constituent nuclear families.

When we turn to applying these comparative considerations to the case of helotage, we encounter several points of uncertainty. There is no direct literary evidence for the nature of the helots' relationship to the landholdings they worked. The nearest piece of evidence is a passage from the geographer Strabo (8.5.4), reporting a statement by the fourth-century historian Ephorus that "it was not permitted for the holder [of helots] either to liberate them or to sell them outside the boundaries". This statement raises several issues whose discussion lies beyond the scope of this article.[20] The essential question, however, is whether the fact that Ephorus mentions only the prohibition of sale outside Spartan territory can be interpreted as signifying that internal sales were permitted.[21] There is currently disagreement on this point.[22] However, even a scholar like Jean Ducat (1990: 21-22),

....

[19] The following discussion is based on Moon 1999: 156-180, 199-236. Although he prefers the term "seigniorial peasants" to the traditional term "serfs", I have retained the latter usage, partly because of its familiarity to non-specialists, partly due to the absence of an obvious substitute for the noun "serfdom".

[20] For fuller discussion, Hodkinson 2000: 117-119.

[21] I interpret the "boundaries" in the passage as a reference to the boundaries of Spartan territory, rather than to the boundaries of individual landholdings as suggested by MacDowell 1986: 35.

[22] For two different recent interpretations, Hodkinson 2000: 119 (Ephorus' text is inconclusive); Luraghi 2002a: 228-229 (the text proves the permissibility of internal sales).

who advocates the permissibility of private internal sales, envisages that they normally took place when landholdings underwent a change of Spartiate owner, so that the helots would remain attached to the land they already farmed. A new Spartiate landowner would surely often want to retain the intimate knowledge which resident helot farmers possessed about the local agricultural terrain, with its diverse microclimates and specialised ecological niches.[23] Hence, even if internal sale were permissible, it would not necessarily be incompatible with the possibility that many helots possessed effective fixity of tenure.

Sale, however, was not the only means by which Spartiate masters may potentially have intervened in the disposition of their helot labour force. By analogy with both American slavery and Russian serfdom, young helots may have been taken off the land into personal and domestic service. We have particular evidence for the important roles played by male helot servants as batmen on campaign and by helot female domestics as wet-nurses of Spartiate children and as sexual partners of Spartiate citizens; sons produced through such liaisons were accorded an honourable place in Spartan society and may have added to the prestige of the citizen household (Hodkinson 1997: 46-55, 2000: 336-337). However, we have no evidence about whether or to what extent the supply of personal and domestic servants was drawn from the helot agricultural population.

Another, potentially more significant, form of intervention was through Spartiate masters' redeployment of their helot workforce. A certain basic level of redeployment may have been necessary as a normal response to regular ongoing fluctuations, such as the changing requirements of agricultural exploitation, the varying demands of Spartiate households and the diverse demographic histories of helot families. In addition, however, we need to consider the impact of more fundamental, long-term changes, which we are now for the first time beginning to perceive through the results of recent intensive archaeological survey. The *Laconia Survey* conducted by the British School at Athens, a survey of some 70 km² of mainly arid, marginal hill territory immediately to the east and north-east of Sparta, has revealed a story of major changes in the area's settlement patterns during the archaic and classical periods.[24] Following a total absence of settlements in previous periods, the sixth century (and especially the half-century between c.550 and 500 BC) witnessed a relatively rapid phase of rural colonisation in a pattern of widespread settlement dispersion, involving the foundation of a minimum of 87 sites,

....

[23] Cf. the reported comments of the wealthy Roman senator Publius Volusius, who declared "that estate most fortunate which had as tenants natives of the place, and held them, by reason of long association, even from the cradle, as if born on their father's own property" (Columella, *De Re Rustica* 1.7.3).

[24] The following discussion is based upon Catling 2002.

mainly of small and medium size from farmsteads to hamlets. Then, within a short period from c.450 BC onwards, there was further radical change: a sharp reduction in the number of sites (from 87 to 46), involving a marked discontinuity in site occupation and a permanent desertion of many of the smallest farmstead sites, along with a proportionate increase in medium-sized sites, especially in the number of hamlets. This growth and subsequent decline in numbers of settlements have been interpreted as signifying an initial intensification of agricultural exploitation of this previously marginal area through the location of farms close to areas of cultivation, followed by subsequent retraction due to a combination of land failure and concentration of land-ownership.

The socio-economic implications of these significant changes are, unfortunately, obscured by uncertainty over the status of the inhabitants of most of the survey area. Plausible cases can be made for viewing them either as helots working Spartiate farms or as *perioikoi* working the land on their own account or with slave labour. It seems certain, however, that most of the western sector of the survey area, closest to Sparta itself, was Spartiate-owned—especially the area embracing the low hills and spurs along the eastern edge of the Eurotas valley from the confluence of the Rivers Eurotas and Kelephina to the state sanctuary of the Menelaion. Within this particular area, there was an initial foundation of 16 sites in the sixth century, comprising 13 small farmsteads (0.01-0.14 ha) and three somewhat larger sites (0.15-0.30 ha). In the later-fifth-century decline, the total number of settlements was reduced to ten. Only six of the 13 original small farmsteads and one of the larger sites continued in occupation; three new small farmsteads were also founded. More detailed analysis of these specific changes lies beyond the scope of this paper, but the general implications are clear. The initial wave of colonisation must have entailed Spartiate masters moving their helots into new settlements to facilitate the new or more intensive cultivation of nearby land. Equally significantly, the subsequent decline and readjustments must have involved the removal of some helot households from the landholdings they had formerly worked and the resettlement of others in different locations. In some cases, of course, removal or resettlement may have occurred at times when a helot household was becoming unviable anyway due to agricultural failure; but it is unlikely that such major changes could have been effected with no element of arbitrary Spartiate intervention or untimely disruption of helot life.

The formation of the agrarian economy

The evidence just considered comes, as already indicated, from just one small area of Spartiate territory and raises again the question whether we can extrapolate the evidence from an area close to Sparta to other areas for which we lack similarly detailed published survey evidence. Here comparative evidence might once again hope to offer some illumination. In general, it seems that the extent of the masters' or landowners' intervention to control the location and disposition of their dependent labour force is often related to the degree to which they themselves were responsible for forming the fundamental elements of the agrarian economy. In Russia the considerable extent of local self-determination had its roots in the fact that "serfdom and the other means by which the 'ruling groups' exploited the peasantry were superimposed on a peasant society and economy which already existed. The ruling and land-owning elites were not primarily responsible for creating the main productive units in Russia's rural economy" (Moon 1999: 66). In contrast, the U.S. plantation system, in which masters exercised strong control over the disposition of their slaves, was the creation of the white masters themselves, and in many states had initially been operated using mainly white indentured servants before the large-scale importation of black slaves (Elkins 1976: 37-40; Kolchin 1993: 8-13). The situation revealed by the *Laconia Survey* is clearly more similar to that of the U.S. plantation system, in the sense that the local agrarian economy was one created by Spartiate landowners themselves. However, the means by which Spartan domination and helotisation were established over more distant areas of Lakonia, and the consequent implications for the formation of their local economies, are unclear.[25]

The case of Messenia might seem, at first sight, more straightforward. A fragment from the late-seventh-century Spartan poet Tyrtaios (*fr.* 5 West) depicts the Spartans as having gained control of Messene two generations previously through act of conquest.[26] Thucydides (1.101) presents a similar picture in his statement that the majority of helots who revolted in 464 were descendants of the "old Messenians" who had been enslaved in the past. To this evidence we may add another fragment of Tyrtaios (*fr.* 23 West), which seems to mention the Messenians as a unified group engaged in military conflict with the Spartans, and also references in later sources to a Second Messenian War (in effect, an abortive revolt from Spartan control) during Tyrtaios' own lifetime.[27] The impression given by this evidence is of a coherent local population which retained its integrity even after its initial conquest—a population whose agricultural practice may not have been massively disrupted by the Spartan conquest. As I myself recently suggested, "after their conquest most Messenian

....

[25] The divergent accounts in classical and later sources are of little historical value: evidence in Cartledge 1979: 348-349; discussion in Luraghi, this volume.

[26] The phrase "fathers of our fathers" may of course have a generic rather than specific temporal reference, but this does not affect Tyrtaios' location of the conquest in time past.

[27] As Luraghi notes (this volume), the first attested reference to the Second Messenian War probably derives from Ephorus (cf. Diod. 15.66).

working farmers presumably became servile cultivators of the same fields they had farmed before the conquest" (Hodkinson 2000: 119).

Although I am not convinced by every aspect of recent revisionist interpretations of the origins and development of helotage (Luraghi 2002a and this volume), I would now present a less simple, more nuanced, picture of the formation of the Messenian agrarian economy under Spartiate rule. I would retain the concept of a mass enslavement of the pre-existing population following a military conquest of Messene, as described by Tyrtaios. His reference to the enemy fleeing the mountain range of Ithome and abandoning their rich farmlands should not be interpreted as signifying a mass desertion of the conquered region. Tyrtaios is surely referring to a wealthy elite such as dominated warfare and landholding in most contemporary Greek communities, including Sparta itself.[28] Their flight would not have involved the mass of the farming population, which was subjected to the servitude described in other surviving fragments of his poetry (*frs.* 6-7 West). Doubt has been expressed about the feasibility of such a mass enslavement, in the light of Orlando Patterson's comparative study, which highlights "a strong tendency on the part of a conquering group not to enslave a conquered population en masse and in situ" and observes that such attempts "were almost always disastrous failures" (1982: 110). In particular, it has been argued that, "a formerly independent group, with a full social structure and its own ruling elites, cannot be reduced to slavery without huge bloodshed" (Luraghi 2002a: 237). However, as the evidence of Tyrtaios suggests, the local population subjugated by Sparta was one already deprived of its full social structure by the flight of its ruling elite, a factor that would have considerably facilitated the initial act of enslavement.[29] Moreover, modern doubters of the basic feasibility of a mass enslavement of a pre-existing population in Greek antiquity should not forget that it was deemed feasible by intelligent later commentators like Thucydides and Theopompos, who also ascribed the Thessalians' domination over the Penestai to the same mechanism.[30]

That said, I would accept that the process of forming the new agrarian regime within the conquered territory of Messene will have been less straightforward and entailed a greater degree of Spartiate manipulation than the simple superimposition of their exploitation on the top of existing structures suggested by the statement in my earlier study. Moreover, I would agree with the revisionist argument on two

....

[28] For what it is worth, Pausanias' account of the episode (4.14.1) states that leading Messenians with foreign *proxeniai* fled abroad, whilst the mass of the populace returned home as before.

[29] That, even so, there remained considerable ethnic solidarity and resistance—as Patterson's thesis would suggest—is shown by Tyrtaios' reference (*fr.* 23 West) to further conflict involving the Messenians (even if one dismisses the later sources' picture of a full-scale Second Messenian War).

[30] Theopompos, *FGrHist* 115F122, *ap.* Athen. 265b-c.

important points: first, that the Spartan conquest of "Messene" mentioned by Tyrtaios probably related to the settlement at the foot of Mt. Ithome and its adjacent territory in eastern Messenia, rather than to any wider geographical area; and, secondly, that it is unlikely that the entire region which later became Messenia had been united before the Spartan conquest, especially as it appears that the region had experienced a widespread break in site occupation during the later eighth century.[31] Exactly when and how the remainder of the region came under Spartiate control is not precisely known. But in these circumstances it seems that, within a framework of potential intra-regional variations, we should expect some degree of scope for the incoming Spartiates actively to mould local agrarian economies. Some support for this probability may be found in preliminary indications from archaeological survey of an increase in settlements in Messenia in the archaic period in comparison with the Geometric period and of a pattern of nucleated settlement under Spartan rule that contrasts with contemporary patterns elsewhere in Greece.[32]

Geographical distance, supervision and absenteeism

We should not imagine, however, that the modalities through which helotage was set in place necessarily exercised a determining impact on Spartiate-helot relations throughout the entire period of Spartan domination. For example, the economic framework of plantation slavery in most regions of Africa was—as in the U.S.A.— a creation of the slaveowners themselves, using newly enslaved imported labour which was typically subjected to close supervision. However, in certain circumstances established second-generation slave villages could become subject to less intervention and gradually assume greater self-direction of their agricultural labour (Klein and Lovejoy 1979: 184-187; Lovejoy 2000: 213). In assessing the development of helotage, we need to give consideration to two further interrelated variables which comparative evidence suggests may have had an important influence. In this section I shall examine the question of geographical distance between owner and cultivator; in the following section, the pattern of residence of the unfree population.

The issue of geographical distance has already been implicitly posed by the fact that both the literary evidence of Xenophon and the archaeological evidence of the *Laconia Survey* suggest a considerable degree of Spartiate intervention in those areas closest to Sparta itself. To what extent should we expect similar levels of intervention further afield? Comparative evidence from a variety of servile systems suggests that the presence or absence of the master or owner can exercise a considerable influence upon

....

[31] Luraghi 2002b; Davis et al. 1997: 452; Alcock et al. in press; cf. also the abandonment of Nichoria around the mid-eighth century: McDonald, Coulson and Rosser 1983.

[32] McDonald and Hope Simpson 1972: 144; Davis et al. 1997: 455-456; Alcock 2002b.

the level of landowner intervention. Within Russian serfdom, for example, there was a marked difference between estates held by petty squires, who normally resided on their estates and ran their domains themselves, giving village communes and their peasant officials little independence, and estates in the hands of the most important noblemen, who were typically absentee landowners on state service in Moscow or in the army. Some absentee landowners did attempt to make use of stewards to impose an authoritarian regime. But on most such estates the management of agricultural production was in practice a shared enterprise between, on the one hand, the land-lord's stewards or estate managers and, on the other, household patriarchs and peasant functionaries elected by the communes, which in most cases were based upon village communities (Kolchin 1987: 200-201). The difficulties that absentee landowners often had (or thought they had) in ensuring that their stewards—who were them-selves normally serfs—performed their duties properly further diminished their capacity for effective intervention. One notable sign of these differential degrees of intervention was that resident landowners almost universally demanded labour services, whereas absentee owners "often preferred to leave their serfs on obrok [dues] rather than worry about the supervisory abilities of their stewards".[33]

As Peter Kolchin's comparative study of American slavery and Russian serfdom has noted, the great majority of U.S. slaves—in contrast to their Russian serf coun-terparts—had resident masters, who managed their plantations directly, usually without even an overseer, and on smaller farms personally directed their labour and even worked alongside them.[34] Under these conditions slave independence of action was severely restricted. Nevertheless, there were exceptional areas, most notably the ante-bellum South Carolina low country, in which absenteeism was common among wealthy slave-owners, who often resided in the town of Charleston rather than on their estates. Some, though not all, absentee landowners appointed a white steward as supervisor; but the key figure in directing work on many estates was usually a black "driver", himself a slave. Hand-in-hand with a lower degree of direct owner interven-tion went a more moderate version of labour services: the so-called "task" system, according to which slaves were assigned given tasks and could cease work for the day on their completion. Within a more flexible, self-managed work regime, slaves were able to devote more time to working for themselves and to accumulate small amounts of property.[35] The huge difference which the presence or absence of the slaveowner can have on the character of farming operations is also emphasised by the Roman agricultural writer, Columella. He strongly advocated the advantages of farming

....

[33] Kolchin 1987: 58-65 (quotation from pp. 64-65), 87-89; Moon 1999: 202-205.
[34] Kolchin 1987: 59-61, 65-68, 1993: 93-132.
[35] Morgan 1983; Kolchin 1993: 31-32.

nearby estates through slave labour working under close supervision by the owner. In contrast, he recommended turning over to tenant farmers distant estates "which it is not easy for the owner to visit", due to the difficulty of controlling the activities of slaves, even when there was a slave overseer (*De Re Rustica* 1.7.5-7).

In the above cases we have been dealing with a relatively sharp dichotomy between the owner's residence on the estate and his absenteeism in a distant town or on state service. As Orlando Patterson (1982: 180-181) points out, however, we should distinguish between such full-scale absenteeism and the simple "living apart" of the master class, as is illustrated by the case of slavery in nineteenth-century, pre-colonial Africa. In various regions of the continent, particular economic and political conditions following the decline of the European slave trade led to the widespread growth of a system of agricultural slavery geared to market production whose most common shared characteristic was the establishment of plantations grouped around the towns.[36] Under this system, residential arrangements of both slaves and masters were varied.[37] On smaller plantations groups of slaves were often housed in a separate section within the compound of the master's family, and owner and slaves worked the fields side by side. On somewhat larger plantations (over about 20 slaves), the owner's family might live apart from their slaves, though at not any great distance; under these circumstances relatively close supervision was still feasible. The largest plantations of several hundred or more slaves often involved separate slave villages, located at a variety of distances from the town, from the immediate suburbs up to a radius of 30 km or more. Given the range of distances involved, the degree of separateness between master and slaves and the extent of intervention from the master varied considerably. Some owners of large plantations, such as government officials, military personnel and merchants resident in the towns, were absentees who relied upon slave overseers. In other cases, however, the plantations might be managed by junior members of the master's lineage. Within one of the most-studied regions, the nineteenth-century Sokoto Caliphate in Islamic West Africa, larger slave-owners appear in general to have been able to maintain a relatively strict and closely-defined regime of labour services, in which the slaves were organised in gangs farming the masters' fields, although they also possessed their own plots which they were allocated time to

....

[36] The economic and political conditions, the prevalence of plantation slavery and its physical manifestations, are sketched in Lovejoy 1979: 1267-1271, and outlined more broadly in Lovejoy 2000: 165-251.

[37] The varied nature of these arrangements is indicated by the semantic range of local terms (such as *rinji* and *gandu*) used to describe larger plantations within the Sokoto Caliphate in Islamic West Africa. These terms could embrace slaves living in the same compound as the master's family through to separate slave villages (Lovejoy 1979: 1279-1280).

cultivate. However, within one region of the Caliphate—that of Nupe in the Bida emirate—the slave villages, which comprised homogeneous populations of captives taken from other areas of Nupe and located together according to ethnic group, enjoyed considerably less intervention, in spite of their relatively recent foundation, organising their own labour regime under village headmen and periodically remitting agricultural tribute.[38] In other regions of West Africa too, such as among the Sherbro of Sierra Leone, "the slave villages, being spatially peripheral to the master's household, slaves were often so little supervised" (MacCormack 1977: 198).

How might these comparative insights illuminate Spartiate-helot relations? The Spartiates all resided in the cluster of villages that constituted Sparta itself. As regards their holdings in the Sparta valley and neighbouring areas, the distinction drawn above between genuine absenteeism and simple "living apart", along with the example of the closely-regulated "suburban" West African slave villages, reinforces the impression we have already gained from both the literary and the archaeological evidence: namely, that, even if there was a residential separation between the Spartiates masters and their helots, the minimal distance between them would not have posed any great barrier to a high degree of intervention in helot farming. Such intervention would have been facilitated by the fact that one of these Spartiate villages, Amyklai, was located in the very centre of the valley, 5 km south of the main cluster. A further indication of Spartiate intervention is the finding of the *Laconia Survey* that the pottery assemblage of most of the settlements in its western sector close to Sparta lacked evidence of storage vessels, suggesting that their agricultural produce was taken for storage to Sparta itself (Catling 2002: 195-196). In several respects, Spartiate management of their estates in the Sparta valley and its environs appears similar to the level of intervention ascribed to the Athenian landowner Ischomachos in Xenophon's *Oikonomikos* (7.29-21.12). Ischomachos and his wife reside in a town house, where the agricultural produce is stored (cf. esp. 9.2-10); but whenever he has no pressing business in town he walks out to his slave-worked farm, where he superintends all the details of the work and implements improvements in method (11.14-18; cf. 21.10).

Many Spartiate estates, however, lay some considerable distance from Sparta. Thucydides (4.3) estimated that Pylos on the coast of western Messenia was "about 400 stades from Sparta", approximately 70 km (cf. Hornblower 1996: 154). Even the eastern Messenian plains were some 40 km distant and parts of the Helos valley in southern Lakonia some 30 km.[39] The impression given by literary sources which describe the Spartiate lifestyle, such as Xenophon's *Polity of the Lakedaimonians* and Plutarch's *Life of*

....

[38] Lovejoy 1978, 1979: 1280-1286, 2000, esp. pp. 196-199, 205-206, 212-216; Mason 1973: 465-466.

[39] I have suggested elsewhere that the Spartiates may have held estates even further south in Lakonia, in the plain of Molaoi some 50 km distant (Hodkinson 2000: 141).

Lykourgos, is that Spartiate life entailed a male citizen's more-or-less continuous presence in or around Sparta itself, so that he would be available for civic duties and especially for the evening meal at his mess group, attendance at which was compulsory except if delayed by sacrifice or hunting (Plut. *Lyk.* 12.2). In contrast, other evidence suggests that periods of individual absence from Sparta were not uncommon: for example, Spartiates are attested as travelling abroad to visit foreign guest-friends and to worship or compete in games at foreign sanctuaries.[40] It is possible therefore that citizens could periodically obtain leave to visit their distant estates. However, since the estates of many Spartiates, and especially the wealthy, were probably fragmented into smaller holdings scattered throughout Lakonia and Messenia, it is unlikely that most male citizen landowners would be able to obtain long enough leave to visit each of their holdings with sufficient regularity to sustain an effective degree of personal intervention. Nor is it easy to imagine that most members of the other major set of landowners, Spartiate women, had the time or opportunity to make such wide-ranging personal visits, given their attested household responsibilities in Sparta (Plato, *Laws* 805e; Xen. *Lak. Pol.* 1.9).[41] Hence, as far as their more distant estates were concerned, the probability is that most Spartiate landowners were effectively absentees.[42]

---

[40] Cf. Hodkinson 1999: 160-176, 2000: 174-175, 294-298, 307-323, 337-352.

[41] Of course, many estates would also be held by minors, both male and female, who were tied to Sparta during their public upbringing; but I take it that responsibility for management lay in the hands of their adult guardians.

[42] See below for discussion of the large inhabited building discovered at Kopanaki in the Soulima valley. It has been interpreted as the home of a Spartiate landlord with his helots living in attendance (Kaltsas 1983; cf. Harrison and Spencer 1998: 162). As indicated below, however, our knowledge of the surrounding settlement pattern is currently insufficient to sustain this conclusion. Moreover, even if the building were the centre of a Spartiate estate, it would not necessarily imply the physical presence of the Spartiate owner. A further piece of evidence is Xenophon's account of the conspiracy of Kinadon, which includes a reference (*Hell.* 3.3.8) to "Lakedaimonians [probably Spartiates] both older and younger", who had visited perioikic Aulon—possibly located in the Soulima valley (Roebuck 1941: 25-26; Lazenby and Hope Simpson 1972: 98 n.101, though there is some uncertainty whether the name signifies a town or a region: Cartledge 1979: 274). Aulon is said to be a place where there were helots, whom Kinadon was ordered to arrest, along with certain of its citizens. The circumstances in which both Spartiates and helots were present in Aulon are, however, unclear. It could be a matter of citizens supervising distant estates: it is not impossible that Spartiates owned land near to perioikic settlements, in which helot farmers also resided. However, the order to arrest Aulonitai and helots could equally indicate that we are dealing with helot fugitives and *perioikoi* harbouring them, and that the visiting Spartiates were on official business (Cartledge 1979: 274-275; Lazenby 1997: 445). This interpretation is strengthened by the fact that the word Xenophon uses to describe the younger Spartiate visitors, *neôteroi,* is the same used in the previous sentence to refer to young men from the elite military squad of *hippeis* who were sent with Kinadon on his mission. Other interpretations of the episode have been suggested by other scholars, such as that the helots were farming perioikic estates or serving a Spartiate garrison (cf. Lazenby 1997: 445). Overall, the context of the episode is too unclear to serve as the basis for any interpretations about the direction of Aulon's agrarian economy.

The obvious question is how absentee Spartiate citizens could ensure the effective management of their distant estates. The comparative evidence considered above suggests that the most common method by which absentee landowners have exploited distant servile agrarian populations is through the agency of individuals drawn from the servile population itself in each locality: serf stewards and communal officials within Russian serfdom; black drivers in low country South Carolina; slave overseers or village headmen within the slave villages of pre-colonial Africa. Similarly, it is *a priori* probable that absentee Spartiate landowners drew upon the services of certain individual helots in the management of their holdings—and not only of their holdings in distant Messenia. Even in the case of estates within the Sparta valley, the Spartiate owner could not be continuously present due to his civic duties, and there will also have been shorter periods when large numbers of owners were unavoidably absent on military campaigns.[43] So too, even under the comparatively strict supervisory regime described in Xenophon's *Oikonomikos*, Ischomachos put his farms in the management of slave bailiffs at times when he was not personally present (12.2). There is, in fact, a piece of evidence which can enable us to identify, at least by their generic name, the helots who probably acted as managing agents on behalf of Spartiate landowners. A gloss which survives from Hesychios' lexicon of rare words refers to the "*mnôionomoi*: leaders of the helots".[44] Drawing upon the evidence of the poem of Hybrias (*ap.* Athenaios 695f-696a), Jean Ducat has concluded that the *mnôia* was a group of slaves living and working on an estate (1990: 63, 74). On this interpretation, the *mnôionomoi* can be viewed as leading men drawn from the helots themselves, men who exercised supervision and control over the persons in their *mnôia*, and through whom a Spartiate owner would be likely to work.

The extant version of Hesychios' text is too brief to indicate any distinctions between the roles played by helot *mnôionomoi* in different geographical locations. In view of the comparative evidence considered above, however, we should expect that differences in levels of Spartiate supervision dictated by geographical distance

....

[43] During the period of Sparta's overseas empire in the late fifth and early fourth centuries, a sizeable number of prominent Spartiates spent substantial periods—sometimes several years—away from Spartan territory (Hodkinson 1993: 153-157).

[44] Hesychios' lexicon, which probably dates to the fifth century AD but drew upon much earlier specialist lexica, focused on rare words in poetry and in Greek dialects. It survives only in a severely abridged form, in which the original lexicon has been reduced to a mere glossary (*OCD*[3], 701-702). The extant text, μονομοιτῶν Εἰλώτων ἄρχοντες (μ1626, ed. Latte, ii.676) has been plausibly emended by Wilamowitz-Moellendorf (1924: 273) to read μνῳονόμοι· τῶν Εἰλώτων ἄρχοντες. Quite apart from the explanatory gloss, the term *mnôionomoi* itself implies a controlling and supervisory role, just as the *paidonomos* had charge of and responsibility for the youths in the Spartiate upbringing (Xen. *Lak. Pol.* 2-4).

will have led to considerable variations in the degree of responsibility for agricultural management possessed by different *mnôionomoi*. Xenophon's Ischomachos, whom we have compared to owners of estates in the Sparta valley, given his ability to walk to his farms, was able to exert a strict regime of supervision and correction over his slave bailiff (*Oik.* 12.2-14.10; cf. 20.16-20; 21.9). Such close supervision would not have been feasible further afield. It is possible (though by no means certain) that, in order to monitor the activities of *mnôionomoi* on their distant estates, some wealthy Spartiates may have appointed outside agents, most plausibly, perhaps, drawn from among the *perioikoi*: men with functions comparable to those of estate managers within Russian serfdom, appointed by landowners to exercise a general supervision over their dispersed holdings. However, the Russian experience (Moon 1999: 202-203) suggests that, even had such a practice been employed, the outcome of such supervision would normally have been a shared responsibility which left plenty of initiative for the *mnôionomos*.

In the absence of the Spartiate owner, how far then might the responsibilities of helot *mnôionomoi* extend? Was their management limited to strictly agricultural matters, such as ensuring the availability of the appropriate equipment, seed and animals, supervising the input of labour, determining the mix of crops to be grown, deciding the timing of sowing and harvest, and ensuring delivery of the owner's share of the produce? Or did it extend to more "structural" responsibilities, such as ensuring that the level of available labour matched the size of the holding and the owner's requirements for produce: responsibilities which might have involved (re)distributing cultivation rights between households or exerting influence over key life-decisions affecting the growth or diminution of helot families? The possibility of such an extended role raises questions regarding the capacity in which the *mnôionomos* performed his role. Clearly, he was in one sense an overseer accepted, if not appointed, by the Spartiate owner; but did his position also reflect, as Ducat (1990: 63) has suggested, the structure of the local helot community? Ducat terms the *mnôionomoi* "des chefs coutumiers"; I would think particularly of the heads of larger and more important helot households.

Residence and helot communities

The proposition that the persons chosen as *mnôionomoi* may have emerged from the structure of local helot society also raises the question whether their roles were confined to individual Spartiate estates or may have had a wider communal aspect. Despite Ducat's understandable linkage of the *mnôia* to a group of helots working a Spartiate estate, the term itself is unspecific in reference and could equally refer to a broader grouping of helots. In approaching this question, it is relevant to examine the issue of helot residence patterns. The comparative material considered above suggests that a relatively high degree of local, communal self-direction of agricultural production may be particularly associated with a nucleated settlement pattern, as in the case of the village communities of Russian serfs and certain groups of African slaves.

This association does appear to apply, both positively and negatively, in the case of helotage. We have already seen that the *Laconia Survey* area adjacent to Sparta itself was one of dispersed, small-scale settlements. Although both archaeological and literary evidence is limited, current indications are that the Sparta plain too contained no sizeable settlements beyond the Spartiate villages and that the helot cultivators were dispersed in a mixture of isolated farmsteads and hamlets (Catling 2002: 232-233). In short, those helot farmers under the closest degree of supervision by their Spartiate masters were settled in a pattern of residence less conducive to collective co-ordination of agricultural production by the helots themselves.

We are sadly ill-informed about residential patterns in other helotised areas of Lakonia. As regards distant Messenia, however, the indications are that settlement patterns were considerably more nucleated than in the areas of Lakonia closest to Sparta. These differential patterns can be seen most clearly through comparison of the results of the *Laconia Survey* with those of the *Pylos Regional Archaeological Project (PRAP)*, which has recently surveyed an area of western Messenia whose distance from any definitely attested perioikic settlements suggests that "there is no overwhelming reason to envisage the residents . . . as anything but of helot status" (Alcock 2002b: 193). Whereas the *Laconia Survey* discovered 87 late archaic and 46 classical sites within the 70 km² of its survey area, the 40 km² of western Messenia surveyed by *PRAP* produced a mere six archaic and four classical sites (Alcock 2002b: 193-195). The principal settlement in the area (named by the survey team "I04, Romanou *Romanou*") was marked by a sherd scatter of some 18 to 22 ha in the archaic period and probably even larger in classical times, compared with a mere 3 ha and 6 ha for the largest sites in the *Laconia Survey* (the perioikic village of Sellasia and the fort of Agios Konstantinos). It was clearly a sizeable conglomeration with a population size well into four figures.[45] Moreover, in both the archaic and classical periods the second largest site within the survey area (a different site in each period) lay close by, a mere 1.5 km distant. In the classical period these are the only securely-attested places of permanent habitation in the entire survey area.[46] Although a complete picture of

....

[45] Population densities for unwalled settlements of some 100-125 persons respectively per ha, which have been suggested by other intensive surveys (Catling 2002: 205-206; Jameson, Runnels and van Andel 1994: 545), would give it a population of some 1,800-2,750 persons in the archaic period.

[46] Of the other two sites, one is probably a shrine; the other is attested by only three sherds and may be a seasonal dwelling or a place of "off-site" rural activity (Alcock 2002b: 195).

habitation within the region is obscured by the fact that the various sectors within the *PRAP* survey area are not contiguous, the survey results indicate an indisputable pattern of residential concentration. Further indications of this pattern have emerged from other, less intensive surveys. The mean size of archaic sites reported by the *University of Minnesota Messenia Expedition*, whose survey area covered the whole of Messenia (and more), has been calculated as approximately 3 ha (Alcock 2002b: 191), equivalent to the sherd scatter from the village of Sellasia, at the top end of the range of habitations in the *Laconia Survey*. Conversely, survey of the "Five Rivers" area by the Gulf of Messenia revealed no evidence of dispersed habitation in farmsteads in the archaic and classical periods, in contrast to the Hellenistic period (Lukermann and Moody 1978: 99; cf. Harrison and Spencer 1998: 160-161). As Richard Catling has recently commented, in comparing the settlement patterns of Lakonian and Messenian helots, "a clear distinction begins to emerge in the ways in which these two groups were distributed in the landscape, and presumably in the ways in which the regions were farmed" (2002: 253).

Not that settlement patterns were necessarily uniform throughout Messenia. One indication of diversity is the eleven-room building (about 30 x 17 m) built around a central courtyard, with thick walls suggestive of a second storey, which was uncovered by rescue excavation in the modern village of Kopanaki in the Soulima valley (Kaltsas 1983). This impressively large structure, whose broad assemblage of domestic pottery including storage facilities marks it clearly as a habitation site, has been interpreted—along with an apparently similar building about 9 km E.S.E. down the valley, near the village of Vasiliko—as evidence of "a plantation-like sort of settlement, with big and isolated buildings forming the centre of large land-holdings" (Luraghi 2002a: 232). Although so precise a conclusion seems premature, given our ignorance—in the absence of intensive field survey—of settlement patterns in the region of each building,[47] their monumental character does suggest a different kind of settlement from those discussed above. Nevertheless, the picture here too seems to be of a population concentrated rather than spread thinly across the landscape.

....

[47] Interpretation of what little evidence does exist is hampered by uncertainty over the period of occupation of the building at Kopanaki. The excavator dated it from the second half of the sixth century to the first quarter of the fifth; but Richard Catling (1996: 34 n.12) has argued that the building's pottery assemblage should be downdated to the second half of the fifth century (perhaps c.450-425). Classical sherds have been noted at two nearby locations: (i) 1km ENE, on the summit of Stylari hill (McDonald and Rapp 1972: 298: Register A no. 233); (ii) 1.5 km W, at one of the tholos tombs at Ano Kopanaki, Akourthi (ibid. no. 234), which constitutes possible evidence of tomb cult (cf. Alcock 1991: 465 no.23; Antonaccio 1995: 85-87). On the building at Vasiliko, Valmin 1941; Pikoulas 1984. The dating of its sherds and inscriptions to the late sixth and early fifth centuries is somewhat generic and beset with some uncertainties: cf. Valmin 1941: 66, 70 n.1, 73; Jeffery 1990: 203 n.2.

The concentration of the Messenian helot population into nucleated rather than dispersed settlements was probably an important factor in ensuring the capacity of helot *mnôionomoi* to act effectively as local co-ordinators of agricultural production. It also makes more plausible the possibility that the *mnôionomoi* may have operated at a broader communal level, perhaps even at the level of a large village like "IO4 Romanou *Romanou*", where they might in effect have been village leaders comprising the more important household heads. Unfortunately, we have no direct evidence for the nature of helot household structures. I have suggested elsewhere that, as part of a strategy to even out some of the above fluctuations and divergences, helot households may have taken the form of co-residential multiple family households (Hodkinson 2000: 125, 386-387). Under such arrangements, the heads of large households would have been notable figures, men of some authority in the wider community. This suggestion, however, must necessarily remain hypothetical.

Whatever the structure of helot households, in considering the kinds of roles that village leaders could potentially have played, we can turn for potential illumination to the best attested case for comparison, namely, the officials of Russian serf communes, who played an important mediating role between absentee landowners and the local serf community. David Moon (1999: 199) has noted that, "communes were the basic institutions of local government in Russian villages . . . guided by state decrees and landowners' instructions, as well as the peasants' unwritten customary law . . . Communal officials were responsible for a wide range of village affairs, including day-to-day administration, sharing out and collecting the obligations communities owed to their landowners and the state, and distributing the village's arable land between households. Communes directed the village economy, especially the three-field system of crop rotation." Of course, in the absence of hard information, we cannot simply transfer the capacities of Russian commune officials onto Messenian helot *mnôionomoi*. We saw earlier that, whereas in Russia serfdom was superimposed on a pre-existing peasant society, there is room for debate about the relative contributions made by the incoming Spartiates and the local farming population to the formation of the Messenian agrarian economy under Spartan rule. Nevertheless, as already noted, the examples of many second-generation African slave villages indicate how even initially disparate groups of slaves transplanted into new territory can, within a context of village residence and landowner absenteeism, come to assume greater self-direction of the agrarian economy. In particular, the aforementioned case of Nupe slave villages, which comprised ethnically homogeneous groups of captives taken from other parts of Nupe territory, shows how the development of semi-autonomous agricultural production can be powerfully facilitated when the servile population shares a common ethnic identity—as was increasingly the case in fifth-century Messenia, whether founded in a longstanding collective identity or spurred by the development of a secondary ethnic consciousness under the common conditions of servitude imposed by Spartan rule (Luraghi 2002a: 238-240). The example of the Russian serf commune, consequently, constitutes an appropriate comparison to think with.

We can reasonably hypothesise that the experience of shared residence will have led many Messenian helot village communities to undertake a number of communal functions. Like any human community, helot villages will have needed to establish mechanisms for regulating anti-social behaviour, maintaining internal law and order, and administering social sanctions. The village was also no doubt the place where helot households working on different estates would interact socially and intermarry. Although evidence from the *PRAP* survey shows that Messenian settlement patterns under Spartan rule were not unchanging, the pre-eminence of the village "I04 Romanou *Romanou*" throughout the archaic and classical periods also suggests a significant degree of permanence and continuity, especially in comparison with the situation within the area of the *Laconia Survey*. Recent research has shown how, even among the fragile servile communities on U.S. slave plantations, physically separated from one another and constantly vulnerable to disruption by their masters, there still existed "extended kinship networks among slaves, who often exhibited impressive awareness of and attachments to more distant familial relations" (Kolchin 1993: 140). Hence, we should expect some meaningful level of kinship relations and community within helot settlements— even among the dispersed, less permanent and more tightly supervised settlements close to Sparta. We can get some sense of the decision-making capabilities of helot communities throughout both Lakonia and Messenia in the Spartans' infamous appeal to the helots "to pick out those of their number who claimed to have most distinguished themselves in the wars" (Thuc. 4.80).[48] Even helot communities in Lakonia possessed, at the very least, effective channels of internal communication, as was demonstrated in 371 when, despite Sparta itself being under siege, a Spartan call for volunteers was disseminated so effectively that more than 6,000 Lakonian helots came forward to enlist (Xen. *Hell.* 6.5.28-29). Under the more favourable and enduring conditions of Messenian helot villages, we should expect a particularly solid network of kinship relations and community; and with it a strong sense of a shared past and an attachment to place which could have served as the basis for

....

[48] "Infamous" because the Spartans subsequently put all those selected to death. This is not the place to enter into the recent debate about the historical authenticity of the episode. At the very least, Thucydides and his source(s) believed the helots capable of such communal decision-making.

the development of communal institutions. Some indication of the sense of attachment that some Messenian communities had to their territory and their past is evident in the "social memories" recently explored by Susan Alcock (2002a: 132-175), in particular through the evidence for local tomb cults, which indicate the operation of some level of communal organisation for the commemoration of the "heroes" of the past buried in monumental Bronze Age tombs.[49] The existence of these local cults in archaic and classical Messenia is an especially notable sign of communal identity, in that comparable tomb cults are considerably less present in other regions of archaic and classical Greece, and are almost totally absent from the helotised parts of Lakonia (Antonaccio 1995: esp. 69-70).

In these circumstances, we should give serious consideration to the possibility that some helot village communities may have taken on a role in the management of agricultural labour and in the fulfilment of the obligations towards the Spartiate landowners whose estates were cultivated by their inhabitants. There is a hint in the case of the Penestai of Thessaly that the obligations of some of their servile communities were organised on a communal level. As Jean Ducat (1994: 90-91) has noted, the term *syntaxeis*, by which Archemachos of Euboia (*ap.* Athen. 264a-b) refers to the dues owed by Penestai to their masters, may carry the connotation of dues rendered collectively rather than individually by each servile household.[50] However, the parallel with the Messenian helots is not exact, in that the very large numbers of Penestai held by the wealthiest Thessalians probably meant that the servile inhabitants of certain Penestic villages, like the serfs of most Russian communes, all owed their obligations to a single master;[51] in these circumstances a collective responsibility for dues would make perfect sense. Although individual wealthy Spartiates reportedly possessed holdings of helots which far exceeded private holdings of slaves in contemporary Athens ([Plato], *Alk. I* 122d), it is doubtful whether any were

....

[49] On Messenian tomb cult, see esp. Alcock 1991, 2002a: 132-175; Antonaccio 1995: 70-102. The spread of these cults throughout diverse parts of Messenia suggests that they cannot be ascribed exclusively to Messenian *perioikoi*.

[50] Ducat squares this evidence with the evidence cited earlier of Penestai being paid monthly rations by suggesting that the difference reflects either the distinction between Penestai directly attached to the master's "palace" and those located in more distant and independent situations, or a distinction between the archaic period when the power of the Thessalian aristocracy was in full flower and later periods when its weakening in the face of the development of poleis had led to a modification in the Penestai's terms of servitude (1994: 91; cf. 118-119).

[51] Ducat 1994: 88-89. As he points out, the fact that Menon of Pharsalos could equip 300 of his Penestai as troops (Dem. 23.199) implies that his total holdings ran well into four figures.

sufficiently large as to encompass an entire village.[52] Hence communal responsibility for dues would have involved co-ordinating payments of produce to a number of different Spartiate owners; if so, this would have entailed a very significant level of communality indeed.

Leadership and politics

This crucial point that, for all their common residence, different helot households would have been working on different plots of land for different masters, subject to a range of variations in their treatment and therefore to different perceptions of their personal requirements and needs, is a useful reminder that even among the most unified human societies there is a point at which impulses towards communal behaviour hit the buffer of household self-interest. Recent research has demonstrated that even the Russian commune, so often idealised as a model of social co-operation and egalitarianism, was itself a hive of village politics dominated by household patriarchs or by factions of wealthier peasants whose power was based on kinship and patronage. In a spirit of collusion between household heads, communal officials and the landowner's bailiff, local village elites "used the power entrusted to them by landowners to oppress and exploit other peasants in pursuit of their own interests."[53] We are not of course able to determine the extent to which helot leaders such as the *mnôionomoi* were able to engage in similar exploitative behaviour over their fellow helots. However, the existence of comparable underlying conditions of economic and social inequality is clearly evident. As in other societies—such as low country South Carolina (Morgan 1983: 120-122)—in which unfree farming populations have enjoyed a certain level of independence, helots were able to accumulate not insignificant amounts of movable property. The ancient sources depict

....

[52] In a recent discussion (Hodkinson 2000: 385-388) I suggested that an "ordinary" Spartiate estate of just over 18 ha might have sustained about 5 helot families and that the average landholding of wealthy Spartiates may have been roughly two and a half times as large at about 45 ha. If we assume, *exempli gratia*, that the wealthiest non-royal Spartiate (I purposely exclude the kings) might have held double that amount, some 90 ha, his estates might have sustained some 25 helot families, or a total population of about 125 helots. Even if all his landholdings were concentrated in one place, on the estimates of village population density of some 100-125 persons per ha referred to above (n. 45), this would imply only a very modest settlement of hardly more than a hectare in extent. In reality, however, most Spartiate estates were probably fragmented into a number of different holdings. If one were to adopt the comparatively low figures for the total helot population proposed by Figueira and Scheidel (this volume), the likelihood of the inhabitants of a sizeable helot village belonging to a single Spartiate would be even more remote.

[53] Moon 1999: 230-236 (quotation from p. 231); Hoch 1996. Cf. the detailed case studies of Hoch 1986; Melton 1993.

helots engaging in private sales (Hdt 9.80), insuring their boats, and expecting to receive rewards of silver (Thuc. 4.26). In the late third century no fewer than 6,000 Lakonian helots were each able to accumulate the sum of 5 Attic minas (500 drachmas) with which to purchase their freedom (Plut. *Kleom.* 23.1). This property accumulation was doubtless rooted in the system of sharecropping, which created possibilities for households enjoying a high ratio of labourers to household size to gain some benefit from agricultural surpluses that they produced.

A necessary consequence of private property accumulation was economic differentiation. In addition to temporary economic differences between helot households deriving from the normal fluctuations of household life cycles, more enduring differentiation will have resulted from divergent demographic histories and consequent differences in household size. Studies of pre-industrial agrarian societies have often noted positive correlations between household size and levels of wealth (Shanin 1972: 63-68). The potential for considerable economic differentiation among a helot-like servile population is suggested by the claim of Archemachos of Euboia (in the passage cited above) that many Penestai were wealthier than their Thessalian masters.[54] The presence of differential prosperity amongst a rural population under Spartiate rule has now been documented archaeologically through the wide variations in ceramic assemblages at different sites within the area of the *Laconia Survey* (Catling 2002: 193-195). Within Messenia, archaeological indications of socio-economic differentiation and the exercise of social control may be present in the evidence for the phenomenon of tomb cult mentioned above. Several recent studies of tomb cults have observed that, while they are in one sense a sign of community solidarity, they could also be used to proclaim the superiority of leading families who claimed to trace their pedigrees back to the heroic age, and in particular to the "ancestor" commemorated in the cult.[55] Excavated finds from the best published example of Messenian tomb cult—that at Tholos F at Nichoria in the Five Rivers region, which dates to the later fifth and early fourth century— suggest that the horizons of some of the cult participants were more than purely Messenian: of 23 recorded items of fine ware, at least 13 (56%), have been identified as either imported items or local imitations of foreign work, with especial links to Olympia and Attica.[56] Moreover, finds of pithoi and amphorae suggest that the

....

[54] As Ducat (1994: 15) notes, the statement is a "paradoxe banal" and is doubtless exaggerated, but makes sense only in the context of economic differentiation among the servile population.

[55] Morris 1988: 756-758; cf. Antonaccio 1995: 142, 257-268; Alcock 2002a: 146-152.

[56] These are my own calculations from the finds published in Coulson and Wilkie 1983. Cf. also Antonaccio 1995: 90-93, although it is unclear how her interpretation that the tomb was reused as a rural or pastoral shelter accords with the presence of fine tableware.

cult's administration included the storage of foodstuffs and liquids for communal dining, a vehicle by which leading helots could perhaps articulate their leadership through the extraction of surplus produce from their own or others' holdings. Thus the administration of tomb cult brings us back to the organisation of agricultural production and to the authority over other helots which the *mnôionomoi*, "the leaders of the helots", may have exercised through their supervision and direction of the agrarian economy. As Jacques Annequin (1985 : 647) has justly remarked, "Surveiller c'est exercer un pouvoir".

Other than the tantalising hints provided by tomb cult, our ignorance of so many of the details of helot society generally prevents us from detecting historical episodes in which more prominent helot households used their position for their own self-advancement at the expense of their fellow helots. One set of episodes in which such personal self-advancement can clearly be seen, however, is the positive response given by several thousand helots, from 424 BC onwards, to Spartan calls for military recruits, often in return for freedom from helot status.[57] Some of these former helot recruits were, indeed, placed on garrison service at Lepreon near the border of northern Messenia (Thuc 5.34), where one of their duties was presumably the capture of runaway helots. Given the evidence of differential status within helot communities and the hint of some communal role in the recruitment process, one wonders whether the composition of these groups of manumitted helots was skewed towards members of the more prominent households. To what extent was the acceptability, indeed desirability, to many helots of military service in Sparta's armies rooted in the social relations of production between helot *mnôionomoi* and their Spartiate masters, in the process of privileged collaboration practised by the *mnôionomoi* in the management of Spartiate estates?

In raising this particular question, of course, we are led logically on to the broader, political question that lies at the heart of modern debates about helot-Spartiate relationships: how, in the face of occasional widespread revolt, the minority elite group of Spartiates, largely confined to Sparta itself, maintained effective control for several centuries over the much larger servile helot population spread around their large and often distant territory. The particular insight to emerge from this article is, I suggest, that the issue of Spartiate collective political management stands parallel to, and may have been interlocked with, the issue of individual Spartiate management of agricultural estates. If the relations of privileged collaboration established in the agrarian sphere between Spartiate masters and

---

[57] E.g. Thuc. 4.80; 5.67; 7.19; 8.5; Xen. *Hell.* 3.1.4; 3.4.2; 6.5.28. Cf. Ducat 1990: 159-166; Hunt 1998, esp. 53-62, 170-175.

the *mnôionomoi* reinforced the authority of wealthy helot households, the influence exercised by those prominent helots within their own communities may in turn have contributed towards the maintenance of order and the stifling, for the most part, of protest against Spartan rule.

Conclusions and prospects

The substantive part of this paper began by asking how helot farming actually worked on the ground, in particular to what extent it was directed by intervention from Spartiate owners, and what the implications were for the fundamental conditions of helot life, including the nature of local helot communities. In addressing these questions, I have attempted to examine certain key variables and general insights suggested by comparative evidence from other systems of unfree agrarian labour, as a means of providing context to and extracting maximum value from the limited ancient literary and archaeological evidence. The first variable to be examined, the nature of helot obligations, was one which took a common form throughout the helotised regions of Spartiate territory: the payment of dues in kind through a sharecropping arrangement. Comparative evidence indicated that the payment of dues was typically correlated with a lesser degree of direct intervention by the owner, although the use of sharecropping may have provided a somewhat greater incentive for such intervention than if the dues had been fixed. The next issue examined was whether helots enjoyed practical fixity of tenure on the land. The ancient evidence regarding the sale of helots proved to be somewhat ambiguous; but the changing agrarian settlement patterns close to Sparta revealed by the *Laconia Survey* suggested that in this region Spartiate owners actively settled their helots onto new agricultural land and subsequently re-settled them when conditions deteriorated. This insight prompted investigation of the underlying issue of responsibility for the formation of the agrarian economy, which comparative study suggested was an important initial influence upon the dominant group's capacity to intervene in agricultural production. It was concluded that, in contrast to the *Laconia Survey* area, Sparta's acquisition of control over eastern Messenia involved the incorporation of a pre-existing farming population within its own territory, although there was probably some scope for the incoming Spartiates to mould local agrarian structures. From here, the observation, derived again from comparative evidence, that subsequent developments in agrarian structures could sometimes override initial patterns of exploitation led to examination of two inter-related variables which have frequently been noted as exercising a significant influence upon social relations of production: geographical distance and patterns of residence among the unfree population. The first of these was, by definition, a factor differentiating different regions of Spartiate territory. Comparative material indicated that the high degree of Spartiate intervention in areas of Lakonia close to Sparta would not have been feasible in regions further afield where, as absentee landowners, Spartiates would have had to manage their estates through helot over-seers, such as the *mnôionomoi*, the "leaders of the helots". This distinction according to geographical distance was seen to correlate with a marked difference between the dispersed settlement pattern of areas close to Sparta and the prevailing pattern of nucleated residence in Messenia. This latter pattern would have created greater potential scope for the development of communal identity and institutions in the context of village residence. Prompted by comparative evidence, however, it was noted that inequalities among the helots may have led to the domination of communal activities by wealthier households who, through their collaboration with Spartiate landowners, could gain private advantage which gave them a vested interest in the maintenance of Spartan rule.

Through use of the comparative method we have been able to reach a deeper understanding, not only of the relationships between Spartiate landowners and their unfree labour force in the operation of the agrarian economy, but also of the implications for certain aspects of helot society, such as their experience of leader-ship and community. Indeed, the insights of this paper regarding the social relations of production between Spartiates and helots could be profitably extended into a more in-depth examination of relations of patronage and of the potential use of helots as a source of socio-political influence. A number of other aspects of helotage, some of them briefly touched on in this essay—aspects such as the use of helots (or ex-helots) in warfare, their employment in domestic service, helot prop-erty ownership, and religious practice—could also be fruitfully explored in the context of other systems of unfree labour, drawing upon a wider range of societies, and in greater depth, than in this initial study. For the present, however, this article has indicated how the practice of comparative history can illuminate the relation-ship between the helots and their masters to a greater degree than is possible through exclusive reliance on the exiguous data available from the ancient world.

Bibliography

Alcock, S. E. 1991. "Tomb Cult and the Post-classical Polis." *American Journal of Archaeology* 95: 447-467.

_____. 2002a. *Archaeologies of the Greek Past: Landscape, Monuments, and Memories.* Cambridge.

_____. 2002b. "A Simple Case of Exploitation? The Helots of Messenia." In P. A. Cartledge, E. E. Cohen and L. Foxhall (eds.), *Money, Labour and Labour: Approaches to the Economies of Ancient Greece.* London and New York: 185-199.

Alcock, S. E., A. Berlin, A. B. Harrison, S. Heath, N. Spencer, and D. Stone. in press. "The Pylos Regional Archaeological Project. Part VII: Historic Messenia, Geometric to Late Roman." *Hesperia.*

Annequin, J. 1985. "Comparatisme/comparaisons: ressemblances et hétérogénéité des formes d'exploitation esclavagistes—quelques réflexions." *Dialogues d'histoire ancienne* 11: 639-672.

Antonaccio, C. 1995. *An Archaeology of Ancestors: Tomb Cult and Hero Cult in Early Greece.* Lanham, MD.

Biezunska-Malowist, I., and M. Malowist. 1989. "L'esclavage antique et moderne: les possibilités de recherches comparées." In M.-M. Mactoux and E. Geny (eds.), *Mélanges Pierre Lévêque, 2: Anthropologie et Société.* Paris: 17-31.

Bradley, K. R. 1987. *Slaves and Masters in the Roman Empire: A Study in Social Control.* New York and Oxford.

Bush, M.L. (ed.). 1996a. *Serfdom and Slavery: Studies in Legal Bondage.* London and New York.

_____. 1996b. "Introduction." In Bush 1996a: 1-17.

_____. 1996c. "Serfdom in Medieval and Modern Europe: A Comparison." In Bush 1996a: 199-224.

Cartledge, P. 1979. *Sparta and Lakonia: A Regional History, 1300-362 BC.* London, Boston and Henley.

_____. 1987. *Agesilaos and the Crisis of Sparta.* London.

_____. 1988. "Serfdom in Classical Greece." In L. Archer (ed.), *Slavery and Other Forms of Unfree Labour.* London: 33-41.

_____. 1993. "Classical Greek Agriculture: Recent Work and Alternative Views." *Journal of Peasant Studies* 21: 127-136.

_____. 1998. "The Economy (Economies) of Ancient Greece." *Dialogos* 5: 4-24.

_____. 2001. "Rebels and *Sambos* in Classical Greece: A Comparative View." Revised reprint in *Spartan Reflections*. London: 127-152. (Originally published in P. Cartledge and F. D Harvey [eds.], *CRUX: Essays in Greek History presented to G. E. M. de Ste. Croix*, London, 1985: 16-46).

Catling, R. W. V. 1996. "The Archaic and Classical Pottery." In W. L. Cavanagh, J. Crouwel, R. W. V. Catling and G. Shipley. *The Laconia Survey: Continuity and Change in a Greek Rural Landscape*. Vol. 2. *Archaeological Data*. (Annual of the British School at Athens, Supplementary Volume 27). London: 33-89.

_____. 2002. "The Survey Area from the Early Iron Age to the Classical Period (*c*.1050-323 B.C.)." In W. Cavanagh, J. Crouwel, R. W. V. Catling and G. Shipley, *The Laconia Survey: Continuity and Change in a Greek Rural Landscape*. Vol. 1. *Methodology and Interpretation*. (Annual of the British School at Athens, Supplementary Volume 26). London: 151-256.

Cooper, F. 1979. "The Problem of Slavery in African Studies." *Journal of African History* 20: 103-125.

Coulson, W. D. E. and N. Wilkie. 1983. "Archaic to Roman Times: The Site and Environs." In McDonald, Coulson and Rosser 1983: 332-350.

Davis, J. L., S. E. Alcock, J. Bennet, Y. G. Lolos, and C. W. Shelmerdine. 1997. "The Pylos Regional Archaeology Project. Part I: Overview and the Archaeological Survey." *Hesperia* 66: 391-494.

Ducat, J. 1990. *Les Hilotes*. (Bulletin de correspondance hellénique, Supplément 20). Athens and Paris.

_____. 1994. *Les Pénestes de Thessalie*. (Annales Littéraires de l'Université de Besançon 512). Paris.

Elkins, S. M. 1976. *Slavery*. Third and revised edition. Chicago and London.

Engerman, S. L. 1996. "Slavery, Serfdom and Other Forms of Coerced Labour: Similarities and Differences." In Bush 1996a: 18-41.

Finley, M. I. 1973. *The Ancient Economy*, London. Second edition, London 1985; updated edition, Berkeley, Los Angeles and London 1999.

Garlan, Y. 1988. *Slavery in Ancient Greece*. Ithaca and London.

Genovese, E. D. 1979. *From Rebellion to Revolution: Afro-American Slave Revolts in the Making of the Modern World.* Baton Rouge and London.

Gill, D. 1983. "Tuscan Sharecropping in United Italy: The Myth of Class Collaboration Destroyed." In T. J. Byres (ed.), *Sharecropping and Sharecroppers.* London: 146-169.

Golden, M. 1992. "The Uses of Cross-cultural Comparison in Ancient Social History." *Echos du monde classique* 11: 309-331.

Greenidge, C. W. W. 1958. *Slavery.* London.

Harrison, A., and N. Spencer. 1998. "After the Palace: The Early 'History' of Messenia." In J. L. Davis (ed.), *Sandy Pylos: An Archaeological History from Nestor to Navarino.* Austin: 147-162.

Hill, P. 1985. "Comparative West African Farm-slavery Systems (South of the Sahel) with Special Reference to Muslim Kano Emirate (N. Nigeria)." In J. R. Willis (ed.), *Slaves and Slavery in Muslim Africa.* Vol. 2. *The Servile Estate.* London: 33-50.

Hoch, S. 1986. *Serfdom and Social Control in Russia: Petrovskoe, a Village in Tambov.* Chicago and London.

_____. 1996. "The Serf Economy and the Social Order in Russia." In Bush 1996a: 311-322.

Hodkinson, S. 1992. "Sharecropping and Sparta's Economic Exploitation of the Helots." In J. M. Sanders (ed.), ΦΙΛΟΛΑΚΩΝ: *Lakonian Studies in Honour of Hector Catling.* London: 123-134.

_____. 1993. "Warfare, Wealth, and the Crisis of Spartiate Society." In J. Rich and G. Shipley (eds.), *War and Society in the Greek World.* London and New York: 146-176.

_____. 1997. "Servile and Free Dependants of the Classical Spartan *oikos*." In M. Moggi and G. Cordiano (eds.), *Schiavi e dipendenti nell'ambito dell'oikos e della familia.* Pisa: 45-71.

_____. 1999. "An Agonistic Culture? Athletic Competition in Archaic and Classical Spartan Society." In S. Hodkinson and A. Powell (eds.), *Sparta: New Perspectives.* London: 147-187.

_____. 2000. *Property and Wealth in Classical Sparta.* London.

Hornblower, S. 1996. *A Commentary on Thucydides.* Vol. 2. *Books IV-V.24.* Oxford.

Hunt, P. 1998. *Slaves, Warfare, and Ideology in the Greek Historians.* Cambridge.

Jameson, M. H., C. N. Runnels, and T. H. Van Andel. 1994. *A Greek Countryside: The Southern Argolid from Prehistory to the Present Day*. Stanford.

Jeffery, L. H. 1990. *The Local Scripts of Archaic Greece. A Study of the Origin of the Greek Alphabet and its Development from the Eighth to the Fifth Centuries BC*. Revised edition by A. Johnston. Oxford.

Kaltsas, N. 1983. "'Η ἀρχαικὴ οἰκία στὸ Κοπανάκι τῆς Μεσσηνίας." ᾿Αρχαιολογικὴ ἐφημερίς: 207-237.

Klein, M., and P. E. Lovejoy. 1979. "Slavery in West Africa." In H. A. Gemery and J. S. Hogendorn (eds.), *The Uncommon Market: Essays in the Economic History of the Atlantic Slave Trade*. New York: 181-212.

Kolchin, P. 1987. *Unfree Labor: American Slavery and Russian Serfdom*. Cambridge, MA and London.

_____. 1993. *American Slavery, 1619-1877*. New York and Harmondsworth.

Lazenby, J. F. 1997. "The Conspiracy of Kinadon Reconsidered." *Athenaeum* 85: 437-447.

Lazenby, J. F. and R. Hope Simpson. 1972. "Greco-Roman Times: Literary Tradition and Topographical Commentary." In McDonald and Rapp 1972: 81-99.

Lotze, D. 1959. Μεταξὺ ἐλευθέρων καὶ δούλων. *Studien zur Rechtsstellung unfreien Landbevölkerung in Griechenland bis zum 4. Jahrhundert v. Chr.* Berlin.

Lovejoy, P. E. 1978. "Plantations in the Economy of the Sokoto Caliphate." *Journal of African History* 19: 341-368.

_____. 1979. "The Characteristics of Plantations in the Nineteenth-century Sokoto Caliphate (Islamic West Africa)." *American Historical Review* 84: 1267-1292.

_____. 2000. *Transformations in Slavery: A History of Slavery in Africa*. Second edition. Cambridge.

Lukermann, F. E., and J. Moody. 1978. "Nichoria and Vicinity: Settlement and Circulation." In G. Rapp, Jr. and S. Aschenbrenner (eds.), *Excavations in Nichoria in Southwest Greece I: Site, Environs and Techniques*. Minneapolis: 78-112.

Luraghi, N. 2002a. "Helotic Slavery Reconsidered." In A. Powell and S. Hodkinson (eds.), *Sparta: Beyond the Mirage*. London: 227-248.

_____. 2002b. "Becoming Messenian." *Journal of Hellenic Studies* 122: 45-69.

MacCormack, C. P. 1977. "Wono: Institutionalised Dependency in Sherbro Descent Groups (Sierra Leone)." In S. Miers and I. Kopytoff (eds.), *Slavery in Africa: Historical and Anthropological Perspectives*. Madison: 181-203.

McDonald, W. A., W. D. E. Coulson, and J. Rosser. 1983. *Excavations at Nichoria in Southwest Greece*. Vol. 3. *Dark Age and Byzantine Occupation*. Minneapolis.

McDonald, W. A. and R. Hope Simpson. 1972. "Archaeological Exploration." In McDonald and Rapp 1972: 117-147.

McDonald, W. A. and G. R. Rapp Jr. 1972. *The Minnesota Messenia Expedition: Reconstructing a Bronze Age Regional Environment*. Minneapolis.

MacDowell, D. M. 1986. *Spartan Law*. Edinburgh.

Martin, R. 1980. "Du Nouveau Monde au Monde Antique: quelques problèmes de l'esclavage rural." *Ktéma* 5: 161-175.

Mason, M. 1973. "Captive and Client Labour and the Economy of the Bida Emirate, 1857-1901." *Journal of African History* 14: 453-471.

Melton, E. 1993. "Household Economies and Communal Conflicts on a Russian Serf Estate, 1800-1817." *Journal of Social History* 26: 559-585.

Moon, D. 1999. *The Russian Peasantry 1600-1930: The World the Peasants Made*. London and New York.

Morgan, P. D. 1983. "Black Society in the Lowcountry, 1760-1810." In I. Berlin and R. Hoffman (eds.), *Slavery and Freedom in the Age of the American Revolution*. Charlottesville: 83-141.

Morris, I. 1988. "Tomb Cult and the 'Greek Renaissance'." *Antiquity* 62: 750-761.

Oliva, P. 1971. *Sparta and her Social Problems*. Amsterdam and Prague.

Patterson, O. 1982. *Slavery and Social Death: A Comparative Study*. Cambridge, MA and London.

Pikoulas, G. A. 1984. "Τὸ φυλακεῖον στὸ Βασιλικὸ καὶ ἡ σημασία του γιὰ τὴν ἱστορικὴ τοπογραφία τῆς περιοχῆς." In Πρακτικὰ τοῦ Β τοπικοῦ συνεδρίου Μεσσηνιακῶν σπουδῶν (Κυπαρισσία 27-29 Νοεμβρίου 1982). Athens: 177-184.

Roebuck, C. A. 1941. *A History of Messenia from 369 to 146 B.C.* Chicago.

Ste. Croix, G. E. M. de. 1981. *The Class Struggle in the Ancient Greek World*. London. Corrected imprint 1983.

Scott, J. C. 1976. *The Moral Economy of the Peasant: Rebellion and Subsistence in Southeast Asia*. New Haven and London.

Shanin, T. 1972. *The Awkward Class.* Oxford.

Skocpol. T., and D. Somers. 1980. "The Uses of Comparative History in Macrosocial Inquiry." *Comparative Studies in Society and History* 22: 174-197.

Smith, M. F. 1954. *Baba of Karo.* London.

Smith, M. G. 1955. *The Economy of Hausa Communities of Zaria.* London.

Tadman, M. 1989. *Speculators and Slaves: Masters, Traders, and Slaves in the Old South.* Madison.

Turton, A. 1980. "Thai Institutions of Slavery." In J. L. Watson (ed.), *African and Asian Systems of Slavery.* Oxford: 251-292.

Valmin, N. 1941. "Ein messenisches Kastell und die arkadische Grenzfrage." *Opuscula Archaeologica* 2: 59-76.

Wilamowitz-Moellendorf, U. von. 1924. "Lesefrüchte." *Hermes* 59: 249-273.

Conclusion

Eleven

Reflections on helotic slavery and freedom

Orlando Patterson

This rich collection of essays tackles many vexing questions in the study of Spartan helotry and it would be rash of me—a professional interloper—to attempt a comprehensive commentary. I will, instead, focus on three issues which, as the specialists themselves here acknowledge, may benefit from a comparative perspective. These are: the problem of the nature of helotry and, more specifically, its relation to the condition of slavery; that of its origin; and—by way of responding to Professor Raaflaub's critique of my work on the subject—the problem of the origins of freedom and its relation to the Spartan system.

1. The nature and origins of helotry

What really was the condition of helots? Was it truly a status between freedom and slavery, a variant of serfdom, as is traditionally believed, or was it more a variant of slavery, as Nino Luraghi and other revisionists have contended? The answer depends partly on what one means by slavery and serfdom; partly on one's interpretation of the available evidence, both in Greece and other pre-modern societies. I will first, briefly summarize my interpretation of slavery, then examine two comparative cases which I think throw some light on the sparsely documented case of Sparta: that of the interplay of slavery and serfdom in Europe during the period of the late Western empire and early Middle Ages; and that of Korea, especially during the Koryo dynasty (918-1392 CE) and the chaotic Three Kingdoms period leading up to it.

When I wrote *Slavery and Social Death* (Patterson 1982), one of my main objectives was to arrive at a crisp definition of the distinctive attributes of slavery, especially when compared with related forms of domination such as serfdom, peonage and debt bondage. I concluded then that the three elements defining the relation of domination called slavery were the near total power of the slaveholder over his slaves, in practice, if not always in law; second, their natal alienation, meaning that they had no claims of ancestry, either because they and their ancestors had been aliens captured in warfare, or had been reduced to the condition of slavery because of grievous crimes against their community, or the shameful incapacity to support themselves or repay their debts. As such, they and their progeny did not belong to the community, were not, according to the deepest Indo-European root meanings of the term "free"—*pri-*, suffix form **priy-o* ; Germanic **friyaz*; OE *freon*—among the "beloved," the "dear" kin of the household, "*as opposed to slaves*" (OED vol. 6: 157; Watkins 1985: 53) and could make no independent claims on it. And third, slavery was a peculiarly degraded condition, an extreme state of dishonor which was distinctive in the parasitic way it enhanced the honor of the master and, in collective ways, the status of all non-slave persons "belonging to the loved ones." This last feature is often neglected or misunderstood. Honorific societies are found all over the world, in many cases without the institution of slavery (Patterson 1982: ch. 3). My point was that there was something distinctive about the dynamics of honor in relations with slaves. In non-doulotic honorific systems, honor functioned symbiotically: patron and client both gained by it in the hierarchy of statuses. The client praised and honored his patron or lord, sometimes advanced his interests, and always enhanced his *dignitas*; in return, the patron was also acutely sensitive to the dignity of his client, not only in guaranteeing protection and access, but in the way his—the patron's—*dignitas* enhanced that of the client in the latter's relation with those beneath him in the status hierarchy. It was, in American parlance, a win-win relation.

Not so, the slave relation. Here the master and all non-slaves gained at the expense of the slave's degradation. This was especially the case with the collective honorific gains of the non-slaves who, by virtue of this simple negation, and by virtue of it only, achieved the status of free men, those who belonged, the "loved ones" who alone could claim a *wergeld*—e.g. the non-*Slav* of the early middle ages, later still, the non-*Black*, which was all that *whiteness* and its near synonym *freedom* could ever have hoped to mean to the lowly whites of the ante-bellum South. There has never existed a condition of free persons in the pre-modern world except in contradistinction to the condition of slaves or some other degraded category of persons whose condition exemplified what it meant to be unfree. Without such a *pre-existing* category of persons the idea of free persons made no sense, was an inconceivable irrelevance. Hegel, I have argued, had some inkling of this in his discussion of slavery and freedom (Hegel 1961: 228-240; Patterson 1982: 97-101, 334-342). To the degree that he saw a fundamental dialectical relation between freedom and slavery, to that degree must he be credited with being the first to articulate this insight. But what he went on to say about the crisis of honor experienced by the master—the paradox of seeking honor from someone you have degraded and therefore in no position to confirm honor—is sheer metaphysical nonsense. The simple solution to the "dilemma" lay right under Hegel's nose, given how well he knew his classical history—the class of men who were not masters, but free by virtue of not being slaves. By enhancing their collective honor, by re-creating them as freemen, this class acquired a vested interest in the state of slavery, and a debt of honor to the all-powerful slave-holder class with whom they felt, as freemen, a bond of solidarity. Thus, slavery solved the problem of honor it created for the master by its concurrent invention of the status of freemen. It was the neatest of all social triangulations, and for the West, one of the most portentous. More on this later, when I respond to Professor Raaflaub.

I still believe that this interpretation of slavery, published some twenty years ago is broadly correct and has stood up to critical scrutiny. However, there is one important respect in which my thinking on the subject has evolved, and it is of some relevance to the issues argued in this volume. I noted earlier that *Slavery and Social Death* was motivated by the search for a rather *crisp* definition of slavery. My view of how one defines a social status, or anything else for that matter, has grown to embrace a somewhat more pluralistic philosophy of definition. To put the matter bluntly: I have learned to take seriously Wittgenstein (1953) and the tradition of cognitive psychology he inspired (Rosch and Mervis 1975), to recognize that entities are often better defined, not only in terms of a specified set of criterial attributes, but more by means of prototypes, which are cases viewed as the clearest examples of belonging to a category. Thus I come to know what a bird is, not by first learning, in Aristotelian fashion, the essential attributes of birds, but by learning that the sparrow outside my window is the prototypical bird, and is far more birdlike than exotic entities such as penguins and ostriches.

My first use of this more hybrid approach is directly relevant to the problems discussed in this volume. It was my reconsideration of the relation between slavery and serfdom in Europe between the period of late antiquity and the eighteenth century (see Patterson 1991: chapter 20). The traditional view that serfdom rapidly replaced slavery over the course of the middle ages is no longer tenable. Both coexisted until well into early modern times. Between the period of late antiquity and modern times what occurred was not the replacement of one Aristotelian entity, slavery, by another, serfdom, but a complex, evolving coexistence during which the two institutions reinforced and mutually reconstituted each other. I have called this a recombinant process, because what basically happened was the socio-historical recombination of the three prototypic elements of slavery into different forms of serfdom, and slavery, from one era to another. This made for fuzzy boundaries. It is sometimes not possible to sharply distinguish slavery from serfdom; and at such times it is best to identify given instances as being more or less slave-like, or more or less serf-like. As Kolchin (1987) has shown, for example, by the mid-nineteenth century Russian serfdom—once so distinctive—had morphed into a mode of domination more like American slavery than what had existed in Russia a century or so earlier.

Between 375 and 975 CE, what I have called a convergent form of serfdom and slavery (Patterson 1991: 352-356) developed in Western Europe. As is well known, several major transitions and recombinations took place during this turbulent era (Bonassie 1985; Brown 1971; Dockès 1982; Ste. Croix 1981; Thompson 1982; Verlinden 1955; Whittaker 1987). Domestically, in late imperial times many slaves "ascended" into the status of tenants attached to the land; at the same time, formerly free tenants descended into what Theodosius called "slaves of the land" although many continued in their former status and, indeed, slavery was on the rise again during the fifth century. These transitions took place in many ways. Many slaves were formally manumitted into hutted status; most seem to have simply arrived at this condition *de facto*. Likewise, some formerly free tenants sometimes became domiciled tenants as a result of debt; others in exchange for protection in what were frightening times; others were first enslaved by the invading barbarians who, however, quickly learned that enslaving a conquered group was not a good idea and promptly "manumitted" them into the statuses of hutted slaves or slave-like, domiciled tenants. In addition, there were those who came from outside with the invaders: some of whom were slaves, who were then domiciled, while others were actually clients and lower order kinsmen of the invaders who rapidly lost claims of kinship in the new, fluid, situation and found themselves reduced to the emerging condition of semi-slaves. In time, all subordinate groups increasingly came to share what had been the most distinctive attribute of classical ancient slavery—the condition of natal alienation. This was a result of the full recognition by the sixth century, that nearly all non-elite persons, whatever their status, were of alien ancestry, including the formerly semi-free *coloni* that had come in with the invaders. However, since many of the new masters were themselves of recent alien ancestry, natal alienation lost its potency as a strong marker of slavery.

The attribute that most distinguished slave from free was honor and name. Non-slaves had an honor price, however meager, payable to them or their kinsmen; slaves had none. The fate of the Latin word, *servus*, nicely illuminates these trends and ambiguities. The old Latin word for slaves increasingly—and accurately— came to apply to all of these converging statuses precisely because they were, in fact, more consistent with the slave prototype than any other status. Nonetheless, people insisted on making distinctions which, though largely honorific, were nonetheless psychologically important: they may have been slaves *de facto*, but they desperately grasped for the empty *de jure* statuses that the clerics and lawyers were busily inventing or reviving to ease their pride and legitimize their lords' claims on them. Interestingly, the legal status and term these semi-slaves most preferred was *colliberti* which echoed the old Roman sentimental confraternity of persons who had been manumitted by the same master. But of equal significance was the term not used to describe their status—*libertas*. That would have been taking too many liberties with reality.

This mutual constitution of slavery and serfdom was not peculiar to Europe. It is strikingly evident in the one eastern society where large-scale slavery and serfdom co-existed for nearly as long as they did in Europe, namely Korea. There, during the nearly two millennia between the founding of Silla (57 BCE) and the end of the Yi dynasty (1910 CE) we find a similar process of enslavement and enserfment that culminated in what seemed like the large-scale enslavement of a native population by its own leaders, especially during the late Koryo and early Yi periods. Unlike Sparta, there is a relative abundance of data on Korea (including even Census data during the Yi period) and our understanding of how this pattern of indigenous slavery emerged offers important comparative clues in our attempt to understand Spartan helotry.

First, by the thirteenth century the vast majority of the slaves (*nobi*) were locally born, of Korean ancestry, and shared a common language and culture with their masters and other free persons (Salem 1979: 634), as was the case in Laconia and Messenia. Is this an instance of the successful mass enslavement of a conquered people, *in situ*, or, more puzzlingly, the large scale reduction of their own formerly free subjects to slavery by an elite? Actually it was neither. From as early as the fourth century, long before the peninsula was united into a single kingdom, slavery was widespread, the result of territorial wars and tribute payment between what were then very different and often warring peoples (Hatada 1969: 17). By the early Koryo period (918-1392 CE), when the Korean peninsula was finally united into a single state, most of the slaves would have been descendants of persons enslaved during the earlier period when there were three distinct states in the peninsula (Silla, Koguryo and Paekche) that were frequently at war with each other, in addition to repeated conflicts with China. Large numbers of prisoners of war were taken in these engagements especially during the wars leading to the Koryo unification. Then, in what historian Ki-baik Lee calls a virtual "social compulsion" on the part of the aristocratic elites of the period, captives were promptly enslaved and resettled in special slave villages within the captors' kingdoms known as *hyang* or *pugok* (Lee 1984: 56). The ranks of this basic stock of hereditary slaves were later supplemented by other forms of enslavement, especially punishment for crimes and self-enslavement due to destitution (Unruh 1976). By the early years of the Yi dynasty (1392-1910 CE) when the slave population was estimated at 30 percent of the total (Shin 1976: 4; for the later period see Wagner 1971: 18-19) the main source of new slaves was "commendation" in which destitute commoners sought refuge from corvée labor and the military draft by enslaving themselves to powerful landlords.

Second, Korean uses of slaves bore remarkable resemblances to those of the Spartan state. As in Sparta, all land, in theory, belonged to the state, its usufruct parceled out to landlords, peasants and tenants. In practice, most land was in the control of private hands, with the crown and large landlords, and the favored Yangban bureaucrats and literati, possessing most of the best lands. During the Yi dynasty, the practice was to assign state land, known as rank land (*kwajon*) to civil and military officers which was returned to the state an the death of recipients. Early in the dynasty so-called merit subjects (*kongsin*) were assigned private ownership of hereditary grants of land, but the theory that all land belonged to the state persisted, and was reflected in periodic state seizure of merit land upon the death of less powerful or "minor merit subjects", the *wonjong kongsin* (Shin 1973: 11-14). A large peasant class of small-holders scraped by on marginal lots. As in Sparta, the elite had little time for the direct management of their farms, so production fell to tenants and slaves in a complex "latifundia-minifundia" pattern which was often under the supervision of slave overseers (Shin 1973). Slaves were either public (*kong nobi*) or private (*sa nobi*). As in Sparta, there were vast numbers of the former, who not only directly served the household of the ruling elite, but farmed its land. Some of these public slaves were given on life-time loans to bureaucrats, military officers and other favored members of the Yangban class residing in the cities. Private slaves, who belonged to individual owners, functioned in all capacities, both in the urban areas where their owners resided, and on their estates, large and small, where they labored under slave overseers. As in Sparta, we find a high level of local absenteeism among the large land-owners combined with partial absenteeism among less wealthy members of the elite Yangbang class (Hong 1979).

A remarkable feature of Korean slavery which may well provide another clue to Sparta, was that slaves were allowed to own land as well as other slaves. Some became quite prosperous. Clearly, there was little prestige attached to the mere farming of land; indeed, the Korean elite seem to have regarded the whole business with as much contempt as their Spartiate counterpart, and was happy to leave it to tenants and so-called "out-resident" slaves, many of whom labored on terms more favorable—such as a fixed fee—than those offered the free share-cropping tenants (Unruh 1976; Lee 1984: 123-124; 188). Slave-holders, and landowners generally, "were either officials or potential officials whose principal aim in life was to rise in prominence and increase their landownings" and this was best achieved by living as absentee landlords in the capital (Hatada 1969: 68).

What then, distinguished slave from free farmer—especially better-off, privately owned slaves who possessed land, or the farm slaves of the palace, most of whom "functioned as small independent farmers in all but name" (Unruh 1979: 634)? Slaves, unlike peasants and free tenants, could be sold or given as gifts, and their status was hereditary, but this was not the decisive factor. In practice this rarely happened. As in Sparta, slave-owners were interested in preserving and increasing their stock of slaves, given the very labor-intensive and unproductive nature of agriculture (Shin 1973: 95-98). And because so many labored on their own in sharecropping arrangements, most absentee owners knew that they were inviting trouble if they sold slaves away from their homes or loved ones. In fact, running away was rampant; and as in Sparta, servile history was dotted with several well remembered major slave revolts (Hong 1983: ch. 8). In Korea, as in Sparta, the decisive factor separating slaves from non-slaves was honor. Ancient Korea was a rigidly stratified social order in which a fundamental distinction was drawn between those who were "good" (*yang*) and those who were "base" (*ch'on*). Baseness was a deep, polluting, and nearly indelible stain, a condition of utter degradation which was not removed in those few cases where slaves were manumitted. In order to become an official, for example, a person had to be able to prove that he was at least eight generations removed from any ancestor who had been a slave (Unruh 1976: 30)!

What do the comparative data on slavery and serfdom in Europe and Korea suggest about Spartan helotry other than what we have already hinted? It is important to note that the question of the origins and status of helots are very closely linked in these papers although both sides of the debate avoid any claim that a conquered group had been enslaved *en masse* and *in situ*. Van Wees (this volume), for example, argues that the helots were primarily a conquered native group who had been enserfed, rather than enslaved. He reinforces this by observing that to the degree that there was intermingling of slaves with serfs in Messenia, the former were brought in from outside. Luraghi (this volume and 2002), on the other hand, insists that helotry was a form of slavery and, as such, could not have originated in conquest. Both agree that there had been intermingling of peoples and statuses, but differ in regard to the primary mode of domination and the main source of the servile population.

Actually, what the comparative data discussed above strongly suggest is that the differences between Luraghi and those holding the traditional view may not be on the "collision course" feared by Professor Alcock (this volume). Let me explain with what may be called a convergent path hypothesis. The argument, derived analogously from the cases discussed above, is that the Laconians had been genuine slaves who had gone through a long process of being hutted up to the status of domiciled, semi-free (or semi-servile) persons. The Messenians, on the other hand, had been free persons resettled in Messenia, who had seen their status gradually reduced to that of semi-free, then virtually enslaved domiciled persons.

Most of the authors here are in agreement that there were striking differences between Laconia and Messenia which recent archeological findings have only reinforced. Van Wees points to several of these differences: the fact that the Laconians had no distinct ethnic identity, in striking contrast with the Messenians; their possibly earlier subjection; their greater loyalty to their Spartan lords, and their continued subjection long afer the liberation of Messenia; and the pathetic way in which they were manipulated by the promise of manumission. There is, further, the archeological evidence tapped most vigorously by Hodkinson (this volume): the more dispersed settlement of Laconia, the more direct involvement of the Spartan lords with them, and the strong hints that the Spartans were initially more directly involved in fashioning its agricultural structure, contrasted with the more nucleated settlements in Messenia with its implication of an incorporated, *partly* pre-existing—though not necessarily native—farming population later augmented with slaves from outside. Finally, there is Figueira's important reminder of the greater fertility of Messenia and, most importantly, the Spartan tendency to depopulate conquered lands and repopulate them with more pliant subjects.

The convergent hypothesis more parsimoniously explains these differences than any other. Slavery, although one that was slowly being changed, best describes the condition of the Laconians, and it is difficult to understand why classicists would want to see anything else. The Laconians were loyal to their Spartan masters and evinced no separate ethnic identity for the simple reason that they never possessed a pre-doulotic identity or culture. Their behavior is most consistent with that of prototypical slave populations that had been recruited—as prisoners of war, as booty, as bought chattels—from disparate sources having no common identity until it was painfully forged on the anvil of their enslavement. American scholars, surely, need not look afar for a perfect example of such a process and such a group: they are called Southern slavery, and African-Americans.

There may have been another reason for the loyalty of the Laconians—their gratitude for the slow change in their status to that of domiciled semi-slaves. Precisely because they had previously suffered the social death of slavery, they eagerly grasped the meager, grudgingly incremental, but emotionally gratifying shift in their position to that of semi-slave tenants. It might even have been that the term *helot* served a face-saving socio-linguistic function similar to that played by *colliberti* and *adscripticius* (the more formal, late Latin term for the domiciled tenant) for the transitional era of late imperial and early Dark Age Europe. In much the same way that every realistic Latin observer of the fifth and sixth centuries who took a good, long look at the emerging servile statuses of his times and brushed away all the fancy revived terminology with the gruff aside that "I know a *servus* when I see a *servus*," so, earlier, might have plain-spoken Greek observers of the

Laconian helots during the fifth and fourth centuries BCE in their insistence (as Luraghi reminds us) on calling a *doulos* a *doulos*.

The case of Messenia is more complicated. The problem the revisionists confront is the widely attested cultural and linguistic unity of Messenians and Spartans and the former's proud insistence on their own Dorian ancestry. This claim, to be sure, cuts both ways. On the one hand, it could be used to defend a pattern of enslavement, deracination and acculturation to the culture of the Dorian master-class similar to that experienced by the Laconians. But this, on the other hand, undermines the otherwise quite attractive second prong of the revisionist argument, advanced by Luraghi, of a rather late, parasitically constructed evolution of Spartan *homoioi* and ritually despised helots (Luraghi 2002: 235).

The solution, offered by several of the authors of this volume (especially Luraghi and Hall), is an ancient instance of the invention of tradition, the deployment of what Hall nicely calls a set of "ancestralizing strategies," by which means the recently liberated Messenians staked their claim to a place in Hellenic historic glory, ably and perhaps cynically, abetted by Athenian propagandists. As a sometime student of modern ethnic identity formation, I am surely tempted to embrace this "ethnic theory of the origins of the helots" as Luraghi calls it. There is certainly something to it, but it is a temptation that, in the final analysis, I feel inclined to resist. To cite a modern example, the "ancestralizing strategies" of modern WASP Americans is full of bombast and fictitious glory-talk about their Mayflower, freedom-loving English ancestors. We *know* that large numbers of the earliest settlers came here as indentured servants. Nonetheless, it remains true that their ancestors all hailed from Britain. Ethnic claims, however puffed up, are not always lies.

Given the heroic tradition of resistance of the Messenians, rightly celebrated in this volume by Cartledge, given the hatred they must have felt for their former Spartan overlords who had so spitefully used and ritually degraded them, I find it hard to understand why they would have wished to do so Tom-like a thing as appropriate the history of these unrepentant and cruel overlords, except for the simple reason that it was true. Data from the ancient world, especially this corner of it, is simply too sparse and precious for us to play social constructionist games with, especially when it is more consistent with other explanations.

The comparative data on early Korea might offer some clues to the origins of the Messenians. It seems unlikely that they were a conquered native population—this appears more true of the *perioikoi*. They were, rather, perhaps in good part an early wave of the migrating Dorians—as the linguistic evidence, and their own traditions suggest—who lost out in the land-grabbing turmoil and military struggles of early state formation during the invasion period. Whatever their reasons for coming, it seems reasonable to surmise that something similar to what evolved in early Korea took place. Waves of primitive warlords—barely more advanced than chiefs and headmen—would have set up petty war-lordships, in the process sometimes killing, sometimes simply politically decapitating then absorbing, sometimes bartering off to other petty chiefdoms prisoners of war taken from their own language group and other peoples. In the struggle for land and power, different groups and waves of invaders would have been treated as the enemy and fair game for take-over as much as earlier indigenous peoples. It is anachronistic to think of the incoming Dorians as a single group with any sense of ethnic identity. The idea that people sharing a common language must have some sense of ethnic identity, and are somehow less loath to slaughter, conquer and enslave each other, is a self-fulfilling late eighteenth and nineteenth century myth, initiated by Johann Herder and his romantic-nationalist followers. Eventually the large number of warring units would have been reduced in a bloody shake-out through alliances and conquests of each other, leading to a single, dominant state. In the process, the losers would have suffered a variety of fates: some, like the *perioikoi,* ended up as semi-dependent, satellite peoples; others, like the Messenians, may have been defeated enemies, but they could just as likely have started off as allies who were later subjected, or independent chiefdoms that had been lured into ill-fated confederations; or prisoners of war; or groups from several petty states and chiefdoms that were incorporated as subject peoples and slaves. And some may even have voluntarily commended themselves to servile statuses to avoid worse fates in the unsettled times. All these outcomes are attested in Korea during the turbulent years of the Three Kingdoms Period leading up to the Koryo unification. They are also found in the Ancient Near East. Indeed, the most famous people of the Ancient Near East—the Hebrews of Egypt—suggest one common mode: a subjected collection of peoples within a state, most of whom had been forcefully resettled there, but a significant number of whom had come voluntarily, who acquired a common identity as a result of their common subjection, and who retroactively constructed an ethnic myth of a pre-existing common identity, as well as an unusual ancestralizing claim of mass enslavement.

All the evidence used by the traditionalists to argue against the slave-like condition of the helots actually does just the opposite. Thus, Paul Cartledge (this volume) notes the frequently cited evidence that the helots were collectively, rather than individually, owned. Let us assume that contemporaries such as Strabo and Pausanias were correct in their observations. There are numerous cases on record of slaves being collectively or publicly owned. We can start with the public slaves of Rome, although it may be protested that their numbers were proportionately small. For most of Korean history, however, as we have already seen, the various dynasties claimed public ownership of all land and a large proportion of slaves. Practice, however, was something entirely different. Some means had to be found for getting nominally public slaves to produce and the best way of doing this was to distribute them to individual masters in varying numbers, depending on their power and status. This, as we have seen, is what happened in Korea. Luraghi and the revisionists are not "finessing" anything in claiming that helots must have been individually controlled and largely owned; they are simply being socio-historically realistic. Until the invention of the modern state in the late eighteenth and nineteenth centuries with its vastly more efficient reach and organizational capacity, state ownership could exist only as an ideal, and a pretty weird one which everyone must have quietly winked or rolled their eyes at. If Sparta was the exception, if it indeed had the organizational capacity to give its ideal of state owner-ship of individuals in so cussedly demanding a sphere as agriculture any but senti-mental meaning, then it is necessary to re-write the history of communism and organizational behavior. The Soviet Union, it had always been thought, was the first state to seriously attempt to do so. Yet, for all its totalitarian might and bureaucratic reach, its agricultural policy was a disaster.

The argument, revived here by Cartledge, that Sparta practiced state manu-mission, really proves nothing. Every large-scale slave system that I know of—including even the ante-bellum U.S. South for all its mean-spirited prohibition on manumission—occasionally resorted to state manumissions. In the Caribbean, which also had relatively low rates of manumission, the British drafted large numbers of slaves to fight the French and Spanish during the eighteenth century and by 1795 almost all the important British islands had corps of slave soldiers. In 1807, in what must rank as one of the most spectacular mass manumissions in the history of slavery, Whitehall manumitted some 10,000 of them (Buckley 1979).

Nothing better attests to the emerging slave-like condition of the Messenians than their ritualized humiliation. As we saw in the case of Korea and early medieval Europe, it is precisely where slaves have acquired a shared culture with their masters due to long centuries of common existence, and where masters do not directly control them, that the compensatory need to ritually humiliate them arises. Rituals of degradation thus become the main markers of the boundary between slave and free: the "base" and the "good," as was said in Korea. Further, the master class para-sitically enhanced its collective honor and sense of superiority through these highly ritualized acts of debasement.

2. Slavery, helotry and the invention of freedom

Kurt Raaflaub's interesting paper raises the issue of the relation of helotry to the development and institutionalization of freedom consciousness and the culture of freedom among the Greeks. He notes that contemporary commentary on the Messenian helots and their struggles for liberation was exceptional for the interest shown in a servile population. He wonders whether the experience of the Messenians prompted the development of freedom consciousness and whether this proved that the simple desire for the negation of slavery was "sufficient impulse" for the construction of freedom. He claims that my view of the origin of freedom implies just such a simplistic, direct causal relation between the experience of slavery and the development of freedom, and he takes issue with it. He sums up his thesis and his disagreement with me as follows:

> By focusing on the perspective of the free, my approach differs starkly from that of Patterson who pays much attention to the point of view of the slaves themselves and considers it crucial for the formation of freedom consciousness in society at large. My reason—and at the same time my thesis—is that slavery as such was able to trigger high consciousness of the value of liberty in a society only if the free, and especially those among them who mattered because they controlled power and set the tone in the community, adopted such consciousness themselves and integrated it into their value system. (above, p. 175)

Anyone who finds himself at odds with a scholar of Professor Raaflaub's eminence must pause and reconsider. In my case the urgency is acute in view of the fact that I relied heavily on Professor Raaflaub's own meticulous earlier studies in the development of an important part of my argument on the origins of freedom (Raaflaub 1981; 1983; 1985). Happily, it turns out that he has misunderstood me, and while a few areas of disagreement certainly exist, we are far more in agreement on the central issues than he allows. In what follows, I will first note the important areas of agreement between us, then I will attempt to show that most our apparent disagreements are based on a misunderstanding of what I said.

First, and foremost, Raaflaub fully agrees with me that slavery was a *necessary* element in the development of freedom consciousness, and second, that in ancient times only the Greeks "raised their consciousness of the value of freedom to a level that enabled them to create an explicit concept of freedom with a differentiated terminology and political emphasis." What's more, in being the first to do so, they can be said to have invented freedom as a cultural system.

It is important to understand that in these post-modernist, multicultural times, such claims immediately make us allies in what is strongly rejected by many as a historically reactionary and philosophically insupportable position. One of the great intellectual ironies of our times is that the very success of the West at diffusing and globalizing its cherished ideal of freedom has led to the situation where intellectuals in many parts of the non-Western world who have come to embrace the ideal now deny its Western ancestry and, along with their Western supporters, are prone to dismiss those who acknowledge its Greek invention as ethnocentric, racist, or (in my case) pathetic dupes of a perverse Western historiography.[1]

Political and other social theorists attack our position from a different, universalist perspective. They begin with the assumption that the desire for freedom is universal—is "written in the hearts of men," as Locke would have it—and that it is a waste of time to even attempt to find its historical origins. If there is no freedom in Booga-Looga, it is only because the Booga-Loogans have not removed the socioeconomic and political constraints on their inherent propensity to be free. Remove these constraints with good public policy and free markets and the Booga-Loogans will be no less passionate about freedom than Americans or Britons.

In such a hostile terrain it is important that the dwindling members of the camp to which Professor Raaflaub and I belong do not end up in fratricidal skirmishes, especially when these skirmishes are based on misreadings of each other. The first of these misreadings is Raaflaub's assertion that I hold the mere existence of slavery to be necessary and *sufficient* for the rise and institutionalization of freedom. This is incorrect. *Slavery and Social Death* had already established that slavery, even sometimes large-scale slavery, was found all over the world. Freedom, on the other hand, was until the twentieth century, almost entirely a Western cultural complex. If slavery alone generated freedom we would have expected to find it all over the world. We do not. Explaining why was the whole point of the first part of *Freedom in the Making of Western Culture*. Like Raaflaub, my problem was to identify those factors which, in conjunction with slavery, sufficiently accounted for the rise of freedom as a central value, and explained the paradox that, as I earlier put it, a set of values "with so degraded a pedigree, and so manifestly dangerous in its propensities" could "come to conquer the culture and consciousness of a people" and a civilization.

First and foremost among these factors was the rise in Greece of large-scale slave society—"genuine slave societies" as Sir Moses Finley called them—for the first time in world history. Second, was the emergence in Athens of an enfranchised farming population that had come close to revolt due to mass debt bondage and the threat of reduction to slavery. Third, was the skillful leadership of renegade members of the Athenian aristocracy—retroactively maligned as Tyrants—who astutely negotiated a substitution of participative political benefits, sweetened with a contradistinctive, solidaristic ideology of shared, Athenian superiority *vis-à-vis* the unfreedom of aliens and metics, for the redistribution of land which was what the

....

[1] See, for example, the hostile review by Martin Bernal of my *Freedom in the Making of Western Culture* in the *American Journal of Sociology*; cf. the more balanced responses to the work by specialists on Asia in Kelly and Reid 1998: chs. 1, 5, 8.

mass of their post-Solonic, debt-relieved, but still land-hungry followers had originally really wanted, in the process creating the first male, mass democracy. Fourth, there was the development of an ancient dual economy in which a "modernized" farm sector of fruit farms and vineyards and an urban and mining sector, both largely manned by slaves, co-existed with a traditional, small-scale economy of own-account, farmer-citizens. Which, fifthly, permanently relieved the mass of small farmers from the economic demands of its elite. All of which, sixthly, eventually created a dynamic urban social space for a large number of manumitted slaves and other skilled, entrepreneurial aliens.[2] Finally, there was the wholly contingent threat of Persian external domination, the successful repulsion of which had three major consequences: mass euphoria about Greek freedom and independence, the likes of which were not to be witnessed again until the revolutionary era of America; the conflation of collective Greek freedom with individual freedom (given that Persian conquest had been identified with mass individual slavery); and the elite ideological appropriation of the triumphalist rhetoric of freedom surrounding the war, by conflating it with their traditional honorific notions of power, glory, valor in warfare, athletic prowess, in short, *aretê*—all that "the free heart displays" as Pindar, the poet of this conflation, eulogized[3]—which, in their view, had inspired their noble leadership and made victory possible.

What emerged as a result of these historical conjunctions over the course of the sixth and early fifth century was a complex tripartite cultural complex—freedom—which I have likened to a chordal triad: freedom as personal, individual liberation; freedom as the participative democracy of free male citizens; and freedom as the power to realize one's wishes, both for oneself and for, as well as in, one's state. Although the historical path to its development was unique, there was nonetheless a remarkable internal coherence to the cultural chord that all Athenians came to call freedom by the fourth decade of the fifth century. At its core, paradoxically, was the notion of power: freedom meant liberation from the absolute power, or threat thereof, of another (archetypally a slave master); it also meant the exercise of power, including power over others (and there was no paradox here, as Raaflaub [1983] himself has shown elsewhere); and it meant sharing in the collective power of the state.

These three notes of freedom emerged at different times before their final convergence around the middle of the fifth century—a convergence that was most powerfully articulated in the funeral oration, as Nicole Loraux (1986) has so brilliantly shown. Each was promoted initially mainly by different groups, but eventually

....

[2] Another first; throughout the Ancient Near East, for example, skilled slaves and those belonging to the elite usually saw no advantage in becoming free.
[3] Cf. Pind., *Pyth.* 2.57 (transl. Bowra).

all three notes were embraced by all, though with different classes emphasizing one or other notes. Personal freedom—raw primal freedom as simple liberation from another's absolute control—was initially an obsession of slaves, abetted by masters who found this a perfect way to motivate them. Freedom as democracy was primarily the work of the farmer-citizen. Freedom as power and exaltation was primarily the construction of the aristocracy and slave-holder class. But however great the emphasis, the chord was always acknowledged.

Two distinctions are neglected by Raaflaub in his summary of my position: that between the mere discovery of freedom and its institutionalization; and that between slavery's role as the foundation of the system that made freedom possible and as generator of the very idea of freedom itself. Most classical historians, including Raaflaub, now agree that large-scale slavery was the economic foundation of this entire transformation. There is still sharp disagreement, however, regarding the more radical claim that slavery also initiated the idea and celebration of freedom. Sir Moses Finley (1959, 1976), for example, while forcefully arguing that slave labor was the foundation of Greek civilization, was not of the view that it generated the idea of freedom. Here, however, Raaflaub like Max Pohlenz (1966)—who greatly influenced us both—shares my view that slavery was at least initially generative of the idea of freedom. Raaflaub appears to believe that there is a major difference between us in the claim that slavery accounts for the *institutionalization* of freedom consciousness, in its extraordinary emergence as a dominant value in Greece but, as I indicated above, there is no such disagreement. It would have violated every professional sociological impulse in me to have argued that the mere discovery of an idea was enough to explain its persistence and institutionalization.

I will not get here into the vexed philosophical issue of whether something can exist without having a name, except to note, once again, that my position is not that different from Raaflaub's. Of course, there will be a lag between the socio-historical construction of a new cultural pattern—especially one as complex and contentious as freedom—and the name that finally settles on it; Raaflaub could hardly disagree with this. Nor with the established fact that terms are often contested, and worse, appropriated, in the process seriously distorting the original meaning and content of the cultural phenomena to which they were originally applied. Consider what Plato did with the previously constructed idea of, and word for, freedom (*Republic* 561D-562C; *Laws* 693B, 701B). Nonetheless, I wholly agree with Raaflaub that, in the long run, if a term does not exist it is very likely that the concept or cultural pattern to which it applies elsewhere also does not. Indeed, one of my main sources of evidence for the non-existence of freedom in the non-Western world is the simple linguistic fact that no word for the idea existed in most of the major non-Western languages until Western contact.

One genuine area of disagreement between us concerns my claim that women were very involved with the original discovery of freedom. The disagreement, however, may be due to Raaflaub's failure to appreciate my distinction between the discovery and institutionalization of freedom. My argument was that women must have been among the first to discover freedom as value, and in conceding that slaves were the first people to discover freedom as an existential imperative of their social condition and their desperate desire to escape it, Raaflaub has no choice but to accept the implication that women were the first to discover it. For it is indisputable that the vast majority of the earliest slaves, in the world of Odysseus as elsewhere, were women. The freedom that women discovered, however, was only the primal, personal note of the triad—the desire for escape from the dread horror of what the free women in Aeschylus' *Seven Against Thebes* could easily imagine as "the house of death, a spear-booty, a slave, in crumbling ashes, dishonorably sacked . . . " They were entirely excluded from the discovery and institutionalization of democracy. And, of course, they were hardly in a position to conceive of, let alone experience, freedom as power over others.

There still remains the question, however, of how far women were able to take the primal discovery of personal freedom. Was the idea still-born among Greek women as was true of women and men all over the non-Greek world? By and large, yes. The institutionalization of personal freedom, it was argued, had to await the full development of the urban slave economy with its enabling social space for freedmen and other members of the metic class, and this came long after the discovery and institutionalization of freedom in the note or form of democracy and the exercise of power. What was first discovered was last institutionalized, precisely because it was first discovered by women and had to await the institutional pressure of successful male metics.

Nonetheless, I did suggest—and here is where we genuinely differ—that something more than mere still-born idea took hold of some Greek women during the late seventh century. Before it was nipped in the bud and they were finally shut out of what Vidal-Naquet (1986: 206) called the male "citizens' club" of classical democracy, marked by its "double exclusion" of women and slaves, something that seems very much like a brief episode of female assertiveness took place in parts of Greece. My main evidence for this comes from outside Athens: Hesiod's notorious misogyny. It is not so much its gratuitous viciousness that is so revealing, as its very expression. It demands explanation, because men in normally patriarchal societies where women are properly in their place find no need to comment on women.

Silence is the normal fate of women in normally functioning patriarchal systems. Only when women are acting out of their place—in other words, not simply imagining, but acting free—do we find men publicly venting their misogyny. There may be a better explanation than this for Hesiod's insistent misogyny, but I am yet to find it.

What does all this have to do with Sparta and its helots? Actually, a good deal more than even Raaflaub suggests. Raaflaub correctly observes that "the helot issue did not automatically trigger conscious concerns about liberty," but he incorrectly concludes that "the slave-free contrast was traditionally viewed at a low level of consciousness or assigned low significance." When we talk about the existence of freedom in any given society, it is important that we distinguish between its structural significance and the extent of its social permeation. Freedom may be highly institutionalized and of great political and ideological importance even though it is restricted to the elite. Indeed, with the exception of fifth and fourth century Athens, this was true of the history of freedom right down to the twentieth century in Europe. To take a few examples, freedom was alive and fully institutionalized in eighteenth century Britain and nineteenth century America but it would take another century before women were truly free, and another century and a half for black Americans. Or consider the extreme case of Apartheid South Africa where freedom was cherished and fully institutionalized among the white elite though denied to the black majority.

Now, as I have argued, what was unique about Athens was that the peculiar conjunction of historical and socio-economic forces, mentioned earlier, led to the revolutionary development and conflation of all three elements of freedom. There is no reason to believe, however, that a more truncated process did not take place elsewhere in Greece, involving, say, only two elements of freedom, and extending to a much more restricted segment of the population. Just such a development may have taken place in Sparta. Indeed, as several of the authors in this volume have observed, for all its peculiarities, Sparta may well have been more typical of Greece in certain respects than Athens.

Luraghi (2002) has tantalizingly suggested that, had it not been for the Solonic reforms the Spartan system, or something more like it, may well have been the course taken by Athens. We know how much certain famous members of its conservative elite admired Sparta. I want to suggest that it is as erroneous to claim that institutionalized freedom and its celebration did not exist in Sparta as it is to argue that it did not exist in Apartheid South Africa, or eighteenth century Britain or the ante-bellum and Jim Crow South. Let us not forget the most famous comment from a contemporary observer of Sparta: that the free there were more free and the slaves more slave-like than in any other part of the Greek world.[4] What developed in Sparta were two, rather than three elements of freedom. First and foremost was the master class' view of freedom as absolute power over oneself (that internal self-discipline and control over one's internal "slave impulses" and base passions, that Plato modeling on Sparta, celebrated) and over inferior others. But Sparta also developed and fully institutionalized a distinctive form of elitist, totalitarian democracy—what the world later came to call *Herrenvolk* democracy. As others, most notably Sir Karl Popper (1962) have shown, it has been the model of this version of democracy throughout the ages of Western Europe, both directly, and indirectly through the malign political "spell of Plato."

Modern Apartheid South Africa and the Ante-Bellum and Jim Crow South instantiate the Spartan model in ways that are often missed. There is really no comparison between the inefficient, absentee farming and land policy of the Spartans and the highly capitalistic, residential farm management of South Africa and the Southern U.S. Where the comparison holds is in the vicious degradation and ritualized humiliation of the mass of South Africans and African-Americans by the white elite, as an integral element of their own *Herrenvolk* conception of freedom as white power and democracy. Sparta's annual declaration of war against the helots; the minstrel-like use of drunken helots as models of negative identification; the Gestapo-like *krypteia*, are all echoed in the modern rituals of debasement practiced in Apartheid South Africa and the ante-bellum and Jim Crow South. Consider the following declaration of a freedom-loving South Carolinian, in 1822, long before the abolitionist movement was taken seriously:

> [Negro slaves] should be watched with an eye of steady and unremitting observation . . . Let it not be forgotten, that our Negroes are freely the JACOBINS of the country; that they are the ANARCHISTS and the DOMESTIC ENEMY; the COMMON ENEMY OF CIVILIZED SOCIETY, and the BARBARIANS WHO WOULD, IF THEY COULD, BECOME THE DESTROYERS OF OUR RACE.[5]

If this sounds all too familiar to every student of Spartan helotry, it is because modern slaveholders were quick to see the parallels between their own versions of freedom and *Herrenvolk* democracy and those of the ancients, especially Sparta. What Luraghi wrote of the "set of practices of ritualized contempt by which the Spartiates' produced a despicable collective identity for the helots," holds exactly

....

[4] Critias 88 B 37 Diels-Kranz.
[5] Cited in Franklin 1956. Uppercase in original.

true of modern *Herrenvolk* practices: that it was "a mirror image of the Spartiates' image of themselves." The most important reason for the study of ancient helotry, then, may well be the fact that the exalted, contradistinctive self-fashioning engendered by the Spartiates' treatment of their helots was the historic prototype of what, until the early decades of the twentieth century, would remain the dominant model of Western freedom.

Bibliography

Brown, P. 1971. *The World of Late Antiquity.* London.

Bonassie, P. 1985. "Suive et extinction du regime escalvagist dans l'Occident du haut moyen age (IV-XIs)." *Cahiers de Civilisation medievale* 28: 307-343.

Buckley, R. N. 1979. *Slaves in Red Coats: The British West India Regiments, 1795-1815.* New Haven.

Dockès, P. 1982. *Medieval Slavery and Liberation.* Chicago.

Finley, M. I. 1959. "Was Greek Civilization Based on Slave Labor?" *Historia* 8: 145-164.

_____.1976. "The Freedom of the Citizen in the Greek World." *Talanta* 7: 1-23.

Franklin, J. H. 1956. *The Militant South, 1800-1861.* Cambridge, MA.

Hatada, T. 1969. *A History of Korea.* Translated by W. Smith and B. Hazard. Santa Barbara.

Hong, S. 1979. "The Slave and Land-Farming in the Koryo Dynasty," *Han ukhakpo* 14. [In Korean. Translated for the author by Hou Keun Song]

_____.1983. *Koryo Society and Slaves.* Seoul.

Hegel, G. W. F. 1961. *Phenomenology of Mind.* London.

Kelly, D., and A. Reid (eds.). 1998. *Asian Freedoms: The Idea of Freedom in East and Southeast Asia.* Cambridge and New York.

Kolchin, P. 1987. *Unfree Labor: American Slavery and Russian Serfdom.* Cambridge, MA.

Lee, K. 1984. *A New History of Korea.* Translated by Edward Wagner. Cambridge, MA.

Loraux, N. 1986. *The Invention of Athens: The Funeral Oration in the Classical City.* Cambridge, MA.

Luraghi, N. "Helotic Slavery Reconsidered." In A. Powell and S. Hodkinson (eds.), *Sparta: Beyond the Mirage.* London: 229-250.

OED = *The Oxford English Dictionary.* Oxford, 1989.

Patterson, O. 1982. *Slavery and Social Death.* Cambridge, MA.

_____.1991. *Freedom.* Vol. 1. *Freedom in the Making of Western Culture.* New York.

Pohlenz, M. 1966. *Freedom in Greek Life and Thought: The History of an Ideal.* Dordrecht.

Popper, K. 1962. *The Open Society and Its Enemies*. Vol. 1. London.

Raaflaub, K. 1981. *Zum Freiheitsbegriff der Griechen*. Berlin.

_____.1983. "Democracy, Oligarchy, and the Concept of the 'Free Citizen' in Late Fifth-Century Athens." *Political Theory* 11: 517-544.

_____.1985. *Die Entdeckung der Freiheit*. (Vestigia 37). Munich.

Rosch, E. and C. Mervis. 1975. "Family Resemblances: Studies in the Internal Structure of Categories." *Cognitive Psychology* 6: 573-605.

Ste. Croix, G. E. M. de. 1981. *The Class Struggle in the Ancient Greek World*. Ithaca.

Salem, E. 1979. "The Utilization of Slave Labor in the Koryo Period: 918-1392." *Academy of Korean Studies, Papers of the 1st International Conference of Korean Studies*. Seoul: 630-642.

Shin, S. 1973. "Land Tenure and the Agrarian Economy in Yi Dynasty Korea: 1600-1800". PhD Dissertation, Harvard University, Cambridge, MA.

_____.1974. "The Social Structure of Kumhwa County in the Late Seventeenth Century." *Occasional Papers on Korea* 1: 9-35.

_____.1976. "Changes in Labor Supply in Yi Dynasty Korea: From Hereditary to Contractual Obligation." Unpublished manuscript.

Thompson, E. A. 1982. *Romans and Barbarians: The Decline of the Western Empire*. Madison.

Unruh, E. 1976. "The Landowning Slave: A Korean Phenomenon." *Korea Journal* 16.4: 27-35.

_____. n.d. "Slavery in Koryo: Sources and Interpretations." Unpublished manuscript.

Verlinden, C. 1955. *L'esclavage dans l'Europe medievale*. Vol. 1. Bruges.

Vidal-Naquet, P. 1986. *The Black Hunter*. Baltimore.

Wagner, E. W. 1971. "Social Stratification in the 17th Century: Some Observations from a 1663 Seoul Census Register." Paper presented to the Columbia University Seminar on Korea, October 15, 1971.

Watkins, C. (ed.). 1985. *The American Heritage Dictionary of Indo-European Roots*. Boston.

Whittaker, C. R. 1987. "Circe's Pigs: From Slavery to Serfdom in the Later Roman World." *Slavery and Abolition* 8: 88-122.

Wittgenstein, L. 1953. *Philosophical Investigations*. New York.

Index